Essays on Indian Literature
POSITIONS

K. Satchidanandan

NIYOGI BOOKS

Published by
NIYOGI BOOKS
Block D, Building No. 77,
Okhla Industrial Area, Phase-I,
New Delhi-110 020, INDIA
Tel: 91-11-26816301, 26818960
Email: niyogibooks@gmail.com
Website: www.niyogibooksindia.com

Text © K. Satchidanandan

Editor: K.E. Priyamvada
Design: Shraboni Roy

ISBN: 978-93-89136-14-2
Publication: 2019

All rights are reserved. No part of this publication may be reproduced or transmitted in any form or by any means, electronic or mechanical, including photocopying, recording or by any information storage and retrieval system without prior written permission and consent of the Publisher.

Printed at: Niyogi Offset Pvt. Ltd., New Delhi, India

CONTENTS

Preface   5

Part One: Looking at Paradigms

- THE PLURAL AND THE SINGULAR   9
  The Making of Indian Literature

- THE MODERN AND THE DEMOCRATIC   45
  Indian Poetry after Independence

- MOTHER TONGUE, THE OTHER TONGUE   67
  Indianising English

- INDIAN LITERARY CRITICISM TODAY   88
  The Challenge and the Response

- INDIAN LITERATURE   109
  Nativism and its Ambivalences

- SEX, TEXT, POLITICS   115
  Women's Writing in India—Problems of Reading

- IMAGINED COMMUNITIES   126
  Collective Aspirations in Contemporary Indian Poetry

- OF MANY INDIAS   142
  Alternative Nationhoods in Contemporary Indian Poetry

- THAT THIRD SPACE   163
  Interrogating the Diasporic Paradigm

- THE POLITICS OF REREADING   171
  The Indian Context

- TRANSLATION AS WRITING   185
  Text, Translation, Authenticity—Towards
  an Indian Perspective

Part Two: Authors and Texts

- ANOTHER LIFE, ANOTHER POETICS   197
  Bhakti, the First Movements

- STRATEGIES OF SUBVERSION 223
  Sramana Elements in Sarala Dasa's *Mahabharata*
- I THINK OF THE ENDS OF THINGS 236
  Some Reflections on Ghalib's Modernity
- MY KABIR, MY CONTEMPORARY 244
- THE PATHOGRAPHY OF NATIONALISM 252
  Tagore's Critique of the Idea of the Nation
- SARATCHANDRA CHATTERJEE AND
  THE DYNAMICS OF RECEPTION 272
- AGAINST THE GRAIN 286
  The Role of Memory in A.K. Ramanujan's Poetry
- TRANSCENDING THE BODY 294
  On the Poetry of Kamala Das
- ON THE LIMITS OF INTERPRETATION 307
  Mahasweta Devi's 'Stanadayini', a case study
- THE TERROR OF THE BLANK PAGE 318
  A Reading of Sitakant Mahapatra's
  'The Other View: Yashoda's Soliloquy'
- BETWEEN TWO CULTURES 327
  On Two Poems of Kedarnath Singh
- SONGS FROM THE UNDERWORLD 336
  The Poetry of Namdeo Dhasal

Acknowledgements 345

Select Bibliography 347

Suggestions for further Reading 350

Index 355

Praise for earlier works of criticism 360

PREFACE

Positions carries a careful selection from my essays on Indian literature written over the last 25 years. Most of these came to be written for presentation as papers or keynote speeches at seminars or for collections on specific themes, while some had their origins as notes for lectures in universities and literary institutions in India and abroad.

The general theme of the book is Indian literature(s). The book carries essays that look for paradigms based on Indian textual practices and reading traditions, while also drawing freely on Indian and Western critical concepts and methods and the close readings of certain texts. The questions discussed include the idea of Indian literature, the poetics of Bhakti, the concept of the 'modern', the location of English writing in India, the conflicting ideas of India, projected especially by the new subaltern literary movements and the issues of literary criticism and of translation. The individual authors whose texts are discussed include Sarala Das, Mirza Ghalib, Kabir, Rabindranath Tagore, Saratchandra Chatterjee, Sarojini Naidu, Kedarnath Singh, A.K. Ramanujan and Kamala Das. I hope these essays will contribute to the growing, yet insufficient, corpus of comparative literary studies in India which, at least since the arrival of scholars like Sisir Kumar Das, has shifted its focus from the discovery of European parallels for Indian literary movements, trends and texts with its Eurocentric bias to comparisons between trends, movements and texts among the different literary languages of India. I consider this a significant and necessary paradigmatic transformation.

I wish to place on record my thanks to all the organisations and institutions whose persistent demands led to the writing of these essays in the first place, to the publishers and editors of journals and books that featured many of them and to Niyogi Books, especially to my former colleague and friend Nirmal Kanti Bhattacharjee, Niyogi's Editorial Director, who realised the academic potential of these essays and took special interest in bringing out this collection.

K. SATCHIDANANDAN

Part One
Looking at Paradigms

THE PLURAL AND THE SINGULAR
The Making of Indian Literature

Whenever I think of Indian literature, a story retold by A.K. Ramanujan comes to mind: Hanuman reaches the netherworld in search of Rama's ring that had disappeared through a hole. The King of Spirits in the netherworld tells Hanuman that there have been so many Ramas over the ages; whenever one incarnation nears its end, Rama's ring falls down. The King shows Hanuman a whole platter with thousands of rings, all of them Rama's, and asks him to pick out his Rama's ring. He tells this devotee from earth that his Rama too has entered the river Sarayu by now, after crowning his sons, Lava and Kusha. Many Ramas also mean many *Ramayana*s and we have hundreds of them in oral, written, painted, carved and performed versions. If this is true of a single seminal Indian work, one needs only to imagine the diversity of the whole of Indian literature recited, narrated and written in scores of languages. No wonder, one of the fundamental questions in any discussion of Indian literature has been whether to speak of Indian literature in singular or plural. With 184 mother tongues (as per Census, 1991; it was 179 in George Grierson's *Linguistic Survey of India*, along with 544 dialects, and 1,652 in 1961), 22 of which are in the Eighth schedule of the Indian Constitution; 25 writing systems, 14 of them major, with scores of oral literary traditions and several traditions of written literature, most of them at least a millennium old, the diversity of India's literary landscape can match only the complexity of its linguistic map. Probably it was this challenging complexity that had forced an astute critic like Nihar Ranjan Ray to conclude that there cannot be a single Indian literature, as there is no single language that can be termed 'Indian'. To quote him as translated from Bengali by Sujit Mukherjee (*Towards a Literary History of India*):

> Literature is absolutely language-based, and language being a cultural phenomenon, it is all but wholly conditioned by its locale and the socio-historical forces that are in

operation through the ages in that particular locale. If that be so, one may reasonably argue that the literature of a given language will have its own specific character of form and style, images and symbols, nuances and associations.

It is true that often 'Indian' tends to imply the values that argue for the cultural unity of India as a whole. The use of English to write about literature in Indian languages seems to reinforce such a view. As E.V. Ramakrishnan observes in his introduction to *Making It New: Modernism in Malayalam, Marathi and Hindi Poetry (ILAS, Shimla)* the framework of grand narratives of history cannot accommodate the subversive function of the new trends in literature unless they become domesticated and canonised.

The levelling effect of history and the domestication implicit in canonicity finally fossilise authors and works, leaving no trace of their relevance to our present. We also have to recognise the fact that the gap between the national and the regional has been problematised by the post-colonial vocabularies of identity and difference, and centrality and plurality.

Comparative literature scholars like K.M. George and Sisir Kumar Das have attempted composite histories of Indian literature, as in the former's *Comparative Indian Literature* and the latter's *A History of Indian Literature*. Sisir Kumar Das tries to locate the points of convergence and parallels on a civilisational terrain of labyrinthine complexity. He looks at the history of Indian literature as a history of 'the total literary activity of the Indian people, an account of all literary traditions, great and little, their ramifications and changes, their recessions and revivals, dominance and decline.' In fact a literary text produced in an Indian language answers a certain need, or performs a historical function in the context of specific linguistic community and its meaning lies essentially in its specificity. This relationship of the text to its context gets blurred or distorted when we abstract a text in an Indian language into the realm of a national literary history. In order to understand how a poet or a fiction writer radicalises the literary idiom, it is necessary to grasp the specific history of that literature along with its social background from which the literary registers spring. There is, in addition, the question of the overlapping of various tendencies at the same juncture in most Indian languages. In Malayalam, for example, even now there are romantic poets following an older idiom jostling with those who consider themselves post-modern and experiment with *avant-garde* idioms. This gets further complicated if we introduce the element of ideology that according to Mikhael Bakhtin is inscribed in the language. In short, there are problems of chronology (or synchrony and diachrony), of ideology and of terminology involved in the consideration of the singular/plural nature of Indian literature.

Let us now look at the other argument. While Nihar Ranjan Ray is not without some followers in contemporary India, it is also possible to interrogate his general approach to literature as something tied entirely and inextricably to the language in which it is originally written. Language cannot be the only criterion of literature; other criteria, social, cultural, political, ethical and aesthetic, have been applied to literature from time to time. It can be, and has been, categorised, read and analysed from the point of view of class, race, caste, gender, myth, archetype, sign, structure, ideology and textual unconscious. For example, Marxist and Marxisant critics from Plekhanov, Lunacharsky, Mikhail Bakhtin, George Lukacs and Walter Benjamin to Raymond Williams, Fredric Jameson, Terry Eagleton, Jacques Ranciere, Ramvilas Sharma, Namwar Singh and E.V. Ramakrishnan have looked at literature from the point of view of class and ideology; women critics like Virginia Woolf, Simone de Beauvoir, Elaine Showalter, Mary Ellman, Sandra Gilbert and Susan Gubar, Gayle Green, Coppelia Kahn, Ellen Moer, Jane Flax, Annette Kolodny, Susie Tharu, Madhu Kishwar and Ruth Vanita have explored the gender dimension of literature; critics like Mulk Raj Anand, D.R. Nagraj and Sharan Kumar Limbale have looked at literature from a Dalit perspective, not to speak of archetypal critics like Northrop Frye, reader-theorists like Stanley Fish or Wolfgang Iser, psycho-linguists like Jacques Lacan, semiologists like Roland Barthes, structuralists like Jean Piaget and Paul de Man and post-structuralists like Jacques Derrida, Michel Foucault and Richard Rorty, who have developed novel ways of reading, reconstructing and deconstructing texts. In all these cases, the language of the text assumes a secondary status under another dominant paradigm.

Secondly, there are many literatures that are known by the name of the nations they belong to rather than the languages they are written in. This is true of American, British, Australian, Canadian, or Indian English literature, where literatures mostly in the same language are given different nomenclatures. On the other hand a category like European Literature cuts across languages, as it is written in diverse languages like German, French, Italian, Spanish or Swedish. And Spanish literature written in South America is considered to have a separate identity, as it belongs to the larger corpus of Latin American literature. Thirdly, crossings of linguistic boundaries are so frequent in Indian literature that we find it difficult to divide our literature solely on the basis of language. In the words of the distinguished Marxist theoretician Aijaz Ahmed, 'multilingualism and polyglot fluidity' are in the very nature of Indian creativity. We have Indian writers of the past like Kabir or Namdev, who wrote in Punjabi and varieties of Hindi, Meerabai who is claimed as much by Gujarati as by Braj and Rajasthani, Guru Nanak who easily switched over from Persian to Kaifi and to Lahudi, Vidyapati who belonged equally to Sanskrit and Maithili and Avahatta. In the modern times we have many writers who belong to the composite Hindi-Urdu tradition that can perhaps be called the Hindusthani tradition, like Premchand; we have bilingual writers who write in Urdu and their mother tongues like the Gujaratis, Mohammed Alvi or Jayant Parmar, or writers like Padma Sachdev who write in Dogri and Hindi with equal ease, not to speak of several bilinguals who write in English as well as their mother tongues: A.K. Ramanujan (Kannada), Jayanta Mahapatra (Oriya), R. Parthasarathy (Tamil), Kiran Nagarkar (Marathi) and Kamala Das (Malayalam) being some well-known examples.

Thirdly, most Indian languages share genres and forms from the *mahakavya, doha, prabandha, prahasana, nataka*, and ballad to sonnet, elegy, lyric, narrative poem, short story and the novel. Fourthly, they also share concepts of poetics, both oriental and occidental, from *rasa, dhvani, alankara, anumana, vakrokti, bhava* and *vibhava* to mimesis, catharsis, metaphor, metonymy, suggestion, myth, archetype and several other, more contemporary, terms, concepts and methods. Fifthly, many literatures in India share literary influences as well as trends and movements like the *Bhakti*, the Nationalist or *Swarajist*, the Progressive or *Pragativadi*, the Modernist or *adhunik* movements and the later trends like post-Modernist or *uttar-adhunik*, nativist or *deseevadi*, ecological or *prakritivadi* or *paristhithivadi*, feminist or *nareevadi*, Dalit and tribal or Adivasi movements. This is besides shared patterns of thought, feeling, concerns and their modes of expression.

These common features must have inspired the famous statement by S. Radhakrishnan popularised by the Sahitya Akademi: 'Indian Literature is one, even while written in different languages.' One problem with this approach is that it is reductive and tends to standardise all the literatures of India and in the process leaves out and thus alienates many literatures like the oral tribal literatures, literatures of the North East and of certain languages and dialects, where the history has proceeded in other directions and which have had little impact of the West. This dilemma was best summed up by U.R. Ananthamurthy, when he said, 'If you look at the diversity of Indian literature, you come to see its unity and if you look for unity, you are struck by its diversity.' This is in fact a dialectical statement that is nearer the truth than the positions expressed by either Nihar Ranjan Ray or S. Radhakrishnan, for, while there have been pan-Indian trends and movements, there have also been regional ones, and even the pan-Indian movements, like *Bhakti*, have manifested themselves in different forms in different Indian languages. It is also not true to say that all the movements have affected all the literatures alike or that the influences from outside the languages, Indian or otherwise, have had the same impact across languages. There are also forms that are unique to certain languages, like, for example, the *thullal* poem, *kathakali* verse, the cartoon poem or the *pattalakkatha* (barrack stories) to Malayalam, or *bijak* or *ramaini* peculiar to ancient Braj as used by Kabir or the *pillaipadal* (lullabies), *chintu* (a kind of song), *akaval* (a metric mode in narratives), *venpa* (for didactic works), *kalippa* (for love poetry and choral music), *vanchapp* (for descriptive situations), *kummi* (a song for dancing women), and *kanni* (a couplet form) in Tamil, *abhang* in Marathi, *vachana* in Kannada, *vakh* in Kashmiri (all forms of Bhakti poetry) or *rubai, maznavi, qavvali, manaqib, nama, qasida* or *quit'a* in Urdu. This is also true of the concepts of poetics. All the languages were not equally permeated by Sanskrit poetics. Tamil, for example, had its own concepts like that of the *tinai* or terrains with their peculiar moods and contexts, their *uri* and *mutal* like *kurinchi* (*mutal*: mountain, *uri*: *punartal* or pre-marital union), *marutam* (*mutal*: lowland, *uri*: *oodal*, or marital union sulking over infidelity), *neytal* (*mutal*: seashore, *uri*: *iranagal* or anxious pining in the state of separation), *mullai* (*mutal*: forest or pasture, *uri*: *iruttal* or patient waiting) and *palai* (*mutal*: desert, *uri*: *pirital* or separation). *Tholhappiyam* also speaks of *meypadus* comparable to the *rasa*s (*uvakai: sringara; nakai: hasya; azhukai: karuna; vekuli: raudra; perumitam: veera; accam: bhayanaka; ilivaral: bhibhatsa* and *marutkai: atbhuta*). There are also concepts like *ullurai* connotatively close to *dhvani*. Urdu has inherited a lot of concepts from the Perso-Arabic critical tradition. One can also see that different languages have appropriated Sanskrit as well as Western concepts in poetics with nuanced semantic shifts. Some forms are common to some languages, but not to all alike; the *ghazal* that came from Persian, was developed in Urdu and then had practitioners in Hindi, Marathi, Gujarati and even in English in India (remember Agha Shahid Ali, for example). This is also true of neo-classical forms like *champu* and *sandeshakavya*, or movements like Dalit literature shared chiefly by, say, Marathi, Gujarati, Hindi, Punjabi, Kannada, Tamil, Telugu and more recently, Malayalam. Even a pan-Indian tendency like the Progressive Literary Movement was stronger in languages like Urdu, Hindi, Oriya, Bengali, Tamil, Telugu and Malayalam than in others. There are too movements and debates confined to one or two languages like *desseevad* or nativism, chiefly observed in Marathi and Gujarati. In short, while languages have interacted from time to time and received forms, trends and movements from other regions and languages, each language has also had periods of isolated growth and its own special genius, just as each region in India has its own customs, celebrations, forms of art and literature and at times even certain temperamental tendencies. Indian culture is a mosaic of cultures, religions, races, languages, attitudes and world views; hence the concept of Indian literature also has to be open, inclusive, dynamic and flexible, so that it accommodates diverse voices, of the majority as well as the religious, linguistic, ethnic and sexual minorities.

2

One glance at the evolution of India's literatures will reveal the dialectical dynamics of its growth and change. I clearly cannot even pretend to narrate the story of a vast and diverse literature with a history of at least 5,000 years in this brief article, even forgetting that such an attempt is doomed to gross simplification from the very beginning. This is only an elementary attempt to discover the connections as well as disjunctions, the continuities as well as the breaks in our long literary history by taking up some of the crucial moments of its constitution.

The roots of Indian literature, can be traced to the oral lore of the earliest inhabitants of India, who seem to have spoken mostly Austro-Asiatic languages and shared a mythopoeiac imagination with the *adivasis* everywhere. Riddles, proverbs, songs related to daily life, labour, magic and ritual, hymns to natural forces and mother-goddesses, poems for occasions like weddings and hunting, songs for dance, uninhibited expressions of love: it had sufficient thematic variety and an often surreal imaginative quality to merit our attention as genuine, if naïve, literature. Many of these tribes, like the Dhangars and Bhils who had created microliths and megaliths have survived to the present day with their songs and stories enriched by their primitive imagination that is close to modern imagination in its modes of signification.

We know little about the literature of the Indus valley since the Saindhava script is yet to be deciphered. It is assumed that those bronze age-people who created the Indus valley civilisation were of Mongolian, Mediterranean, Alpine and Proto-Austroloid stocks and their language was close to Sumerian, Cretan and Elamite. These people must have come from some restricted locality with little room for expansion. At the same time, they had a highly developed civilisation in their homeland, as the Indus Valley Civilisation—recent excavations show that they went beyond the Indus valley—shows knowledge of agriculture, brick-making, construction and proper grouping of houses and some military technique. Several of its features, like the citadel mound, the 'great bath' probably meant for fertility rites, seals carrying Gilgamesh-type of heroes, terrifying terracotta figurines showing women with bird-marks and the Saindhava script prove the proximity of the Indus Valley Civilisation to Sumerian, Babylonian and Mesapotamian civilisations. From the Babylonian and earlier records, it is evident that the island of Bahrain, in the Persian Gulf, was the Tilmun of the Mesopotamian legend. Here the legendary, deathless Sumerian Noah Zinsudda spent his days, after surviving the deluge and was sought out by the hero Gilgamesh in search of the secret of immortality. The cuneiform clay tablets that speak of trade through Bahrain conducted by a special class of merchants, the *alik Tilmun* have been amply confirmed by modern excavations. They later traded under the protection of the Assyrian king who took a major share of the profits but was also probably their greatest customer. The Mesopotamians seem to have called the Indus region, Meluhha. All mention of Meluhha ceases by about 1750 BCE, which means that the trade contacts were then presumably interrupted by invaders. Those dwellers of the Indus valley who for the first time brought to India gods like Mayon (Krishna) and Peyon (Muruga), Siva and Ganesa and goddesses like Kottavai (Parvati) and Kali, seem to have been defeated or driven away in the 18th century BCE by another tribe that came from Central Asia that worshipped Indra, Varuna, Mitra and Yama and used the dialect in which the Vedas have been written. A good number of historians, including D.D. Kosambi, believe that the vanquished tribe of short dark people with not-so-prominent noses ('*anasikas*') mostly moved to the South, while a few remained in the river valley to get integrated into the victorious tribe and become part of a composite priestly class. Once this conflict was supposed to have been between 'Dravidians' and 'Aryans', but contemporary historians like Romila Thapar have no doubt that 'Dravidian' and 'Aryan' are only names of groups of languages and it is wrong to view them as the names of two races in combat (see *The Aryan* and *Which of us are Aryans?*). The people who spoke the languages of these groups must have been of various ethnic stocks. There are others who think that only some people who spoke the Aryan languages were called 'Aryans'. The army of Xerxes, son of Darius, had 'Aryan' contingents and the Medes who preceded the Persians formerly bore the name, 'Aryans'. Iran is derived from '*aryanam*' (the country) of the Aryans. Alexander's contemporary historians used 'Aryan' to refer only to one section of the people speaking Aryan languages: those settled on the right bank of the Indus, tribes who, by philological evidences, seem to have come from the northern regions of Eurasia. Whether 'Aryan' is a race or not, we know that their chief wealth was cattle, they had horse-drawn chariots that gave them superiority in battle, and their social organisation was patriarchal. Mitannian records around 1400 BCE show that the people worshipping Indo-Aryan Gods in an Aryan language were settled near Lake Urmiyeh in Iran. The same gods had been worshipped by the Persians till the arrival of Zoroaster in the late sixth century BCE. *Avesta* mentions the Punjab as a recognised 'Aryan' territory. Some of the Indo-Iranian heroes came from the shores of the Caspian, in what is now Gilan and Mazanderan. The Iranian records speak of the 'var' of King Yima, a rectangular place into which neither death nor the winter's cold would penetrate, till someone sinned. The good King Yima saved his people from general punishment for the broken taboo by taking death upon himself, to become the first mortal. In India Yama of the Rigveda was also the first mortal, the old ancestral death-god, and still remains a god of the dead. Rectangular enclosures discovered by archaeologists in Uzbekistan have the exact traditional dimensions of the 'var' of Yima in Iranian religious books. The 'var' reappears in Greek myths as the Augean stables cleansed by Herakles.

The Aryan family of languages has spread right across the Eurasian sub-continent. Sanskrit, Latin and Greek were the classical Aryan languages. The Romance languages like Italian, Spanish, French and Rumanian developed from Latin; the Teutonic languages like German, English and Swedish and the Slavic languages like Russian and Polish are also sub-groups of the Aryan linguistic group. The Indo-Aryan languages from Pali or Magadhi and the various Prakrits to the modern Hindi, Punjabi, Bengali, Oriya, Marathi, Gujarati, etc., developed from Sanskrit or some earlier form that had given rise to Sanskrit, Prakrits and Pali. The languages of the South like Tamil, Kannada, Telugu, Tulu and Malayalam are considered Dravidian languages. The Archaemenid emperor Darius I (d.486 BCE) calls himself *Hakhamanisiya* (Archaemenid), *Parsa* (Persian) and 'an Aryan of Aryan descent' in his inscriptions, from which we may guess that the term Aryan had been prevalent in those days too, whether it denoted just 'noble', a race, a family or a group of languages. The oldest Indian documents, the Vedas also speak of the 'Aryans' as the people who venerated the gods worshipped in the Vedas; here again it may mean only the 'noble' people. Linguists have proved that *Rigveda* was the earliest of the Vedas, followed by *Yajurveda* (in two branches, the Black and the White), the *Samaveda*, and much later by the *Atharvaveda*. That concentrates upon witchcraft. Some historians guess that the *Rigveda* refers to events that took place in the Punjab around 1500–1200 BCE.

Vedic poetry written in simple meters is part of the most beautiful body of poetry produced by ancient man, with its magical quality and rare cadences, reflecting a society not yet divided into classes and castes. This is particularly true of the *Rigveda* that has more than 1,000 hymns arranged in 10 *mandalas* that reveal a kind of pantheistic faith that associate divinity with the elements. Rigvedic hymns were memorised syllable by syllable by those who chanted it for centuries and were committed to writing with commentary only in the second half of the 14th century AD in South India. The *Rigveda* is also significant for its poetic quality and its invocation of an undivided human society that Marx would have called a 'Primitive Communist' society, as it was broadly egalitarian and there was no concept of private property. *Ekam vipra bahudha vadanti* (It is the same One who is called different by scholars) shows a monotheistic tendency that could absorb all deities into a unitary divine concept.

It is difficult to separate Vedic myth from historical reality. Indra, the chief of Gods in the Vedas, might well have been a war-leader, according to D.D. Kosambi. There are references to many teeming strong places shattered by Indra, described as 'pregnant with black embryos', which might be a metaphoric reference to the dark people who occupied these places. Indra's 'freeing of rivers' might refer to the destruction of the dams built by the peasant communities of the Indus valley, as those rivers are said to have been 'brought to a standstill' by 'artificial barriers'. The demon, Vritra, lay like 'a great snake across the hill-slope'. And when the demon was smashed by Indra, 'the stones rolled away like wagon wheels' and 'the waters flowed over the demon's inert body'. Indra was 'Vritrahar', the killer of Vritra; the same word was transformed in Iranian as 'vetretraghna' and then to 'Ahura-Mazda', the supreme Zoroastrian god of light. There are several references to the tribes destroyed by Indra in the *Rigveda*. Probably it was the destruction of agriculture that had forced the majority of the Indus valley people to move towards the South. The main people, thus, destroyed are called 'Panis'. One Rigvedic hymn suggests that the Aryans demanded a tribute in cattle from the Panis that they rejected, leading to a battle between them. Coin is *'pana'* in Sanskrit and a trader is a *'vanik'*; trade goods are *'panya'*. These words might have come from 'Panis'. The people who had migrated to India were clearly people on a lower level of culture than the urban people they destroyed, since there is no characteristic post-Indus valley pottery or tool, and the *Rigveda* says nothing about fixed settlements, or about reading, writing, art or architecture. Music was restricted to ritual chants, and technology to the construction of chariots and tools and weapons for war. Gambling, chariot-racing and dancing were the chief entertainments; weaving was the women's special skill. There is Rigvedic evidence for the rise of a new professional Brahmin priesthood and also the emergence of slavery. *Dasyu*, the word for enemy is related to *dasa* or slave. Probably some of the vanquished tribes were kept by the victors as *dasas*. The *Yajurveda*, along with the attached

Satapatha Brahmana, inform us about the later life of the victors in the Iron Age with the growing importance of agriculture and of metals. The victorious tribes now began to break into groups and move in different directions. The caste system began to develop in the tribes and *varnas* developed, based on their vocations. The *gotras* (literally, cow-pen) or clan-units also began to evolve. Kinship groups were called *gramas,* which later came to mean villages. The various *gramas* together formed the tribal kingdoms or the *rashtras.* A regular class-based state mechanism that would altogether dispense with tribal unity was in the making.

The Upanishads and the Brahmanas tend to reveal the sacred as a structure of human consciousness and revel in the mystery of the metaphysical. The Upanishads, some of the pinnacles scaled by human thought until then, have for their central concept the Brahman, the ever–unknowable, indefinable, infinite and omniscient spirit or energy that pevades the cosmos. (*'na tatra chakshurgacchati,na vaggacchati, na mana; na vidmo, na vijaneemo yathai thadanu sishyaat'*: Kenopanishad) Kenopanishad collapses the self and the divine so that once one realises oneself, the divine, which belongs to the realm of imagination, becomes redundant. The wealth of ancient folk narratives in India is contained in anthologies like Somadeva's *Panchatantra* and *Kathasaritsagara,* Kshemendra's *Brihatkathamanjari* and Gunadhya's *Brihatkatha.*

The epics, which are the most comprehensive artistic products of the folk tradition form another founding moment of India's literatures. The tales of Puru, Kuru, Yadu and Naga tribes seem to have been integrated into the *Mahabharata,* developed over the years through revisions, retellings and additions. The *Mahabharata* has several versions in the languages and in the folk and performing traditions, though the version ascribed to 'Vyasa' has been the most popular among scholars. It is a polyphonic work that has been read from varying perspectives. Critics and scholars like Iravati Karve and Kuttikrishna Marar have found it to be an immortal record of the complex human condition and a mirror held to the various masks we wear. This version of *Mahabharata* refuses to idolise its characters, unlike some popular versions of the *Ramayana*, where Rama is an adorable and infallible hero. No character here is beyond questioning. Contradictions assail their character; at the same time the conduct of each character is justified in his/her specific context. Iravate Karve in her *Yugant* has shown how even epic heroes and heroines are not above human failings: Duryodhana's anger is not baseless as he had been disgraced by the Pandavas. The wise Bhishma is trying to bring peace; but the attempt leads to great injustices. The events that follow lead to the feud between the families and finally ruins both. Gandhari, who is upheld as an ideal wife, had actually been tricked into marrying the blind prince and walked blind-folded to remind the family of her husband of their cruelty and generate in them a sense of guilt. The noble Arjuna, the great warrior that he is, falters before the enemy and is shown to be weak before the kin and the teacher he has to fight. And the same warrior has little hesitation in committing genocide—destroying the whole race of the Nagas—joining hands with Krishna and Agni. Even Draupadi, one of the most celebrated women of all time, suffers from arrogance and obstinacy that cause her a lot of pain. Krishna, who is supposedly an incarnation of Vishnu, is Machiavellian in his plans against the Kauravas. In fact, these characters, and many others, appear as our contemporaries or our own images in their strengths as well as weaknesses. This ability to address the present and relate to different contexts in life is one of the major qualities of this epic. The *Mahabharata* is one of the finest products of our folk tradition. It has grown over time, taking in various strands of philosophy and literature. Its first version was *Jaya* that had only 8,800 verses. Later it grew into *Bharata* with 24,000 verses chanted by Vaisampayana during Janamejaya's *sarpasatra* (the serpent-sacrifice). It was during the *yajna* conducted by Saunaka in the Naimisaranya that it attained its present form with more than a lakh of verses. It is said to have been sung by Sootha and Ugrasravas on the request of Saunaka. In its present form it is almost an encyclopedia of ancient Indian culture, a compendium of myths and legends from varied sources. D.D. Kosambi has observed how Krishna was deified and the *Bhagavatgeeta* was appended to the text much later, thus 'brahminising' the whole epic. The origin of the epic is connected to the hymns of the *Rigveda,* and literary genres like *itihasas, akhyanas* and *puranas*. Several *gathas* and episodes like the *Saparnyakhyan* relating the tale of Kadru and Vinata in the *Asthikaparva* are later added. The chanters have also added many narrative poems and genealogies of dynasties; these singers are also known by the names of the stories or characters they added to the main narrative. For example, the one who sings the tale of Yayati is called *Yayatika*. The tales detailing Brahmin versions of philosophy, justice and law were also added. Many of these tales, like those of the *sarpasatra,* of Garuda, Ruru, Chyavana, Savitri, Risyasringa, Agastya, Vasishta and Viswamitra are meant to frighten people of other varnas, including the princely Kshatriyas, into submission. Another stream is that about the *rishis* and *parivrajakas* belonging to different clans inhabiting the forests. This includes moral tales, parables, legends, fairy tales, legends about monks, etc. These appear in the form of dialogues in the epic, mostly in the *Santhiparva* and *Anusasanaparva*. The longest of such additions are perhaps the *Bhagavatgeeta* and *Anugeeta*. R.N. Dandekar is right in observing that the present Indian life is least influenced by the Vedic 'Aryan' elements. The Vedic gods are no more important and the jurisprudence too has undergone sea change. Still the epics fascinate us and have a deep impact on our moral imagination, thought and life through its profound human element that is subject to various kinds of reading. *Mahabharata* in its present form is eight times as big as the *Odyssey* and *Iliad* put together. The saying, '*Vyasocchishtam jagat sarvam*' ('The whole world is but the remains of Vyasa', meaning there is nothing in the world that has not been dealt with by the poet) expresses the comprehensive nature of the epic. The text itself puts forward the claim, '*yadi nasti tadanyatra, yanye nasti na tatkvachit* (No where else can you find that, which is not in this). No wonder not only scholars from the East as well as the West, but writers and artists all over the world keep on rereading and rewriting the *Mahabharata* from diverse perspectives, even today. If the Feminists have found a protagonist in Draupadi, the Dalits have discovered in Ekalavya a typical victim of Brahmin injustice and cruelty. There are hundreds of stories, novels, plays and poems based on the *Mahabharata* and they keep getting written almost every day.

Like the *Mahabharata,* the *Ramayana* too is not an individual text, but a multiple tradition that carries different voices in its diverse sung, written and performed versions. As Romila Thapar says in her critique of the televised *Ramayana, Ramayana* does not belong to any *one* moment in history, because it has its *own* history embedded in the many versions, which were woven around the theme at different times and places. The appropriation of the story by a multiplicity of groups means a multiplicity of versions through which the social aspirations and ideological concerns of each group are articulated. Father Camille Bulcke (*Ramkatha*) and Paula Richman (*Many Ramayanas: The Diversity of a Narrative Tradition in South Asia; Questioning Ramayanas: A South Asian Tradition* and *Ramayana Stories in Modern South India*) have acquainted us with hundreds of *Ramayanas* produced in diverse circumstances and with diverse ethical and aesthetic implications. In many Telugu folksongs sung by women, Sita and not Rama is the main character, as pointed out by Velcheru Narayana Rao and they interrogate Rama's wisdom and sense of justice in relation to Sita. Even Shanta, Rama's elder sister gets special attention here, not to speak of the detailed treatment of Sita's wedding and labour. And it is women who take the initiative in resolving issues; men's role becomes nominal on most occasions. In the Buddhist *Ramayana,* The *Dasaratha Jataka,* Rama returns to his kingdom of Benares and establishes his benevolent rule and restores moral and spiritual order; In Jaina *Vasudevahimdi,* in Kannada folk tradition as sung by *tamburi dasayyas,* Sita is Ravana's daughter and in some Telugu folksongs, Sita is conceived by Ravana, there called Ravula. In *Paumachariya* (Prakrit for *Padmacharita*) by Vimalasuri, the Jain Ramayana, Ravana is a noble devotee of the Jain masters, a learned man who earns his magical powers and weapons through austerities, a tragic hero undone by a passion he had vowed against. In another Jain version, Sita is Ravana's daughter; his ignorance of this leads to a tragic oedipal situation. And it is Lakshmana, and not Rama who fights Ravana here; Lakshmana and Ravana are the eighth incarnation of Vasudeva and Prativasudeva, a hero and an antihero destined to fight in life after life. Lakshmana goes to hell for assassinating Ravana while Rama, an evolved and non-violent Jain soul, attains salvation. In *Patalaramayanam,* a Malayalam folk version, Patalaravana, the King of the netherworld helps his friend Ravana by abducting Rama and Lakshmana from the battlefield into the netherworld, from where Hanuman releases them after killing the abductor. Sita is the goddess of agriculture for the Bhils of Gujarat and the Baiga and Bhumia communities of Madhya Pradesh. According to the Bhili *Ramayana, Rom-Sitma ni Varta,* Ravana's soul resided in a wasp hidden in the Sun's chariot. Lakshmana threw this wasp into boiling oil, causing Ravana's death. There are too many interesting episodes in this tribal version, like a boy being born to Hanuman in a fish that had gulped down his generative fluid while sitting on an arrow shot by Rama, while crossing the ocean to go to Lanka. The child grows into a great water warrior called Matsyaraja. The Bhili *Ramayana* also gives a lot of importance to birds, beasts and plants that play a major role in the evolution of the narrative. The many written *Ramayana*s in the Indian languages—like those by Ezhuthacchan in Malayalam, Pampa in Kannada, Kambar in Tamil, Ranganatha in Telugu, Krittivasa in Bangla, Madhav Kandali in Asomiya, Balaramadasa in Oriya, Girdhara in Gujarati, Eknatha in Marathi or Tulasidasa in Avadhi—these are only some popular *Ramayana*s; there are so many in each language, Malayalam alone having 197 works based on the *Ramayana* story, also show great diversity in the setting, the relative importance given to characters and episodes, the choice, depiction and interpretation of incidents and the form of narration. These are by no means translations of any previous text in the current sense of translation and most of them draw from different sources, including regional folk versions, Valmiki's *Ramayana* being only one, though a major one. The relationship between the 'great tradition' and the 'little traditions' in India, to follow A.K. Ramanujan's terms, is by no means one of hegemony and subalternity, but of adaptation, exchange and original creativity. Hence it will be a grave error and gross simplification to consider one *Ramayana* more 'authentic' than another: All the writers mentioned above have been admired as original poets, and not as translators, as they had chosen the Rama story as a space for the free play of imagination and a context to express the specific genius of their languages. That is why many of them are also considered the very makers of their languages. This heterogeneity is reflected also in the contemporary versions, depictions and readings of the *Ramayana*. You find a great poet like Kumaran Asan interrogating Rama's sense of fairplay in his dramatic monologue, *Chintavishtayaya Sita* (Sita in Meditation), and Sara Joseph putting on trial the whole ethics of the *Ramayana* from a feminist and subaltern point of view, in her stories based on the *Ramayana* episodes (now available in English versions, published by Oxford University Press, *Retelling Ramayana,* with my introduction) or the Dalit writers finding in Sambooka a wronged hero and devotee. This is also true of the *Mahabharata* that has any number of old and contemporary versions.

I dwelt on the Ramayana tradition and its sub-traditions for a short while, only to show how even our major epic tradition is plural and far from uniform. Just as there is no one *Ramayana* that is 'essential' whose 'phenomena' the other *Ramayana*s are, there is no Indian literature out there as an 'essence' (*satta*) whose 'phenomena' (*pratibhasa*) the regional literatures are. This resistance to standardisation is a unique quality of our literary scenario that is also the basis of its democratic character and its potential response to the hegemonic homogenisation and the bulldozing of cultural difference that is part of the pernicious agenda of the champions of neo-Hindutva or of globalisation. Let us also remember that when we discuss the epic tradition, we tend to forget, ignore or suppress more than a hundred oral epics in dialects and tribal languages like *Malle Madeswara* (from Karnataka) or *Pabuji* (from Rajasthan) to take just two texts, whose English versions are available. We will come across more such examples as we follow the trends further.

The age of the Epics was followed in the North by what is often called the golden age of Sanskrit literature (circa third century to 14th century AD), an age that produces poets and playwrights like Kalidasa, Bhasa, Bhavabhuti, Visakhadatta, Soodraka, Banabhatta, Bodhayana and finally Jayadeva, the poet of *Gitagovinda,* an erotic Bhakti text. Pioneering plays like *Abhijnanasakuntalam, Vikramorvasiyam, Malavikagnimitram* (Kalidasa), *Swapna vasavadattam, Oorubhangam* (Bhasa) and *Mricchakatikam* (Soodraka) set the standards for Indian drama integrating diverse elements from myths, legends, epics, rituals and folklore. Kalidasa's poetry with its deep understanding of human passions, the seasons of nature, history, traditional morality, customs, manners and speech forms as testified by his verse plays as well as his works of lyrical and epic poetry (*Ritusamharam, Meghadootam, Raghuvamsam*) had all the elements of a specific poetics that many scholars identify as Indian poetics. That the society had by that time begun to be divided into classes, and patriarchy was on the rise, is clear from the ideology inscribed in the language of the time: Kalidasa uses Prakrit for his women characters as well as those from the lower classes. It may also be interesting here to note the difference between the Sakuntala of the *Vyasabharata* who is an assertive and independent woman and the Sakuntala of Kalidasa, who is a beautiful, coy, vulnerable, weak and gullible woman. It was this latter Sakuntala who suited the tastes of the Orientalists, as the paragon of female virtue and appealed to their imagination as the model of the frail Oriental beauty. This according to Romila Thapar (*Sakuntala*) is one of the reasons for its popularity in Europe. Linguists like Panini, Patanjali and Bhartrhari, exponents of dramaturgy like Bharata and of poetics like Bhamaha, Kuntaka, Abhinavagupta, Anandavardhana, Mammata and Mahimabhatta conceptualised the linguistic/poetic/dramatic practice as obtained in their time, chiefly in Sanskrit, in different ways.

Two bodies of writing co-existed with the mainstream Sanskrit literature: one consisted of Buddhist and Jain texts, mostly dealing with the lives of the Buddha and Mahavira as well as their teachings. These works were in Sanskrit, Pali, Prakrit or Apabhramsa. Asvaghosha, the author of *Buddhacharitam*, Santideva, Aryadeva, Nagarjuna and Vasubandhu were among the important writers of this strain. King Hala's anthology of love poetry in Prakrit, *Gathasaptasati* is a good example of the terse, suggestive and often erotic poetry of the period.

The second was a collection of works of rare merit in Tamil, a corpus referred to as *Sangam* literature that featured scores of excellent writers, often writing under pseudonyms, and mostly following the *tinai* poetics. Ilango Adigal's *Silappadikaram* and Chathanar's *Manimekalai* are two epic narratives of the period. Anthologies of domestic or love poetry (*aham*) and socio-political (*puram*) poetry like *Purananooru, Ahananooru, Pathittuppathu* and *Kalithokai* preserved the literature of the period for posterity, while *Tholkappiyam*, a book of grammar and poetics and *Thirukkural*, a book of ethics with marks of Jain influence, codified the thought of the age. Here again we hardly find any uniform literary principle or modes of praxis followed synchronically across the whole country.

3

The Bhakti movement, the next constituting moment in Indian literary history too was no monolith. It shows great diversity in its central icons (Shiva, Vishnu, Shakti and their regional variants), modes of worship, forms of expression, organisation and propagation and the forms of art—murals, sculpture, architecture, music, dance— it gave birth to. It also had its hegemonic and subaltern elements and though pan-Indian in a broad sense, there were regions and communities not directly affected by the movement, especially tribal ones who had their own gods and goddesses, systems of faith and worship and cosmologies independent of what has been called Hindu. Let me also add that calling Bhakti a 'movement' is an act of retrospection, as it was spread over several centuries from the sixth to the 19th and did not happen simultaneously in all languages and regions. Still the 'movement' in most parts had certain common features, though expressed in different ways and forms natural to the language and the culture of the people. (1) Most of the Bhakti movements and their creative leaders had a predilection for pre-vedic gods (like Shiva, Vishnu/Krishna, Sakthi/Kali for example) and their patterns of life and thought as implied in the rejection of Brahmin privilege, its egalitarian philosophy and the tribal character of its collective worship. (2) they emphasised the similarities among different religions/cults, finding them to be only different paths leading to the same goal, and even attempted syntheses of religions as in Sikhism, founded by Guru Nanak, and the different Sufi cults. (3) Most of them rejected the *varna-jati* system and the superiority of the priestly class. (4) They problematised and often rendered superfluous the institution of priesthood by directly addressing God. (5) They privileged the oral tradition against the written. (6) They de-privileged Sanskrit language and chose to compose in the regional languages and dialects. (7) They were often multilingual, easily traversing regions and crossing language barriers (eg; Meera, Kabir, Nanak, Namdev, Vidyapati). (8) They created and introduced new forms of composing, singing, dancing and performing (like *doha, pada, bijak, ulatbasi, vakh, abhang, bharud, barahmasa, qasida, rasa, vachana, kummi, prabandha; kirtan, bhajan, dhun, jatra, harikatha, burrakatha, angkiyanat, nagarasankirtana, tungi, Ramlila, Krishnalila; tullal, kathakali, yakshagana, Bharatanatyam, Kuchipudi, Manipuri, Odissi*). (9) Poetry and philosophy co-existed and supported each other, and the barriers between the physical and the metaphysical grew thin in their aesthetic-religious practice. (10) They developed a symbolism of their own, mixing traditional symbols like water, fire, river, sky, bird, tree, etc., and symbols chosen from the kitchen and the workplace like the loom, wheel, knife, ladle, bellows, veil, sindoor, bangles, etc. (11) Many of them formed alternative egalitarian communities like the Veerasaivas of Karnataka and the Warkaris of Maharashtra. Thus, looking back, it looks like a comprehensive cultural revolution with profound ideological, aesthetic and practical implications that attempted to create an alternative religion of the people, articulating subaltern aspirations at the material as well as spiritual levels.

The 'movement' had exhibited most of these features in its very initial phase in the Tamil Bhakti poetry (sixth to 13th centuries, A.D.), especially in the poetry of the Siddhs or 'Chittars' qualified by Rev. Robert Caldwell as the 'anti-Brahminical cycle' considering its thrust against caste-system and priesthood. Thirumular, the sixth century mystic proclaimed in his *Thirumantiram,* 'Caste is one and God is one' (Verse 2104). He decried bigotry and preached equanimity in an age torn by cult rivalries. Chivavakkiyar also reflects this sentiment, when he declares that the chanting of the Vedas, the study of the sacred scripts, the smearing of holy ashes and the muttering of prayers will not lead anyone to God. (*Chittar Jnanakkovai,* 21). He was also against idol worship: 'Do gods ever become stone?' (Ibid). 'Of what use are temples/And of what use the temple tanks?' (Ibid, 29). Chivavakkiyar also denounced the theories of the transmigration of the soul and of rebirth: 'Milk does not go back to the udder/Likewise butter can never become buttermilk;/The sound of the conch does not exist once it is broken;/The blown flower, the fallen fruit, do not go back to the tree? The dead are never born again, never!' (Ibid, 123). Pambatti Chittar states: 'We will set fire to the divisions of caste,/ We'll debate philosophy in the marketplaces/We'll have dealings with despised households/We'll go around in different paths.' Tradition tells us that the Siddhas came from the lowly and they included shepherds, temple drummers, artificers, robbers, potters, fishermen, hunters, weavers, washer-men, oil-pressers, pariahs, etc. *Periyapuranam,* the 12th century hagiographical work narrating the lives of 63 Shaiva saints supports this, as it says the Siddhas came chiefly from the Vellalas (farmers) and Vanigas (merchants), well below the Brahmins in caste hierarchy. By imagining an impersonal Godhead, they liberated themselves from rituals and similar observances. Like the India Sufis, they rejected the mechanical and dreary aspects of Bhakti and cherished love, tenderness and compassion. They also considered the body sacred, like the *vachanakara*s of Karnataka later ('*Kayaka* is Kailasa,' says Basavanna).

I mentioned these features of Tamil Bhakti poetry only to show how from the very beginning it had all the features of what Victor Turner and A.K. Ramanujan call an 'anti-structure', developed out of the elements of the structure they reject. Many of these elements go into the poetry of the later Bhakti poets, like Allama Prabhu, Basavanna, Devara Dasimayya, Dasreswara,, Vemana, Thikkana,Tukaram, Namdev, Jnandev, Chokhamela, Karmamela,

Kabir, Raidas and others, who share many of these concerns and perspectives in different ways. For example, look at some *vachana*s of Basava:

> You can make them talk
> if the serpent
> has stung
> them.
> You can make them talk
> if they're struck
> by an evil planet.
> But you can't make them talk
> if they're struck dumb
> by riches
> Yet when poverty the magician
> enters, they'll speak
> at once,
> O lord of the meeting rivers.
> —(Vachana, 132, *Speaking of Shiva,* Tr A.K. Ramanujan, Penguin Books, New Delhi, 1973, p.77)

> They plunge
> wherever they see water.
> They circumambulate
> every tree they see.
> How can they know you
> o Lord
> who adore
> waters that run dry
> trees that wither?
> —(Vachana 581, Ibid. p. 85)

> In a Brahmin house
> where they feed the fire
> as a god

when the fire goes wild
and burns the house
they splash on it
the water of the gutter
and the dust of the street,
beat their breasts
and call the crowd
These men then forget their worship
and scold their fire,
O, lord of the meeting rivers!
—(Vachana, 586, Ibid. p. 85)

The rich
will make temples for Siva.
What shall I,
a poor man,
do?
My legs are pillars,
the body the shrine,
The head a cupola
of gold.
Listen, O lord of the Meeting Rivers,
Things standing shall fall
But the moving ever shall stay.
—(Vachana, 820, Ibid. p. 88)

Now look at some verses from Namdev, the Marathi-Hindi saint poet (1270–1350):

Give up all worship,
All debates, all activity.
Give up all distinctions,
Keep your mind on Govind.
—(Pada 63, *The Hindi Padavali of Namdev*, Winand M. Callewaert,

Mukund Lath, Motilal Banarsidas Publishers Ltd, Delhi, 1989, p. 180)

> These clowns with their sacred beads
> And rosaries know nothing about truth.
> They see nothing but claim to
> Give insight to others.
> Can deception lead to liberation?
> —(Pada 64, Ibid. p. 181)

> I gather no leaves for ritual offerings.
> There is no god in the shrine.
> —(Pada, 65, Ibid. p. 182)

Chokhamela (d.1338), the Mahar saint, looks at God as a worker:

> He dusts and cleans, and fetches water,
> the upholder of dharma;
> saves from the searing flames of nirvana.
> He keeps the cows at the milkman's house
> and happily with others
> breaks the pot of curds.
> He pulled a wall for
> Dhyaneshwar, made Changdev
> famous; weeded the beds
> for Saavata the gardener,
> and fired pots for Gora.
> He loves more than his own self
> goldsmith, cobbler and Namdev the tailor.
> —(Verse 284, *Songs of Chokhamela,* Tr. Rohini Mokashi Punekar, The Book Review Literary Trust, New Delhi, 2002, p. 61)

Tukaram, the Marathi saint (1608-1650) has a take on Brahmins:

> In this Age of Evil, poetry is an infidel's art:

The world teems with theatrical performers.
...They cite Vedic injunctions, but can't do themselves any good.
—(*Says Tuka,* Tr. Dilip Chitre, Penguin Books, Delhi, 1991, p. 115)
...His teaching begins when the sun goes down.
Drawing mystic squares on the ground,
Decorating them too, he worships occult designs.
Placing lamps in all four corners and behind curtains
He assumes a posture and demonstrates tantric gestures.
As an oblation he wants to be offered sweets
Nothing short of a divine feast
His preaching over, time to start the feast
Forget about sipping water from the palm of the hand at the end of the meal
Committing sacrilege is his means of livelihood:
He sends his followers into the bottomless pit.
—(Ibid. p. 116)

Don't kill a snake
Before the eyes of a saint
For the saint's being
Includes all living things
And he is easily
Hurt.
A single hair plucked from one's body
Causes instant pain
And the soul that perceives
Life as a community always suffers.
—(Ibid. p.155)

And here is Kabir:

When learned priests
forget their stuff,
they read the good old Vedas—
without their books

they don't have a clue
to the secret of things
—('Sapling and Seed', *Kabir, The Weaver's Songs,* Tr. Vinay Dharwadker, Penguin Books, Delhi, 2003, p. 149)

I went on hajj to the ka'aba,
but on the way I ran into God.
Picking a fight with me, he said:
who told you to go there?
—(From *Adigranth*, No.7, Ibid. p. 176)

The Sufi poets like Mullah Dawood, Bulle Shah, Baba Farid, Shah Husain, Shah Sharaf, Ali Hyder, Hashim Shah and Shah Abdul Latif also laugh at Muslim priesthood, reject rituals and hierarchies and believe only in the four paths to God, *shariat* or disciplined life, *tariqat* or following the *murshid* or guru, *haqiqat* or enlightenement and *marafat* or realisation of truth and merger in the Divine reality. Bulle Shah, the Sufi saint, like the bhaktas, rejected religion in its insular sense:

Lumpens live in Hindu temples
And sharks in the Sikh shrines.
Musclemen live in Muslim mosques
And lovers live in their clime.
—(*Sain Bulleh Shah, the Mystic Muse,* Tr. K. S. Duggal, Abhinav Publications, Delhi, 1996, p. 189)

Or

The Mullahas and Qazis show me the light
Leading to the maze of superstition.
—(Ibid. Quoted in the Preface, p. 12)

Wipe off Kalma from the sight
Bulleh has found his lover within.

Others grope in the pitch dark night...
—(Ibid. p. 159)

A lover of God?
They'll make much fuss;
They'll call you a Kafir
You should say—yes, yes.
—(Ibid. Quoted in the Preface, p. 13)

Women saints like Andal, Mahadeviyakka, Meerabai, Gangasati, Bahinabhai and Lal Ded add a gender dimension to the movement finding bhakti to be a path of emancipation from a patriarchal world. Akka Mahadevi, the 12th century Kannada Veerasaiva saint, expresses the tension of having to serve two masters simultaneously:

Husband outside,
Lover inside,
I can't manage them both.
This world
And the other,
Cannot marriage them both
O lord white as jasmine,
I cannot hold in one hand
Both the round nut
And the long bow....
—(Mahadeviyakka, Verse 114, *Speaking of Shiva,* p. 127)

She wanted to overcome her sexuality by rejecting the body:

My body is dirt,
my spirit is space:
which
shall I grab, O lord? How,
and what
shall I think of you?

> Cut through
> my illusions,
> lord white as jasmine
> —(Ibid. Verse 12, p. 116)

Like Akka, Lalleswari (Lal Ded, Lalla Arifa) the 14th century Saivite poet of Kashmir also walked naked, overcoming her physical sense of shame. She too was rejected by her husband, and her *vakhs* are full of references to the treatment she received at her in-laws. Meerabai, the 16th century Rajasthani saint poet also had to suffer ignominy at home; there was even an attempt made to poison her.

> Rana
> sent me poison
> I drank it
> happily
> I am in love
> who cares
> what happens
> next
> —(Mirabai, Tr. Rahul Soni from *Eating God, A Book of Bhakti Poetry,* ed. Arundhati Subramaniam, Penguin Ananda, Haryana, 2014, p.114)

These and similar feelings are echoed by many women saints including Ayadakki Lakkamma, Satyaakka, Kadire Remmavve and other Saivite saints. The Bhakti-Sufi movements once again demonstrate the unity as well as the diversity of Indian literary genius as a composite of the genius of individual writers, of the respective languages and communities.

4

The Bhakti-Sufi movements may be said to have laid the foundational values and principles of the modern literatures of India in definite ways as they interrogated hierarchies, promulgated the egalitarian ideal, upheld the freedom of the spirit and were secular-spiritual. It was these ideas that inspired later movements like the anti-colonial and reformist trends in pre-Independent India. The trends began to surface strongly in the second half of the 19th century that was again a defining moment of turbulence in Indian history, both social and literary. The spread of education, translations of Sanskrit and Western classics into modern Indian languages giving them norms and standards to aspire to, the arrival of the printing press, the rise of prose genres like the novel, the short story, the prose play, the essay, literary criticism, the travelogue, the autobiography and the biography, the arrival of new forms of poetry like the lyric, the sonnet and the dramatic monologue, the emergence of literary journals and associations of writers and readers: a 'public sphere' in the Habermasian sense had clearly emerged in most languages by the beginning of the 20th century. The literature of the period had two chief preoccupations: resisting British colonialism and reforming Indian society from within. The poetry of Ghulam Mehjoor, Rabindranath Tagore, Nazrul Islam, Sumitranandan Pant, Maithilisaran Gupt, Bhaivirsingh, Keshavsut, Subramania Bharati, Bharatidasan, Vallathol, Kumaran Asan, N.S. Bendre, Veeresalingam and others, while celebrating the virtues of India's unique intellectual and spiritual traditions and popular resistance against oppressors is also critical of the inequality, poverty, caste system, superstitions and meaningless rituals that haunt Indian society. The secular spirituality of this literature is also akin to that of the Bhakti-Sufi movements. The early Indian novels, say, of Bankim Chandra Chatterjee, Govardhan Tripathi, H.N. Apte, C.V. Raman Pillai, O. Chandu Menon and others also reflect a deep awareness of the paradoxes of Indian life as felt in their own regions. The West is a strong presence in these novels in several ways. It is there as a culture received through modern education, to be encountered, made use of, challenged or exorcised. Tagore's *Gora* is in some sense a paradigmatic text, setting the agenda for those who wish to fight colonialism. In his anxiety to be authentic to himself, Gora, the protagonist, has to abandon not only his urbanism and fanaticism but his self-righteousness as well: this is an anxiety carried on by several post-Independence novels, like U.R. Ananthamurthy's *Samskara*. The Progressive Movement, influenced by Gandhian as well as Marxian ideals, was an offshoot of the reformist literature with which it co-existed and linked to the debates over decolonisation and the nature of the post-colonial nation-state that was to come into being. Pioneered by Mulk Raj Anand, Sajjad Saheer and Premchand and blessed by writers like Tagore, the Movement brought together people from diverse ideological backgrounds, who however shared a concern for the society in the making. There were very few writers in India totally unaffected by the ideals of the Movement. The fact that writers as diverse as Thakazhi Sivasankara Pillai, Vaikom Mohammed Basheer, G. Sankara Kurup, Niranjana, Sri Sri, Jayakanthan, Vinda Karandikar, Tarashankar Bandopadhyay, Subhas Mukhopadhyay, Saadat Hasan Manto, Ismat Chughtai, Ali Sardar Jaffri, Yashpal, Nagarjun and Abdur Rahman Rahi associated themselves with the movement proves its broad and inclusive base in the early days. The ideological field of the nation of this time exploded into a terrain of struggle for several social and political forces that were getting organised around issues ranging from gender, caste and religion to class, language and region—a struggle inflected by the anti-Imperialist struggles in Asia and Africa and the anti-fascist struggles in Europe. The writers in the Movement, along with a large body of co-travellers outside it represented 'an energy, a stubborn force engaging as a committed and recognisable voice in language and society with a whole slew of issues, all of them having to do with a combination of enlightenment and emancipation or freedom', to use the qualification that Edward Said attributes to the modern intellectual. While its impact was felt across the country, the Movement was stronger in certain languages like Hindi, Urdu, Punjabi, Tamil, Telugu and Malayalam. The concerns varied according to the regions, as also the communities that sought representation in the literary discourse and those that represented them. Dalits and tribals, for example, were most often represented through the non-Dalits say, like Thakazhi Sivasankara Pillai or Gopinath Mohanty or later by Mahaswetadevi.

Even women were not necessarily represented by women writers and the gender issue was seldom foregrounded as class was the defining category. Still the origins of several recent literary movements based on identity—like the Dalit, Adivasi, feminist and nativist—can be traced to the Progressive Movement, though the Movement itself got fragmented later for ideological reasons. The realism of the Progressives in the late 1930s and 1940s was to be challenged in the 1950s and the 1960s by the Modernists when the personal, subjective element came to the fore, obscuring the objective, social element, which was not entirely absent from the Modernist works. From the 1970s onwards realism of a kind seems to have been on a strong comeback trail in many of the language literatures of India..

This brief examination of some key moments in the evolution of India's literature is enough to prove the variety as well as the common sources and concerns of our literatures. After more than five decades of independence and 500 years of imperial and colonial rule, it is imperative that we rethink concepts like Indianness and Indian literature. One may then be able to unveil the complicity of these concepts with the ideology of colonialism on the one hand and globalisation on the other. We have come a long way since the German romantic theorist Wilhelm von Schlegel used the term Indian literature to mean Sanskrit literature (1823). Since then many other scholars have used the term as being synonymous with Sanskrit literature, at the most extended to include Prakrit, Apabhramasa and Pali literatures. M Garcin de Tassy's two-volume *History of the Literature of of Hindu and Hindustani* in French (1839-47; later revised and enlarged as a three-volume edition in 1870-71), Albrecht Weber's *History of Indian Literature* in German (1852), George A. Grierson's *Modern Vernacular Literature of Hindustan* (1889), Ernst P. Horowitz's *A Short History of Indian Literature* and Maurice Winternitz's *History of Indian Literature* (1908-1922) in German as well as Herbert H Gowen's *History of Indian Literature* (1931) have all contributed to the constitution of the category of 'Indian literature'. Most of these do not represent, or under-represent, the literatures in the modern Indian languages that were fully grown by the time and many even had their own histories of literature written in the concerned language itself. Sanskrit was posited by them as the classical code of early India, congruent with new linked conceptions of classicism and class. One has also to see that many Indian texts like *Bhagavad Gita, Manusmriti* and *Arthashastra* were translated by the Orientalists for colonial rulers so that they can better understand the people they had to deal with and control. Tejaswini Niranjana has closely looked at the colonial agenda behind the translation of such texts into English that were mostly done by Western scholars, as the masters did not trust native translators. Literary works were also translated with this purpose in mind and as Kate Teltscher says, into a European code. She points out how the English translation of Kalidasa's *Sakuntalam* echoed Shakespeare and how it was treated as a romantic comedy. Romila Thapar too, in her book, *Shakuntala: Texts, Readings, Histories*, has looked at the reasons for the rare reception the play received in the West as Kalidasa's heroine, unlike Vyasa's independent and assertive Sakuntala, fitted well with the Orientalist concept of the coy, vulnerable, naïve and beautiful exotic Oriental woman. Sakuntala was also, metaphorically, the wild, feminine and rustic India while Dushyanta was the urban, powerful and masculine England. These representations have larger implications, as the whole colonial epistemology is based on the positivist belief in a non-political and unbiased science, whose objectivity was ensured through a distanced neutrality. The whole Enlightenment rationality was based on a denial of coevalness, such as that we find in the science of anthropology, which objectifies its subjects of study and posits them in a distant time. Colonial historiography too looks at Europe as universal and the European male as the ultimate human being, thus placing cultures in an unreal hierarchy in an evolutionary pattern of time, where India will be seen as Europe's past and Europe as India's only possible future. It is essential thus to escape the colonial paradigm to freely look at India's history as well as Indian literature for, as Michel Foucault says, it is not enough for us to liberate the individual from the state and its institutions, but to liberate us both from the state and the type of individuation linked to the state so that we develop and promote new forms of subjectivity. India and Indian literature were constituted as a site of knowledge in the context of its encounter with Europe and, hence, today we need to decolonise ourselves by critiquing all those attitudes and processes that give rise to discourses that 'other' the Eastern nations and cultures.

Indian thinkers too have discussed the category of Indian Literature: Sri Aurobindo, Krishna Kripalani, Suniti Kumar Chatterjee, V.K. Gokak, Umashankar Joshi, Sujit Mukherjee, Sisir Kumar Das, K.M. George, Ganesh Devy, etc., have elaborated the concept as a posited unity of diverse language formations or as the articulation of 'Indian Culture'. Aijaz Ahmed in his essay on Indian literature in *In Theory* has acknowledged the difficulties of positing such a unitary category. T.R.S. Sharma has pointed to the European neglect of the Indian languages in his introduction to *Ancient Indian Literature*, an anthology edited by him for the Sahitya Akademi, 'While many European scholars had translated entire works of Sanskrit, few of them had ventured into Prakrit and Apabhramsa and none into Kannada'. This is also true of other languages, often including classical languages like Tamil. As P.P Ravindran remarks in an article ('Genealogies of Indian Literature', *Economic* and *Political Weekly*, 24 June, 2006), 'Even today European scholars of modern south Asian languages and literature feel compelled to legitimise themselves and their fields of study, working as they do in departments of south Asian studies—at times designated, even now, as departments of Indology—that are dominated largely by classical Sanskrit scholars.'

Pointing to the introduction of *Narrative Strategies: Essays on South Asian Literature and Film* by Vasudha Dalmia and Theo Damsteegt (Leiden, 1998), where they claim to let the world know 'the seriousness' of their discipline, he points out how their statement is unabashedly Eurocentric and ignorant or deliberately neglectful of the enormous scholarship that has been produced on Indian literature by scholars of various hues from the South Asian subcontinent. It is disgraceful that the attitude of European scholarship to this mighty archive remains unchanged since the 19th century. All these works also share the class and caste prejudices of the tradition of the Sanskrit-based

Hindu orthodoxy. Only recently have some scholars like Sheldon Pollock begun to realise this, as is evident in his introduction to *Literary Cultures in History: Reconstructions from South Asia* (New Delhi, 2003), where the language literatures have been treated in isolation, as also in relation to other language literatures in India. Sheldon Pollock says:

> With very few exceptions, European histories of Indian literature remained histories of Sanskrit and its congeners... The real plurality of literatures in south Asia and their dynamic and long-term interaction were scarcely recognised, except perhaps incidentally by Protestant missionaries and British civil servants who were prompted by the practical objectives of conversion and control.

Pollock also examines how the Subaltern school of historiography has sought to redirect the study of 19th and early 20th century Indian society and politics 'toward the popular, the vernacular, the oral, and the local, and to recapture the role of small people in effecting big historical change.'

Contemporary analyses of colonialism have shown how new Indian pasts with real-life social consequences, such as the traditionalisation of the social order by the systematic miscognition of indigenous discourses on caste were created by colonial knowledge. They have demonstrated at the same time, how discourses, such as Nationalism, which were borrowed from Europe entered into complex interaction with local modes of thought and action that, through a process not unlike import substitution, appropriated, rejected, transformed or replaced them. Pollock goes on to say how the reexamination of theory, practice and history of areas, especially driven by the analysis of globalisation, has made us aware of the artificiality of geographical boundaries of inquiry.

Today we need to develop alternative genealogies that go beyond the hegemonic canon and travel to the deepest springs of popular creativity. Rather than a mechanical unitary concept we need to develop a comparative concept, a fresh literary cartography, marking areas of isolation and interaction, patterns specific to languages and influences that they share. Only then will we be able to overcome the binary opposition between the singular and the plural as irreconcilable antinomies and arrive at a dialectical concept of Indian literature in its twin aspects of unity and diversity.

THE MODERN AND THE DEMOCRATIC
Indian Poetry after Independence

Let me begin again with some stories. Dhoorjati, the 16th century king of Madurai once declared a prize of 8,000 gold coins to a poem adjudged the best by the scholars and critics in his court. The land was passing through a terrible famine, and an impoverished farmer approached Lord Siva, asking him to give him a poem so that he may present it in Dhoorjati's court and win the prize that might assuage his poverty. The farmer promptly took the poem to the court in earnest confidence, as it had been composed by the Lord himself. The poem met with general approbation from the court, but one critic, Natkeeran, while agreeing that the sentiment, the embellishments and the features of the poem were perfect, objected to one usage: the poem had said that women's hair is naturally fragrant. This was against common sense, as also *Alamkara-shasthra*. Siva himself appeared before the court to defend the poem and said the Parvati's hair was naturally fragrant; but Natkeeran was not impressed. He said Parvati was a goddess and it did not apply to human beings. It was a mockery of traditional poetics. Siva now revealed his third eye; but Natkeeran was adamant; he said the poem was defective, even if the poet had eyes all over his head. Siva then cursed the critic and turned him into a leper. The story can be interpreted at many levels; but I would like to see it as a demonstration of experience and imagination challenging and transcending *status quo* poetics. Poetry, all literature, advances by rendering the laws of poetics redundant or inadequate, rewriting them and creating new laws, as the new experiential context demands.

The second story, a folktale retold by A.K. Ramanujan, is about a wood-cutter who claimed that the axe he used had been handed over to him through generations. Asked whether the handle had never been changed, he would say, of course, how could the same handle function for so long? Asked about the blade, he would have a similar answer, yes, it has been changed many times too. Yet he would never concede that the axe was different from the one used by his forefathers. The story gives us a new insight into tradition: what we call tradition is nothing but a series of innovations; its seeming continuity is a matter of faith rather than reality.

The third is not really a story, but a poem by Baudelaire, titled 'Loss of a Halo' published posthumously. One day a reader of poetry finds the poet he adores in the most unlikely of circumstances, in a dark and dingy backyard of the city where beggars, criminals and prostitutes live. He is shocked and asks the poet how he happened to be there. The poet tells him the other day he lost his halo while travelling along the busy city street. He could not pick it up as vehicles were rushing past and his life was more valuable than his poet's halo. The reader tells him he could have advertised the loss and retrieved the halo; but the poet answers that now he feels it is better not to have a halo so that without being identified, he can visit the backyards of the city and see how ordinary people live; he can be a man among men. The poem is about the loss of the romantic aura around poetry that has made poetry more mundane, more real and closer to people.

All the three stories are relevant to what I have to say here as they sum up the transformation that has been happening to poetry over the last one century or so. While this is true of world poetry in general, it is especially true of Indian poetry that has been changing continuously in its attempt to capture the modern reality growing more and more complex everyday and to be the voice of the marginalised millions in the country.

Two seemingly antithetical yet overlapping projects characterise the poetry of independent India: modernisation and democratisation. By modernisation I mean that radical transition of sensibility, perception and idiom that overtook Indian poetry in most languages in the 1950s and 60s. By democratisation, I mean the engagement of literatures with collective destinies reflected in content as well as the employment of everyday language and folk traditions at the level of form.

While independence was greeted by several poets with celebratory odes, quite a few considered it a false dawn: either because they felt, like Nazrul Islam, that the *swaraj* did not bring anything for the hungry child or because it was a flawed and fissured freedom since the gift was a divided India. Memories of the communal holocausts were still fresh in people's minds. Telugu poets like Dasarathi and Arudra still yearned for the sun of freedom that had not yet risen in the Hyderabad of Nizam and the Razakars. Umashankar Joshi, the Gujarati poet confessed, 'However much I might try/to force a chuckle on my lips/there is no real cheer in the desert of my heart.' Armando Menzes heard 'the angry gnashings' of 'monsters agape for food' in the 'wintry fold'. The deepest anguish was expressed by the poets of the Punjab and Bengal directly affected by the Partition. Annada Shankar ray found the Partition to have been 'an elemental psychic experience'; Bishnu Dey found the experience 'life-in-death or death-in-life.' People who had lost a country were panting in the shade: 'some here, some there, some in Barisal, some in Dacca'. In the Punjab, Amrita Pritam invoked Waris Shah as the symbol of the undivided Punjab: 'Corpses entomb the fields today. Blood overflows the Chinab'. Faiz Ahmed Faiz wrote from the other side of the border, 'This is not the longed-for break of day,/ Not that clear dawn in quest of which our comrades/Set out.' The crisis moved hundreds of poets from Makhdoom Mohiuddin, the Urdu poet to Somorendra, the Manipuri poet. (Fiction reflected this murderous attack on the millennial continuum of Indian history and civilisation in the new narratives, the stories of Saadat Hasan Manto, Amrita Pritam, K.S. Duggal, Nanak Singh, Krishan Chander, Sunil Gangopadhyay and Rajinder Singh Bedi, novels like Khushwant Singh's *Train to Pakistan*, Qurratulain Hyder's *Aag ka Dariya*, Yashpal's *Jhoota Sach*, Bhisham Sahni's *Tamas*.)

The mutual recriminations, communal tensions and orgiastic demonstrations preceding and following Independence climaxed in the assassination of Mahatma Gandhi on 30 January, 1948: now came the time for prayerful introspection and novel beginnings in India's national life. The death of the Mahatma signalled the end of a great era in the nation's life that had turned the most ordinary of men and women into heroes and heroines prepared to sacrifice even their lives for the nation's freedom. Selflessness slowly gave way to selfishness in politics; the common people victimised by the landlords, the capitalists and the bureaucrats felt estranged from the society they had created. Gajanan Madhav Muktibodh, a pioneer of the new poetry (*nayee kavita*) in Hindi, declared in 1953 that 'the face of the moon is crooked' and the hegemonic political formation was a 'wooden Ravan'. Kedarnath Singh spoke of the *anagat*, the one who had not yet arrived, whose wings were lost in the golden shadows and feet were trembling in the mist. A catastrophic vision like that of W. B. Yeats in 'The Second Coming' seemed to penetrate literature, for, the best appeared 'to lack all conviction' and the worst were 'full of passionate intensity'. Bishnu Dey, the Bengali poet, expressed his concern for the death of the village, the rude aggression on nature, and the thoughtless urbanisation that seemed to disturb the harmony of life:

> Why in this land is man
> dumb and helpless?
> Why are rivers, trees and hills
> so uncared for?
> How long do we roam about
> carrying our tents?
> When does the alien
> set up his own house?

The same feeling was echoed by N.N. Kakkad, the Malayalam poet, who compared the city evening to a made-up whore, roaming about the park in search of customers, when a giant figure was going up the mansions, spilling blood and thorns behind him (*Paarkil*, In the Park). Ayyappa Paniker, in his poems like 'Kurukshetram' and 'Mrityupooja' echoed similar frustrations and dilemmas, both social and moral; Gopalakrishna Adiga, in poems like 'Frog in the Well' and 'Do Something, Brother' too attacked the passivity and complacency of the Indian middle class that hardly responded to the misery around. Akhtar-ul-Iman, the modern Urdu poet, found in the child lost in the city's glare and stampede, a symbol of 'the Indian youth torn from his roots'. 'The Hungry Poets' of Bengal inspired by Allen Ginsberg, especially Sunil Gangopadhyay and Shakti Chattopadhyay and the 'Digambara poets' of Andhra Pradesh like Nagnamuni, Jwalamukhi and Nikhileswar gave birth to a new poetry of anger and frustration with Dadaist and Surrealist elements in their modes of imagination and expression. Free verse and prose came to be increasingly used; images replaced older figures of speech; poetic imagination and idiom were both freed from conventional habits and clichés. Annada Shankar Ray said that there was nothing foreign about these changes: 'We went surrealist without reading about it. Ionesco's absurd world had descended upon us.'

These similarities of impulse and formal experimentation not withstanding, Modernism emerged under different circumstances in different languages. Even its names differed: it was *nayee kavita* (there were other movements too like *akavita*) in Hindi, *adhunik kavita* in Bengali and Malayalam, *navya* in Kannada and *puthukkavitai* in Tamil, though all these mean the new or modern poetry. The idioms and approaches often differed from language to language and even ideologically it was no monolith. For example, in Hindi, Bengali or Telugu the new poetry had a predominantly progressive character, as the movement had been pioneered by Muktibodh, Bishnu Dey and Sri Sri, who had a radical socialist impulse in them, while in Marathi, Malayalam and Kannada the thrust was individualistic as in B.S. Mardhekar, Ayyappa Paniker or Gopalakrishna Adiga, who were primarily for the sovereignty of the individual, though their poetry seen in retrospect was not without social implications, expressed often negatively, in terms of escape or of agony. It is possible to build a whole approach to Indian modernism based on these attitudes as has been done by E.V. Ramakrishnan in his study—perhaps the only book-long study of modern poetry in India so far—*Making It New: Modernism in Malayalam, Marathi and Hindi Poetry* (IIAS, Shimla, 1995) though such a division between what he, following Fredric Jameson, calls 'high modernism' that is essentially form-based and individual-centred and what he, following Peter Burger calls 'the avant-garde', that is radical in content and questions the very institution of literature. He questions the approaches of V.K. Gokak, U.R. Anantha Murthy, et al., to assert that the 'rightist Adiga and the leftist Muktibodh' cannot explore the same states of mind and there are conservative and radical strains within the modernist camp. He also complexifies the question further by pointing to the poets who are still wedded to certain kinds of romantic or non-Modernist poetry that is traditional in tone and design and rural in vision and inspiration: can we say that they are not responding to modern reality at all?

If our use of the term 'modernism' is haunted by bad faith in the Indian context, it is because of the large segment of Indian reality it cannot accommodate within its aesthetic matrix. The other India, which is untouched by print journalism and lives beyond the written word, is nevertheless a strong presence, which an Indian writer has to come to terms with.

Ramakrishnan uses the terms 'high modernism' and 'the avant-garde' to describe how various writers within the modernist group respond to the presence of such a subaltern domain of counter-culture constituted by underprivileged classes. The avant-garde tradition in Indian languages, according to him, constitutes an attempt to indigenise Western Modernism through the deployment of indigenous forms of articulations and through the accommodation of greater segments of Indian reality within these forms. High modernism, to him, is confined to the realm of the aesthetic and he considers that realm to be autonomous. It is when such a formulation is made and the aesthetic crystallises as an independent category, that the avant-garde begins to clearly recognise the social cost of such a purely aesthetic project. Ramakrishnan takes up for special study the poetry of Kedarnath Singh, Dilip Chitre and K. Satchidanandan in the last three chapters of his book, in order to exemplify the distinctions he makes. These poets are taken primarily as avant-garde poets who had started as modernists. He has also looked at the Dalit poetry in Marathi as practised by Namdeo Dhasal, Raja Dhale, Daya Pawar, Vaman Nimbalkar, etc., and the nativist 'Dravidian' poetry in Malayalam, like that practised by Kadammanitta Ramakrishnan as other examples of poetic practices that interrogate the status quo.

He says that the avant-garde idiom is inseparable from that of 'high modernism' initially because both have a common agenda of interrogating the patriarchal assumption that had become institutionalised in the literatures of Indian languages. U.R. Ananthamurthy and D. R. Nagaraj in the introduction to *Vibhava*, the first-ever anthology of modern writing in India, have spoken of these patriarchal icons in all the languages who represented the nationalist-romantic views and personified all that was stereotyped and stale in poetry. They call this the 'Tagore syndrome'.

In terms both of style and ideology, one can notice a surprising similarity among the father figures of different Indian literatures. Cultural nationalism, romantic love, nature, mysticism, metaphysical leanings and an ideal of nation building formed the common ethos of the Tagore syndrome and the concoction they produced had become a little too sweet and stale. The dominant form in poetry was the lyric and the fiction writer's creed was realism. When this type of patriarchal authority became too much to bear the new generation had to free itself from the clutches of what it thought was an overbearing literary culture. It is in this act of defiance, this urge to commit patricide if need be, that we see the beginnings of this movement.

Tagore, as Amiya Dev suggests, was a poet of faith in God, nature and man while the modernists were poets of doubt and at times despair. Tagore had his parallels in other languages like Vallathol or G. Sankara Kurup in Malayalam, N.S. Bendre in Kannada, the poets of the Ravikiran Mandal in Marathi, Umashankar Joshi in Gujarati, the Chhayavadi poets in Hindi, or Bharatidasan in Tamil. But it may be wrong to assume that they completely negated the legacy of such poets; it was redeployed in the new poetry in various ways. Amiya Dev has shown how the important variables like Sanskrit connection, the Western impact and the Tagore tradition operate in the modern poetry of Jibanananda Das, Sudhindranath Datta, Budhadeva Bose and Amiya Chakravarty in diverse ways. In fact we need to read individual poets closely in the context of their languages and the larger context of modernism to properly expose the hidden contours of the modernist moment in the literary history of Indian languages.

I fear there is some sociological as well as stylistic reductionism in E.V. Ramakrishnan's approach where two kinds of modernism are counter-posed against each other as black and white and the folk is bluntly identified with the social. The actual practice of poets—the so-called 'high modernists' as well as the 'avant-garde'—militates against such a clean categorisation as one often finds in the same poets both the tendencies expressed at the different stages of their evolution or in different poems. At the most, one can only speak about 'dominants' and not divide poets cleanly into the two categories. That is why, based on the concept of 'difference' I have tried to look at the emerging identities in modern Indian poetry as 'alternative nation-hoods' ('Imagined Communities: Collective Aspirations in Contemporary Indian Poetry' in *Indian Literature: Positions and Propositions*, 1999 and 'Many Indias: Alternative Nationhoods in Contemporary Indian Poetry' in *Authors, Texts, Issues*, 2003) and have also examined them as stages in a process of ontological evolution ('The Quest for the Dominant: Towards an Ontology of Modern Malayalam Poetry', *Indian Literature: Positions and Propositions*). In these attempts, I have tried to show how the monolithic idea of a nation is slowly giving way to a democratic and pluralistic idea where each group relates itself to the idea of the nation in its own special way. In the context of the threat of a forced homogenisation and cultural globalisation, difference becomes the key creative concept that defines the Indian avant-garde while all the essentialist ideas about 'Indianness', most of which have been inherited by our nationalists from the Orientalist constructions of a Hindu India stand challenged. Such a construct will be an act of civilisational violence as it involves a negation of heteroglossia, a silencing of ethnic diversity and religious pluralism and a bulldozing of diverse worldviews and cosmologies that together constitute the federation of Indian culture. The salient features of that characterisation were the denial of empirical reality, the inability to distinguish the self from the non-self and exterior from interior, a neglect of universal human nature, a refusal to create synoptic systems and the consequent construction of an illogical bricolage of tools and systems, the theories of *karma* and *samsara*, the hierarchies of caste, the hegemony of *vedanta* in philosophy or of *dhwani* in literature or *rasa* in theatre, each of which has not merely exceptions but parallels and alternatives. Cultural nationalism today has become synonymous with a carnivorous revivalism that seeks to recreate the past in its own image and impose its oppressive authority over the present, the truth and strength of which lies in its cultural pluralism. India is a republic of languages, literatures, religions and ethnicities, each of which is authentically Indian and not 'regional' as they are often dubbed.

Whatever the paradigm we choose, the modern experience in India can be seen as a composite of many elements that had in their background the larger context of industrialisation and urbanisation. Initially, at least it was the revolt of a sensibility threatened by imminent decadence on the one hand and the ominous intimations of the loss of rural life on the other. The existing culture was under shock, stimulated by the retreat of Gandhian values from political life, the huge city-oriented demographic movements prompted by rural unemployment, the trauma left by Partition, the demon of hunger stalking the city slums as well as the villages, the tensions bred by colonial education, the alienation, angst and solitude felt by the sensitive urban populace, many of whom had their moorings in the village, the challenges posed by the uprooted masses to the secure sense of tradition and the native ways of seeing and feeling and the terror and ecstasy of the new world without a Supreme Ruler. Even collective ideologies seemed to have lost their charm to many and the simplistic idea of continuous progress was in question: the interminable complexities of experience compelled writers to seek alternative styles of thought, image and expression. It is in this process that they came to reject the *status quo* ways of perception and articulation in their predecessors. It was a natural outcome of their quest and need rather than a deliberate posture as U.R. Anantha Murthy, et al., seem to suggest. The criticism that modernism was some kind of *pastiche*, as raised by progressive critics like Jaidev, and conservatives in all the languages, does not stand scrutiny. While it is true that the modernists had learnt lessons from poets across the world, as has been done by the pioneers of most of the later movements in Indian writing, it is wrong to look at their poetry as some kind of mimicry or soulless imitation. They were answering a demand of literary and social history to mould a fresh idiom that could express the new complex reality of their regions and reform the poetic style in their languages that was drowning in clichés. Western models might have been employed as tools of subversion; but the agenda for the new aesthetic was set by our own literary history. It initiated a dialogue between the subaltern and the hegemonic, breaking through the Progressives' distrust of new textual strategies.

By 1965–70, Indian writers in different languages had already produced a body of poetry that strove to capture the multi-layeredness of Indian life with its uneasy co-existence of different time-worlds, of the rational and the spiritual, of the real and surreal, in their startling images, syncopated rhythms, employment of novel patterns, dream-like mixing and substitution of time and space, unexpected leaps of thought and fancy, transgressions of established norms of decency and propriety, odd combinatorial plays of the folk and the classical, indigenous and exotic elements, re-mappings of Indian mythology in the fresh contexts of life and language, forays into legends and archetypes and conscious use of everyday language. Navakanta Barua's *Mor aru Prithvir* (Of Mine and the Earth's), Hiren Bhattacharya's *Bibhinna Dinar Kavita* (Poems of Different days) and Neelmani Phookan's *Surya Heno Namiahe ei Nadiyedi* (The Sun is said to come Descending this River) in Assamiya, Shakti Chattopadhyay's *Jete Pari Kintu Kena Jabo* (I Can Go, but Why Should I?), and Nirendranath Chakraborty's *Ulanga Raja* (The Naked King), the poems of Buddhadev Bose, Amiya Chakravarty, Subhas Mukhopadhyay, Sudhindranath Datta, Samar Sen, Premendra Mitra and Sunil Gangopadhyay in Bengali, G.M. Muktibodh's *Chand ka Muh Tedha hai* in Hindi, the poems of Kunwar Narain, Kedarnath Singh, Vinod Kumar Shukla, Shamsher and others, Suresh Joshi's *Pratyancha* and Sitanshu Yashaschandra's *Magan poems* in Gujarati, the poems of Ravji Patel and Labhshankar Thaker, Gopalakrishna Adiga's *Bhoomigeete, Bhoota* and *Koopamanduka* in Kannada, he poems of K.S. Narasimhaswami, S.R. Ekkundi, Chandrasekhar

Patil, Channaveera Kanavi and G. S. Shivarudrappa in Kannada, M. Govindan's *Jeevitathil, Maranathil,* (In Life, In Death) Ayyappa Paniker's *Kavitakal,* (Poems) N.N. Kakkad's *1963,* Madhavan Ayyappath's *Jeevacharitrakkurippikal* (Notes for a Biography) and the poems of Attoor Ravivarma and Cherian K. Cherian in Malayalam, the poems of Nachiketa in Maithili, Dina Nath Nadim's *Ba Geva Na Az* (I Will Not Sing Today) and the poems of Rahman Rahi, Amin Kamil, and G.R. Santosh in Kashmiri, L. Samarendra Singh's *Khula Amagi Wari* (The Story of a Village), Thangjom Ibopishak's *Narak-Patal-Prithvi* (Hell, the Netherworld and the Earth), the poems of E. Neelakanta Singh and N. Biren in Manipuri, the poems of B.S. Mardhekar, Dilip Chitre, Arun Kolatkar and P.S. Rege in Marathi, Bhanuji Rao's *Bisad eka Ritu* (Despair, a Season), Sachi Rautroy's *Kabita* series, Ramakant Rath's *Sri Radha* and the poems of Sitakanata Mahapatra, Guruprasad Mohanty, Hara Parasad Das and Soubhagyakumar Mishra in Oriya, Harbhajan Singh's *Rukte Rishi,* Amrita Pritam's *Sunehere* (Messages) and Shivkumar Batalvi's *Luna* and in Punjabi, Sundara Ramaswamy's *Nadunisi Naikkal* (The Midnight-Dogs) and the poems of Ka. Na. Subramanyam, Jnanakoothan, C.S. Chellappa, S.Mani, T.K. Doraiswamy and others in Tamil, the poems of Ismail, Ajanta, and others in Telugu and of Firaq Gorakhpuri, Akhtar-ul-Iman, Balraj Komal Shehryar, Makhdoom Mohiuddin and others in Urdu, were responsible for giving new formal devices and aesthetic dimensions to Indian poetry in the last decades. While they were united in their urge to discover a new idiom of poetry, they differed at many levels, of the specific linguistic situation and genius, of ideological moorings and the models, if any, they looked forward to in other languages. This was paralleled in fiction where modernism was best represented by writers like Nirmal Verma, Krishna Baldev Vaid and Vinod Kumar Shukla in Hindi, Navkant Barua in Assamiya, O.V. Vijayan, M. Mukundan, Paul Zacharia and M.P. Narayana Pillai in Malayalam, U.R. Anantha Murthy, Poorna Chandra Tejaswi, Chandrashekhara Kambara and B.C. Ramachandra Sharma in Kannada, Mowni, Pudumaipithan and Sundara Ramaswamy in Tamil, Suresh Joshi in Gujarati, and Bhalchandra

Nemade in Marathi. Anantha Murthy's *Samskara*, Nirmal Verma's *Antim Aranya*, K. B. Vaid's *Bimal in Bog*, Vinod Kumar Shukla's *Nowkar kee Kameez*, Sundara Ramaswamy's *J.J. Sila Kurippukal* and O.V. Vijayan's *Khasakkinte Itihasam* may be taken as the paradigmatic texts of modernist Indian novel. The movement also produced playwrights like Vijay Tendulkar, Chandrashekhara Kambara, C.J. Thomas, C.N. Sreekantan Nair and Girish Karnad. There were parallel movements in painting, sculpture and architecture too.

Modernism—what E.V. Ramakrishnan calls 'high modernism'—became a way of documenting the dehumanisation of society in India after independence with its attendant alienation, morbidity and loss of identity. There was a 'shattering of the gestalt' as Dilip Chitre calls it in his introduction to the *Anthology of Modern Marathi Poetry* edited by him. The political conservatives and progressives alike had grown cynical and frustrated about the authoritarian tendencies of the nascent State and the economic and moral deprivation and both were on the look-out for new ways of documenting the outer, as well as the inner, reality of the new age.

2

The democratic tradition of Indian poetry—I have elsewhere called it the *sramana* or *samanya* tradition—as different from the more elitist, esoteric and exclusive *Brahmana* or *Brahima* tradition, following the distinction in world-view made by Patanjali, Jains and Buddhists—('Strategies of Subversion: *Sramana* Elements in Sarala Dasa's *Mahabharata*', *Authors, Texts, Issues*) can be traced back to the tribal and oral lore of the ancient past that voiced the perceptions, concerns and dreams of the community in simple, imaginative and sonorous verses informed by a deep respect for the cosmic order, a profound understanding of human suffering and a mythopoeic imagination that infused nature and life with a strange sense of mystery and surrealism. The epics, constructed from the oral lore, extended and transformed this tradition, providing it a lasting form and a polyphonic content that could be read in several ways. The

Buddhist and Jain literature enriched this tradition further, giving it an ethical foundation and the *Sangam* literature of the ancient Tamils provided it with ecological and social dimensions through a poetry of landscapes, love, domesticity and public life. The *bhakti* movement, essentially subaltern in nature, having been championed by peasants, craftsmen and common men and women from the so-called lower castes, created a radical spiritual poetry that revolted against all forms of man-made hierarchies like caste and class, rejected priesthood, used the languages of the people, in place of Sanskrit, for its compositions, gave rise to myriad forms of music, dance and theatre and created an alternative religion of the people, where earthly power, caste-superiority and riches could no more hold sway. The poetry of the anti-colonial and social reform movements and the Progressive Movement that followed marked another advance towards the democratisation of Indian poetry. From the 1970s onwards, this tradition has flowered like never before, with the emergence of several so-far marginalised sections of the society getting empowered by democracy. This poetry has emerged from a series of transversal struggles that have been raising the issues of decentralisation, right to cultural difference, caste and gender power, ecological balance, the rights of the tribals to land, language and culture, and sought to fight the intrusion of the market in everyday life, the consequent reduction of liberty to mere consumer choice, the forced standardisation of culture sought by capitalist and communal forces, the valorisation of competition, suppression of autonomy, the subtle imperialism of the unipolar world in the wake of globalisation and the cultural amnesia imposed on the Indian people with their glorious intellectual and artistic traditions and their unique ways of knowing and responding to the world. The individualistic tendencies of some of the modernists began to be interrogated as new collective identities got forged and a new literature of opposition and an aesthetics of resistance began to evolve in almost all the languages of India in the 1970s. These writers tried to evolve their own concepts of community and nation where the voices of the silenced and the marginalised would be heard aloud and listened to, and where they will have a decisive say in shaping the national destiny. It is to be noted here, as so eloquently argued by Ramachandra Guha in his recent book, *India after Gandhi: The History of the World's largest Democracy* that Indian democracy has survived and grown exactly as it could accommodate varied voices, communities, languages and religions without privileging one or the other, even when the civil society goes on throwing up movements that seek to foreground this section or that. Each citizen and each community has the right to imagine his/her/its own nation; the moment you try to define this nation, name it and turn it into a religious, cultural or linguistic monolith, the nation evaporates and divisions begin to take over. India's pluralism has always resisted imposed unities, like the ones that the champions of the Hindu right or of Hindi as the one 'national' language—not merely the 'official' language—have sought to do. They are simply enemies of diversity and thus of our democracy.

Poetry reflects these emerging collective identities through diverse idioms and modes of articulation. One such collectivity is formed by the poets who share a deep social concern, even while differing in ideological pursuits. There is a wide spectrum of dissenters who are democratic, but find the present system inadequate to reflect the aspirations of the common people. They include Gandhians, the followers of Ram Manohar Lohia and M.N. Roy and Communists of different denominations and liberal humanists of diverse hues. All of them recognise the existence of class inequalities and dream of a more egalitarian society. They differ from the old Progressives in their use of the new modes of poetry, some of which were introduced by the Modernists—irony, black humour, free verse, prose in differing tones, fresh images, surrealist metaphors and new forms like the sequence poem, poetic cycles, the long poem, the extended lyric and the like. In short, they share the socialist vision of the Progressives and the contemporary sensibility of the Modernists. Their poetry is also informed by an awareness of the complexification of life in our times as also their urban experience. The poetry of Raghuveer Sahai, Dhoomil, Sarveswar Dayal Saxena, Vijay Narayan Sahi, Kunwar Narain,

Kedarnath Singh, Vinod Kumar Shukla, Manglesh Dabral, Rajesh Joshi, Arun Kamal, Vishnu Nagar, Riruraj, Asad Zaidi and several others of the younger generation can be cited as examples from Hindi alone, not to speak of poets from other languages like Jagtar, Pash or Surjit Patar from Punjabi, Chandrashekhara Kambara or P. Lankesh from Kannada, Bishnu Dey, Samar Sen, Subhash Mukhopadhyay or Joy Goswami from Bengali, J.P. Das or Jayanta Mahapatra from Oriya, Narayan Surve or Chandrakant Patil from Marathi, Mafat Oza, Chinu Modi or Sarup Dhruv from Gujarati, Ali Sardar Jafri or Javed Akhtar from Urdu, Kadammanitta Ramakrishnan, K. Satchidanandan or K.G. Sankara Pillai from Malayalam, SivaReddy or Varavara Rao from Telugu, to cite just a few familiar examples. Some of these poets, like Kadammanitta and Kambara have rediscovered the folk idiom with fresh nuances, while some of the Maoist poets like Subbarao Panigrahi, Cherabanda Raju, Saroj Dutta, Murari Mukhopadhyay, Gaddar and Civic Chandran have created a new symbolism that marks the arrival of a revolutionary romanticism. Many of these poets have fashioned a sharp, unsentimental, ironic and concrete language to express their distaste for the system. Look at Pash, the Punjabi poet: 'No, I don't think now about/such things as/the fine hues of red/when the sun sets over the village/nor do I care about how she feels/when the moon glides over the threshold/at night./No, I don't worry about such trifles now.' ('No, I am not Losing My Sleep Over...') Dhoomil says: 'A man/severs the neck of another/from torso/As a mechanic separates a nut/from a bolt/You say; This is murder. I say: This is the dissolution of a mechanism.' He takes his readers 'to the territory of poetry/In the wilderness of language/where cowardice has run away/ Throwing an empty revolver/and defiance has gone forward/in then dark.' In 'Twenty Years After' he asks: '...is freedom only the name/of three tired colours/dragged by a single wheel?' Kunwar Narain in the poem 'To Delhi' comments:

> A familiar sight, then, as now,
> Abject, pitiful, dragged
> Behind victorious horsemen'

> Hands tied together, pitiful,
> Who was it this time,
> On the road to Delhi?
> None knows.
> Only a pair of hands, tied together,
> Made it there.

Or look at P. Lankesh speaking of his mother:
> My mother, black, prolific earth,
> Green leaf, a festival of white flowers
> With every burn the earthier,
> With every pang more fruit and petal...

She has 'limbs that thrill to children's kicks'. Her life was spent in raising millet, swilling water for each clod of earth, to nourish pepper and peas and grain, hiding her youth in a tatter of sarees. She grew into a hag bent double, weeping for coin, for dead calf and ruined grain, roaming villages for an ancient run-away buffalo. She was not Savitri, Sita or Urmila, not a heroine of history books, tranquil, fair, grave, in dignity:

> ...Did not worship the gods,
> Nor listen to holy legends, nor did she wear
> Like a good auspicious wife
> any vermilion on her brow...

The poet calls her 'a wild bear leaving a litter of little ones', snarling and grumbling like a hurt bitch, rearing a husband, saving coins in the knots of cloth, ready to scratch like a monkey.

> A wild jungle bear has no need for your Gita:
> My mother lived
> for stick and grain, labour and babies
> for rafter overhead, rice, bread, a blanket:
> to walk upright among equals.

Her death is so casual; she lays down the basket on her head, groans and closes her eyes, never again to open them. It was as if she were leaving home for the fields, 'cool in the middle of small talk'.

Writers of fiction like Chandrashekhara Kambara, Srikrishna Alanahalli or P. Lankesh in Kannada, Mahaswetadevi or Nabarun Bhattacharya in Bengali, M. Sukumaran or Pattathuvila Karunakaran in Malayalam, Jayakantan or Imayam in Tamil, Birendrakumar Bhattacharya or Indira Goswami in Assamese and Kamaleswar or Rajendra Yadav in Hindi are also deeply concerned with social reality. This can be said also of the plays of Vijay Tendulkar, Mahesh Elkunchwar, G.P. Deshpande, Prasanna, Satheesh K. Satheesh and others.

3

Another imagined community is that of the women-poets, scores of whom have emerged with strong Feminist inclinations in the last three decades in several Indian languages. Though India has a tradition of women's poetry extending from the Buddhist nuns of the sixth century BCE through the poets of the Bhakti, such as Akka Mahadevi, Meerabai, Andal or Lal Ded to poets of the last generation like Mahadevi Varma and Balamani Amma, a poetry consciously committed to the cause of women's emancipation, taking gender as the organising principle of experience and body as central to their language is a rather new phenomenon. It can be said to have begun with poets like Kabita Sinha, Nabaneeta Dev Sen, Amrita Preetam and Kamala Das and has now several spokeswomen from Eunice D'Souza and Sujata Bhatt of English to Mallika Sengupta of Bengali, Pravasini Mahakud of Oriya, Pratibha Nandakumar of Kannada, Tarannum Riaz of Urdu, Manjit Tiwana of Punjabi, A. Jayaprabha of Telugu, Rajathi Salma of Tamil, Anuradha Patil of Marathi, Anamika of Hindi or Savitri Rajeevan of Malayalam and several other poets represented in popular anthologies like Arlene Zide's *In Their Own Voice* and Susie Taru and K. Lalita's *Women Writing in India: From the 6th Century to the Present*, besides individual collections and anthologies in different languages. These poets challenge the norms of the phallocentric discourse, interrogate patriarchal canons and try to forge idioms adequate to express the specifically feminine experiences of pain, solitude, desire and pleasure. But women's poetry is no monolith, it has enough space for regional variations, specific geniuses of languages, diverse traditions, a large variety of forms and different approaches to experience. For example, the poetry of urban Muslim women like Mallika Amar Seikh or Imtiaz Dharker, exiles like Panna Naik or Meena Alexander or Dalit poets like Prajna Lokhande or Hira Bansode reflect their specific community experience within the broader frame of women's poetry. They have realised, with Eunice D'Souza that 'the histories they know are not fit to print' and that 'the perfect book is one long cry in the dark'. Nabaneeta Dev Sen compares love to a bird whose fixed phrases pour honey into her ears and then 'in private, jingles its chains in raucous laughter to itself and sheds its feathers in empty space.' Kamala Hemmige knows class divides even women: 'You grow cactii/in flowerpots and wear roses in your hair/ do you know/about the nude women/worshipping their God in Chandragutthi?/you skilful one/who can drink tea without smudging your lipstick/do you know the story of the girl/who was stripped naked/for wanting to eat?' Savitri Rajeevan compares herself to a worn-out kitchenware elevated into an icon. Indira Bhavani speaks of the ten avatars of the male in total sarcasm; smacking his lips over smutty books as Fish, hiding himself in his shell when invited to act strongly like Tortoise, falling flat on his face in an ocean of booze like a Pig... taking pleasure in different houses like Krishna and so on. There are too poets identifying themselves with Radha deceived by Krishna (eg; Sugatakumari, 'Where is Radha?'), with Draupadi insulted in the royal assembly (eg; Lakshmi Kannan, 'Draupadi') or with Akka Mahadevi who roamed naked battling against male wits (eg; Bhagya Jayasudarshana, 'For Akka') A Muslim woman poet of Bombay like Malika Amar Sheikh looks at the city from its margins in her series of poems, 'Metropolis'. People in the city, she says, haven't slept for years: 'By night men are transformed/Into different kinds of hungers/And one kind of hunger swallows another.... We've often lost ourselves/in the jungle of intestines/Even a white hot bread/conquers us completely'. Another Muslim woman poet, Imtiaz Dharker meditates over the purdah in her series of poems, 'Purdah' where the veil grows into a paradoxical sign of oppression as well as security: 'One day they said/She was old enough to learn some shame./She found it came quite naturally.' In the beginning the purdah is a place to hide, but soon it grows into a coffin and the cloth that fans out against the skin is like the earth that falls on that coffin. She feels she is a clod of earth; roots inside her scratch for a hold between the ribs. A Dalit woman poet like Hira Bansode interrogates the Buddha, who had left his wife and son under cover of night. Addressing Yashodhara, she says:

> I don't have the audacity to look at you.
> We were brightened by Buddha's light,
> Bu you absorbed the dark
> Until your life was mottled blue and black...
> Listening to your silent sighs
> I feel the promise of heavenly happiness is hollow.

Women fiction writers from Vaidehi of Kannada, Volga of Telugu, Nabaneeta Dev Sen or Bani Basu of Bengali, Krishna Sobti, Maitreyi Pushpa and Alka Saraogi of Hindi, Pratibha Ray or Yashodhara Mishra of Oriya, Madhavikkutty, Sara Joseph, Gracy, Chandramati, S. Sitara, Indu Menon or K.R. Meera of Malayalam, have developed their own ways of dealing with women's reality in a world dominated by men.

4

Dalit poetry has been mainstreamed in Kannada, Marathi and Gujarati and has emerged strongly in Punjabi, Hindi, Bengali, Tamil, Telugu and Malayalam. It is no more a mere expression of the despair and indignation of the Dalit communities who had been relegated to the bottom of the caste hierarchy for over 30 centuries, but an assertion of Dalit values and of the community's rightful claim to all the privileges democracy gives its people. The movement has produced an extremely innovative poet like Namdeo Dhasal in Marathi, while it has been enriched by the contributions of scores of poets like Siddalingaiah of Kannada, S. Joseph, Raghavan Atholi, M.R. Renukumar and M.B. Manoj of Malayalam, Sivsagar, J. Gautam, Maddoori Nageshbabu, Paidi Thereshbabu and Satish Chander of Telugu, Anpathavan, Yakkan, Bharati Vasanthan, Puthiya Matavi and Idayavendan of Tamil, Soorajpal Chauhan, Rajnee Tilak, Om Prakash Valmiki, Mohandas Naimishrai, Susheela Taksore, Asang Ghosh and Kusum Meghval of Hindi, Gurdas Alam, Sant Ram Udasi, Manjit Khader and Lalsingh Dil of Punjabi, not to speak of Marathi poets like Arjun Dangle, Daya Pawar, J.V. Powar, Arun Kamble, Arun Kale, Sharan Kumar Limbale, Prakash Kharat, Arun Chandra Gavli, Dinkar Manwar, Mahendra Bhavre, Asha Torat, Meena Gajbhiye, Urmila Pawar, Jyoti Lanjewar and Kumud Pavade and Gujarati poets like Harish Mangalam, Jayant Parmar, Yoseph Macwan, Mangal Rathod and Kisan Sosa, to cite only a few names. The Dalit poets have created their own aesthetic that often goes against the injunctions of traditional poetics, using expressions that used to be dismissed as *gramya* (rustic), *chyutasamskara* (culturally corrupt) and *asleela* (obscene) and questioning rules like *dhvani* (suggestion) and *ouchitya* (propriety). They have brought into poetry a whole new lexicon rich with community dialects, slang, street language and rarely known sayings and usages. They have redrawn the map of Indian literature by discovering and exploring a whole continent of experience, so far left to silence and darkness. The Dalit writers have also overcome the stagnation that was looming large over many literatures through a cleansing renewal, disturbing the complacency of the dominant social groups, challenging set mores and conventions of looking at reality and forcing the community to refashion its critical tools and observe itself critically. In this attempt they have re-visioned myths and reread the epics from the perspectives of a Sambooka or an Ekalavya, subverting the middle-class notions of poetry and poetic language.

Dalit poets at times make fun of even concepts like patriotism. Baburao Bagul says: 'You who have made themselves a mistake of being born in this country/must now rectify it: either leave the country or make war.' Chokha Kamble advises himself: 'There is no cloud, no shower/or open sky or sun for me/and yet, my stupid foolish mind,/don't give in to despondency.' Yashvant Vaghela says: 'The stones of centuries have piled up over us/a pyramid of tears/Here today we are mummies stuffed with wailing voices/but forging destiny in our smithies.' Pravin Gadhvi opens his 'Shadow' with a line from Lorca: 'O, Woodcutter, cut my shadow.' The shadow in the poem is the shame of having been born a Dalit: 'I can be a Hindu,/a Buddhist/a Muslim./But this shadow/shall never be severed from me.' Jayant Parmar challenges Manu: 'One day in front of my house/on the neem tree I will hang you naked/I will split open your veins to see/how much blood of my elders you have drunk.' Siddalingaiah asks: 'Who has stopped the timely rain? Who has slashed the stars with a rainbow? Who is hiding the sun so that darkness may float and swell?/O World, I must get to know you/and so I must have a word with you.'

Dalit fiction has found its best spokesmen/women in writers like Bama, Sivakami (Tamil), Devanoor Mahadeva, Mogally Ganesh (Kannada) Laxman Mane, Laxman Gaikwad, Sharan Kumar Limbale, Rajan Gawas (Marathi), Joseph Macwan, Harish Mangalam (Gujarati) and others.

5

Along with the Dalits, the tribal communities of India have also woken up and begun to claim their rights for land and life and retrieve their history from amnesia. They have realised that they were the first poets, the first philosophers, the first cosmologists, the first peasants, the first myth-makers and the first artists and scientists. The Vedas, the Upanishads and the epics were created by the ancient tribes. Human history has also been the history of their marginalisation and alienation from the so-called mainstream. They have also a history of struggles against foreign invaders; the Bhils of Gujarat, the Kurichyas of Kerala and the Santals of Bihar were the first to fight the dominance of the British. It is strange that heroes like Birsa Munda, Siddhu Kanhu, Chand Bhairav, Thilak Majhi, Tantiya Bhil, Khajya Nayak and Rumalya Nayak find no place in official histories. Vinayak Tumram has defined the new tribal literature as 'the verbalisation of the primal pain of the maimed life of the *adivasi*s'. The new tribal writing opposes the *varna* system that pushed them out of the society and upholds the ideal of an egalitarian, non-hierarchical, non-exploitative and non-violent society. *Prakriti, sanskriti and itihas* (nature, culture and history) equally inspire their writing and they celebrate the positive tribal values of camaraderie, sharing and concern for nature. Besides Santali and Bodo that have found a place recently in the eighth schedule of the constitution, languages like Bhili, Mundari, Gondi, Garo, Gammit, Bhartari, Mizo, Lepcha, Garhwali, Pahadi, Kokborok, Tenydie, Adi and Ho have thrown up a lot of new writing that connects with the specific oral traditions through their mythopoeic imagination and yet are distnctly contemporary. Anil Bodo, Ramdayal Munda, Nirmala Putul, Mamang Dai, Paul Lingdoh, Kympham Nongkinrih, Bhujang Meshram and Vinayak Tumram are only some of the champions of the new tribal writing of dissent and assertion.

The nativist or *desivadi* writers have been celebrating cultural pluralism and questioning the hegemonic canons of the market and of the revivalists seeking to create an India that suits their projects. They feel that our geo-political and linguistic federalism is being undermined in the everyday practices of governance and reassert the need for multiculturalism and heteroglossia that have defined the Indian culture through the ages. The attempts by the *bandaya* poets of Kannada like Chandrasekhara Patil, P. Lankesh and Siddalingaiah, to retrieve the cultural memory of the Shudras, the de-Sanskritisation of Malayalam sought by poets like M. Govindan, N.N. Kakkad and Attoor Ravivarma, the conscious employment of local dialects by several poets in Malayalam and Telugu, the use of local history, provincial archetypes, myths and nature in Kadammanitta Ramakrishnan, K.G. Sankara Pillai, P.P. Ramachandran or Rafeek Ahmed of

Malayalam, Arun Kolatkar of Marathi or Kanji Patel of Gujarati, the use of orality and the evocation of rural life in the *uttar-adhunik* Bengali poets like Anuradha Mahapatra, Ekram Ali and Amitabha Gupta, ('the roots lie deep into the soil, loud sophistries are but a desperate invocation', says Birendra Chattopadhyay) the deliberate assertion of Tamil tradition and identity in Tamil poets like Jnanakkoothan, Manushyaputran, Vallikkannan, Pasuvayya and others, the forging of a specific Punjabi identity by poets like Gul Chauhan, Surjit Patar, Minder, Swarjbir, Mohanjit, Jaswant Deed and others, the return to Bhakti to initiate a contemporary spiritual discourse in poetry as in H.S. Shivaprakash, S.R. Ekkundi or Dilip Chitre, the evocation of Maithei history and Manipuri landscape by Manipuri poets like Y. Ibomchasingh, Thangjom Ibopishak, Mouchambi Devi and Saratchandra Thiyam, these are all attempts to bring back regional hues strongly to the cultural map of India that is turning increasingly monochrome under the pressures of the market forces, as well as the Hindu theocrats.

MOTHER TONGUE, THE OTHER TONGUE
Indianising English

Poacher! Pirate! We reject your authority. We know you, with your foreign language wrapped around you like a flag: speaking about us in your forked tongue, what can you tell but lies?
—Salman Rushdie, *Shame*

It is wrong to pit English writing against the whole regional writing; how can we compare a part with the whole? How can you put a literature that is over a thousand years old against one that is scarcely hundred years old and only finding its true voice?... There is a failure of criticism to put this writing where it belongs, in its right context, relating it instead to literature with which it has nothing in common except the language.
—Shashi Deshpande, from her article in *The Hindu*

...Why not let me speak in
Any language I like? The language I speak
Becomes mine, its distortions, its queernesses
All mine, mine alone. It is half-English, half
Indian, funny perhaps, but it is honest,
It is as human as I am human, don't
You see?...
—Kamala Das, *An Introduction*

The question of Indian writing in English and in the languages, I fear, has so far been posed from totally false premises, looking at them as oppositional categories rather than as two ways of articulating the same reality. It is time we accepted English as a legitimate language of literary expression in India, as relevant and significant as any Indian language despite its 'foreign' origin, though one can hardly deny its kinship with Sanskrit and other languages of the Indo-Aryan group, as they all come from a common stock of Indo-Germanic tongues. The proof of this kinship is not far to seek; it is evident at the morphological, lexical and semantic levels in these languages, even in their present form, as in the most ordinary words like father/*pita* or mother/*mata*, as well as several shared grammatical features of Sanskrit, German and old English.

Even if we choose to ignore this common fact, we cannot write off the two centuries of the presence of English in India. If it had been the language of colonial domination, it had also been the language of anti-colonial resistance; our national leaders including Mahatma Gandhi and Jawaharlal Nehru had employed it in the service of the freedom struggle arousing the nation to fight the Empire. We may also remember it was our own decision to retain English as a link language and a language of intellectual, emotional and imaginative articulation even after the British had left the country. Today India is the third-largest English-using nation in the world; only the U.S.A. and U.K. have greater number of users of the language. It is used in India by five per cent of the population; some of the languages of the Eighth Schedule of the Constitution have far less than the 35 million users that English has. English is also the state language of some of the Indian states in the North-East; it is our associate official language and the chief link language for not only international but even inter-regional communication. India has a large network of newspapers, journals in English besides several publishing houses that bring out books only in English. In fact, India today is one of the three largest publishers of books in English. Salman Rushdie's Aurora Zogoiby (*Moor's Last Sigh*) was not far wrong when he said, 'Only English brings us together.'

More importantly, English is getting absorbed into Indian languages and also enriching itself by assimilating them in turn. It has acquired a specific cultural identity in India and entered India's linguistic and literary creativity, not to speak of its undeniable presence in the everyday speech of the educated Indian. Several English words have merged indistinguishably with Indian languages that have not even bothered to find indigenous equivalents for them, or even where there are, they seldom care to use them. Words like school, desk, bench, book, party, machine, factory, computer—and all its parts— wine, soap, box, trunk, bus, car, truck, stock, share, godown and scores of others have entered into common speech across classes in the country. It is true that the 'post-colonised' can never retrieve the pristine purity of their languages, as Simon During observes. English has acquired new structures and tonalities in India, in the process of adapting it to native use. At a time when we have ceased to speak of Queen's English and speak instead of many Englishes, we need no longer be apologetic about Marathi/Gujarati/Bengali/Tamilian English that carry the tonalities and inflections of these mother tongues. When Vikram Seth's novel, *A Suitable Boy* was translated by Gopal Gandhi into Hindi as *Ek Accha sa Ladka,* the author saw it as an act of retrieval since the cultural subtext of the original really belonged to the Hindi milieu and some extracts from poems and songs were restored to their originals. Mulk Raj Anand once told me in a conversation that he would first think in Punjabi whatever he would later write, rather translate into, English and that is what gave a Punjabi flavour to his English. Jayanta Mahapatra's claim that he is an Oriya poet writing in English can also be seen in this linguistic context, though later the poet began to actually write in Oriya also. At a deeper level, Indian language writing and English writing share concepts, experiences, world views and belief systems as a comparison between, say, U.R. Ananathamurthy's *Samskara* and Raja Rao's *Kantapura* or Premchand's *Godan* and Mulk Raj Anand's *Coolie* or O.V. Vijayan's *Khasakkinte Itihasam* (The Legends of Khasak) and R.K. Narayan's *Malgudi Days* might reveal. There is also a sharing of discoursal devices and indigenous genres. For example, R.K. Narayan's *Malgudi Days* and Raja Rao's *Kanthapura* are *sthalapuranas* or local histories; Allan Sealy's *Trotternama* is a *nama* like the Moghul chronicles; Kiran Nagarkar's *Cuckold* is a kind of hagiography and Vikram Seth's *The Golden Gate* is an epic narrative in verse. Agha Shahid Ali and more recently, Jeet Thayil, have tried *ghazals* and *qasidas* in English, like Lorca did in Spanish. V.S. Naipaul claims he was inspired by the Indian epics in the writing of *A House for Mr. Biswas.* Shashi Tharoor's *The Great Indian Novel* also takes off from the *Mahabharata* in an ironic vein. Raja Rao had this comment to make on the way Indian creative writers should handle English:

> One has to convey in a language that is not one's own, the spirit that is one's own... We cannot write like the English, we should not. We can write only as Indians. We have grown to look at the large world as part of us. The tempo of Indian life must be infused into our English expression even as the tempo of American or Irish life has gone into the making of theirs... and our paths are paths interminable... we tell one interminable tale. This was and still is the ordinary style of our story telling.

Let us also remember that writings and translations in English have had a decisive impact on Indian writing. Many of our early novels were modelled on English novels, like O. Chandu Menon's *Indulekha* (1889) that according to the author's own confession followed *Henrietta Temple*, a popular British novel of the times written by Disraeli in 1837, while the historical romances in Malayalam, Tamil and Marathi were deeply impacted by the works of Walter Scott. O. Chandu Menon sums up his reasons for writing *Indulekha* in his dedicatory letter to his translator, W. Dumergue:

> First my wife's oft-expressed desire to read in her own language a novel written after the English fashion, and secondly a desire on my part to try whether I should be able to create a taste amongst my Malayalee readers not conversant with English, for the class of literature represented in the English language by novels, of which at present they (accustomed as they are to read and admire works of fiction in Malayalam abounding in events and incidents foreign to nature and often absurd and impossible) have no idea, and... to illustrate to my Malayalee brethren the position, power and influence that our Nair women, who are noted for their natural intelligence and beauty, would attain in society, if they were given a good English education; and finally to contribute my mite towards the improvement of Malayalam literature, which I regret to observe is fast dying out by disuse as well as by abuse.

In fact Chandu Menon had first tried translating *Henrietta Temple* and abandoned it to go for a fresh novel that took after it. Here we find the supernatural in the earlier novels yielding place to the new manifesto of the Indian novel that was oriented towards literary innovation as well as social reform. Nand Shanker Mehta, in his introduction to his Gujarati novel, *Karan Khelo* (1866) also says something similar: 'The former education inspector of our state Mr Russell has expressed to me his desire to see Gujarati books written along the lines of English novels and romances. I have written the novel according to that plan.'

Samuel Pillai, the Tamil novelist of *Piratapa Mutaliyar Charittiram* (1879) tells us that his object was 'to supply the want of prose books in Tamil' and that he has 'represented the principal personages as perfectly virtuous, in accordance with the opinion of the great English moralist, Dr Johnson.'

Even later, Western trends, movements and techniques like realism, surrealism, symbolism, imagism, modernism and post-modernism have profoundly influenced Indian language writing, though each language adopted these as suited to its own specific genius. To take the case of Malayalam, Robert Browning and Edwin Arnold had an impact on Kumaran Asan's poetry, the British Romantics as well as the French Symbolists on the poetry of Changampuzha Krishna Pillai, poets like Yeats, T.S. Eliot and the European Modernists on the Modernists and the Black and Latin American writing on the radical poets of the 1970s. Western Feminist writing, the Stream of Consciousness novel, the post-Modernism of Rushdie, Beckett, Pynchon and others have all had their effects felt on Malayalam and certainly several other language literatures. This is not to deny their indigenous nature, but only to show that writing in English and received through English has not been without a positive impact on our language writing. This is also true of genres like the short story, sonnet, lyric, dramatic monologue, elegy, sequence poem, burlesque, essay, etc.

The charge of 'elitism' against Indian writing in English is also hard to sustain as a lot of modern Indian writing in the languages too is considered 'obscure' and 'inaccessible' by some readers and critics. This is not in fact a question of the medium or class, but of the varying levels of sensibility. Some complain that the English writers cater only to the urban middle classes and hence deal only with the issues that concern them. Even if this was the case, we cannot neglect this 20 per cent of our population that has a major say in the affairs of the State; but this is not a true complaint either, as writers from Mulk Raj Anand, R.K. Narayan and G.V. Desani to Shashi Deshpande, Amitav Ghosh and Arundhati Roy have dealt with village life and the subaltern classes with great sympathy and understanding. A lot of writers in the languages too deal with the problems of the middle class as they constitute the majority of Indian readership in either case and as it is an interestingly varied, struggling and mostly upwardly mobile class. Indian writers living in India whatever the language they write in, live in the same milieu, undergo similar experiences, think and feel more or less in the same way and dream in the same way too. There is, no doubt, a difference in the writers who have spent most of their life abroad, a difference that is obvious in their concerns with issues like migration and their often outsiderish, exoticising gaze that packages 'Indian' life for a largely foreign readership.

2

We may briefly examine the ways in which English is being indigenised by Indian writers. From 1960 onwards a distinct Indian English idiom has been taking shape in poetry. The new poets abandoned the high rhetorical flourishes and colourful overstatements of their predecessors like Sarojini Naidu and Toru Dutt. Nissim Ezekiel, Kamala Das, Adil Jussawallah, A.K. Ramanujan, Jayanta Mahapatra and Arun Kolatkar helped this nativisation in various ways. In his *Rough Passage*, R. Parthasarathy wondered:

> How long can foreign poets
> Provide the staple of your lines?
> Turn inward; scrape the bottom of your past.

He stated later that his task was 'one of acclimatising the English language to an indigenous tradition' and 'to initiate a dialogue between myself and my Tamil past.'

A.K. Ramanujan began searching for his Tamil and Kannada roots and translating the saint poetry of both the languages at the same time. He declared:

> I must seek and will find
> my particular hell only in the Hindu mind.
> ('Conventions of Despair')

Ezekiel attempted to recreate Indian characters in their natural situations. He employed colloquial speech rhythms and conventional tones in poems like 'The Professor', 'Goodbye Party for Miss Pushpa. T.S.', 'Hangover', 'Healers', etc. Here is a sample from his 'Hangover':

> No Indian whisky sir all imported this is Taj.
> Yes sir soda is Indian sir.
> Midnight.
> Taxi strike. George Fernandez...
> Half the day hazy with the previous night.
> Three other samples:
> Remember me? I am professor Sheth
> Once I taught you geography Now
> I am retired though my health is good...
> If you are coming again this side by chance,
> Visit please my humble residence also
> I am living just on opposite house's backside.
> ('The Professor')

> Come again
> All are welcome whatever caste
> If not satisfied tell us
> Otherwise tell others

> God is great.
> (Irani Restaurant Instruction)
>
> You are going?
> But you will visit again
> Any time, any day
> I am not believing in ceremony
> Always I am enjoying your company.
> (The Patriot)

Several Indian words and expressions like goonda, guru, mantra, ashram, bhikshuks, chapati, pan, burkha, Indirabhen, Rama Rajya, etc., keep appearing in Ezekiel's poems. They illustrate Ayyappa Paniker's statement that national sensibilities are based on racial or cultural factors.

The fabric of A.K. Ramanujan's poetry is woven out of myriad threads of Indian myth, history, culture, heritage, topography and environment. He remembers his mother when he sees a buxom woman beside a wreckage van in Hyde Park Street in London:

> Something opened
> in the past and I heard something shut in the future, quietly
> like the heavy door
> of my mother's black-pillared nineteenth century
> silent house, given on her marriage day
> to my father, for a dowry.
> (Still Another for Mother)

> father when he passed on
> left dust
> on a table full of papers,
> left debt and daughters,
> a bewildering grandson
> named by chance after him
> a house that leans
> slowly through our growing

years on a bent coconut
tree in the yard.
Being the burning type
he burned properly at the cremation
as before, easily
and at both ends.
Then the son picks up the half-burnt spinal discs:
To pick gingerly and throw
facing east as the priest said where the three rivers
met near the railway station.
(Obituary)

Ramanujan's poetry keeps recalling his aunts and uncles and his childhood in Karnataka. He has made an honest statement about the sources of the Indian poet writing in English in his personal context:

> English and my disciplines give me my outer forms—linguistic, metrical, logical and other such ways of the shaping of experience, and my first 30 years in India, my frequent visits and field trips, my personal and professional pre-occupations with Kannada, Tamil, the classics and folklore gave me my substance, my 'inner' forms, images and symbols. They are continuous with each other, and I no longer can tell what comes from where.

Jayanta Mahapatra is Indian by his closeness to Oriya reality, rather than tradition, and his sympathetic understanding of the plight of his people. For example in 'Death in Orissa', he sees

nothing but the paddy's twisted throat
exposed on the crippled earth, nothing but
impotence in lowered eyes,...
nothing but the cries of shriveled women
cracking against the bloodied altar of Man, nothing
but the moment of fear
when they need a God whom can do them some good.'

Again, look at Kamala Das:

> Bereft of soul
> My body shall be bare
> Bereft of my body
> My soul shall be bare
> (The Suicide)
> You called me wife; I was taught to break saccharine into your tea and To offer at the right moment the vitamins... I lost my will and reason.
> (The Old Playhouse)

Here the Indian character comes from a philosophical approach to things as in the first quotation or from an awareness of the state of women as in the second.

One can go on multiplying examples. Arun Kolatkar's poems like *Jejuri, Sarpa Satra* and the poems in the *Kala Ghoda Poems* are Indian in so many ways, at the levels of myth, ritual and the modern urban reality as felt in a city like Bombay. Rukmini Bhaya Nair's poetry is not only deeply Indian in the ways it confronts social and individual experience, but in the use of certain forms borrowed from Sanskrit like *stuti* or hymn too, as in her *Ayodhya Cantos*. Meena Alexander brings into her poetry memories of her early life in South Kerala. Several poets writing today, from Arvind Krishna Mehrotra and Dilip Chitre to Ranjit Hoskote, Arundhati Subramaniam, Jeet Tayil, Vijay Nambisan, Anand Thakore and others are deeply Indian in their themes, sensibility and their way of looking at things. Poets like Keki Daruwalla have an ironic relationship with Indian reality as seen in his satirical writings.

The Indian English novelists too, at least since the 1930s have been self-assured and confident enough to bend the language to their will. Mulk Raj Anand was perhaps the first conscious experimenter followed by Raja Rao and Bhabani Bhattacharya. They, with G.V. Desani, took liberties with diction and syntax. They drew from the resources of Indian languages and infused English with their essence. Meenakshi Mukherjee in her *Twice-born Fiction* points to certain linguistic problems the Indian writers in English face: one, they have to write in English about people who do not normally speak or think in English; two, they have to write in an acquired language which is a situation very different from those of the American, Australian, Canadian or West Indian writer who can make use of living speech. Look at Vic Reid using, in his *New Day,* Jamaican dialect for poetic effect, V.S. Naipaul using the West Indies Indian dialect in his *A House for Mr Biswas* or Derek Walcott bringing in special effects from the Creole dialect of St. Lucia. American novels like *Huckleberry Finn, Catcher in the Rye,* or *Herzog* use slang and dialect with great effect. But Indians dealing with non-English people in non-English situations do not have this option. They have to convey through English a vast range of expressions, observations and experiences whose natural vehicle is an Indian language. This problem becomes especially acute in writing dialogue, and one reason for drama remaining the poorest genre in English in India, with very few exceptions like Asif Karim Bhoy or Mahesh Dattani, may be precisely this difficulty.

It is the sum of differences in attitudes, world views and responses that makes his/her novel 'Indian'. Here again the word 'Indian' needs to be used with caution, since writers in English too belong to specific geographical regions or languages but for some who are regular mavericks. This gives their works a local quality. As we have noted, Mulk Raj Anand conveys a Punjabi flavour and is not very successful when he writes about regions other than his own. *Private Life of an Indian Prince* is an example. In R.K. Narayan's fiction one can easily perceive the presence of his region in the customs and manners he deals with and the language he employs that has Tamil overtones. Raja Rao's *Kanthapura* shows conspicuous use of the nuances of Kannada, Bhabani Bhattacharya's fiction has something Bangla about it, Vikram Seth has Hindi beneath his English and Arundhati Roy's first novel has the flavour of Malayalam. But as Meenakshi Mukherjee rightly notes, this regional dimension is missing in the 'public school English' of the novels of Shanta Ram Rau, Kamala

Markandeya or Manohar Malgonkar, who are not rooted in any specific Indian culture. This forces many writers to try exotic or Orientalist Indian themes or catchy phrases in order that their works look Indian on the surface.

Many Indian writers in English experiment with diction, literally translating idioms, or with syntax, transforming the structure of the sentence. The literal translations can be seen mostly in Mulk Raj Anand. Look at some examples: 'Is this any talk?', 'Are you talking the true talk?', 'May I be your sacrifice'. There are Punjabi-Hindi expressions like 'counterfeit luck', swear words and abuses used by the peasants in Punjab as also proverbs like 'Your own calf's teeth seem golden' (*The Road,* p.24), 'A goat in hand is better than a buffalo in the distance' (Ibid, p.22) 'The camels are being swept away, the ants say, they float' (*The Big Heart*, p.206). Khushwant Singh also has a similar flavour to his English: 'Sardar Saheb, you are a big man and we are but small radishes from an unknown garden' ('I shall not Hear the Nightingales'). Bhabani Bhattacharya translates a Bengali saying: 'When an ant grows wings and starts flying in the air, it is not far from its doom.' (*A Goddess named Gold*). There are also expressions in him like 'childling', 'wifeling', 'starveling', 'villagefuls of folk', 'joy-moments', 'picture-play' (for cinema), etc. He also uses Bengali idiom like the typical short sentences: 'Why speak? What use? Trees and rocks have a heart. Not man. Why speak?' (*So Many Hungers*, p.76). Raja Rao also uses phrases like 'that-house people', 'next-house woman's kitchen', 'milk-infant', 'ten-eleven year-old child' etc. Sometimes, words in other languages are used directly, as in Mulk Raj Anand: 'angrez-log', 'yar'; there are created verbs like 'burburred in his sleep', 'sisking with cold', 'thak-thakking at a cauldron'; at times the spellings indicate the speaker's illiteracy: 'yus' (yes), 'notus' (notice), 'Amrika' (America) or 'Girmany' (Germany).

Raja Rao uses Kannada figures of speech etc unobtrusively: 'Postman Subbayya, who had no fire in his stomach and was red with red and blue with blue.' (*Kanthapura*, p.154), 'You are a Bhatta and your voice is not a sparrow voice in your village and you should speak with your people and organise a Brahmin party. Otherwise,

Brahminism is as good as kitchen ashes.' In *The Serpent and the Rope*, he tries changes in structure: 'He is so tender and fine-limbed, is my brother' (p.12), 'His Sona, one who is dead, was once tied to a tree and beaten.' (p.149). Arundhati Roy in her *God of Small Things* uses Malayalam words directly, at times mixed with English words: '*Poda, pattee*', '*Valare* thanks', 'Thanks, *ketto*', '*Naley*', '*Chacko Saar vannu*', '*Veluthe! Ividay! Veluthe*', '*mon*', '*mol*', '*kochamma*', '*paravan*', '*pulayan*'. She uses Malayalam words like these in English script and does not care to give a glossary. Her descriptions invoke typical Ayemenem landscapes through their use of pepper vines, tapioca, etc.

In Salman Rushdie, as it has often been said, English is in dialogue with Indian languages. This is especially so in *Midnight's Children*, his best work so far. Upamanyu Chatterjee's *English August* also at times uses a mixed language as in the expression 'hazar-fucked', a typical marriage of Urdu and American slang. Amitav Ghosh has used multi-lingualism most effectively in his *Sea of Poppies*, though the tendency is evident in his other works like *The Hungry Tide* and *Glass Palace*. In the *Sea of Poppies* he uses the tonal music of Bhojpuri, the language of its woman protagonist, very effectively and even brings in Bhojpuri folk songs; he also uses Hindustani in many forms, at times mixed with English as in the slang used by the crew of the ship, *Ibis*. There is a self-conscious questioning of the boundaries of language in many of the works I referred to; often they bring languages into comic collision, testing the limits of communication between them. They celebrate India's linguistic diversity and take over the English language to meet the demands of the Indian context. In this process they also question the 'purity' of Indian culture and prove that it is a mixture, receiving influences from outside the subcontinent. English thus becomes part of the polyphony and its colonial authority is relativised when it enters the complexity it describes.

But English as a language has been associated with colonialism, modernity and the elite. The new writers are aware of this and hence refuse to privilege either tradition or modernity (Look at Upamanyu Chatterjee's *English August* or *The Last Burden*, Amitav

Ghosh's *Glass Palace* or *A Sea of Poppies* or Rushdie's *Midnight's Children* and *Shame* for example). The new writers after Rushdie are also more playful and confident; their abrogation of standard English is also seen as a sign of a certain cultural weightlessness, the deracinated insouciance of elite college boys, alienated from the natural community. Altaf Tyrewala's 170-page *No God in Sight* is a slap in the face to the tradition of 'the Great Indian Novel'. He uses a plain-spoken and condensed language to capture the psychic inner life of Mumbai. He deals with ordinary people, especially, Mumbai's Muslim middle class struggling for survival and dignity within a political landscape transformed by Shivsena. The novel gives voice to critical dissent in relation to the one-sided success story narrated through campaigns like 'India shining'. Aravind Adiga's *White Tiger* is another novel of critical dissent, where he pits the Darkness of the rural world of India's poor against the Light of the new world of the rising upper-middle-class; here too he invents a language that is apparently light and full of fun, yet adequate to portray the horrors of Indian reality. Several graphic novels from Saranath Banerjee's *Corridor* to Amruta Patil's *Kari* explore the genre to create new models of reality as well as fiction. Chetan Bhagat's *One Night@the Call Center*, set in the world of a call centre at Gurgaon, is also critical of the new lifestyle, which is seen as a re-colonisation of the city. Here again he uses colloquial English, the lingua franca of the urban middle class. The author is not concerned with literariness, but with the possibilities of identification. He freely mixes *Mahabharata* and James Bond, Western pop and Indian fables. Novels like Samit Basu's *The Simogin Prophecies* and Rana Dasgupta's *Tokyo Cancelled* attain a new level of freedom by reflecting the new global space created by the market through their multiple locations. Their language reflects the new texture of life in India, a world where jazz and Bob Dylan are as popular as Bollywood film songs and ghazals. It is an openness that calls for interrogation as it traces the inner cartography of liberalised India that switches between cultures and is rooted nowhere. It also raises the ethical questions like that of our behaviour toward immigrants and refugees.

3

Indianisation also happens at the thematic level. We have quite a few novels about freedom and Partition like Mulk Raj Anand's *The Sword and the Sickle* and *The Private Life of an Indian Prince*, K.A. Abbas's *Inquilab*, Raja Rao's *Kanthapura*, R.K. Narayan's *Waiting for the Mahatma*, Nayantara Sahgal's *Rich like Us*, *A Situation in New Delhi* and *Storm in Chandigarh*, Shashi Tharoor's *The Great Indian Novel* and *The Riot*, Khushwant Singh's *Train to Pakistan* or Salman Rushdie's *Midnight's Children* and *Shame*. These works look at the questions of colonialism, communalism, Partition, post-Colonial governance and society, etc., from different angles. East-West encounter as in Tagore's *Gora* is the theme of another set of works like K.S. Venkataramani's *Murugan the Tiller* that dramatises the tension between pre-industrial modes of life and mechanisation, Nayantara Sahgal's *A Time to be Happy* and *This Time of Morning*, D.F. Karaka's *Just Flesh* and *There Lay the City*, Raja Rao's *Serpent and the Rope*, Anand's *Across the Black Waters*, Attia Hosain's *Sunlight on a Broken Column*, Amitav Ghosh's *Circle of Reason* and *The Hungry Tide*, B. Rajan's *The Dark Dawn*, Shanta Rama Rau's *Remember the House* or Kamala Markandeya's *Some Inner Fury*. The conflict happens at many levels in these novels: of values and world views, epistemologies (as in *Serpent and the Rope*, personal relationships and racial prejudices, individual fulfilment and family obligations, tradition and modernity etc. According to Clyde Kluckhohn, the American sociologist, the bases of all value systems are relation to nature, relation to men and the conception of time, and in these novels we find different value systems at work. Novelists like Kiran Desai (*Inheritance of Loss*) Salman Rushdie (*Grimus*) and Jhumpa Lahiri (*Namesake*) have dealt with the immigrant experience and the question of identity. The relation between idealism and renunciation and the pragmatic world has been explored by many novels like Arun Joshi's *The Strange Case of Billi Biswas* and Raja Rao's novels including *Cat and Shakespeare*. Murthy in *Kanthapura*, Govindan Nair in *Cat and Shakespeare*, Gautama in Anita Desai's *Cry the Peacock*, the narrator of Nayantara Sahgal's *A Time to be Happy*, Raju in R.K.

Narayan's *Guide,* Mynah in Sudhir Ghose's *The Flame of the Forest,* Kalo in Bhabani Bhattacharya's *He who Rides a Tiger,* or Gyan Chand in Anand Lall's *Seasons of Jupiter* explore this theme in various ways. At times the novelists laugh at the false gurus and fake *sadhus*. You find such characters in Anand's *Coolie, Untouchable,* and *The Road,* K. Nagarajan's *Adhawar House* or G.V. Desani's *All about H. Hatterr.* Novels like Anand's *The Village* and *Big Heart* deal with the changed village. Menon Marath's *The Wounds of Spring* looks at the changes in the *tharawad,* the old joint family in Kerala, while Attia Hosain in her *Sunlight on a Broken Column* looks at the transformation of a Muslim family in Lucknow. Arundhati Roy deals with life in Aymenem in the Travancore region of Kerala with humour and compassion in *The God of Small Things.* We have also unchanging villages like Narayan's Malgudi and critiques of the city like Amitav Ghosh's *Calcutta Chromosome.* Altaf Tyrewala and Vikram Chandra look at life in Bombay with understanding as well as anger.

Myth is invoked in novels like *Kanthapura* where we have Rama and Krishna myths. *The Man-eaters of Malgudi* has the structure of the *Purana,* Sudhir Ghose uses the Krishna myth in *The Cradle of the Clouds.* Anand uses the Sita myth ironically in *The Old Woman and the Cow.*

Not only has the empire been writing back through English novels, but the nation too gets re-written in the process. Anita Desai once said, 'Rushdie showed English language novelists in India a way to be post-colonial.' The history of Saleem Sinai in *Midnight's Children,* a paradigmatic post-colonial novel, reenacts the key moments in the nation's history, including Jallianwalabagh and the Indo-Pak wars and reflects the salient debates and competing visions for an independent India mapped by Gandhi, Nehru, et al. The novel also examines the values of modernity and tradition through Adam Aziz, Saleem's progressive father and Tai, the Kashmiri boatman. Saleem represents the need and effort to contain all of India and the impossibility of doing so. He says, 'There are as many versions of India as Indians.' *Shame* shows Pakistan as the failure of a dreaming mind, an insufficiently imagined place. The nation here is narrated through a portrait of its corrupt and shameless ruling elite: a densely metaphoric meditation on the various embodiments of national shame in the public sphere of male power and the private sphere of women's oppression and the management of their sexuality. *Satanic Verses* was an attempt to give voice and fictional flesh to the immigrant culture and examine the metamorphosis of the immigrants, their divided selves resulting from negotiating two or three cultures simultaneously. It also examines the nature of revelation from a secular point of view and the conflict between religious faith and religious doubt that unfortunately led to a public controversy and almost cost the author his life. *The Moor's Last Sigh* completed the cycle by revisiting Bombay: it is a celebration of hybridity, of mixtures and impurities. We see here many communities and cultures jostling with Saleem Sinai and Moraes Zogoiby. The saga of the Vasco de Gama and Zogoiby families compares with the nation's saga. Rushdie is still productive, though with a semi-historical magical novel like The *Enchantress of Florence*, the pleasure principle seems to have marginalised his spirit of historical enquiry.

Now Rushdie has a whole generation that follows him, a generation that interrogates the nature of India's unity and proposes several ways of imagining the nation. 'India is cracking up like my multi-channelled mind,' says the narrator of Rukun Advani's *Beethoven among the Cows* (1994). His novel deals with the loss of innocence of the narrator as well as the nation. The assured unity of the nation is questioned from the boundaries by Shama Futehally's *Tara Lane* (1993), while the loss of the nationalist self is the chief concern in Amit Choudhuri's *A Strange and Sublime Address* (1991) and *Afternoon Raag* (1993). Kiran Nagarkar's *Ravan and Eddie* and *The Little Soldier* examine the ironies of religious faiths and the destiny of communities; Amitav Ghosh in his novels from *Shadowlines* to *A Sea of Poppies* looks at the continuing tradition of India's cultural exchanges across the Indian ocean from an anti-colonial, subaltern point of view; Allan Sealy's *Trotternama* is an example of post-colonial history writing, as opposed to colonial historiography that leaves out everyday life; Mukul Kesavan's *Looking through Glass* uses photograph as a metaphor, suggesting that history can only provide a lens that frames and refracts and not a clear window to the real. Vikram

Chandra's *Red Earth and Pouring Rain* (1995) networks history and myth and presents the idea of India as an endless narrative potential. Vikram Seth's *A Suitable Boy* (1993) is an allegory of nationhood set in the 1950s. It asserts the inevitability of bourgeois life, subscribes to the idea of Indian history as a progress towards the goal of a secular commercial society of a Western model and exhorts the middle classes to come out of its nostalgia and its obstructive concern with traditional identities to pursue the secular liberal economic mode. Shashi Deshpande is concerned with the fate of urban middle class women in the new nation in her novels like *The Dark Holds No Terrors* (1980), *Roots and Shadows* (1983), *That Long Silence* (1988) and *Small Remedies* (2000). Urmi, the heroine of *The Binding Vine* sums up her liberating vision as she discovers her mother-in-law's trunk, full of poems and diaries after she had been killed by her husband and also Sakuntala whose daughter had been beaten and raped. They bring Urmi out of the trauma of her daughter's loss. Gita Hariharan's *A Thousand Faces of Night* posits Indian women in relation to the Orientalist idea of woman and questions it and *The Time of Siege* exposes the dark forces behind the neo-fascist Hindutva ideology.

4

There are critics who tend to view Indian writing in English as a pan-Indian phenomenon born with the Bengal Renaissance of the 19th century, since many of its first exponents like Raja Rammohun Roy, Henry Derozio, Radhakant Deb, Toru Dutt, Michel Madhusudan Dutt, Aurobindo and Vivekananda were products of that Renaissance. The constraints that Indian literature in English encounters have best been articulated by one of its living practitioners, Shashi Deshpande, in an article she wrote in *The Hindu*. One is, of course, its lack of a long tradition and the assurance that comes from it. There is hardly any archive, cultural register or community memory that it can fall back upon for drawing its images, archetypes and cultural symbols. It tries to make good at times by drawing on the larger 'Indian' mythology and epics or Greek, Roman or Persian traditions, thus making it difficult to locate it specifically: this is particularly evident in Indian poetry in English as poetry depends, more than fiction does, on cultural memory to achieve its vertical semantic and associational dimension. The range of verbal associations available to the language poet is also unavailable to the poet writing in English. This may also be why poets like Ramanujan, Arun Kolatkar, Dilip Chitre, Kamala Das and Jayanta Mahapatra, chose to be bilingual, writing also in their mother tongues. English writing also suffers from the potential danger of standardisation of experience as the language flattens regional, linguistic and dialectal differences and annihilates the local colour, tone and texture so prominent in language writing, especially, fiction. English writing in India also, as pointed out by Shashi Deshpande, has a tendency to inflate itself and tends to exoticise, present or explain India and package it for a foreign audience, as it happens mostly with the writers living outside the country. It does not have a close-knit community of readers as the language writing mostly has. This amorphous nature of the audience it addresses also leads to an ambivalence in English writing, regarding what it can expect from the readers. This uncertainly of context is besides the ambiguity about its own historical positioning. One may well ask why there are no movements, like the Dalit movement for example, in English, but for *Touch* a recent novel by Meena Kandasamy. The more intelligent of the writers in English are aware of these issues and are, as we have seen, trying to find the means to overcome them.

The task of the critic at this juncture is not to sensationalise the opposition but to look at the texts: their strategies of the absorption and nativisation of experience and the differences at thematic, emotive, signifying, ideological and structural levels with their Indian language counterparts in order to bring out the nuances of their linguistic and existential negotiation. If we need to fight English as a language of power and hegemony in India and a potential threat to the existence and development of Indian languages, it is not by opposing the creative use of English as a literary language where it is like any other Indian language, with the constraints outlined, but by reframing the priorities in our system of education, for example, by making the study of at least one Indian language compulsory up to a certain stage, after which the students may exercise their option. As a literary language in India, English needs neither to be privileged nor de-privileged: it is just one of the several languages in which the multilingual Indian creativity chooses to express itself.

Indian critics of Indian writing in English like M.K. Naik, C.D. Narasimhaiah, Meenakshi Mukherjee, Makarand Paranjape, Shyamala Narayan, P.K. Rajan and Vinay Kirpal, besides scores of academics who have been contributing to anthologies, have tried to explore the field in varied and useful ways. It is clear that neither the old Sanskrit poetics nor the new Western literary theories can adequately explain or interpret this genre of writing. Any meaningful criticism of this genre should necessarily take into account the multicultural milieu from which these writers emerge as they come from different regional cultures and linguistic backgrounds often woven into their texts. A common 'Indian' paradigm may not do. It should be sensitive to the problems of language and style. It needs to look, especially in the case of fiction, at the history-fiction interface, the ways in which history is treated and transformed. It needs to do a symptomatic reading of the texts, as there may be contradictions between the projected worldview and the actual content. It has also to read these texts in relation to regional writing as well as world writing. In short, it calls for a new comprehensive comparative critical method.

Let me conclude my observations with some relevant lessons from the African and Caribbean encounters with English. They have fought the hegemony of English by creating their own English, infusing it with the tones, timbres, rhythms and expressions of native speech as has been done by Derek Walcott or Sam Selvon. There are writers like Ngugi who have chosen to shift their creative writing into heir own languages—in this case Gikuyu—and persuade others to write in pidgins, creoles and other dialects of English rather than 'standard' English. Zimunya of Zimbabwe too admits that English can be stifling and inflexible, while translating from Shona, his mother tongue. (In his own words, 'we only render the meaning, but not the feeling; the feeling is lost, the feeling!') Gabriel Okara, the Nigerian poet, also speaks of the 'untranslatability' of Ijo experiences. Poets like Christopher Okigbo, Okot p'Bitek, Kofi Awoonor and Dennis Brutus bring into their writing the qualities of oral poetry, thus collapsing orature with ecriture. Chinua Achebe considers English richer than his language, Igbo, though his expression is also impacted by native speech. Writers also engage in code-switching and code-mixing, just as G.V. Desani in India had allowed the intrusion of Sanskrit compounding in *All about H. Hatterr.*

While we ought to resist the cultural imperialism of English that might promote the enfeebling of other languages, and the erasure of language writing, we may also well remember that English itself has been used as a tool for subversion, as in Derek Walcott's *Dream of the Monkey Mountain* that inverts Shakespeare's *Tempest* and tries Shakespeare for crimes against humanity, in Aime Cesaire's *Une tempete* where Creole and Kiswahili are employed to subvert the Queen's English or in J.M. Coetzee's *Foe* that turns the slave of Daniel Defoe's Robinson Crusoe into its protagonist, empowered by the knowledge of the master's language. Let us not forget that every language carries in its armoury tools of introspection and weapons of self-subversion like satire, irony, parody and structural inversion, all of which it can turn upon itself.

INDIAN LITERARY CRITICISM TODAY
The Challenge and the Response

Traditional Indian poetics is in a crisis today. Its categories are proving clearly insufficient to explain several of the modern genres, forms and movements in Indian literature. This often unacknowledged crisis had already begun with the maturing of Indian languages that declared their independence from Sanskrit, centuries ago, even while retaining some of its aspects that they found useful to their flowering and growth. These languages had their own literary traditions, mostly oral, that informed their new developments. Some of them, like Tamil, had a different poetics altogether. Their canons were formed not only with the examples from Sanskrit literature, many of which they got translated or adapted, but by Western, especially English, classics, as well, that were either translated or emulated as models. The inadequacy of the existing paradigms became acute in the nineteenth century, when, mostly under the Western influence, new prose genres like the novel and the short story, and even modern prose drama, began to develop in our languages. Criticism, for some time, continued to fight shy of these genres and to confine itself to poetry and verse drama, since it hardly had any tools to explain and interpret the new forms. The crisis began to affect even traditional forms like poetry with the advent of new genres like the sonnet, the pastoral, the elegy, the new lyric or the sequence poem and new movements like Modernism that replaced the simile and the metaphor with the symbol and the image and experimented with free verse and prose as the vehicles of poetic imagination. Imagination itself had grown unconventional with new modes like symbolism, surrealism, antipoetry and the like. Then came the new movements like Dalit writing, women's writing, tribal writing, nativism, ecocentric writing and modern folk writing, not to speak of the Indian variants of post-Modernism, all of which sprang from the new social awakenings and carried a new intellectual and verbal energy that could hardly be explained by traditional poetics.

Behind all these were the radical changes happening in Indian life itself: the complexification of life brought about by the changed environment, the new textures of urban living with its contradictory aspects of penury and luxury made possible by new technologies, the intensification of alienation among the intelligentsia, the angst of the new awareness of space and time, the growing consumer instinct, the loss of traditional values and the growth of the new post-industrial ethos, the continued intervention of the modern State in every aspect of the lives of its subjects, the revolutionary awakenings of the marginalised and oppressed sections of the people based on caste, class, religion and gender, the threats of war, poverty and terrorism, the search for new identities and the new structures of feeling generated by these transformed environments of existence. The canons were being constantly changed, the institution of literature itself was under threat, the status-quoist concepts were being challenged and the paradigms proving hopelessly inadequate to meet the hermeneutic needs of literary criticism.

The history of Indian criticism in the last few decades has been the history of the varied responses to these challenges and the attempts to arrive at some critical canon that might help unlock and explain contemporary Indian texts.

2

One response, call it a form of enlightened revivalism, has been an attempt to extend, develop and reinterpret traditional poetics in order to apply its concepts to modern texts and genres, at times incorporating the concepts of Western poeticsin the process. Indian poetics has often been identified with Sanskrit poetics, though there is a whole parallel tradition in Tamil and in Urdu— derived from the Persian tradition—not to speak of individual texts—like *Kavirajamarga* in Kannada—available in the languages and the poetics implied in our oral literary practices. Traditional scholars, like M. Hiriyanna, S.K. De, P.V. Kane, V. Raghavan, K.C. Pandey, K. Krishna Moorthy, S.K. Chari and Krishna Chaitanya, along with foreign scholars, like Daniel H.H. Ingalls and Anand Coomaraswamy, have played a major role in giving it this pan-

Indian status through their books in English. Indian languages also have scholars like Kuttikrishna Marar of Malayalam, who have interpreted language texts in the light of Sanskrit poetics, as well as those like K.P. Narayana Pisharody of Kerala or Ramaranjan Mookherjee of Bengal who have interpreted classical Sanskrit poetics texts for the language readers. There are also those like M. Leelavathy or Joseph Mundassery of Malayalam who have tried to compare Eastern and Western concepts of poetics or even combine them in their critical analyses.

Critics like Krishna Rayan have read Sanskrit poetics in the light of the new theories from the West and have come up with extended and flexible interpretations of the central concepts of Sanskrit poetics like *dhvani, rasa, rasadhvani, vakrokti* and *anumana* along with peripheral concepts like *abhidha, lakshana, vibhava, anubhava* etc. In his book, *Text and Sub-text* (1987) Rayan looks at the theory of suggestion and tries to establish that suggestion—the production of unstated, subsurface, indirect, multiple, emotive meaning—is what distinguishes modern literature from the literature of earlier periods. Rayan examines texts like Tennyson's *Becket,* alongside T.S. Eliot's *Murder in the Cathedral,* Christopher Fry's *Curtmantle* and Jean Anouilh's *Becket ou L'Honneur de Dieu.* Four of Thomas Hardy's novels exploring the notion of a return to the roots are analysed in relation to novels by Margaret Drabble that pursue a similar theme. The book also looks at the practice of suggestion and evocation in Milton's *Paradise Lost* and the poetry of Yeats and the minimalist, micro-suggestive, poetic practice of the *Review* poets like Ian Hamilton, David Harsent, Colin Falck, Hugo Williams and Michael Fried. The critic quotes critical passages from Mallarme, T.S. Eliot, Arthur Symmons, Yeats, A.C. Bradley, Edmund Wilson and W.K. Wimsatt to relate the theory of suggestion to the symbolist practice, as well as the Sanskrit concept of *rasadhvani*. He also considers the binary oppositions like emotive/referential meaning (I.A. Richards) oblique/direct (E.M.W. Tillyard), local texture/logical structure (J.C. Ransom) and intensive/extensive meaning (Allen Tate) to be renamings of the suggestion/statement distinction found in Eastern as well as Western poetics. He also associates concepts like 'depth language' (Philip Wheelwright) and 'interiority' (W.J. Ong) with *dhvani*/suggestion. In *Burning Bush: Suggestion in Indian Literature* (1988) Krishna Rayan extends the *rasadhvani* concept to modern subcontinental texts in various languages, by authors like Nirmal Verma, Kiran Nagarkar, M.S. Sarna, Pranabjoti Deka, Lokenath Bhattacharya, Rajinder Singh Bedi (fiction) P. Lankesh, Kumaran Asan, Jayanta Mahapatra, Nissim Ezekiel, Dina Nath Nadim, Soubhagya Kumar Mishra (poetry), Shrikant Shah, Ediriwira Sarachchandra (play) and others, besides some older texts from classical Tamil and Sindhi, in order to demonstrate the applicability of the theory to different languages, genres and periods. In *Sahitya: A Theory*, Rayan produces an eclectic theory for Indian critical practice by bringing together Sanskrit, Tamil and Western concepts with plenty of examples and quotations. *Natyasastra* and *Tholkappiyam* are referred to as two basic texts. Here, he also establishes parallels between the *rasa*s of *Natyasastra* and the *meypadu*s of *Tholkappiyam*. For example, *sringara* is identified with *uvakai*, *hasya* with *nakai*, *karuna* with *azhukai*, *raudra* with *vekuli*, *vira* with *perumitam*, *bhayanaka* with *accam*, *bibhatsa* with *ilivaral* and *atbhuta* with *marutkai*. The critic looks at the diverse aspects of literature like literariness, image, narrative, character, style, rhythm, landscape and evaluation. In the chapter on landscape, he introduces the *tinai* concept of *Tholkapiyam* with the accompanying *uri* and *mutal* viz., *kurinci* (*mutal*—mountain, *uri-punartal* or premarital union), *marutam* (*mutal*—lowland or riverside, *uri*—*oodal* or marital union sulking over infidelity) *neytal* (*mutal*—seashore, *uri-iranagal* or anxious pining in the state of separation), *mullai* (*mutal*—forest or pasture, *uri-iruttal* or patient waiting) and *palai* (*mutal*—desert, *uri-pirital* or separation). The landscape here is the signifier and the bond that holds it to the signified is arbitrary and fixed by conventions, which were sustained for several generations during the *Sangam* period. Ayyappa Paniker has also tried to apply the *tinai* theory to Thakazhi Sivasankara Pillai's *Kayar*, while V.J. Sebastian has done it to a series of contemporary poems. S. Carlos (Tamilavan) has also tried to extend and apply the theory to modern texts in Tamil.

While these are interesting experiments, the method can work fully only in a stable static culture with a lot of received assumptions and capable of a large number of shared responses. The theory of *rasa*s is also too limited and rigid to make it critically effective, while applied to modern texts where the boundaries of emotions are blurred, moods are in a flux and responses more complex. Behind these theories is a whole static world view and a fixed view of literature and literariness. They have also a tendency to look at literature, especially poetry, as a craft, detached from its time and society. Both classical Sanskrit and Tamil poetics, therefore, fail to historicise its texts and themselves need to be historicised to be understood. Concepts like *dhwani* and *ouchitya* and the linguistic injunctions against *asleela, gramya* and *chyutasamskara* can hardly be isolated from the class that has generated them and hence do not apply to several subaltern forms and movements, both ancient and modern. The traditional concepts of *pratibha* or genius, *sahridaya* or the competent reader, the *sahitatva* or the fixed togetherness of the word and the meaning—compared to the bond of Parvati and Parameswara, meaning as something deposited in the work by the author, and the authorial institution itself, emerge from an idealist philosophical premise. The concept of reader as the producer of meaning, of the text as a flux, and the absence or the eternal deferance of a 'final meaning', literariness itself as the effect of reading, and the historical and ideological determinations of the text are alien to this aesthetic ideology. While the concepts of *dhwani* and *anumana* do take the reader into account, it is an abstract reader outside real history. It is seldom bothered with the question of the historical construction of subjectivity and hence fails to answer several questions about writing, reading and authorship. This also applies to Persian poetics that deals exclusively with forms available in classical Persian or Arabic from which Urdu has adopted them— like *masnavi, nazm, ghazal, rubai, qavvali, manaqib, nama, qasida, qit 'a* (or *muqatta 'at*) etc, their prosody, rhyme patterns, rules of composition, style and evocation of moods and feelings. The tradition is still alive in the criticism of traditional poetry, but while discussing the new poetry and fiction, critics often depend on modern Western theories as can be seen in the practices of Shamsur Rahman Faruqi, Shamim Hanfi or Gopichand Narang.

3

Quite a few critics, in English as well as the languages, have been employing Western theoretical tools to analyse Indian texts, both old and new. The influence of Western criticism was evident from the very beginning of modern criticism in India that had emerged along with the new genres like the short story, the novel and the modern prose-play. Only the credos and fashions have changed with the changes in Western theory. If initially it was only English criticism that had influenced our critics, later Russian, French and German schools also began to have their impact. This began chiefly with the emergence of Marxist and Freudian analytical modes. The early Marxist models were often reductive, as the critics were not yet familiar with the works of Antonio Gramsci, the Frankfurt School—like those of Adorno, Habermas or Horkheimer, or even of Michael Bakhtin, Ernst Fischer, Ernst Bloch, Walter Benjamin, and Raymond Williams and the later theorists—like Louis Althusser, Pierre Macherey, Fredric Jameson or Roland Barthes—not to speak of the post-Structuralists—and thinkers like Slavoj Zizek, Georgio Agamben and Jacques Ranciere—were yet to emerge. In that circumstance the models were chiefly from the Soviet Union and Eastern Europe: Zhadanov, Lunacharsky, Plekhanov, Lukacs and others. No wonder they equated Modernism with decadence, upheld socialist realism as the sacred model for committed writers to follow and often pursued a narrow class-reductionist approach. One of the reasons for the fall of the Progressive Literary Movement was this exclusionist approach that would not try to read literary works using modern tools to grasp their progressive implications or interpret commitment in a larger context where it could also involve social concerns of various kinds, other than purely class concerns. They would not have committed this mistake if they had carefully read even Marx or Lenin. Marx was a great admirer of the Greeks and of Shakespeare and in many of his analyses he exposed the contradictions in the self-proclaimed committed writing (eg: his detailed critique of Eugene Sue's *The Mysteries of Paris* in *The Holy Family,* where he brings out the contrast between the authorial claims to radicalism and the reactionary implications of the text itself) while upholding certain other forms of writing that did not make any claim to commitment. Macherey has looked closely at Lenin's symptomatic reading and appreciation of Tolstoy as the 'mirror of the Russian revolution' as against Plekahanov's accusation that Tolstoy was a reactionary, as he was a Catholic and an aristocrat by birth. Here Lenin goes beyond the empirical biographical facts to the truth of the text itself that transcends the author's class origins and proclaimed opinions. A similar hermeneutic conflict can also be seen in the well-known argument over Kafka between Lucaks on one side and Benjamin and Bloch on the other. To Lukacs, Kafka represented decadence and morbidity, but Benjamin and Bloch read Kafka politically to see in his works a sharp critique of bureaucracy, an expression of the solitude of the individual cut off from the community and the premonitions of the Nazi nightmare. The exclusivist approach of the early Progressives blurred the distinction between party literature and literature itself. While their method could partly explain 'Progressive' literary works as they understood them, it was incapable of understanding more complex works of literature that contained many voices and grappled with many contradictions. The result was that some of the better writers of the period, whose multiple articulations did greater justice to the society of the times, were kept out of the Marxist canon. In Kerala for example, fiction writers like D.M. Pottekkatt and poets like Kedamangalam Pappukkutty were hailed as revolutionaries, while fiction writers like Basheer and Uroob and poets like Edassery and Vailoppilly, who captured the deeper contradictions of their society, remained outside the canon. Only recently have some unorthodox Marxist and Marxisant critics begun to develop a more open approach to literature taking into account the post-Colonial and post-Structuralist insights into the working of language, unconscious and society. Early Freudian criticism too suffered from reductionist attitudes that analysed the characters as though they were living beings and attributed their motifs to their author. Only after Lacan, Deleuze and Guattari has Freud begun to be understood in all his complexity, as also his concept of unconscious that is structured like a language.

If Sydney and Arnold had held sway for some time in liberal Indian criticism, later they were replaced by T.S. Eliot and I.A. Richards. This happened especially during the emergence of Modern poetry that came to be associated with Eliot's modes and mores. Eliot did have an influence on early Modernist poets like Mardhekar, Muktibodh, Bishnu Dey, Navkant Barua, Gopal Krishna Adiga, Kaa. Naa. Subramanyam, Ayyappa Paniker and others. But they chiefly imbibed Eliot's iconoclasm in terms of form while their poetry was by no means a 'pastiche', but was sufficiently indigenous and their formal innovations sprang from the inner need of their own literary histories. They were no more 'Elioteans' than the new novelists like Nirmal Verma, Krishna Baldev Vaid and Ananthamurthy were 'Joyceans'. The new critical tools were patently inadequate to understand the new writing in Indian languages, as they also had their deeper social roots in the urbanisation of the country, the alienation of the intellectuals and the disillusionment with the system and the values it stood for. Semantics and semiotics would have helped grasp the verbal plays and the deployment of symbols and metaphors in the new writing, but not their socio-spiritual environment. Existentialist and Phenomenological tendencies dominated the critical scene in the 1960s when literature was conceived as the apotheosis of solitude and the articulation of metaphysical angst and alienation. Northrop Frye's archetypal patterns were at times contextualised and put to effective use, especially in the study of poetry. Another interesting development is the developing dialogue between Marxist and post-Structuralist approaches to writing. Roland Barthes's political semiology and his concept of the death of the author and the distinctions he draws between the 'work' and the 'text', Jacques Lacan's theory of the unconscious as the 'discourse of the other' and the mode of symptomatic reading that derives from it as illustrated by Louis Althusser and Pierre Macherey, Jacques Derrida's strategies of deconstruction meant to subvert the hegemonic discourses and institutions by reading them from the margins and bowing them up by developing their contradictions and Michel Foucault's theories of the power-knowledge nexus and the construction of subjectivity combined with Bakhtin's concept of ideology 'inscribed' in the linguistic sign, of dialogic imagination and of the carnivalesque and Gramsci's concept of the 'popular'—all these can liberate Marxist criticism from the sociological reductionism and the mechanical application of the class theory that had characterised its earlier phases. In fact this is happening in a big way in languages like Malayalam and Bengali, where, as Octavio Paz said of Latin America, the Marxist concepts and terms have become natural components of social and literary discourse. This is chiefly being pursued by young academics seeking an escape from the empiricist-positivist or idealist-iconic models offered by conventional English criticism, thus de-Anglicising and indirectly decolonising, the critical discourse.

Re-readings of canonical texts, side by side with the discovery of buried and forgotten texts, has certainly unleashed a lot of radical energy in the realm of criticism. Critics like B. Rajeevan, V. C. Sreejan, S.S. Sreekumar, E.V. Ramakrishnan, P. Udayakumar, V. Sanil, S. Saradakkutty, J. Devika, Dileep Menon, M.T. Ansari and others have been consistently rereading texts from various, mostly subaltern, points of view. They have been trying to expose the ideological determinations that underlie representations, especially of Dalits, muslims, *adivasis* and women, in the texts they choose to re-read. The new readings of Sreenarayana Guru and C.V. Raman Pillai by P. Udayakumar, the reading of Pothery Kunhambu's *Saraswativijayam*, a Dalit novel, by Dileep Menon, the readings of Chandu Menon by M.T. Ansari, the readings of some texts of Kumaran Asan by S. Saradakkutty and V. Sanil illustrate this trend. P. Udayakumar, for example, has looked at the evolution of the concept of the body in Sreenarayana as he moves from works like *Mananateetam, Siva Satakam* and *Indriya Vairagyam* to *Atmopadesa*

Satakam, Advaita Jeevitam and *Suddhipanchakam*. Sreenarayana denies ontological status to the body, but gives it epistomological status and discovers a subtle body (*sookshmasareera*) within the gross body (*sthoola sareera*). The body can attain purity once it is liberated from the gross body. Then it will be capable of spiritual bliss. This is the moment where community enters Sreenarayana's system, for, the reforms within the communities—in education, economy, health, etc.,—enable societies to attain this bliss, as the material and spiritual arrangements need to be co-ordinated like the organs of a body to lead to enlightenment, to recall his statement in *Advaitajeevitam*. Here he reminds us of Tirumular, the Tamil Saivite saint, as well as Basava, the Kannada Saivite reformer, both of whom accepted the interdependence of the body and the soul. It is the body that bears the organic marks of distinction in man; the caste marks and caste titles are an aberration that hide these organic markers. So there are only two castes among the humans—men and women. Sreenarayana thus views caste as a false distinction, religion as nothing more than a matter of opinion, and the community as the locus of concrete action. In 1916, Narayana declared that he does not belong to any caste or religion. Human community, he said, will be born only when false distinctions and hierarchies disappear. This was the basic principle of the Renaissance that was soon to transform the society in Kerala.

Dileep Menon's reading of *Saraswativijayam*, a novel by Pothery Kunhambu published in 1892, looks at Kunhambu's project closely to discover that initially he too had thought of reforming Hindu society, but later abandoned it as impossible. The author, an Ezhava who was often called Pulayan Kunhambu for his concern for the Pulaya community, found that tradition is impervious to modernity. The novel is an example of the spatial delineation of issues of power, hierarchy and inequality as the characters traverse different territories of freedom and knowledge. Travel becomes a metaphor of individual redemption here as the cruel landlord, Kuberan Namboodiri travels to Kasi; Marathan, the Pulaya protagonist travels to Madras and Subhadra, the Namboodiri's daughter, falsely accused of extramarital relations and banished from her caste, travels to Kannoor to escape from the enclosed space of historical memory. Kuberan has a change of heart, Marathan converts to Christianity, studies law and becomes a judge; Subhadra too converts and becomes a teacher and gets reunited with her husband, who also converts to Christianity. Christianity is the mediator of modernity in the text. Kunhambu did share the creative tension between the possibility of an internal critique of Hinduism and the pragmatic and robust alternative of empowerment through colonial education, though finally he found that liberation is unattainable within the Hindu fold, a fact that Ambedkar too was to discover later though his choice was not Christianity, but Buddhism. *Saraswativijayam* is not a revenge novel, nor a conversion tract; conversion here is a metaphor for the new possibilities opened up by colonialism and modernity. It may be noted that while elite thinkers like Ramakrishna, Vivekananda and Dayanand Saraswati championed an internal critique of Hinduism and found habitation within reformed religion, most of the subaltern thinkers found a solution to caste inequality only in conversion. Sreenarayana was an exception, as, through a pilosophical inversion, he could free himself from all religions.

Romila Thapar has reread Kalidasa's *Abhijnana Sakuntalam* from a historical point of view to reveal the Orientalist determinations behind its reception. She has shown how Kalidasa's Sakuntala is delicate, shy, meek, faithful and unquestioning in her obedience, returning with tears from Dushyanta's court when he disowns her, as different from the Sakuntala of *Adiparva* in the *Mahabharata*, where she is strong and independent, and boldly interrogates Dushyanta's sense of justice and decorum. She puts certain conditions even before she enters into a *gandharva* relationship with the king. Kalidasa's description fits in very much with the romantic concept of the innocent forest virgin embarrassed by the awakening of desire. In fact there is a whole romantic opposition at work here between the simple, picturesque ashram in the woods that represents rusticity and innocence and the splendid palace of the king that stands for the urban with its accent on power and cunning. Kalidasa's Sakuntala was the kind of ideal heroine that the romantics were looking for. Goethe describes her as 'a rustic girl', a 'child of nature' with elegant limbs and graceful undulating gait. Popularised in the West through Monier Williams' English translation, from which the German translation was done by Georg Forster in 1791, *Abhijnana Sakuntalam* fitted very well with the Orientalist project of romanticising the East, reflected equally well in colonial photography and the Company paintings. The Germans also exulted in the racial bonds between the ancient Indians and Europeans, whom they considered 'Aryans', whatever that term stands for. For French Indologists, like Sylvane Levy, and Russian Indologists like Oldenberg, Sakuntala was part of their fantasy about India. She was the ideal Hindoo woman also for the Indian middle class Nationalism, who like the Orientalists bemoaned the 'fall' of the ideal Indian womanhood. Rabindranath Tagore also upheld Sakuntala, combining in his approach the British Orientalist attitudes of the 19th century, the nascent nationalist sentiment and Victorian moralism. Romila Thapar upholds Shantaram's portrayal of Sakuntala in his film *Stree* as being faithful to her portrayal in the *Mahabharata*, as also the contemporary interpretation one comes across in Nachiket Patwardhan's *Anant yatra,* which brings Sakuntala to modern Bombay where Dushyanta is a business executive. The film hints that any appreciation of the naïve and frail Sakuntala today can only be an escape from today's oppressive patriarchal urban reality.

Post-Colonial readings, especially informed by Edward Said's theoretical insights have helped unearth the colonial prejudices behind a lot of work on India—not literature alone, but also photographs and paintings. These interrogations, while at times reductive or eclectic, have helped make writers and readers conscious of the dangers of (mis) representation. At the same time the post-Colonial theory makes certain assumptions that need to be reexamined. Arun P. Mukherjee has summed them up like this[1] (a) The theory claims that the major theme of literatures from post-Colonial societies is discursive resistance to the now absent coloniser.

---

1. Harish Trivedi and Meenakshi Mukherjee, eds., 'Some Uneasy Conjunctions', in *Interrogating Post-colonialism: Theory, Text, Context* (Shimla: IIAS, 1996).

(b) It unproblematically assumes that the writers who write back to the centre are representing the people of their society authentically. (c) The theory downplays the difference between the settler colonial and those colonised in their home territories using the term 'colonised' for both of them. It trivialises the experience of those who suffered genocide and pauperisation under colonial rule, not to mention cultural deprivation. (d) In its use of terminology like 'the oppressed', 'the colonised peoples' and 'the indigenous' to describe post-colonial societies, the theory suppresses internal hierarchies and divisions in these societies. It does great disservice to the minorities in these societies by deflecting attention away from their oppression by using a unitary vocabulary which confers a 'subaltern' status on the entire post-colonial world, disregarding the fact that it is ridden with hierarchies. This last erasure is particularly dangerous as it glosses over the distinctions of class, caste, race and religion in these societies. I also feel that the post-colonialists often assume that history begins with colonialism, which is exactly what the colonialists want us to believe. The paradigm has also been used by the right-wing to promote their agenda of a revival of pre-colonial practices and justify hierarchies like the *varna* system and even superstitious practices like astrology, *sati* (eg. Ashis Nandy) and nude worship (eg. U.R. Ananthamurthy). Another strange fact about its application is that only the Indian writing in English is considered to be post-colonial by the academics. It may be true about some works like those of Mulk Raj Anand (*Untouchable, Coolie*), Khushwant Singh (*Train to Pakistan*), Salman Rushdie (*Midnight's Children, Shame*) or Kiran Nagarkar (*The Little Soldier*), while post-colonial reality is expressed with greater authenticity in language texts like *Kayar* (Thakazhi Shivasankara Pillai), *Dharmapuranam* (O.V. Vijayan), *Abhayarthikal, Marubhoomikal Undakunnathu* (Anand), *Bharatipura* (Ananthmurthy), *Kusumabale* (Devanoor Mahadeva) *Malapally* (U. Lakshmi Narayana), *Karukku, Sangati* (Bama), *Kosla* (Bhalchandra Nemade), *Uchalya* (Laxman Gaikwad), *Upara* (Laxman Mane), *Akkarmashee* (Sharan Kumar Limbale) *Angaliyat* (Joseph Macwan), *Aranyer Adhikar, Agnigarbha* (Mahaswetadevi), *Parsa* (Gurdial Singh), *Maila Anchal* (Phaneeswar

Nath Renu), *Tamas, Madhavi* (Bhisham Sahni) *Zindaginama* (Krishna Sobti), *Kitne Pakistan* (Kamaleswar) *Iyaru Ingam* (Birendrakumar Bhattacharya) and *Aag ka Dariya* (Qurratulain Hyder), just to take a few random samples from the novel alone. The post-colonialists also do not see the distinct ways in which the elite and the downtrodden reacted to colonialism—like Ambedkar and Sreenarayana Guru welcoming the reformative and egalitarian aspects of the colonial rule. They also fail to see the neo-colonial forces seeking hegemony in the post-colonial India, now masquerading as globalisation.

Said's formulations in *Orientalism* have also been challenged by a host of theoreticians. Aijaz Ahmad[2] has shown how Said is silent about the modes by which the colonial subjects received, challenged, changed or rejected the Western conceptualisations about them. Patrick Williams and Laura Chrisman[3] have also pointed to Said's neglect of the colonial subject's power of resistance. Sara Mills[4] is rightly critical of Said's neglect of gender: did the Western woman share the Western man's fantasies about the Oriental woman as the passive subject of desire? There are too other objections: historians feel that colonial discourse analysis tends to make large generalisations based on a limited number of largely literary texts. It also de-historicises and treats all texts as synchronic, as if they existed in an ahistorical, unchanging textual continuum. The textualism and idealism of colonial discourse analysis occurs at the expense of materialist historical inquiry and politicised understanding.

4

Feminist critics have also responded to the crisis by using gender as the organising principle of writing as well as reading. Feminist scholarship has retrieved a lot of forgotten or suppressed writing in

---

2. Aijaz Ahmad, *In Theory: Classes, Nations, Literature* (New Delhi: Oxford University Press,1992).
3. Patrick Williams and Laura Chrisman, eds., *Colonial Discourse and Post-colonial Theory* (New York: Columbia University Press, 1994).
4. Sara Mills, *Discourses of Difference: An Analysis of Women's Travel Writing and Colonialism* (London: Routledge, 1991).

the Indian languages done by women in the past, the most famous example being *Radhikasantwanam,* Muddupalani's Telugu text of the 18th century, proscribed by the British Raj and willed into oblivion by indigenous patriarchy, including the nationalists as a frank, and hence threatening, expression of female desire. The patriarchal canons are being interrogated, myths revisioned, texts decoded and literary history revised. Susie Tharu and K. Lalita have traced in their introduction to the anthology *Women Writing in India, Sixth Century B.C. to the Present* the evolution of women's writing in India across centuries. Uma Chakravarty, Vijaya Dabbe, Sonal Shukla, Madhu Kishwar, Leela Mullati, Parita Mukta, Vijaya Ramaswamy and others have explored the poetry of women saints like Lal Ded, Akka Mahadevi, Satyakka, Kadire Rammavve, Ayadakki Lakkamma, Muktayakka, Andal, Karaykkal Ammayar, Meerabai, Gangasati, Janabai and Bahinabai to show how Bhakti was to them a tool to escape gender distinction, patriarchal oppression and domestic confinement, just as it was to the Buddhist nuns like Mutta, Ubbiri or Sumangalamata of the sixth century. God becomes a way of dissolving an otherwise impossible situation in these saints. Their worldly marriages, actual as well as potential, represent both the lure and the bondage of the world, while their relationship to God represents a renunciation of the world and the woman's traditional roles in it. Like Susie finds the lyrics of *Terigatha* to be, their poems are epiphanic experiences in which the painful constructions of secular life fall away and the torment of feelings subsides, as the peace and freedom of nirvana are attained. While they exult in their new life transformed by Bhakti, they also contrast it to the painful worlds they have left behind. These poets created an alternative family, resisted the oppressive social role imposed upon them by the male-dominated society and simultaneously created a parallel language of experience and emotion.

A lot of scholars and academics like Nabaneeta Dev Sen, Malashree Lal, Vrinda Nabbar, Brinda Bose, Ruth Vanita, Gayatri Chakravarty Spivak, J. Devika, Anita Devasia, A.K. Jayasree and S. Saradakkutty have also done considerable research in women's discourses and the representation of women in literary texts by men. The complexity of gender construction in India is a challenge to the students of gender as it is overdetermined by other formations like class, caste, religion, regional cultures and languages, specific traditions, taboos, laws of marriage, sexual kinship and inheritance and the contradictions between the country and the city and the feudal moral codes and the new roles popularised by the indigenous and the Western media. Feminist enquiry in literary historiography means discovering the past from the women's angle, questioning the existing modes of periodisation, examining past texts for feminine inscriptions, unburying the marginalised, relating literature to the differential articulation of the various levels of the superstructure and defining and explaining the breaks and continuities in the history of women's writing in the country. In literary theory it means challenging the patriarchal canons, deconstructing the phallocentric creative and critical discourse, defining the feminine literary texts in the Indian context, unearthing the ideological determinations that lay behind the reception and rejection of literary texts in the different periods, relating their formal constituents to the specific environment and regional traditions, thus developing an indigenous semiotics that connects signs to their specific space and lineage, decoding gender as an organising principle of experience and relating forms of feminine articulation to the changing social, racial and conceptual permutations in our history—for example, the employment of dialects and images of domesticity in the quest for deliverance in the Bhakti period, the tactical redeployment of hegemonic discourses to constitute a new enlightened middle class female subject in the colonial-reformist period, the creation of new enunciative modalities and rhetorical strategies to articulate the gender-class nexus in the Progressivist writing and the caste-gender nexus in Dalit writing, or the use of body-imagery, emphasis on female bonding and open defiance of the set norms and structures of writing in more recent, openly feminist, writing. While the Western feminist critical theories, right from Virginia Woolf, Simone de Beauvoir, Elaine Showalter, Kate Millet and Sandra Gilbert and Susan Gubar to Helene Cixous, Annette

Kolodny, Ellen Moer, Mary Ellman, Gayle Greene, Coppelia Kahn, Jane Flax, Julia Kristeva and Barbara Smith will certainly be of use, and have been used, in Indian feminist criticism, we may also come across some areas of resistance to Western theories in Indian literary practice. While the Bhakti poets provide a fine example to such resistance, contemporary texts, say of Ismat Chughtai, Kamala Das, Sara Joseph, Bama, Amrita Pritam, Mahasweta Devi, Krishna Sobti, Alka Saraogi, Arundhati Roy, etc., again to take some fiction writers, also have a lot that is specifically Indian or regional about them that call for different critical strategies.

Eco-criticism is another response to the existing theories that focus entirely on the text without looking at its organic relationship with nature and the larger universe. Even though it was William Rueckert (*Literature and Ecology: An Experiment in Eco-Criticism*, 1978) who introduced the term, it was Joseph Meeker's *The Comedy of Survival: Studies in Literary Ecology* (1974) that first defined the subject. According to Meeker, literary ecology was concerned with the biological themes appearing in literature. Its aim was also to discover the role of literature in human ecology. Literary works, he said, often reveal man's beliefs about the truth of natural processes and the cultural ideologies that have brought the human race to the modern environmental crisis. Cheryll Glofelti who edited the first eco-criticism reader (1996) describes eco-criticism as an attempt to unravel the exchanges between nature and culture. It has one leg in literature and the other on earth: as a theoretical discourse it connects equally with human beings and non-human ones. The writers' world is not only the social world, but the ecosphere itself. Earth, she says, is at the centre of eco-criticism, just as gender is at the centre of feminist criticism and class at that of Marxist criticism. Eco-Criticism according to Lawrence Buel, brings space into the critical agenda that has so far been confined to the theme, plot and characters. He sees it as an umbrella term that embraces various modes and approaches. It has also been called 'ego-criticism' (Sven Birkerts, *Only God can Make a Tree: The Joys and Sorrows of Eco-Criticism*) as it tries to discover what literature has to say about man's ego-centrism, greed and craze for wealth and power. Some eco-critics also draw strength from Engels' *Dialectics of Nature*, Raymond Williams's insights into the city-country contradictions and the works of Adorno, Walter Benjamin and other new Marxist thinkers. The anthology *Haritaniroopanam Malayalathil* (Green Criticism In Malayalam) edited by G. Madhusoodanan carries 76 different samples of what can be broadly called eco-criticism in Malayalam—along with 16 theoretical pieces—that began to grow with the environmental awareness generated by the struggle against the proposed dam in the rainforests of the Silent Valley. The book carries applications of the concepts of eco-Marxism, eco-Feminism, eco-Ethics and eco-Spirituality in literary criticism.

The emergence of strong Dalit writing in Marathi, Gujarati, Hindi, Punjabi, Telugu and Tamil has given rise to a Dalit poetics that, though not fully defined, finds its expression in the works of D.R. Nagaraj, Daya Pawar, Arjun Dangle, Saran Kumar Limbale, Chandrakant Patil, Mulk Raj Anand, M.S.S. Pandyan, Cho. Dharman, G. Lakshmi Narasiah, Malay Dewanji, Arun. P. Mukherjee, S.P. Punalekar, A. Satyanarayana, Jyotsna Macwan, Kalpana Rentala, Eleanor Zelliot, K.K. Kochu, K.K. Baburaj and others. It was perhaps Sharad Patil's book in Marathi, *Abrahmani Sahityanche Saundaryasastra* that first launched an attack on Brahmin aesthetics and spoke of the need for a counter-poetics. Sharan Kumar Limbale in his book, *Towards an Aesthetics of Dalit Literature* has attempted a critique of status-quoist Marathi aesthetics as also of the adulatory as well as negative criticism of Dalit literature by the *savarna* critics. He points out that Dalit literature is not meant to entertain the readers, but to provoke them into rethinking their society and its ethics and aesthetics. It is impossible to investigate the Dalit writing with its rebellion, rejection and commitment with the established critical tools meant for the literature of acquiescence and consent. He does not agree with critics like Yadunath Thatte who want to enlarge the *rasa* theory to include revolt and cry as the tenth and eleventh *rasa*s. What is needed is a new aesthetics that takes into account the differentness of Dalit writing in content as well as form. Aestheticist criticism cannot digest the non-traditional stance of Dalit literature.

For that freedom will have to be recognised as an aesthetic value. The intensity of experience, the way the experience is socialised, its power to cross the boundaries of time and space—these are the standards Limbale proposes for the evaluation of Dalit literature. D.R. Nagaraj in his book, *The Flaming Feet: A Study of the Dalit Movement in India,* has gone deeper into the specifics of the Dalit sensibility and Dalit imagination and the problem of cultural memory in the context of the cosmologies of caste and the realism in Kannada fiction. He traces the cultural memory of the Dalits to the subaltern, radical, traditions, folk cosmologies, rural myths and oral narratives which are getting lost in the oppressive process of sanskritisation pursued by the Hindu revivalists. He looks at the cults of Madeswara and Manteswamy in Southern Karnataka as examples. He points out how the cultural paradigm of the nationalists had no place for the Dalit cultural traditions and practices. The monolithic cultural model erected on the basis of Vedanta by the Hindu Right also precludes all the philosophic and cultural expressions of the Dalits. Nagaraj makes a very insightful comparison between U.R. Ananthamurthy's *Samskara* and Devanoor Mahadeva's *Kusumabale* to show how caste has been an important factor in determining their modes of representation and imagination. *Samskara* gives the readers an insight into the self-image of the Brahmin by allowing them to see the world through the eyes of Pranesacharya, whose attempts to break the system miserably fail, as against that of Naranappa, his alter ego, who completely breaks free of tradition and its taboos. This is also the failure of the novel as it cannot establish the sexual contact between the Brahmin and the non-Brahmin as a possible way to break free of the oppressive caste society. Realism frustrates the novel's radical ambitions. But *Kusumabale* rejects the notion of verifiable reality at the very outset and follows a folk narrative form. While *Samskara* ignores the socio-economic power structures, thus turning its concern more metaphysical, *Kusumabale* counterposes the personal and the political realms of the caste structure, and finds that sexual contact like the one in *Samska*ra can only lead to violence within the existing power structure. Devanoor Mahadeva revives the Dalit mode of imagination as when a cot tells a story and a lamp turns into a woman who comments on the events of the day. The narrative is open and works at multiple levels while *Samskara* is highly centred and has an ending that closes the narrative.

Dalit literature has created a new poetics by redrawing the map of literature, discovering and exploring a whole new continent of experience that had so far been left to darkness and silence, by helping literature overcome stagnation through a cleansing renewal, by disturbing the sterile complacency of the dominant social groups, by challenging their set modes of looking at reality and their stale habits of ordering knowledge, beauty and power and their established literary canons, bringing to focus marginalised or suppressed aspects of experience, vision, language and reality and forcing the community to refashion its tools and observe itself critically from a fresh and different angle. Dalit writing has thrown overboard classical virtues like propriety, balance, restraint and understatement, using a deliberately subversive diction that celebrates Dalit values and challenges the middle-class notions of linguistic decency. It has renewed literary language by bringing in fresh words, usages and modes of imagination kept out by the so-called mainstream literature. The new tribal literature emerging in languages like Santali, Bodo, Bhili, Tenyidie, Angami, Ao, Gondi, Mundari and others, also share many of these characteristics, while celebrating the tribal vision of the world and nature, demanding an alternative poetics.

There are also independent attempts like Bhalchandra Nemade's *Teeka Swayamvar* that uses a methodology drawn from Marathi literary history itself to describe the evolution of the Marathi novel, Namwar Singh's *Doosari Parampara* that speaks of a second tradition in Indian thought and literature, E.V. Ramakrishnan's *Making It New*, a comparative study of modern poetry in Hindi, Marathi, Malayalam and Gujarati, Sisir Kumar Das's *History of Indian Literature* that tries to develop a history of Indian literature without ignoring the regional and linguistic differences and Ayyappa Paniker's *Indian Narratology* that seeks to found a theory of Indian narrative practices. I am in the process of exploring an alternative democratic poetics that I have temporarily called *sramanic*—as against the dominant *brahmanic* poetics, which alone can explain the second tradition in Indian literature that includes the tribal, oral and folk literature, the literature of Bhakti and Sufi movements, Buddhist and Jain literary practices, anti-colonial literature, and contemporary subaltern writing done by women, tribals, Dalits, socialist radicals and other dissenters to the system.

Let me conclude with a statement made by Terry Eagleton in his *Significance of Theory* that seems relevant to our discussion:

> Theory on a dramatic level happens when it is both possible and necessary for it to do so—when the traditional rationales, which have silently underpinned our daily practices stand in danger of being discredited, and need either to be revised or discarded. This may come about for reasons internal to those practices, or because of a certain external pressure, or, more typically, because of a combination of both. Theory is just a practice forced into a new form of self-reflectiveness on account of certain grievous problems it has encountered.[5]

---

5. Terry Eagleton, *Significance of Theory* (Oxford, UK: John Wiley and Sons Ltd., 1992).

INDIAN LITERATURE
Nativism and its Ambivalences

Nativism, in its positive and progressive aspects, is a celebration of the pluralism that is at the very core of Indian culture and literature, an interrogation of the existing canons that are most often a continuation of the orientalist notions of 'Indianness' governed by wrong premises like the privileging of high textuality, the marginalisation of the non-canonical, performative and counter-hegemonic texts and trends, simplifications of our overdetermined literary contexts and movements, aesthetic reductivism and revivalist nostalgia trying to retrieve a supposedly lost metaphysical past, and an exploration into the possibilities of alternative genealogies that take into account indigenous elements of our popular creativity, or what A.K. Ramanujan would call our 'little traditions.' No doubt, we need from time to time to problematise the idea of cultural homogeneity that has been haunting the dominant discourse in the country, not in order to discard the idea of unity, but to re-emphasise diversity and to revise our understanding of unity, to see it as a continuous and evolving process of open dialogue and creative interaction among our different languages and cultures, including the marginalised ones of the minorities, of the Dalits and of the tribals, rather than as the hegemonic presence of some central voice, say, of a caste from the past or a class from the present that bulldozes all unevenness and crushes all differences. Indian culture is no monolith and Indian literature is not a monologue; they have many tongues and many voices, many hues and many world views. The dominant and the subaltern, the high text and the popular text, the great tradition and the little tradition, the *margi* and the *desi*, the written and the oral/performative have co-existed in the Indian literary landscape for centuries, giving and taking, teaching and learning from one another.

We have, for example, as many *Ramayana*s as we have languages and traditions, even as we have arts, for, besides the various written *Ramayana*s from those of Valmiki and Tulsidas to those of Pampa and Kambar and Ezhuthachchan, we also have the very different

*Ramayana*s of the Buddhist and Jain traditions, the visual texts from our murals and miniatures, as also the performed texts from Harikatha to Burakatha, from Yakashagana to Kathakali to Ramleela. None of these texts can claim to be more authentic than any other; privileging one at the expense of another will be a violation of what I may call 'textual democracy'.

No discussion on Nativism today can steer clear of cultural politics. On the one hand the very concepts of 'India' and 'Indianness' have almost been hijacked by the ideologues of religious revivalism of various hues and shapes; on the other we are fast developing into a competitive market-society whose interpretation of freedom abhors autonomy and reduces cultural diversity to a variety of changeable fashions and marketable life-styles that easily become the investments of a flourishing culture-industry with its mushrooming pulp-literature factories, multi-cultural cook-books, pop-music discotheques, formula films, television soap operas, video-parlours and ethnic exports. Alternative ways of life, thought and art are resisted by a culture that believes in uniformity and standardisation. The basic democratic idea of geopolitical and linguistic federalism is being diluted day by day in the actual practices of our governance. Any discussion of Nativism in this context will have to define the concept against a kind of revivalistic cultural nationalism as also against political separatism, against a mere atavistic retrieval of an ethnic past, as also against the pressures of the culture-market that is eager to absorb and trivialise everything native, turning it into another cultural commodity that would adorn the drawing rooms of the West's odd fantasies of oriental ethnicity. A clear and constructive concept of plurality alone can salvage the sinking project of India's unity at the level of the people, as different from what we listen to in the daily rhetoric of the political demagogues.

2

The human self is composed of multiple identities and roles, familial, territorial, linguistic, class, religious, ethnic and gender, being the most prominent of them. Ideologies of identity are constructed by foregrounding anyone/some of these elements; imagined communities from groups to nations are projections of these ideologies. Nativism too is such a literary-cultural ideology, spatial and verbal at the same time, projecting the language—with its dialectal variants—of a place or a community along with the ways of life and thought and the structures of feeling peculiar to that community and its space. Its relationship with other ideological formations like the nation, class, gender, religion, race and caste is extremely complex and highly mediated since the language community often cuts across these divisions. It receives its political content from the context in which it is invoked, as well as the ways it is employed. In Dalit literature, for example, we find Nativism put to a class/caste use, while it can also go beyond class distinctions, as in the times of a language-based struggle, like that for the restoration of the old script in Manipur or the resistance in Tamil Nadu. Nativism is post-colonial in its battle against the invasion of alien sensibilities and modes of feeling and articulation, while it is post-modernist in its emphasis on cultural difference. The Nativists seem to consider social class an inadequate basis for an enduring collective identity because of its limited emotional appeal and lack of cultural depth. Classes are also, like gender divisions, often territorially dispersed and are likely to be subdivided on the basis of differences in income and levels of skill. Economic factors are also subject to rapid fluctuations over time; economic self-interest alone cannot form the basis of stable collective identities, since it is again an area of conflicts of identity. Religious communities transcend classes; but in a multi-religious society like ours, they too can become divisive and promote conflict along communal lines, as we find happening in many parts of India today. Even ethnic communities often use religious criteria of differentiation to create specific identity (e.g. Sikhs in India, Sinhalese in Sri Lanka, Serbs and Croats in erstwhile Yugoslavia, Catholics and Protestants in Northern Ireland).

A proper national identity, however, is larger than the concept of community implicit in Nativism, for the former requires, besides a language and territory, common myths and historical memories, a common mass public culture and common legal rights and duties for all members. We all have to differentiate also between the nativist ideology and that of 'the state' for the majority of the 'states' today are not true nation-states, where the total population of the state shares a single ethnic culture, but are 'plural' states inhabited by different communities, religions and races and speaking different languages, as is the case with India. Nativism, on the other hand, is a configuration of ethnic and linguistic ties that seeks literary articulation in a specific region. An ethnic community or ethnic, to use the French term, has the following attributes: a collective proper name, a myth of common ancestry, shared historical memories, one or more differentiating elements of common culture, an association with a specific 'homeland' and sense of solidarity for significant sectors of the population. We may add a common language also to this list, in order to define the bases of the Nativism ideology. A nationalist language and symbolism are still broader as they connect the ideology with the mass sentiments of wider segments of the designated population through slogans, ideas, symbols and ceremonies. Nationalism is primarily a political ideology with a cultural doctrine at its centre, while Nativism is primarily cultural-linguistic. However, it has the potential of developing into a full-fledged political ideology, when it develops links with the movements for regional autonomy, like the Jharkhand and Uttarakhand movements in India. Democracy will be able to accommodate such movements so long as they demand only cultural parity and a little more autonomy within the structure of a multi-national state (as in the case of several Catalan, Scots and Flemish nationalists); it can tolerate even the demand for the creation of a separate state within the federal polity; but it can hardly cope with the separatist demand for outright independence and secession, as in the case of the Khalistan movement in the Punjab. Nativism, taken to this extreme, will cease to be a positive literary ideology and instead become a pernicious political ideology that can spell the ruin and fragmentation of India.

3

While opposing this extreme, one may also do well to caution against the other extreme that has become the bane of India's cultural policy: that is the marginalisation or even eradication of all intermediate bodies and local differences in the interests of cultural and political homogeneity. Here the state becomes the agent of the 'nation-to-be' and the creator of a 'political community' and 'political culture' that is to replace the various ethnic cultures of a heterogeneous population. Such forced homogenisation and the bulldozing of cultural differences, while being dangerous in themselves as they destroy the very essence, character and richness of our heterogeneous culture, become all the more dangerous when they work in association with any particular religion. The pluralistic religious tradition of India has been inclusive and democratic enough, even to accommodate non-theistic and materialistic strains championed by say, Charvak or the Buddha or Mahavira. Indian culture too is a mosaic made up of components from various traditions, including what the revivalist's views as 'foreign' cultures. Sufi poetry, Persian literary forms, Moghul and Gothic architecture, Christian legends, Arabian stories, the novel, which in its present form is primarily a Western contribution, European painting, Western science have all become part of our heritage and have played a great role in shaping our sensibility and to exorcise them is neither possible nor desirable, as all of them have enriched our culture along with our home-grown cults, movements, systems and forms.

The present Indian culture has *margi, desi* and *videsi* elements that keep on productively interacting with one another; our identity is multiple by definition. To reduce it to just one of its components can impoverish our culture. Nativism is progressive in so far as it fights any revivalistic destruction of our native plurality; it can also be regressive if it just creates an alternative past and obstructs the growth of genuinely modern perception and attitudes, for nothing is necessarily good because it is native; our rural traditions have a whole feudal baggage of patriarchal, anti-egalitarian and anti-democratic values, along with their more positive and cheerful aspects. Nativism can degenerate into a form of rustic revivalism and an uncritical valorisation of feudal values, if it falls into less enlightened hands, with no awareness of modern egalitarian values, objective temperaments and futuristic orientations.

While acknowledging the positive aspects of Nativism as an attempt to indigenise our modernism, one can hardly forget that Indian literature has never been divided on linguistic lines. Shared themes, forms, concerns, experiences, influences, directions and movements, along with multi-lingualism and inter-language translations still keep the ideas of 'Indian literature' dynamically alive. Indian writers continue to be Indian, whatever language they write in. This is as true of 'nativists' like Balchandra Nemade and Kanji Patel, as of Indian English writers like R.K. Narayan or Arundhati Roy. We must accept the historical fact that Indians have been condemned by the forces of the past, as well as of the present, to live together or to perish and that our highly over-determined literary context demands an integrated approach and genuinely inter-linguistic and inter-disciplinary studies for its full understanding. The Nativist task of deconstructing the Indian Tradition must be part of a greater project of constructing unity at a higher and more realistic conceptual level, of heteroglossia, cultural plurality within the nation's boundaries and intertextuality within culture.

SEX, TEXT, POLITICS
Women's Writing in India—Problems of Reading

Any meaningful discussion on women's writing today is, by compulsion, part of the larger enterprise of empowering women and this, in turn, joins hands with other 'transversal' struggles for social justice on various fronts, may they be of the Dalits and tribals against caste hierarchy, of the radical democrats against imperialist economic and cultural interventions, of the workers and peasants against class exploitation, of the health activists against unethical medical practices, of the pacifists against nuclear proliferation and war-oriented planning, of the critical academics against the enslavement of knowledge to hegemonic power, of the secular intellectuals and people against verities of communalism, of the civil rights activists against the suppression of individual and collective rights, of the environmentalists against pollution, poverty, deforestation and the disastrous displacement of populations in the name of a development that often benefits only the upper strata of society, and of the marginalised minorities, regions and languages against the forces that oppress them. These are not only struggles against dominant groups and ideologies but are also movements for democratic plurality, creative difference, cultural heterogeneity, healthier environment, better living standards, active peace and active non-violence, a liberating pedagogy and an egalitarianism that transcends distinctions of gender, class, race and community: in short, for a truer and fuller democracy that combines a concern for the nation with a concern for our own endangered species.

Patriarchal power is one among many forms of power that tyrannise the species today, one that upon action making them easier or more difficult, using induction, seduction and incitement, structures their possible fields of action and even defines the nature and strategy of resistance. Power brings into operation a whole micro-physics of differentiation, legitimation, institutionalisation and rationalisation. It only weighs on us as a force that suppresses and negates but traverses and produces things, induces even forms of pleasure and produces 'truth-effects'—a whole 'regime' of truth to use Michel Foucault's term—through the technologies of control, of production, of the sign and of the shelf. A conscious reading of women's writing today, as also a reading of men's writing for women's point of view, will have to deconstruct it, lay bare the play of power and locate the zones of resistance built into it. Such a symptomatic reading will have to travel from the text to the world and back, making constant references to historical and contemporary reality, while, at the same time, admitting the translucent and polyphonic nature of the text as a linguistic artifact.

In the specific context of India, we do not require an Edward Said to tell us of the interrelation between the world of words and the world of events; the everyday breaks in upon our textual explorations so much so that the borders between imagination and reality often appear to dissolve and all the claims of language to autonomy and of the text to an auto-erotic semiotic play appear suspect, despite all our theoretical rigour and vigilance. Listen to a contemplative hymn by Meerabai or Lal Ded and some woman rejected by every hearth wails for alms at your door: read Mahasweta Devi's tales of valiant tribal heroines like Draupadi and a destitute tribal woman forced to sell herself in the marketplaces of civilisation stares at you from the street: read a novel like Ismat Chughtai's *Terhi Lakeer* or Krishna Sobti's *Mitro Marjani* with their uninhibited portrayals of feminine desire and watch an advertisement that exploits woman's sexuality for simple commerce: read Kamala Das's *A Doll for a Child Prostitute* or Lalitambika Antarjanam's *The Goddess of Revenge* and hear that one more group of impoverished girls has been trapped in the red-light areas of Bombay; follow the fate of the pathetic girl child in Balamani Amma's poem 'At the pond' or Sugathakumari's poem 'Girl child in the Nineties' and let the newspaper tell you another girl sold to an Arab, another minor raped, another bride burnt by her-in-laws: why, widows of our 19th century novels still instill guilt in you, begging at Vrindavan, sacred to the mythical great lover. These frequent interjections of sordid existence into the fables of imagination make the world and the text appear almost a seamless continuum, so that we are forced to warn ourselves for reasons of objectivity that the literary text is after all a verbal construct and even its semblance of reality is only an effect of the discourse (as Roland Barthes has convincingly demonstrated in his study of Balzac's story 'Sarrasine' (S/Z). Events do exist in the world externally to thought; but their specificity as objects is constructed within a discursive condition of emergence and depends upon the structure of the discursive field. This does not, however, mean that we cannot relate literary texts to history—the history of the period of their origin as works, as well as of the periods that receive them and constitute them in different ways, within different epistemes and problematiques possible in that age and that society.

Only recently has women's writing begun to receive special attention among students and scholars in India and to be read from subaltern and gender points of view. Our regional languages do have a long tradition of women's writings, especially poetry, but they have become visible on pan-Indian and international planes chiefly through anthologies of translations like *Women Writing in India, The Slate of Life, Truth-Tales, Inner Courtyard, Inner Spaces, In Other Words, Under the Silent Sun* and *In Their Own Voice,* translations of individual works by Qurratulain Hyder, Ismat Chughtai, Kamala Das, C.S. Laxmi (Ambai), Mahasweta Devi, and Tamil Sangam women poets, besides women's magazines and studies on women's writings from different points of view. Women writers have also begun to receive fairer representation in literary anthologies and journals and fairer treatment from publishers. We now have a substantial body of women's literature, the roots of which go well into the past, from the 19th-and early 20th-century writers like Swarnakumari Devi and Ras Sundari Devi of Bengal, Ramabai Ranade and Lakshmibai Tilak of Marathi and Bandaru Acchamamba and Tallapragada Viswasundaramma of Telugu, to the 17th and 18th-century writers, like the long-suppressed Muddupalani of Telugu, Sanciya Hosannamma of Kannada, Bahinabai of Marathi and Mahlaq Bai Chanda of Urdu, to the devotional poets of the 12th to 15th centuries, like Akkamahadevi of Kannada, Mirabai of Gujarati, Janabai of Marathi and Aatukuri Molla of Telugu, the medieval folk songs and to the Sangam poets of Tamil, like Neccellaiyar and Velli Vitiyar of the last century BCE, the Pali songs of the Buddhist nuns of the 6th century BCE, like Sumankalamata and Ubbiri and the tribal songs of the earliest inhabitants of our country.

A lot of buried or censored writing by women has been unearthed and retrieved from amnesia, thanks to the efforts of feminist scholars like Susie Tharu and K. Lalita. Indian women poets and fiction-writers in English have also contributed to a new awareness of women's issues among their urban middle-class readership, complementing in a way, the contributions of Indian language writers to the raising of gender-consciousness. This has a long, though discontinuous, tradition in the Indian languages and rose to visibility in the 19th and early 20th centuries, along with the nationalist and social reform movements and more recently pioneers like Lalitambika Antarajanam, K. Saraswati Amma, Madhavikutty, Ismat Chughtai, Qurratulain Hyder, Ashapurna Devi, Mahasweta Devi, Krishna Sobti, Amrita Pritam and Balamani Amma, have been joined by a lot of apparently more militant counterparts in all the languages. These writers perhaps have a more native awareness of the issues that concern ordinary women and write from a more authentic cultural milieu, even though it would be simplistic to assume that they are pristinely rustic, innocent of all urbanisation and derivative consciousness.

This difference, however, does not, I hope create a cleavage in the ranks of the woman writers who, despite differences in their perception and articulations of the issues, as between the feminist and non-feminist, or between the socialist feminist and the lesbian feminist or Dalit feminist and upper- or middle-class feminist, share certain common concerns and visions of a democratic society, where woman's voice will be heeded and woman's status upheld. These differences of positions, attitudes, language, themes, patterns and mornings, on the other hand lend a healthy heterogeneity to our woman's writings, which are otherwise likely to suffer from a dull monotony and redundance, a potential threat to the literature of any collective movement.

Along with this spurt in women's writing, feminist reading of literature of both men and women, have also come up, questioning androcentric approaches to literary and social theory. If the close reading of the Bhakti women poets by Uma Chakravarty, Vijaya Dabbe and Robert Zydenbos, Ruth Vanita, Sonal Shukla and Madhu Kishwar is an initial effort to read ancient women's writing, Gayatri Chakravarty Spivak's 'Dayini' is a unique, though highly westernised, effort in the analysis of contemporary women's literature. A lot of other women scholars from Susie Tharu and Meenakshi Mukherjee to Vrinda Nabbar, Jancy James and Tejaswini Niranjana, have also done considerable research work in women's literature or the portrayal of women in men's literature. However, it is doubtful whether we have really involved an indigenous way of decoding gender and reading texts foregrounding the feminine. This is, however, part of a general post-colonial situation where the decolonisation of culture, outlook and methods of reflection has been hampered or slowed down by various factors, including a neo-colonial onslaught. One has, however, to be extremely cautious about any discussion of decolonisation today, since the idea has practically been hijacked by the revivalist discourse that in our context here boils down to an invocation of the Vedic ideal of Aryan womanhood and a celebration of piety, submission to the father and the husband and the son, and even the practice of Sati. Orientalists like William Jones and Indologists like Clarisse Bader had idealised this ascetic endurance of the ancient Indian women as against their later 'fall' into sensuousness. Indian nationalist historians also had invoked the same passive ideal in their anxiety to answer the accusations of utilitarians like James Mill, critics like Katherine Mayo and the Evangelicals who attacked 'the Hindu paganism' and the imperialists who found in India's moral degradation an opportunity to legitimise the colonial rule. Decolonisation, obviously, does not mean the retrieval of a romanticised 'golden' past; in the context of our discussion it means an objective realisation of the complexity of gender construction in India, overdetermined as it is by other formations like class, caste, religion, regional cultures and languages, specific traditions, taboos, laws of marriage, sexual kinship and inheritance and contradictions between the country and the city, feudal moral codes and the new roles popularised by the indigenous and Western media.

In literary historiography it means discovering the past anew from the woman's angle, questioning the existing modes of periodisation, examining past texts for feminine inscriptions, unburying the marginalised, relating literature to the differential articulation of the various levels of the superstructure and defining and explaining the breaks and continuities in the history of women's writing in the country. In literary theory, it means challenging the patriarchal canons, deconstructing the phallocentric creative and critical discourse, defining the feminine in literary texts in the Indian context, unearthing the ideological configurations that lay behind the reception and rejection of literary texts in different periods, relating their formal constituents to the specific environment and regional traditions, thus developing an indigenous semiotics that connects signs to their specific space and lineage, decoding gender as an organising principle of experience and relating forms of feminine articulation to the changing social, racial and conceptual permutations in our history; for example, the employment of dialects and images of domesticity in the quest for spiritual deliverance in the Bhakti period, the tactical redeployment of hegemonic discourses to constitute a new, enlightened middle-class female subject in the colonial reformist period, creation of new enunciative modalities and rhetorical strategies to articulate the gender-class nexus in the period of progressive literary trends, or the use of body-imagery, emphasis on female bonding, appeal to the pre-oedipal phase of mental development and open defiance of the set norms and structures of writing in more recent, openly feminist, literature.

Of course, it is impossible to wish away the influence of various Western feminist critical trends on our reading of women's literature. First of all we have little choice in the matter. Our turn towards the West was a command, as Gayatri Chakravarty Spivak remarks in one of her interviews. This is especially so for a critic writing in English, since she is by necessity a participant in an international critical discourse on which she, the subject, an intellectual, demands this involvement. Our system of education has also forced us to internalise the 'universal human being' of western metaphysics as our model and our hero. Secondly, contemporary global knowledge would only help the fulfilment of that Western fantasy of an Oriental Eden that helps the occidental to escape the pressures and tensions of modernisation. Thirdly, theoretical enterprises anywhere in the world from Marxism to Relativity to Post-Structuralist linguistics have a global dimension. Fourthly, the post-structuralists like Derrida, Foucault, Lyotard, Lacan, Deleuze, Althusser, Barthes or Rorty are themselves engaged in a struggle to dismantle the western metaphysical tradition from within and the feminist in the West are collaborators in this deconstructive enterprise that must find its natural ally in the feminists of the East. Fifthly, fighting revivalist closure, nostalgia and ahistorical quests for purist positions is as important in our cultural context as fighting the epistemic violence of imperialism and the essentialist discourse in Western theory where the Universal is equated with White, upper-class, male. What is required is to recognise the structures of oppression within the post-colonial space. The feminist agenda today may include developing the Marxist idea of labour so as to include domestic production, integrating the narrative of the mode of production with that of the mode of reproduction, saving the women's issue from a class-reductionist approach, promoting the awareness of the micro-political in society, analysing and exposing the operational tactics and alienating and subjectivising strategies of male-oriented ideologies and institutions in our society and foregrounding women in interpretations of history and literature. Literary studies, thus, form part of a social programme though this, by no means, a reification of aesthetics into sociology. Only we must be conscious of the dangers of a liberal approach, since the 'modern secular democratic' subject of the dominant discourse in India has seldom meant anything other than the high-caste, middle class, Hindu male.

The strategies of reading will differ, depending on the nature of the text: eg. The reading of a highly patriarchal ancient text may require an approach that is different from a sympathetic text that represents the gendered subaltern; though in both cases the critic's task is to make visible the assignment of subject-positions by unravelling the text. Wrenching the text out of its proper context and putting it within alien arguments may be at times necessary to draw out its use; it also can demonstrate the limits and limitations of the arguments from various forms of Western feminism—the Marxist, the liberal, the lesbian, the American and French theories of female writing and the inscription of the body—thus forcing the reader to re-situate the text within its context and obtain an insight into the continued subalternisation of the so-called 'third-world' literatures. She may also begin to understand why the kinds of feminist criticism that naturalise the experiences and issues of Western feminism are easily co-opted by the academy and align themselves with the apparatus of power. She will come to know that in order to intervene meaningfully in the Indian critical scene she will have to reconstitute the self, gender, knowledge, social relations and culture without resorting to linear, teleological, hierarchical, holistic or binary ways of thinking and being and to do so in our own socio-historic and cultural context. She may not neglect her Elaine Showalter and Kate Millet, her Ellen Moer and Sandra Gilbert and Susan Gubar, her Patricia Mayer Spacks and Mary Ellman, her Gayle Greene and Coppelia Kahn, her Jane Flax and Annette Kolodny, her Helene Cixous and Julia Kristeva, even her Barbara Smith, as she dances adroitly through the theoretical minefield and liberates the madwoman from the attic. At the same time she may also warn herself against the procrustean set of critical procedure and the straitjackets of prescriptive categories provided by many Western feminists, since they might not help her to understand the differences of her Indian author from her western counterpart, though they might help her understand certain similarities at the very fundamental biological and pre-linguistic levels. She will come to know that the universalising theories of Western feminism alone cannot explain Janabai's fervent appeals to Vithoba, the relationships of Meera and Raidas or Mahadeviyakka Basava, Mahasweta Devi's accounts of the tribal Jashoda or Draupadi, Sugathakumari's vision of Devaki dreaming in her prison of Krishna, Qurratulain Hyder's forays into Indian childhood and sexuality; Kamala Das's concepts of love and transcendence or Sarah Joseph's hair-symbolism that turns woman's long hair into a sign of gender identity and struggle and a site of torture for her oppressors. This resistance of the Indian text to western theories is certain to be experienced by any reader who attempts to decode that gender is constructed, despite biology, within a specific social, cultural and psychological milieu, using elements innate to them.

To attempt a comprehensive reading of Meerabai, for example, it is essential to place her in her context. A late-comer in the Bhakti movement, her writing is imbued with a rebellious spirituality. The movement itself is deeply embedded in India's social history, a history of literature and of philosophy. Even to call this age 'medieval', though empirically true, may recall the dark ages of European history, while in fact it was in India a great period of tremendous social and literary upheavals. Of course dogmatic Marxists have evaluated the Bhakti movement as an assertion of feudal piety and devotion to the Lord as the worldly master as well as the other worldly-one. This is obviously a highly reductive approach as they completely miss the democratic value of the movement that was dominated by subaltern elements, workers, peasants and women that had preached egalitarianism and questioned the Brahmin orthodoxy and the caste hierarchy and broken the hegemony of Sanskrit in literary discourse by using the languages of everyday speech and even created a new poetics employing folk rhythms, patterns of popular imagination and images from the ordinary life of the home and the workplace. The women poets of the movement did not have to confine themselves to places considered holy by the priestly class; every place was sacred and poetry left the places and the temples for the peasant's field, the artisan's work place, the common woman's kitchen and the endlessness of open streets. Poetry became direct, its contexts familiar and its emotions extremely human as when the poet loves, chides, derides, cajoles and quarrels with her God. Historiographers like Neera Desai, I.H. Qureshi and Tara Chand have tried to see the whole movement in purely religious terms as a reaction of the medieval Hindu society to the threat posed by the Muslim invaders, or a subtle attempt by Hindus to woo Muslims into their fold or as a synthesis of the two traditions in confrontation with each other. Susie Tharu is right in pointing out that these too are reductive approaches as they speak of Hinduism as a monolithic religion, and also lose sight altogether of the socio-political roots and the broader implications and impact of the movement in different sections of the society including women. Add to this Mirabai's personal contexts of her early life as a Rajput aristocrat—of leaving the palace, being tortured and poisoned and subjected to dirty gossip, seeking Raidas, choosing to learn spirituality from a common worker-saint, equating Krishna with love and liberty and beginning a life of wandering with the mendicants to the ire and vexation of her sister-in-law.

Patriarchal traditions have canonised Mirabai as a harmless devotional poet with little streak of revolt in her; however, an examination of her texts clearly reveals the dimension of her rebellion within the family and the kinship group and her fight against the injustices and discriminations she had to suffer just because she was a woman. The Rajput aristocrats who had developed an intricate system of patriarchal control through the segregation and seclusion of women, a fierce insistence upon woman's chastity and filial piety and the consequent valorisation of woman's sexual virtue, sanctions against remarriage and widow remarriage and the celebration of individual Sati, as well as its collective form called Jauhar, must have been shocked by Mirabai's declarations of freedom and outright rejection of the conventional image of women written into her texts, so well brought out by Madhu Kishwar and Ruth Vanita in their presentation of Mirabai.

A study of Mirabai also ought to place her in the context of the Western Rajasthani and Brajbhasha traditions of language and oral poetry besides analysing her relationship to the Krishna cult, to the pan-Indian concepts of the Divine, as also to her body, herself, her community and her God. Her class too is inscribed in her imagery, as unlike other Bhakti poets who use imagery from the kitchen and workplace in their poetry, Mirabai uses symbols like *suhag-sindoor*, bangles, head ornaments and fine dress materials all denoting in her case a bondage to convention, class, and male power that forces woman to beautify herself and obstructs her self-realisation. An intimate reading of Mira will also have to take into account her reception in her own society, her image in popular perception, her interpretation in Nationalist discourse, as in Gandhi's many references to her as a symbol of woman's emancipation from the tyranny of possessions as well as of man, and her representations in music, film, picture-stories and media. Western theories have little to offer by way of content in such a reading; they may only offer some very broad methodological guidelines, some semiotic insights and some grasp of the working of the ideologies of class, gender and spirituality and perhaps some psychological notions. Our purism needs not stand in the way of using their help, as we do in any other area of enquiry from economics and anthropology to physical sciences.

IMAGINED COMMUNITIES
Collective Aspirations in Contemporary Indian Poetry

Contemporary literature, even when deeply rooted in the past cannot but reflect contemporary experience—the experience of a world fast moving away from the truth to state-of-the-art merchandise, from the aristocratic responsibility of authoritarian families to the polluted sunshine of the shopping malls and the permissiveness of the modern-day beach resorts and holding out the gruesome promise of the end of ideologies, including the visionary ideologies that represented the principle of hope. Liberation movements across the 'Third World' seem to have dried up overnight as commitment to the market system has become sheer 'common sense' and no longer a political programme. All values, other than those of business society seem to have been abolished and any discussion of the issue of ends, to have become anathema. The intellectual caste, especially those in the echelons of power, celebrates with euphoria the 'end of history' and seals the acquisition of its own professional guild values like 'freedom' of speech and 'free' elections and holds out a hand for money to that great champion of freedom, the United States that is gearing up for local 'defensive' operations round the world, buying nationalised industries on the cheap and reaping the benefits of the cheap labour being thrown open to the multinationals by the collapse of national states and the deterioration of the former 'second World' into a 'Third World' status. The emergence of the new, aggressive, ruthless capitalism has already sounded the knell of autonomous development in the 'Third World', including South Asia, forcing the people to become either avaricious consumers or immiserated labourers for foreign capital. The days of the grand social engineering projects seem to be over; the dreams of a better society are dismissed offhand as flights of fancy or declaration of subversive intent. Alternative ends are invalidated of the strength of the proved ineffectuality of means. A jubilant valorisation of the careeristic values of a competitive society appears to be the only ethical possibility. The only voices heard are of the preachers of maxims like 'everyone for himself', the free-for-all ideologists. The seduced are happy as they have resources to complete and the rules of the game are positively in their favour. To the oppressed however, the rules seem to be working against their very survival. Liberty has boiled down to mere consumer choice: poverty is a positive disqualification in a world that privileges the rich.

The market interpretation of freedom translates communal needs into acts of individual acquisition. It also abhors autonomy and reduces cultural diversity into a variety of changeable fashions and marketable life-styles that easily become tribals dancing on a TV screen in a city hotel. They no more belong to the inner world of the politics of life. Tolerance here degenerates into estrangement, instead of leading to solidarity. It reduces social bonds into surface gloss. Difference is considered safe as long as it is confined to the airy world of the symbolic game of representation and does not spill over into the realm of daily co-existence, when it is perceived as a threat. The other's inferiority is justified by difference; thus tolerance becomes fully compatible with social domination. The promise of equality is withdrawn, as difference means distance, non-cooperation and hierarchy. The global origin of problems, economic, ecological and cultural, is effectively hidden from view as new sensitivities are confined to neutral, de-politicised technological discourse. The political issue of democratic control over technology, their purpose and desirable limits, the question of self-management and collective choice, is always left outside. The rich countries are busy selling their poison as the poor people's food and transferring provenly dangerous technologies and polluting production units to nations like ours.

The remedy of social ills is also privatised. This clash between the social nature of risks and the privatised means of their containment is one of the contradictions of late capitalism. True, the patronage-state has collapsed with its suppression of democratic opposition and individual freedom and its monopoly of needs, satisfaction and social status. But, is the open market with the consumer society the only alternative? Should the obvious failures of the statist model of socialism lead to passive submissions of the norms of a business society? Don't we require a new mood, a new methodology and an introspective or reflexive dialectic that befits a situation where the relationship between the individual and system seems fluid, even dissolved? Don't we need a fresh vision of radical social transformation illuminated by the objective experience of the majority of our people and inspired by indigenous egalitarian ideas and experiments? And a political aesthetic that affirms the primacy of the present, the present of struggle and suffering, and grapples with the seemingly elusive totality of our complex experience, free from the ideological reductionism that stifled the artistic movements of the past? Remember that the totalitarian systems punish the dissenting artist with prison, exile or even death, while the market society absorbs and contains him, turns him into a show piece and thus incapacitates him, subverting the very intent of his rebellion. It permits even opposition, as long as it is marketable.

How do the writers of our country react to this situation where their identity is either eroded or turned into a purely private, personal, saleable commodity? Let me take the case of Indian poetry. The early modernists of the 1950s had a background of the development of debilitating post-industrial urban infernos with their massification of human beings. I will not say that the modernist problematique is obsolete; there are and will be contexts where the private has to be upheld and defended against the encroachment of the public and the omnipresent gaze of the modern state that turns individuals into subjects without will, passive participants of the hegemonic designs. The dark days of the mid-1970s belong as much to the reality of the immediate past as to the possibility of the immediate future. Still, the modern state is different from the authoritarian regimes of the left and the right varieties, precisely in that it privatises and diffuses dissent rather than collectivising it and prompting it to accumulate into an explosive energy that shatters the system. This compels writers to evolve counter-strategies for the collectivisation of dissent. Literary modernism in its Indian form had meant an articulation of the angst and alienation, the divided self, of the Indian caught between the gilded image of his pre-colonial past and his squalid present that roamed the crowded thoroughfares of the post-industrial metropolis. At the ontological level, it meant a search for the lost identity of the individual: a quest that often bordered on the metaphysical. B.S. Mardhekar, Dilip Chitre, G.M. Muktibodh, Harbhajan Singh, Sitanshu Yashaschandra, Gopalakrishna Adiga, Kaa.Naa. Subramaniam, N.N Kakkad, Ayyappa Paniker, Navakant Barua, Sachi Routray and other pioneers of modernism in Indian poetry responded to the modern environment in this way. Their responses are not without social dimensions, but their central concern seems to have been the destiny of the individual in modern mass society rather than that of communities caught in the maelstrom of exploitative modernisation. However, roughly from the 1970s onwards, Indian poetry begins to concern itself with collective destinies. A glance at the present poetic landscape in India reveals certain radical concerns whose boundaries often cross one another.

2

The most dominant of these streams may be termed progressive-modernist, but the attitudes of the poets embraced by the term are by no means uniform. At one end of the spectrum stand the votaries of armed peasant struggles like the Naxalite poets of Bengal and Andhra Pradesh, whose action poetry combines a virile modern idiom with a sincere moral indignation. At the other end stand the followers of Gandhi and Lohia and Liberal humanists whose frustration with the system is as intense as that of the Naxalites; only they hold on to indigenous ideals of peaceful social transformation. What unites these writers is their recognition of the existence of class inequalities; this, however, is combined in the best representatives of the trend with a deeper awareness of the complexity of human experience and an introspective search for their own selves in relation to the world of outer reality. These tendencies, along with their subtler and newer sense of form and idiom, rescue these poets from the slogan-mongering and rhetorical mode of some of the early progressives.

Nagarjun, Kunwar Narain, Kedarnath Singh, Vinod Kumar Shukla, Asad Zaidi, Vishnu Nagar, Rituraj, Mangalesh Dabral, Surjit Patar, U.R. Ananthamurty, P. Lankesh, Chandrasekhara Patil, H.S. Shivaprakash, Ali Sardar Jafri, Nida Fazli, and K.G. Sankarapillai may broadly be said to belong to this genre. Some of these poets, like Chandrasekhara Kambara and Kadammanitta Ramakrishnan have moulded a folk idiom to present themes, issues and structures of feeling related to the life of the rural folk and the marginalised sections of the society. The insurrectionary political poetry of the Maoist activists and their co-travellers was an attempt to subvert both the solipsistic ideal of high Modernism and the sentimental romanticism of the earlier decades. Look at the poem, 'Love' by Murari Mukhopadhyay of Bengal:

> When in love,
> Do not become the moon.
> If you can,
> Come as the sun.
> I'll take its heat
> And light up the dark forest.
> When in love,
> Do not become the river.
> If you can,
> Come as the flood.
> I'll carry its passion
> And break the dams of despair.
> When in love,
> Do not become a flower.
> If you can,
> Come as the thunder
> I'll lift its roar to my breast
> And send forth the battle-cry to every corner.
> When in love,
> Do not become a bird.
> If you can,

Come as the storm.
I'll borrow its force
And destroy the palace of sin.
The moon,
The river,
The flower,
The stars,
The birds—
We can look for them later
But today,
In the darkness,
The last battle is yet to be fought.
What we need now in our hovel
Is—Fire.

The poet rejects the usual objective correlatives of love employed in romantic poetry; especially symbols and metaphors like moon, river, flower, stars and birds. He replaces them by the warm sun who would illumine the dark woods, the flood that would break the barrages of despair by revolutionary passion, the thunder that would help the poet carry his war-cry to all parts of the world, the storm that would lend him strength enough to pull down 'the places of sin' and fire in the hovel that would burn down the decrepit, decadent, old world. It is difficult to say that the poem is anti-romantic; rather it inverts old romanticism and creates a revolutionary romanticism that employs energetic signs like flood, fire, sun, and thunder. A similar rejection is seen in Pash, the Punjabi poet, when he says: 'No, don't think now about/such things as/the fine hues of red/when the sun sets over the village/nor do I care about how she feels/when the moon glides over her threshold/at night./No, I don't worry about such trifles now' (No I am not losing my sleep over...). Pash does it again when he asks the nightingale to leave her sanctuary in the scented garden and come to town as her song cannot conform to anyone in these rotten times and her charming melody fades in memory like evaporated dew (O, My sweet nightingale). The Naxalite movement also led to a regeneration of the oral folk literature, in an attempt to communicate to the villagers in their own idiom and to bridge the gap between the elite urban sensibility and the rural one that demanded another language and another kind of knowledge. Activist-poets like Subbarao Panigrahi (who later became a martyr) and Gaddar of Andhra Pradesh actually went to the villages to learn their idiom, while urban co-travellers like Varavara Rao felt they would never understand the worker: 'The truth that the worker's sweat will never utter.../Call a drop of ink from a poet's pen/ever express it?' Poets like Dhoomil of Hindi fashioned a sharp, unsentimental language full of concrete images in order to articulate the new experience: 'A man/severs the neck of another/from a torso/As a mechanic separates a nut/from a bolt/You say: This is murder. I shy: this is the dissolution of a mechanism.' He takes his readers 'to the territory of poetry/In the wilderness of language/where cowardice has run away/Throwing an empty revolver/and defiance has gone forward/in the dark.' There were also many poems flavoured by a special brand of humour, a mixture of self-mockery and self-defence. The more complex attitudes were expressed in varying degrees of irony: bitter, playful, whimsical, tragic, self-flagellatory.

The later poems in this category are often like confessions or sighs of frustration. Cherabandaraju, the Telugu radical poet, admits, 'Today the helm is no longer in my hands; it is me who is in its hands.' Civic Chandran of Malayalam joins in, 'Our legs were short and the alleys unfamiliar.' Surjit Patar expresses the mood of the survivors poignantly:

To go back home now is difficult.
Who will recognize us?
Death has put its mark on the forehead,
Friends have left their footprints on the face.
Another face stares at me from the mirror.
My eyes sparkle with a dead glow
Like the light from the broken roof of a house.

It would however be wrong to think that his trend is entirely past, as there are quite a few poets especially in Telugu, Bengali and Hindi who refuse to give up all their hopes about a Communist revolution. Poetry has not abandoned its social critical function, even in poets who have no direct commitment to revolution. One such poet is Kunwar Narain of Hindi. See his poem, *To Delhi* for example:

A familiar sight, then, as now,
Abject, pitiful, dragged
Behind victorious horsemen.
Hands tied together, pitiful,
Who was he this time,
On the road to Delhi?
None knows.
Only a pair of hands, tied together,
Made it there.

3

The Dalit poetry in Marathi, Gujarati, Hindi, Punjabi and Telugu, and the Bandaya poetry in Kannada together constitute another dissenting collective, another alternative nationhood that articulates the silent anguish and indignation of the so called 'untouchables' relegated to the bottom of the caste-hierarchy for more than 30 centuries. To these poets, the socio-cultural phenomenon of the caste is more real than the economic category of 'class' (though 'caste' may be considered a 'social class' in the sense in which Nicos Poulantzas uses the term). There is indeed a diversity of attitudes even among the Dalit poets that springs chiefly from their ambivalent relationship with the Buddha, Marx or Ambedkar. Some deify Ambedkar while some long to go beyond him. Arun Kamble, Yaswant Manohar, Arjun Dangle, J.V. Pawar, Namdeo Dhasal, Daya Pawar, Prakash Jadhav, Bhujang Meshram and Meena Gajabhiye of Marathi; Joseph Macwan, Jayant Parmar, Mangal

Rathod, Kisan Sosa, Praveen Gadvi and Raju Solanki of Gujarati and Siddhalingaiah of Kannada are some of the prominent Dalit poets writing today. Dalit literature has created its own alternative aesthetic by redrawing the map of literature in discovering and exploring a whole new continent of experience that has so far been left to darkness and silence, by helping literature overcome stagnation through a cleansing renewal, by disturbing the sterile complacency of the dominant social groups, by challenging their set mores and fixed paradigms of looking at reality, their stale habits of ordering knowledge, beauty and power and their established literary canons, bringing to focus neglected, suppressed or marginalised aspects of experience, vision, language and reality and forcing the community to refashion its tools and observe itself critically, from a fresh and different angle. Dalit poetry rejects the norms set by Brahminic poetics and throws overboard classical values like propriety, balance, restraint and understatement. The diction of these poets is deliberately subversive as it challenges the middle class notions of linguistic decency.

Dalit poets at times make fun even of concepts like patriotism. Baburao Bagul the Marathi pioneer of Dalit poetry says, 'You who have made the mistake of being born in this country/must now rectify it: either leave the country or make war.' He advises the rebel to go towards the settlements like Jesus and speak to them like Tathagata, as the untouchable, the beloved son of the revolution, lives there. Chokha Kamble advises himself: 'There is no cloud, no shower of rain/nor open sky or sun for me/and yet, my stupid, foolish mind/Don't give in to despondency.' Namdeo Dhasal's highly imagistic poems like *Mandakini Patil* and *Hunger* combine violent images with intense experiences. He asks 'the innumerable suns' ablaze in his blood to 'march on city after city, setting each on fire.' Yashvant Vaghela, the Gujarati Dalit poet says: 'The stones of centuries piled up over us/ A pyramid of tears/Here today we are mummies/Stuffed with wailing voices/but forging destiny in our smithies.' Jayant Parmar, another Gujarati poet challenges Manu who legitimised the Varna system: 'One day in front of my house/ on the neem tree I will hang you naked/I will split open your veins to see/how much blood of my elders you have drunk.' Siddalingaiah, the Kannada Dalit poet asks: 'Who has stopped the timely rain? Who has slashed the stars with a rainbow? Who is hiding the sun so that darkness may float and bulge?... World, I must get to know you/and so I must have a word with you.' Dalit women poets like Mallika Amarsheikh, Hira Bansode and Meena Gajabhiye have given a feminist slant to Dalit poetry in their poems that are more introspective and less given to sloganeering and abuse. See for example *Yashodhara* by Marathi poet, Hira Bansode:

O Yashodhara:
You are like a dream of sharp pain,
Life-long sorrow.
I don't have the audacity to look at you.
We were brightened by Buddha's light,
But you absorbed the dark
Until your life was mottled blue and black,
a fragmented life, burned out,
O Yashodhara:
The tender sky comes to you for refuge
Seeking your shining but fruitless life
And the painted stars shed tears.
My heart breaks,
Seeking your matchless beauty,
Separated from your love, dimming like twilight.
Listening to your silent sighs,
I feel the promise of heavenly happiness is hollow.

The new phase of Dalit writing seems to be more mature, sober, larger in its concerns, more conscious of form, less angry and complaining. There is even a tone *of* the celebration of Dalit identity in the new generation poets.

4

This takes us straight to the third form of collective poetic dissent: that of India's women poets. India has always had great women poets, such as Akkamahadevi, Meerabai, Mahadevi Verma and Balamani Amma. It is perfectly possible and legitimate to deconstruct their work from the feminist perspective. However, a committed feminist poetry that emphasises difference in terms of gender and seeks to rewrite the patriarchal discourse and challenge the phallocentric order of things is a more recent aesthetic phenomenon in India. These poets are engaged in revisionist mythmaking and the establishment of a parallel semiotics centred round the female body. Poets like Amrita Pritam, Kamala Das, Gauri Deshpande and Nabaneeta Dev Sen were the first to create a sacred zone for the female subject; they have now been joined by literally scores of women poets from all Indian languages, from Savitri Rajeevan and Vijayalakshmi in Malayalam, M.R. Kamala and S. Usha in Kannada, A. Jayaprabha and Kondepudi Nirmala in Telugu, Chandrakanti and Indira Bhavani in Tamil to Kabita Sinha and Mallika Sengupta in Bengali, Pravasini Mahakud and Ranjita Nayak in Oriya, Manjit Tiwana in Punjabi, Gagan Gill and Katyayani in Hindi, Panna Naik and Sanskritani Desai in Gujarati, Anuradha Patil and Aruna Dhere in Marathi to Meena Alexander and Eunice D'Souza in English, to cite only a few names. Together they seek a libidinal economy and a new politics of Desire that can restructure the male-dominated world on the basis of love, freedom and equality.

Kamala Das, and the women poets after her, have brought great diversity into feminine and feminist poetry reflecting their varied regional traditions and different social circumstances and experimenting with different forms. They have recognised, with Eunice D'Souza that the histories they know are not fit to print and that 'the perfect book is one long cry in the dark.' Marnata Dash, the Oriya poet, invites the murderer to take her life as she feels mauled and defeated: 'Come, murderer/Step into my sacred courtyard/you're my last guest, after all, aren't you?/Come, today I feel, you also are my final love.' Nabaneeta Dev Sen from Bengal compares love to a bird whose fixed phrases pour honey into her ears and then 'in private, jingles its chains in raucous laughter to itself and sheds its feathers in empty space.' Kamala Hemmige, the Kannada poet, is conscious of class that even divides women when she asks: 'You who grow cactii/in flower pots and wear/roses in your hair/do you know/about the nude women/worshipping their God in Chandragutthi?... You skillful one/who can drink tea/without smudging your lipstick/do you know the story of the girl/who was stripped naked/for wanting to eat?' Indira Bhavani, the Tamil writer, speaks sarcastically about the 10 avatars of the male: smacking his lips over smutty books as Fish, hiding himself in his shell when invited to act strongly like Tortoise, falling flat on his face in an ocean of booze like the Pig, making the worker dance and clawing the files like Narasimha, longing for undercover bribes like Vamana, rooting out people he does not like, like Parasurama, taking oaths of monogamy in bed like Rama, taking pleasure in different houses like Krishna. Savitri Rajeevan of Malayalam compares herself to a worn out kitchenware elevated into an icon. A. Jayaprabha of Telugu warns the avaricious ogglers: 'A day will come/when women in this country have/thorns/not only in their eyes/but all over their bodies. There are too occasions when women poets identify themselves with Radha deceived by Krishna (eg. Sugathakumari: *Where is Radha?*), with Draupadi insulted in the royal assembly (eg. Laxmi Kaman: *Draupadi*) or with the Saint poet Akkamahadevi who roamed naked and battled against male wits (eg. Bhagya Jayasudarshana, For Akka) in an attempt to find their roots.

5

Equally significant is the search for regional and linguistic identity in Indian poetry. This may be seen as a natural continuation and fulfilment of the process of cultural decolonisation that had accompanied India's struggle for political independence. It is a celebration of the pluralism that is the very essence of India's culture, an interrogation of the hegemonic canons flaunted by the bourgeois market as well as by the revivalist Hindu communalism, canons that are often a rehash of the orientalist notions of Indianness governed by wrong premises like the privileging of high textuality, the marginalisation of non-canonical, performative and counter-hegemonic texts and trends, aesthetic reductivism and revivalist nostalgia striving to recreate an imagined golden past. Many writers feel that the basic democratic idea of geopolitical and linguistic federalism is being undermined everyday in the practices of our governance, and that only a constructive concept of multiculturalism and heteroglossia can fight the atavistic retrieval of an ethnic past and the pressures of standardisation imposed by the culture-market. The battle of course is not between the ideals of integration and disintegration; but between two different concepts of unity: one that believes in an insipid uniformity imposed from above, a forced cultural compound, a superficial tinsel collage, and the other that places its faith in a genuine fraternity of our diverse cultures and languages, each permitted to retain and encouraged to develop to the full, its distinct mode of popular creativity.

This centripetal tendency expresses itself in various forms. In the languages of the South, it appears primarily as a quest for a Dravidian poetics implied, say, in the works of the Tamil Sangam poets and the Kannada Vacanakaras. The post-Subramania Bharati period in Tamil poetry, as represented by poets like Bharatidasan and Na. Pichamurty has shaped regional consciousness, distinct from the earlier pan-Indian patriotism. The Kannada poetry after Adiga has demonstrated the gap between the rich cultural memory of the Sudras and the outcastes and their present political experience of marginalisation, as is evident in the poetry of P. Lankesh, Chandrashekhara Kambara, Chandrasekhara Patil or Siddhalingaiah. Poets like S.R. Ekkundi and H.S. Shivaprakash have invented an indigenous progressive poetry that draws a lot from Kannada saint-poets and philosophers like Madhvacharya and Basavanna. In Malayalam this regionalism appears chiefly as a celebration of local myths, especially counter-myths like that of Onam, which worships Mahabali, the great demon king whose reign is praised in songs and thus indirectly denounces

Vamana, the impish avatar of Vishnu who pushed Mahabali down into the nether world—an attempt to discover a tradition distinct from the pan-Indian one. There are also attempts to de-Sanskritise the poetic language as represented by (late) M. Govindan, N.N. Kakkad (in his later phase) and Attoor Ravivarma (in his recent poems). Traditional metres, familiar rhythms, provincial archetypes, regional rituals and cultural symbols and local flora and fauna are staging a comeback, constructing an eco-aesthetics of racial retrospection and introspection.

Ayyappa Paniker's long poem 'Gotrayanam' (The Passage of the Tribe) is an attempt to reconstruct regional history at the level of myth. Kadammanitta Ramakrishnan's poems with their folk-rhythms are also intensely regional. The Dalit poets of Marathi and Gujarati and the revolutionary poets of Andhra have also drawn freely on regional forms, rural dialects and tribal languages, thus giving their poetry an intensely native idiom. North-eastern dialects like Nagamese and Kokborok have also begun to produce their first generation poets, who, like the poets in Manipuri, draw largely on tribal myths and local customs and beliefs. The Punjabi poets of our time like Surjit Patar, Gul Chauhan, Minder, Swarjbir, Mohanjit, Jaswant Deed and others have also attempted to forge a typical Punjabi idiom with references to local history and regional heroes and saints. The Uttar-Adhunik (post-modern) poets of Bengal like Amitabha Gupta, Anindya Chaki, Bipul Chakravarty, Ekram Ali, Gautam Basu, Gita Chattopadhyay and others have made a similar gesture. They constantly go back to local themes, rituals, festivals and heroes and make innovative use of folk-rhythms and metres. 'The roots lie deep into the soil, loud sophistries are but a desperate invocation,' says Birendra Chattopadhyay, who denounces bookish education and loves to learn from the rustic peasant. Amitabha Gupta says about his language:

> This is the embryo and the fire.
> At dawn, with none else awake,
> The wedding signals

Touched the chirping of children.
I am the vermilion of her light,
I am the lustre of her womb.

While it is futile to try to discover a single 'post-modern' movement in contemporary Indian poetry, it can safely be said that since the 1970s every fresh poetic initiative has been in some way stimulated by a conscious or unconscious desire to re-establish poetry's deep and meaningful relationship with nature and society, without at the same time losing sight of the decisive stylistic revolution brought about by modern poetry. With some risk of generalisation, we may note the following features as the common contexts of our indigenous 'postmodernisms': (1) A revolt against the solipsistic tendencies of early modernism and the consequent longing to communicate even with the public traditionally kept out of poetry's sacred grove (2) a pursuit of the politics of difference reflected in an attempt to forge collective identities based on differences of class, caste, gender, region, language and culture as a response to the homogenisation of Indian culture sought by hegemonic forces (3) a non-atavistic revival of the past that at times results in a kind of bricolage, a frequency of quotations of elements from previous styles and periods illuminating a present situation by comparison or contrast, and at times simply contributing to a process of amnesia that follows the modernist cultural amnesia (4) a growing perception that the status-quoist ideas of progress do not take into serious account cultural differences and variations in world views (5) a consequent suspicion of all universalising ideologies that conceal differences, or reduce them to a single dimension (6) the loss of the *modernist* confidence that *high* or *avant-garde* art is intrinsically more valuable than *low* or *popular* art (7) a growing disbelief in the modern project that was supposed to be valid for all mankind but found mankind divided into one part confronted with the challenge of complexity and the other with the ancient task of mere survival (8) an awareness of issues beyond class struggle: of caste, gender, war and ecology (9) a preoccupation with post-cognitive and ontological questions like: 'Which world is this? What is to be done in it? Which of my selves is to do it? How are worlds constituted? How do they differ? What happens when different kinds of world are placed in confrontation, or when the boundaries between worlds are violated? What are the modes of existence of the text and the world?' And (10) a multi-directional movement within the poetic scene in general and a polyphony within specific poetic texts resulting from these perceptions that go against all forms of standardisation natural to consumer societies.

OF MANY INDIAS
Alternative Nationhoods in Contemporary Indian Poetry

'Do you still love this land?'...
'...But not this India, not this valley of Skeletons'
—K. Satchidanandan (*Fever*)[1]

The Parable and the Lesson

A.K. Ramanujan concludes his informal essay, 'Is there an Indian Way of Thinking?' by narrating a parable told by the Buddha: 'Once a man was drowning in a sudden flood. Just as he was about to drown, he found a raft. He clung to it and it carried him safely to dry land. And he was so grateful to the raft that he carried it on his back for the rest of his life.'[2]

The concept of a cultural Indianness that transcends the contexts of language, caste, class and gender is not unlike this raft: it has saved us from drowning on many an occasion in the past, the last one being during our struggle against British colonialism. But cultural nationalism today has become synonymous with a carnivorous revivalism that seeks to recreate the past in its own image and impose its oppressive authority over the present whose truth and strength lie in its cultural pluralism. India is a republic of languages, literatures, religions and ethnicities, each of which is authentically Indian and not 'regional' as they are often dubbed; any attempt to standardise Indian culture is more than likely to invite the disaster of Balkanisation. Constructing an India over the tomb of cultural differences that constitute the mosaic of its culture is certain to please the Orientalist with his perceptions of a homogeneous Indian culture, the globaliser who seeks to hand India packaged in a comprehensible and easy format over to the alien consumer awed by its inaccessible plurality, and the obscurantist who seeks political hegemony through biased cultural representations that entirely marginalise the women, Dalits, tribals and entire linguistic and religious minorities of India with their different, often subaltern if not subversive, traditions and perceptions of Indian culture. The construction of a monolithic Indian culture, character or literature is thus an act of civilisational violence that inevitably involves a negation of heteroglossia, a silencing of ethnic diversity and religious pluralism and a bulldozing of diverse cosmologies and world views that together constitute the federation of Indian culture. This is not to deny certain shared patterns of literary evolution, linguistic kinships and intercultural ties developed over centuries of co-existence. The foreign observer looking from a distance does find a semblance of cultural unity in India, but coming closer one begins to see hundreds of *Ramayanas* and *Mahabharatas,* dozens of philosophical systems and religious cults, which were never called Hindu until the 19th century, as many modernisms as there are languages, as many different ways of negotiating foreign influences and as many ways of ethnic and linguistic expression that reflect the genius of the Indian people. 'Indian culture' and 'Indian Literature' are no more than convenient umbrella terms that embrace diverse cultures and literatures, whose historical and geographical co-existence has led to certain exchanges and at times produced examples of multilingual creativity. The raft that saved us is gradually, imperceptibly, turning into the old man in the Sindbad story pressing us down, suffocating our cultures and silencing our many voices, reducing them all to a mere stammer.

We are not unfamiliar with the European stereotypes of India, both positive (e.g. Max Muller) and negative (e.g. Hegel). The salient features of this characterisation are: the denial of empirical reality, the inability to distinguish the self from the non-self and interior from exterior, a neglect of universal human nature, a refusal to create synoptic systems, and the consequent construction of an illogical bricolage of tools and systems, the theories of *karma* or of *samsara,* the hierarchies of caste, the hegemony of *vedanta* in philosophy or of *dhvani* in literature or *rasa* in theatre: but each one of these has not merely exceptions but parallels and alternatives. A.K. Ramanujan in the essay cited earlier, labours hard to discover and define a certain movement in Indian thought from the context-sensitive to the context-free. He points out how the Indian concept of *dharma* has always been particular, bound as it is to region and caste. No Indian literary text, even the dateless and anonymous ones, until the 19th century comes without a context or a frame and that every story within the epics is encased in a meta-story like the tale of Nala told by a sage to a dependent Yudhishtira in his exile in the woods, which itself is part of the macrotale called *Mahabharata*. The taxonomy of landscapes in Tamil *cankam* poetry is another example of intense contextualisation, where the character and mood are related to the patterns of landscape, labour and food. Again, Ramanujan points to the collapsing of nature and culture as against the Levi-Straussian opposition, a metonymic view of man in nature or an expression of culture that is enclosed in nature. Such a pattern of concentric containments, like when the little Krishna swallows the three worlds and his mother sees herself and her son also within his open mouth, is then supposed endemic to Indian cultural representations. Even space and time are particularised and each kind of soil, each type of house, each season, each hour of the day has its special mood and character. Thus from the caste-system in society to the *raga* system in music, everything seems to reflect context-sensitivity. Hence all counter-movements in India according to Ramanujan are attempts to be context-free: *rasa* in aesthetics, *moksa* in the *purusharthas* (or the aims of life), *sannyasa* in the *asramas* (or the stages of life), *sphota* in semantics and *bhakti* in religion define themselves against a background of inexorable contextuality. They are universal and generalised and betoken a liberation from the context—let it be from relational social roles as in *moksa,* from worldly ties as in *sannyasa,* from the particularity of *bhavas* as in *rasa,* from the sequence and time as in *sphota* or from caste, ritual, gender and custom as in *bhakti*. If in the West, the revolt is against a status-quo that is abstract, universal and context-free, in India, the rebellion is against the context-bound, to create universals. Ramanujan sees modernisation in India as a movement towards context-free systems and practices: Gandhi's egalitarianism as against Manu's hierarchies, the singing of *ragas* free from the time-contexts of convention, or borrowings from Western culture re-aligned to fit earlier context-sensitive needs, for example.

Let us look at some samples of contemporary Indian poetry that militate against the monolithic idea of a past or projected 'Indianness' and assert the plurality of the perceptions of India in the present context. They are context-sensitive in the strictest sense of the term but also contain within them the desire to be free of certain contexts of class, caste or gender, for example—to arrive at a society where cultural difference is not bound to oppressive categories but springs from creative regional and linguistic contexts. The poets I choose here, like hundreds of their contemporaries, seem to believe that it is necessary to problematise the concept of India in order to fight its oppressive implications and to re-contextualise poetry in order to build a free democratic society in the country. In the context of the threat of a forced homogenisation and cultural globalisation, difference becomes the key concept that defines the poetry of the Indian *avant-garde*.

A cow has slopped its dung on the map of India...

In 'Twenty Years after Independence'[3] Dhoomil (real name: Sudama Pandey, 1935–1975), one of the most radical of political poets in Hindi, interrogates the very concept of free India symbolised by the national flag. The warnings seem to have overcome the dangers they foresaw: once again the poet sees the jungle before him as a solid green sea, where trees have lost their identity. Signals have all turned green: everything is permitted here; the moral scruples at work during the struggle of Independence no more operate.

> Twenty years later
> I ask myself —
> How much endurance does it take
> To turn into an animal?

Only silence answers the poet. He finds it 'almost dishonest' to follow one's impulses, 'to go chasing the little leaves/blowing about in blood.' It is the autumn of the heart: the fall before the chill winter of death. The poet finds the houses around locked, suggesting martial law, mourning, curfew or hartal. The growing violence of the present is suggested in the lines that follow, a disaster written in the language of bullets buried in the walls and shoes scattered in the street. Obviously there has been a protest march and a shooting by the police. The image of violence is juxtaposed against the grotesquely comic picture of 'a cow that has slopped its dung on the map of India flapping in the wind.' Something dies in the poet's heart: it is nothing but the image of a peaceful, just and prosperous India dreamt of by the freedom fighters. The map is but a representation of that beloved country now covered by the dung of shame. The word 'shame' immediately follows: it is not the time to measure the shame of a scared people. The poet wonders whether the policeman or the saint is the country's greater misfortune: the former represents a mockery of law and the latter, in the context of the poem, a mockery of religion since this 'saint' has nothing to do with the tradition of Kabir or Tukaram: he is the venomous fundamentalist presiding over the *dharma samsads,* the 'religious parliaments,' the saffron-clad politician, the communaliser, the pseudo-moralist and the censor. The policeman and the 'saint' here represent two forms of violence: of the state, and of the obscurantist forces in the civil society. The poet dares not go back to the street he had fled during the encounter to retrieve his shoes. Only he passes through the deserted lanes 'like a thief' and asks himself:

> ...is freedom only the name
> of three tired colours
> dragged by a single wheel?

The colours and wheel of the flag that used to signify abundance, purity, youthfulness and the commitment to *dharma* and the welfare of the people have lost their meaning: they denote nothing when people are shot down like rats on the streets. The poet's question about the significance of the flag remains unanswered; this silence suggests an absent, yet unborn, India, just as do the lines quoted at the beginning of the paper from my own poem 'Fever'.

The poem 'Bharat' by Pash,[4] the Punjabi poet-martyr (1950–1988), whose real name was Avtar Singh Sandhu also projects an alternative, subaltern, idea of nationhood: for the poet the word stands for the sons of the soil who measure time with the shadows of trees that follow the Sun's movement, who can munch their own bones when they are hungry, who consider death a deliverance and life a convention. The poet wants to hurl his cap in the air when someone speaks of one Bharat or of national integration, so that he may put into his head the idea that Bharat has many meanings and that it has nothing to do with the name of Bharat, the son of King Dushyant and Sakuntala. About those meanings the poet says: 'They register themselves in the fields/where all the corn grows/and so many burglars go.' The poem is characterised by an assertion of the India of the peasants and has also a hidden 'Punjabiness' about its commitment to the corn field and the landless peasant.

There was soil...
Kudal (The Spade), a Hindi poem by Kedarnath Singh,[5] reflects the conflict between two Indias: the India of the rural peasant and that of the city dweller. True to Kedarnath Singh's method of choosing symbols from ordinary life—a mode probably inherited from the Bhakti poets, in this poem he chooses a *kudal*, a spade, as the symbol of India's agricultural civilisation juxtaposed against the urban one, though the poem reveals many more levels of meaning and of conflict. The poet's eyes are disturbed by the sight of a spade left by the gardener at his door. It looks quite out of place there. At the same time, he is fascinated by its 'strange, curvaceous, dust-laden beauty.' The word 'dust' is very important here as it is a recurring symbol in Kedarnath's poems. In the poem '*Kasbe ki Dhool*' (The Dust of *Kasba* [small town]) he says: 'I am aware because/this dust is the most living/and lovely thing of my land/the most restless/the most active/the earth's most nascent/and the most ancient dust.' In a conversation the poet says:

Dust represents the whole Indian life itself. It is always active and flying in the atmosphere. The darkness and sadness are there in dust.

The slowness of its movement represents the rhythm of semi-rural Indian life I am familiar with.

This dust is also related to the past, for the poet sees the spade 'in the pale light of the departing day' (*Jate hue din ki dhundhali roshni mein*). The departing day implies also the disappearance of a whole culture represented by the spade:

> There was work
> It is over
> There was soil
> It has been dug to the roots
> And now this spade
> Stands at the door
> Like a silent challenge.

The spade has already done its work; the rustic cultures of the peasant have contributed to an awareness of our roots. Perhaps it also suggests that the village has already played its role in the shaping of the poet's vision and sensibility.

The poet thinks of taking the spade inside the house and leaving it in some corner. First he thinks of keeping it in the drawing room; why not the spade if he can keep the *nagphani* there? But immediately he discovers that the presence of the spade will upset the balance of the whole house. What about the kitchen? But the kitchen had a 'fresh-washed sacredness' before which the dusty spade looked out of place. The products of the peasant can enter the kitchen, but not the peasant himself, nor his earth-laden tool. The spade cannot be kept in the darkness under the cot. It will be an act of cowardice—like concealing one's true origins. The house may, however, become warmer by that odour of mystery that will fill the air. A spade under a cot is a strange image; it makes the poet laugh.

Finally, the poet stops by the spade for a while to meditate over it. He feels he is standing in some invisible court, with the spade on his shoulder, to witness the being of the spade on earth.

One cannot but acknowledge the presence of the peasant and his contribution to man's making and civilisation. But for him the cities would not have been; but for him we would go without food and even without culture, for the roots of our literary culture lie in the great oral traditions and our music, dance, painting, sculpture and architecture; even our wisdom, owes much to the folksingers, ritual dancers, carpenters, masons and other artisans, all products of a rural culture with agriculture at its centre. Not only India's marvellous temples are products of rural artistry; our classical dances and music can easily be traced to their folk roots, and our epic *Ramayana,* if we can believe the legends, was authored by a hunter-turned sage, and *Mahabharata* by the son of a fisherwoman. The post-industrial culture of the cities may try to conceal these beginnings by hiding them in the darkness under their cots and sleeping over them. But its presence is undeniable, and poetry is perhaps the last witness to that ancestral civilisation. This is why the poet feels the gardener has raised 'the most difficult question of my century'.

The final stanza sounds like a warning. It is like the 'village encircling the city.' As it grows darker, the spade's blade seems to be growing; it is dangerous to leave it at the door. Throwing it to the streets is also impossible. We cannot disinherit or disown our fathers. If Cavafy's people of the city wait for the barbarians to destroy their culture and offer an alternative, the poet here is caught between two cultures, the rural and the urban, the agricultural and the industrial. The poet does not resolve the question; his project is only to present the poser, to highlight the ambivalence of the culture we live. Such an ending is quite natural to a poet who sees the emptiness of the postcard as a message that tells us, 'to write is to see the whole world including the blind' ('Postcard' in *Uttar Kabir*).

A wild jungle bear has no need for your Gita...
P. Lankesh's Kannada poem, 'Mother'[6] rejects the stereotypes of the Indian tradition in order to celebrate the illiterate rural woman struggling hard to bring up her children.

> My mother, black, prolific earth,
> green leaf, a festival of white flowers
> With every burn, the earthier,
> With every pang more fruit and petal.

She has 'limbs that thrill to children's kicks.' Her life was spent in raising millet, swilling water for each clod of earth, to nourish pepper and peas and grain, hiding her youth in a tatter of sarees. She grew into a hag bent double, weeping for coin, for dead calf and ruined grain, roaming villages for an ancient run-away buffalo.

> No, not Savitri, Janaki, nor Urmila
> nor a heroine out of history books,
> tranquil, fair, grave, in dignity
> nor like the wives of Gandhi
> and Ramakrishna. Did not worship the gods,
> nor listen to holy legends, nor did she wear
> like a good auspicious wife
> any vermilion on her brow.

The poet calls her 'a wild bear leaving a litter of little ones,' snarling and grumbling like a hurt bitch, rearing a husband, saving coins in the knots of cloth, ready to scratch like a monkey.

> A wild jungle bear has no need for your Gita
> My mother lived
> For stick and grain, labour and babies
> For rafter overhead, rice, bread, a blanket;
> To walk upright among equals

Her death is also casual; she lays down the basket on her head, groans and closes her eyes, never again to open them. It was as if she were leaving home for the fields, 'cool in the middle of small talk.' The whole poem is a tribute to a woman who lived in mud and soil, rejecting the role models assigned to her by the 'great' Hindu tradition. The poet's position can perhaps be appreciated better if we compare this poem with a poem like Sitakant Mahapatra's 'Father' that opens with the lines 'Behind all his action/lurked one desire: *Vaikuntha.*/He would not slip out of the house/without taking the name Durga Madhay.'[7]

Her fierce hunger may I put into the forest fires...
Attoor Revivarma's 'Metamorphosis'[8] a Malayalam poem, speaks of the transformation of such a woman into an embodiment of revenge. The speaking middle-class subject feels a sense of sin that he wants to expiate, carrying the rotten corpse of that woman-servant inside him. He goes about with fingers stuck in his nostrils; but the odour keeps everyone away. As a child he had seen this maid, a leech in his eyes; her child had died of overeating from hunger. She had a woman's head by birth, but the sea never roared in its ears; it had eyes only to be closed at midnight, its lips were the edges of a silent wound. She went to bed after every star had slept and woke up with a start much before the sun did. She has walked a thousand miles and yet is where she was; kicked and trodden a thousand times she has not yet woken up. She is

> The stump of a broom,
> a stinking swab, a gruel plate with a warped rim
> a lump of earth.

The second part of the poem is like a magic ritual where the poet wants to rouse and transform her into a beast of prey. He would like to dismantle the unlaid ghost of her soul like a machine and cautiously fasten it to another body:

> Not to the body of a woman
> creeping like a leech
> but to a man-eating tiger
> on the prowl from hunger.

He would like sleeping children to hear its growl, moving closer to their home. He longs to take her tongue and fasten it to the 'throat, not of a stray bitch relishing left-overs', but of a 'hungry wolf that rounds up and kills and dines on its prey.' He would put her fierce hunger into the forest fires that beset and burn cities and settlements, her agony in the twilight sky dripping with pus and blood. He would infuse her curse into the sun, which scorches the fertile fields. Her death thus becomes a sacrifice to the goddess who sows the seeds of small pox, represented by the sky with the stars for pockmarks. The poem with its dense imagery and radical symbolism, characteristic of much of the Indian poetry of the 1970s sums up the dreams of subaltern India, of transforming the society through a purifying act of violence.

I don't know politics...

How does a woman poet reconstruct her India? Look at Kamala Das's much-discussed poem 'An Introduction'[9] that works simultaneously at the individual and social levels proving once again the truth of the feminist slogan, 'the personal is the political'. 'An Introduction' is a polyphonic text with several of the poet's voices seeking articulation in a single verbal construct. The opening statement, 'I don't know politics', has an ambiguous tone that comes from a woman's marginalised position in society. Outwardly it is a confession of ignorance, but it also conceals in it a potential irony, as the society does not expect a woman to deal in politics. She is never the master in politics, only the victim, hence her lack of knowledge of the names of those in power, who have no content for her. Then she situates herself more specifically using nationality, complexion, place of birth and the languages known, an ironic filling up of an ungiven form. The 'language she dreams in', again is ambiguous enough to warrant many interpretations: it could be that of imagination, woman's language, English, or Malayalam, her mother tongue. She also justifies her choice of English as she believes she is using it with her own angularities and eccentricities. It is the voice of her instinct as is the lion's roar and the crow's cawing. She recalls the unconscious terrors of her childhood as she tries to differentiate herself from trees: monsoon clouds and rains bring in the locale of Kerala. Speaking of adolescence, her female body inscribes itself on the text and she remembers too her first encounter with masculine violence that belongs to the same frightening world of trees in the storm and the mutterings of the funeral pyre. References to swelling limbs, growing hairs, the pitiful weight of breasts and womb and the 'sad woman body' emphasise the corporeal ground of woman's experience, female physicality often identified with female textuality.

It has been said that women suffer cultural scripts in their bodies and women writers are like the mythic woman warrior who went into battle scarred by the thin blades which her parents literally used to write fine lines of script on her body. Woman herself becomes the text and this may explain women writer's preference for confessional modes of writing. (However a crude emphasis on the difference of the body can even be dangerous as that is also the foundation of gender discrimination against women, hence the ironic comment, that the identity of woman's literary practice must be sought in 'the body of her writing and not the writing of her body.') The woman cannot change her body; so Kamala changes her dress and tries to imitate men. But the voices of tradition would force her back into sarees, the saree becoming here a sign of convention. She is pushed back into her expected gender roles: wife, cook, embroiderer, quarreller with servants: the gender role also becomes a class role. The elders fill her world with taboos asking her to be her parents' Amy, her friends' Kamala or her readers' Madhavikutty (her pen name in Malayalam). Every deviation from the norm is looked upon as perversion or mental illness. Her hurt humiliated soul goes on begging for love; the nature similes of the hasty river and the waiting ocean reemphasise the element of instinct that drives the woman in her. The many ontological dimensions of her being—lover's darling, drinker of the city nights, one who makes love, feels shame, sinner, saint, beloved, betrayed—are tied together at the end of the poem, where the poet's ego dissolves in others, as soon as it is asserted.

If the poet finds the male ego, 'tightly packed like the sword in its sheath,' violent, arrogant and exclusive, she finds her identity to be a moment of difference, before a final dissolution in others, as she recognises her joys and aches to be the same as those of her readers. The poet dreams of another India, where the female body is free from the oppressive male gaze and the patriarchal violence that it engenders, where women do not have to play the roles assigned to them by the conventions of the family and the canons of literature, but can be everything until she becomes a true person, a human being with all possible dimensions.

One kind of hunger swallows another...
This feminine discourse, however, is not uniform as it gets qualified by caste and religion. A Dalit Muslim woman poet in Marathi like Malika Amar Sheikh (b. 1959) looks at the city from its margins as in her *Metropolis—24*.[10] People in the city, she says, haven't slept for years.

> By night men are transformed
> Into different kinds of hungers
> And one kind of hunger swallows another.

Men suspended from the tree of passion fly by night towards blind bodies. This is the moment when the hungry woman sells herself, tempted not by flesh but by food. 'We've often lost ourselves/in the jungle of intestines/Even a white-hot bread/conquers us completely.' This language of pure biology reflects the play of instincts: of hunger answering lust. During the day robots rule the city; night is the women's empire. Yet no one even thinks these dark women exist; only 'a poet or two' have this suspicion. This invisibility comes from the complete marginalisation of the woman, particularly the Dalit woman in contemporary India. The poet suggests no alternative: it is as if there is the India of eternal present juxtaposed against the glorious image of India and Indian women projected by the champions of the past.

A Muslim woman poet like Imtiaz Dharker (b. 1954) is forced to meditate over the purdah. In 'Purdah, 1'[11] the purdah grows into a paradox of simultaneous oppression and security.

> One day they said
> She was old enough to learn some shame.
> She found it came quite naturally.

The woman overcome by shame finds some safety in the purdah, where the body finds a place to hide, but soon realises that it is almost a coffin and the cloth that fans out against the skin is like the earth that falls on the coffin. The purdah also sharpens her vision: she begins to notice the angles people make in the light as they stand up or sit down, notice their sly, slanting eyes. She also remembers her secret liasons and carries a sense of sin between her thighs. The cloth grows closer to the woman's skin; light filters inward through the body's walls. The voices inside grow louder: she stands outside herself, inches past herself. She feels she is a clod of earth; roots inside her scratch for a hold between her ribs. As she passes out of her own hands into the corner of someone else's eyes, doors keep opening inward: thus the purdah that keeps her hidden from the world forces her to travel into the inner world: hers is also an experience of double marginalisation: first as a member of a minority community, then marginalised by that community's patriarchy.

Pravin Gadhvi, the Gujarati Dalit poet (b. 1951), opens his Shadow'[12] with a line from Lorca, 'O, Woodcutter, cut my shadow.' The shadow in the poem is the shame of having been born a Dalit.

> I can be a Hindu,
> a Buddhist
> a Muslim.
> But this shadow
> Shall never be severed from me.

Even conversion does not seem to offer a solution. He has thrown away the caste marks, the sweeper's bucket and the broom, but the shadow sticks. Even after changing the name, the job, the village, even the caste, the shadow of ostracisation, of estrangement, gathered over generations, stays with him. The language and the dress and the gestures have changed; yet the shadow resolutely plods on. A new *smriti,* different from *Manusmriti* that legitimises *chaturvarnya,* the four-caste system, a new constitution that proclaims equal rights to all citizens, a new penal code that punishes the practice of untouchability: none of these seems to help to change him into a confident new man. The shadow, the poet feels, will stick to him forever. Thus being born in India in a so-called low-caste becomes a curse without redemption, forcing another Dalit poet, Baburao Bagul, to say 'You who have made the mistake of being born in this country must now rectify it: either leave the country or make war.'[13]

In what language shall we fight for freedom?

Language and region are other key-concepts that define the dissent in contemporary Indian poetry. Raghuvir Sahay's (1929–1990) poem 'Hindi', for example, speaks of the battle between two Hindis: Hindi as the language of power and hegemony and Hindi as the creative expression of the ordinary people. The poem begins with the direct thought:

> We were fighting
> a language battle to change society.
> But the question of Hindi is no longer simply
> a question of Hindi—we have lost out.

In a mood of self-examination typical of this Hindi poet that militates against the manufactured consents that inhibit our voices and the idea of a liberation achieved through an external agency, the poet asks the soldiers in the battle for Hindi whether they and those on whose behalf they fought had been the same folk, or whether they had at best been sympathetic, well-meaning and well-schooled agents of their oppressors. This is a moral question very much like: can the rich liberate the poor, can the Brahmin fight for the Dalit, can man take up women's battles for emancipation from patriarchy? Clearly, this poet thinks that any battle without the victims' involvement will only be a proxy war that does not finally free the victims but only creates new masters: a fact proved again and again by history. Raghuvir Sahay expresses himself in a characteristic paradox:

> Those who are masters are slaves.
> Their slaves are those who are not masters.
> If Hindi belongs to the masters,
> then in what language shall we fight for freedom?

The poet then plays on the relationship between English and Hindi in India as two languages fighting for hegemony. The demand for Hindi, he says, is no more a demand for rights: it wants preferential treatment; this demand is put to the slave-masters by the agents who use Hindi in place of English. The difference is only that the masters use English in place of Hindi. This looks more like an exchange-deal than a victory. Only those who expose this power-game, being played within the upper class—the rich, the bureaucrats, the elite intellectuals—will really be able to liberate Hindi from its slavery.

> This will be the one who when he speaks Hindi,
> will show us what simple folk really feel.

In a related poem, 'Our Hindi',[14] Raghuvir Sahay compares Hindi to the state of a widower's new wife who talks, eats and sleeps too much. The widower goes on making new ornaments for her, makes her get fat while she smuggles the stuff out to her mother. She envies the neighbours, quarrels over garbage disposal; she is kept in the house with all that she requires, a *Mahabharata,* a *Ramayana* by Tulsidas and one by Radhesyam, the story of the film *Nagin,* its lyrics, a *Kokashastra,* a textbook of lovemaking, printed in the spoken language, a maid to make a mess of household things, a middle-aged husband to quarrel or make love with, an untended garden, many rooms like prison cells, dirty linens for washing at the well, soiled pillows, falling glasses, crumpled clothes, darkness in the house, five kilograms of gold, a child with an enlarged liver being taught to squat over monthly magazines, a plot of land to build a house for Hindi (the *Hindi Bhavan*). The poem, full of irony, ends up saying 'let the faultfinders say what they will/our Hindi is a married woman, she's faithful, she's happy/ she wants to die before her husband dies/everything's okay but first her husband must survive her/for how else can she have her wish.' Thus practically Hindi becomes the expensive, much fondled keep of English that's certain to survive the mistress. Similar anxieties have been expressed for other languages too—for example for Malayalam, by me[15] or Gujarati by Sitanshu Yashaschandra.[16]

While seeking what is lost...

Attoor Ravivarma's Malayalam poem '*Pandi*'[17] (A form of percussion in Kerala) foregrounds the regional against the national. The speaking subject in the poem—the poets' own alter ego—is one who leaves his native village in search of a job. The poet only says he had gone to the east giving up 'his mango and tamarind trees/his plot of land/ his moonlight and darkness.' He reaches a town where he joins a big hotel as a waiter. He spends his time following orders, carrying plates in haste and visiting a temple, sitting on the beach or watching a film in the evenings. While alone, he tries to recollect the shapes of the flowers of his village. He has come across several great men whose pictures appear in the newspapers, who pull crowds on the street, whose names dance on every tongue; he has watched them speak and smile and eat. As years go by, the trains run faster, yet he stops going to his village for its festivals, he forgets several words of his language, even his dreams dry up. Then one day the owner of the hotel dies on his chair, food loses its natural taste, visitors change, the dining hall is rebuilt, new waiters replace old ones. After 30 years he goes back to his village, only to find that all his friends and relatives have gone, even his enemies have left the place; plants and beasts do not recognise him; the sterile hill, the dried-up stream and the perplexed star do not remember him. He tries to locate what is lost. Suddenly he hears the ancient drums of the village temple: the beating rods have changed, the pipes and ears have changed; yet in that percussion he recognises himself and retrieves his identity.

The whole poem can be viewed as a complex metaphor where the big hotel with its din and its strange visitors stands for the concept of the 'national' with its diffuse identity clearly juxtaposed against the local/regional represented by specific trees (mango, tamarind), names of festivals (*onam, pooram*) and finally the percussion typical of Kerala. The 'nation' alienates the subject dissolving its identity in a motley crowd who speak different languages, eat different kinds of food, and dress differently while the region defines it, giving it definite shape, definite cultural and natural memories and definite language.

These few examples from contemporary Indian poetic practice must be enough to convince us of the operation of a poetics of difference that governs this practice and surfaces as a centripetal tendency in recent poetry. The women poets emphasise difference in terms of gender and seek to rewrite the patriarchal discourse challenging the phallocentric order of things. Many of them are engaged in revisionist myth-making and the establishment of a parallel semiotics centred round the female body, creating a sacred zone for the female subject and delving into the possibilities of retrieving a buried mother tongue, a secret language of female bonding that resists the male linguistic gaze. The Dalit poets too have redrawn the map of literature by discovering and exploring a whole new continent of experience that had so far been left to darkness and silence, by helping literature overcome stagnation through a cleansing renewal, by disturbing the sterile complacency of the dominant social groups, by challenging their set mores and fixed modes of looking at reality, their stale habits of ordering knowledge, beauty and power and their literary canons, bringing into focus neglected, suppressed or marginalised aspects of experience, vision, language and reality and forcing the community to refashion its tools and observe itself critically from a different angle. Dalit poetry also throws overboard the dominant poetics of *dhvani, rasa* and *ouchitya* by interrogating values like understatement, fixed moods and conventions, propriety and restraint and by challenging the middle-class notions of linguistic decency and employing words that are *asleela* (obscene), *chyutasamskara* (uncouth), and *gramya* (rustic), all proscribed by conventional poetics. The poets who foreground the local and the regional renew poetry by retrieving lost rhythms, deploying provincial archetypes and cultural symbols, alluding to regional rituals, festivals and local flora and fauna, thus constructing an eco-aesthetics of racial retrospection and introspection. This assertion of pluralism is a revolt against the felt erosion of geo-political and linguistic federalism in the everyday practices of the country's governance. The nativists hold that only a constructive concept of multiculturalism and heteroglossia can fight the pressures of standardisation imposed by the culture-market.

Cultural pluralism has never been a threat to the unity of the country at the peoples' level, and creative diversity has never stopped the people from enriching exchanges. The general thrust of our cultural evolution has been from the unitary to the plural, from the domination of a single language to a federation of many languages and the present context of democracy and decolonisation demands a retrieval of the regional as well as the foregrounding of the marginal against an assumed 'Indianness', which unfortunately implies a suppression of the non-canonical and the counter-hegemonic, a privileging of high textuality, aesthetic reductivism and revivalist nostalgia striving to construct a golden past, which never existed in real history for the majority of the people. Let us remember that literatures in India have a whole parallel history of counter-poetic practices with their own poetics that disapprove of the hegemonic aesthetics: a second tradition that includes the hundreds of oral, written and performed *Ramayana*s and *Mahabharata*s in the languages and dialects, the Buddhist and Jaina literature, the Bhakti and Sufi poetry of the period from the 6th century to the 20th century, the poetry of the freedom struggle especially of Kumaran Asan, Subramania Bharati, Nazrul Islam and others, the progressive poetry of poets from Sri Sri to Faiz Ahmad Faiz and the contemporary subaltern and nativistic poetic trends. It is not accidental that a Punjabi Dalit poet, Sant Ram Udasi, pays homage to the great *chamar* saint-poet Ravidas whose hoe 'tore up ugly illusions' and whose needle 'sewed up the wounds of the people',[18] the Marathi Dalit poet Daya Pawar reveals a radical Buddha 'speaking and walking amongst the humble and the week with torch in hand',[19] and the Kannada feminist poet Bhagya Jayasudarshana addresses the Kannada woman saint Akka Mahadevi with her 'thunders and rains' and her 'freedom from constraints imposed from within and without'.[20] Any essentialist attempt to construct a standard Indian literature, Indian culture or Indian character, without addressing the question of this inherent and enriching plurality will only end up creating a parody of Indian reality.

Notes

1. U.R. Ananthamurthy (ed.). *Vibhava*. Bangalore: Panther. 1992, p. 199; tr. poet.
2. Vinay Dharwadker (Gen. ed.). *The Collected Works of A.K. Ramanujan*. New Delhi: Oxford University Press. 1999, p. 51.
3. E.V. Ramakrishnan. (ed.). *The Tree of Tongues*. Shimla: Indian Institute of Advanced Studies. 1999; pp. 194-195, tr. Vinay Dharwadker.
4. Tejwant Singh Gill. (tr.). 75 *Poems of Pash*. Delhi: Sahitya Akademi. 1999, p.1.
5. Kedarnath Singh. *Uttar Kabir our Anya Kavitayen*. Delhi: Rajkamal,. 1995, pp. 16-18. Also see my analysis of this poem along with that of another Kedarnath Singh poem, 'Tuta hua Truck' (The Broken-down Truck) in Satchidanandan, K. *Indian Literature: Positions and Propositions*, Pencraft International, Delhi, 1999. ('Two Poems of Kedarnath Singh,' pp. 162–70).
6. *Vibhava,* pp. 139-40 (tr. A.K. Ramanujan).
7. Sitakant Mahapatra. *Death of Krishna and Other Poems*. Delhi: Rupa. 1992, pp. 18-20.
8. K. Satchidanandan (ed.). *Signatures: One Hundred Indian Poets*. Delhi: National Book Trust., 2000, pp. 1978 (tr. Ayyappa Paniker).
9. Kamala Das, *Only the Soul Knows How to Sing*. Kottayam: D.C. Books 1996 (pp. 96-7). Also see my Introduction to the book.
10. *The Tree of Tongues,* p. 97. (tr. Ravindra Kimbahune).
11. Vinay Dharwadker and A.K. Ramanujan (ed.). *The Oxford Anthology of Modern Indian Poetry*. Delhi: Oxford University Press. 1994, pp. 1701.
12. K.M. Sherrif, (tr. ed.) *Ekalavyas with Thumbs*. Ahmedabad: Pushpam Publications. 1999, p. 43.
13. Daniel Weissbort and Girdhar Rathi, (ed.). *Survival*. Delhi: Sahitya Akademi, 1994, pp. 7-8, (tr. Harish Trivedi, Daniel Weissbort).
14. *The Oxford Anthology of Modern Indian Poetry,* (tr. Vinay Dharwadker), pp. 105-06.
15. K. Satchidanandan, 'Languages' from 'Delli-Dali,' *How to Go to the Tao Temple,* Delhi: Haranand, 1998, p. 19 (tr. poet).

16. Sitanshu Yashachandra. 'Language,' *The Tree of Tongues,* pp. 124-8 (tr. Roomy Naqvi, poet).
17. Attoor Ravivarma. *Attoor Ravivarmayude Kavitakal.* (Collected Poems), Kottayam: D.C. Books, 1995, pp. 101-02.
18. Daya Pawar. 'The Buddha', *The Oxford Anthology of Modern Indian Poetry,* pp. 59-60, tr. Eleanor Zelliot, Jayant Karve.
19. Sant Ram Udasi, 'Tor Bhagat Ravidas,' *Indian Literature,* Delhi: Sahitya Akademi, No. 185, p. 25, tr. Tejwant Singh Gill.
20. Bhagya Jayasudarshana. 'Tor Akka' from *In Their Own Voice* (ed. Arlene R.K. Zide), Delhi: Penguin. 1993, tr. Poet.

THAT THIRD SPACE
Interrogating the Diasporic Paradigm

> *I reorganise my living room*
> *asking each piece*
> *Where it would like to be placed.*
> *I give a new spot to the sofa and the lamp,*
> *Change the drapes, and*
> *Replace the old rug with a wall-to-wall carpet.*
> *When everything is just right*
> *I begin to wonder:*
> *Where among these*
> *Should I place myself?*
> —Panna Naik, 'The Living Room', *Journal of South Asian Literature*,
> Vol. 21, No. 1, Winter, Spring 1986.

> (If the exile's) body cannot appropriate its given landscape... the substantial body dwindles into phantasm... Language... degenerates into a dead script when the bodily power of a people no longer instils it with particularity, no longer appropriates it in the expression of a emergent selfhood... In the battle between the body and the spirit, the outworn script of English as we find it here must be made to open its maw and swallow, swallow huge chaoses, the chaoses of uninterpreted actuality.
> —Meena Alexander, *Exiled by a Dead Script* (1977)

> ...It is from those who have suffered the sentence of history—subjugation, domination; diaspora, displacement—that we learn our most enduring lessons.
> —Homi K. Bhabha ('Post-Colonial Criticism': *Redrawing the Boundaries*, ed. Greenblatt and Gann)

While one does not doubt the enduring value of the diasporic experience as a spring of agonised inspiration, multiple identities, new subjectivities, creative memories and fresh perspectives on language and life, a stage seems to have come when one should problematise the concept of the diaspora, not to deny to it its authenticity as a state of experience but to qualify, complexify and interrogate it in order to understand it better.

For one thing, there has been a tremendous quantitative and qualitative change in the phenomenon of diaspora owing to the great demographic upheavals of the last century, especially its last decades, and to the unprecedented growth of the technologies of communication including the maturing of the multi-media communication systems and cyber technologies. Even though the word 'exile' continues to be fashionable and is not yet entirely devoid of significance, the new speed, reach and dimension of communication networks including the dimensions of vision, sound and movement, and the increased possibilities of forming a little real—not 'imagined'—community of one's own people who are from the same country and perhaps even speak the same language have definitely changed the nature of the experience of exile: it is no more solitary in, most cases; it is a shared experience. One may well argue that it is only like shifting your confinement from a closed solitary cell to a more open prison with a few jailmates who share the anxieties of return: but those who think it is the same have never experienced the pangs of sequestration in the maddening darkness of a closed prison. Arjun Appadurai and Anthony Smith have also pointed out how large communication networks erode national boundaries even as they promote intense interaction between members of diasporic communities: but these communities remain local and provincial even as they acquire transnational characteristics. The homeland becomes at once remote and accessible due to the contradictory phenomena of migration and cyber communication. Consequently, as Nalini Natarajan points out the contemporary episteme is ruled not by experience but by images that by their sheer proliferation and scope have become more real than anyone could have anticipated even a few decades ago.[1] These images, verbal, auditory and visual play a crucial role in shaping diasporic subjectivities. She points out how the impact of these

---

1. Nalini Natarajan, 'Reading Diaspora,' Introduction to *Writers of the Indian Diaspora,* ed. Emmanuel, S. Nelson, (Greenwood: London, 1993).

images unites the sartorial, culinary, literary, cinematic and religious, for instance in the videochannels for Indian diasporic viewers. It has also been noted how these images combine memory, experience and desire in suggestive ways juxtaposing mythological images with those of advertisement, thus creating new discourses that bring together religion, consumerism, cosmopolitanism and national identity. While challenging the media hegemony in the metropolis, they also reinforce other hegemonies within the community: of religion, class or caste.

Questioning the assumptions

While the word 'diaspora' may be used as an umbrella-term for immigrant writers, it also conceals the differences in their backgrounds as well as contexts. The first general assumption is that the diaspora refers to those who write in English as presumed by Emmanuel S. Nelson in his bio-bibliographical source book, *Writers of the Indian Diaspora*. Where does a Malayalam writer in Oman, a Tamil writer in Singapore, a Bengali writer in Paris or a Hindi writer in Mauritius, figure? Or is writing in English, which paradoxically enough is international writing at least by aspiration, the inevitable precondition for being qualified as diasporic?

The second general assumption is that the diasporic writer occupies a kind of second space, of exile and cultural solitude. But maybe Homi Bhabha is right, when he calls it a third space, a hybrid location of antagonism, perpetual tension and pregnant chaos.[2] The reality of the body, a material production of one local culture, and the abstraction of the mind, a cultural sub-text of a global experience, provide the intertwining threads of the diasporic existence of a writer: this is a neither/nor condition that Sura P. Rath calls 'Trishanku' in his article 'Home(s) Abroad: Diasporic Identities in Third Spaces'.[3] The products of this hybrid location are 'results

---

2. Homi Bhabha, *Location of Culture* (London: Routledge, 1994).
3. Sura P. Rath, 'Home (s) Abroad: Diasporic Identities in Third Spaces', *Journal of Contemporary Thought* (Baroda, M.S. University, Summer, 1999).

of a long history of confrontations between unequal cultures and forces, in which the stronger culture struggles to control, remake, or eliminate the subordinate partner'.[4] Bhabha sees individual and local experiences of diasporic writers as a part of the larger processes of historical change. The inter-subjective and collective experiences of nationness, community interest or cultural values are negotiated in the emergence of the interstices, the overlap and displacement of domains of difference. 'The negotiation of cultural identity,' he says, 'involves the continual interface and exchange of cultural performances that in turn produce a mutual and mutable recognition (or representation) of cultural difference'. The representation of difference, as he warns, is not to be hastily read as the reflection of pre-given ethnic or cultural traits set in the fixed tablet of tradition. 'The social articulation of difference, from the minority perspective, is a complex on-going negotiation that seeks to authorise cultural hybridities that emerge in moments of historical transformation.'

Forms of othering

The context of immigration also can alter the nature of the diasporic experience. Earlier diasporas of the neo-colonial and post-colonial world were often a product of forced immigration, of people running away from religious and other political or social persecution. But several Indians who migrated to America in the mid-1970s and afterwards, were going in search of a better life, greater promises of prosperity and material success. They did not have to burn the bridges with their past, at times, especially in the case of many academics, who had to strengthen those connections since they had to teach in South Asian departments. The new immigrant was a new kind of coloniser, taking full advantage of the war-time labour market, at the same time having no intention of ruling over the land. They had a home to go back to and an identity to protect; they were 'resident aliens' who kept up their citizenship and indulged in and even theorised

---

4. Lavie, Smadar and Ted Swedenburg, eds., *Displacement, Diaspora, and the Geographies of Identity* (Durham: Duke University Press, 1996).

a politics of identity, say, like Gayatri Spivak or Amartya Sen, thus taking full advantage of their status. I would suggest that one may have to look more closely at the class component of the diasporic experience: and there one can hardly ignore the difference between a refugee Bangladeshi or Philippine worker in Saudi Arabia and an academic capitalising on his/her scholarship in his/her language or literature in an American university. One can hardly compare their state to the pagan Indian, Chinese or Mexican immigrants of the 19th century or, worse still, the African immigrant workers who were treated as filthy, uncivilised slaves and beasts.

Like the class factor, the language factor also counts, as the experience of someone writing in English from England, U.S.A., Canada or Australia, especially in terms of accommodation, negotiation and reception, is certain to be different from that of a writer writing in English in France or Gujarati in England. Again there is the gender factor. The diasporic experience is also a gendered experience when it comes to the writing of Indian women abroad, say Meena Alexander, Panna Naik, Malati Rao, Sudha Chandola, Sujata Bhatt, Anita Desai, Kamala Markandeya, Bharati Mukherjee, Suniti Namjoshi, Jhumpa Lahiri and others.

The minority-majority status too contributes to the intensity or otherwise of the felt alienation. A Tamil in Ceylon or an Indian in Mauritius is even perceived as a threat by the dominant community there because of the size and confidence of these migrant populations. Again, the experience of the second generation or third generation migrant is very different from that of the first generation migrant: home becomes unreal to them, just a space of imagination rather than of nostalgic recollection. I have seen this transposition of Kerala from memory to imagination in the second generation American immigrants from my state. They reconstruct their homeland from fragments of information gathered from hearsay or from the Internet. For them, home is not a place to return to, but a place to fantasise about, or may be to visit some time as a guest or a tourist.

One has, in short, to take into account different forms of 'othering' experienced within the diaspora, as also different levels of identity.

Imagining the other is not necessarily a crippling experience; it also defines one's Self and reassures one about one's own distinct identity. The narrative production of home assumes many strategies according to one's relation to the place one came from, the place one came to and the place one belongs to. The idea of home is also related to time that transforms it into history or myth. Post-colonialism seems to come full circle in those writers who inhabit the third space, live the third culture and shape the third history.

The diaspora within

We are living at a time when the idea of 'Indianness' is being interrogated from different perspectives of Dalits, tribals, women, gays, lesbians and minorities, for example. The essentialist, often Orientalist, conception of India derived from Colonial-Indological and nationalist discourses is beginning to give way to a more federal democratic perspective of a polyphonic India, a mosaic of cultures, languages and literatures and worldviews. But the critical discourse on the diaspora still seems to swear by that exotic, eternal India, which is also at times woven into the diasporic writer's own perception of the country, while several Indian writers writing in the languages today are engaged in projecting different imagined communities, alternative nationhoods.

According to Homi Bhabha, the discourse of the wandering peoples of the diaspora marks a 'shifting boundary that alienates the frontiers of the modern nation'. Thus it interrupts the monologic discourses of modern metropolises with their imperial memories. It is a moment of the disinherited unsettling imperial inheritance and thus challenging the monolith of the modern Western nation; but it can also foster cultural nationalism by suggesting, say, a Hindu hegemony, while pulling down another. Patriarchy, class structure and ethnic conflicts too can well be reproduced and reinforced by diasporic ideologies. I have seen sections of Indians in the United States practising a kind of apartheid worse than that of the Whites against the Coloured, while they should by normal logic and just politics have identified themselves with them. Distinctions of class and sect and patriarchal norms within the family are also often reproduced by the diaspora as part of the reproduction of structures at home, often viewed as the structures of the lost golden past, and hence also of the Promised Future. Fortunately, more and more diasporic writers are becoming aware of the relativity of the concept of the diaspora, its inherent contradictions, with its multiple possibilities of alienation and assimilation, retreat into remembered patterns and revolt against them, of being the coloniser and the colonised, marginal and central.

Finally, I would like to point to the diaspora within. Now that the old concept of a unisonant nation with a single unified culture is being challenged, it may be possible to extend the concept of the diaspora at least in relative, linguistic and regional-cultural terms, within the country: the Malayali diaspora in Delhi, the Tamil diaspora in Bangalore, the Bengali diaspora in Bombay, or a Santhali diaspora in Calcutta, for example: mostly these populations of migrant workers, officers, media-persons, businessmen and academics, are concentrated in cities giving them a cosmopolitan character, and in turn finding a kind of solace in these many-tongued, multi-cultural milieu. I can speak with some authenticity about the Malayali diaspora that has made significant contribution to Malayalam literature especially since the 1960s. Even some genres of writing have entirely been products of diasporic consciousness: for example, the 'military fiction' (*Pattalakkatha*) came from writers like Kovilan, Parappurath, Vinayan and Nandanar who were in the army and thus got exposed to people and languages from different parts of the country. These are stories and novels that depict the life in the barracks in all its complexity. Many of the stories and novels of the diasporic writers are marked by the presence of non-Malayali characters who are even protagonists at times. Significant novels like M. Mukundan's *Delhi,* O.V. Vijayan's *Pravachakante Vazhi* (The Way of the Prophet), V.K.N.'s *Arohanam* (The Ascent) and Anand's *Alkkoottam* (The Crowd) and *Marubhoomikal Undakunnathu* ('How Deserts Are Made' published by Penguin in English under the title *Desert Shadows*) are pan-Indian in the range of their experience and the spread of their characters and at times reflect this cosmopolitanism even in their style and linguistic structure. Words and even sentences in other languages, particularly Hindi, are interwoven with Malayalam in the texts of some of these novels. Modernism in Malayalam, fiction in particular, is entirely a creation of diasporic Malayali writers living in Delhi, Bombay and Calcutta. O.V. Vijayan, V.K.N., M. Mukundan, Kakkanadan, M.P. Narayana Pillai, Sethu, Kamala Das, Punathil Kunhabdulla, Paul Zacharia: all these pioneers of the new fiction lived, at least in their formative years as writers, in cities outside Kerala, experiencing an alienation, a solitude, a torment of the absurd and the irrational and an existential angst as intense and as creative as that of say, Kafka, Beckett, Sartre or Albert Camus, whom many of them identified with in the early1960s. Some of the pioneers of modern poetry, like M.N. Paloor, Madhavan Ayyappath and Kadammanitta Ramakrishnan also lived in the cities outside Kerala. However, urban life affected them in a different way and appears in their poetry as distrust in the system, fear of the crowd, the experience of boredom, philosophic detachment, fragmentariness of expression and a kind of nostalgia for their lost villages in Kerala that get transformed in their poetry into emerald green imagined spaces of pristine purity and simplicity.

THE POLITICS OF REREADING
The Indian Context

Re-readings and counter-readings are a way of retrieving texts and making them available to the contemporary readers in new ways in which they can easily relate to them, as also to diverse aesthetic and ideological uses. The theoretical premise for re-readings was prepared hugely by reception theorists like Wolfgang Iser, Roman Ingarden and Jonathan Culler and thinkers and analysts like Pierre Macherey, Roland Barthes and Jacques Derrida. There are many factors that make re-readings radical: the social and historical premise; the ideological tools being used; the reader's (critic's) positions vis-a-vis gender, social class, caste, race, sexuality and majority/minority, which could be status-quoist and hegemonic or revolutionary and counter-hegemonic/subaltern. I am speaking here only of re-readings, which however cannot completely be extricated from re-writing to which examples abound in contemporary literature, especially works of subaltern writers who have rewritten episodes from epics like the *Mahabharata* and *Ramayana*, religious texts like the Bible, as well as regional myths and legends. But that is subject enough for another essay. As an example I may just point to *Ramayana Stories in Modern South India* edited by Paula Richman (University of Indiana Press) as one anthology where several rewritings of episodes from the *Ramayana*—by Kumaran Asan, N.S. Madhavan, K.B. Sreedevi, C.N. Sreekantan Nair, K. Satchidanandan, Kuvempu, Vijaya Dabbe, Subramania Bharati, Pudumaipithan, Ambai, Chalam, Volga, and others, have been brought together. Writers like Pratibha Ray, M.T. Vasudevan Nair, P.K. Balakrishnan, S.L. Bhyrappa, Girish Karnad, Ratan Thiyam, Mahasweta Devi and others have attempted rewritings of episodes and re-visioning of characters from *Mahabharata*, while others like Paul Zacharia, Sara Joseph and Anand have rewritten tales from the Bible.

These re-readings are not without a social and literary context: the complexification of life brought about by the changed environment, the new textures of urban living with its contradictory aspects of penury and luxury made possible by new technologies, the intensification of alienation among the intelligentsia, the angst of the new awareness of space and time, the growing consumer instinct, the loss of traditional values and the growth of the new post-industrial ethos, the continued intervention of the modern State in every aspect of the lives of its subjects, the revolutionary awakenings of the marginalised and oppressed sections of the people based on caste, class, religion and gender, the threats of war, poverty and terrorism, the search for new identities, and the new structures of feeling generated by these transformed environments of existence. The canons were being constantly changed, the institution of literature itself was under threat, the status-quoist concepts were being challenged and the paradigms proving hopelessy inadequate to meet the hermeneutic needs of literary criticism. The history of Indian criticism in the last few decades has been the history of the varied responses to these challenges and the attempts to arrive at critical canons that might help unlock and explain old and new Indian texts in the context of changing social mores and literary concerns. Re-readings are part of this larger scenario of revising the canons and revisiting the history of writing and reading in India. Every rereading is also an attempt, direct or oblique, to unsettle one or more existing, often hegemonic, mode(s) of reading.

Re-readings of canonical texts side by side with the discovery of buried and forgotten texts has certainly unleashed a lot of radical energy in the realm of criticism. Just to take examples from a single language, Malayalam, critics like B. Rajeevan, V.C. Sreejan, S.S. Sreekumar, E.V. Ramakrishnan, P. Udayakumar, V. Sanil, S. Saradakkutty, J. Devika, Dileep Menon, M.T. Ansari and others have been consistently rereading texts from various, mostly subaltern, points of view. They have been trying to expose the ideological determinations that underlie representations, especially of Dalits, Muslims, *adivasi*s and women, in the texts they choose to re-read. The new readings of Sreenarayana Guru and C.V. Raman Pillai by P. Udayakumar revealing little-noticed nuances of their vision, the reading of Pothery Kunhambu's *Saraswativijayam*, a Dalit novel, by Dileep Menon locating it in the context of the social discrimination of the author's time that justified conversion and demanded education as a prerequisite for social emancipation, the readings of the novels of Chandu Menon and C.V. Raman Pillai to reveal their anti-Muslim prejudices by M.T. Ansari, the readings of some texts of Kumaran Asan by S. Saradakkutty and V. Sanil to critique some of his gender prejudices as in the former case or to discover new symbolic meanings as in the latter, illustrate this trend. B. Rajeevan and P. Udayakumar, for example, have looked at the evolution of the concept of the body in Sreenarayana Guru as he moves from poetic-philosophical works like *Mananateetam, Siva Satakam* and *Indriya Vairagyam* to *Atmopadesa Satakam, Advaita Jeevitam* and *Suddhipanchakam*. Sreenarayana denies ontological status to the body, but gives it epistemological status and discovers a subtle body (*sookshmasareera*) within the gross body (*sthoola sareera*). The body can attain purity once it is liberated from the gross body. Then it will be capable of spiritual bliss. This is the moment where community enters Sreenarayana's system, for, the reforms within the communities—in education, economy, healthcare, etc., enable societies to attain this bliss, as the material and spiritual arrangements need to be coordinated like the organs of a body to lead to enlightenment, to recall his statement in *Advaitajeevitam*. Here he reminds us of Tirumular, the Tamil Saivite saint as well as Basava, the Kannada Saivite reformer, both of whom accepted the interdependence of the body and the soul. It is the body that bears the organic marks of distinction in man; the caste marks and caste titles are an aberration that hides these organic markers. So there are only two castes among the humans—men and women. (The third gender was probably theoretically invisible at that point of time) Sreenarayana thus views caste as a false distinction, religion as nothing more than a matter of opinion, and the community as the locus of concrete social action. In 1916, Sreenarayana declared that he does not belong to any caste or religion. Human community, he said, will be born only when false distinctions and hierarchies disappear. This was the basic principle of the Renaissance that was soon to radically transform the society in Kerala.

    Dileep Menon's reading of *Saraswativijayam*, a novel by Pothery Kunhambu published in 1892, looks at Kunhambu's project closely to discover that initially he too had thought of reforming the Hindu society, but later abandoned it as impossible. The author, an Ezhava who was often called 'Pulayan Kunhambu' for his concern for the Pulaya community, found that tradition is impervious to modernity. The novel is an example of the spatial delineation of issues of power, hierarchy and inequality as the characters traverse different territories of freedom and knowledge. Travel becomes a metaphor of individual redemption here as the cruel landlord, Kuberan Namboodiri travels to Kasi; Marathan, the Pulaya protagonist travels to Madras and Subhadra, the Namboodiri's daughter falsely accused of extramarital relations and banished from her caste, travels to Kannoor to escape from the enclosed space of historical memory. Kuberan has a change of heart, Marathan converts to Christianity, studies law and becomes a judge, Subhadra too converts and becomes a teacher and gets reunited with her husband, who too converts to Christianity. Christianity is the mediator of modernity in the text. Kunhambu did share the creative tension between the possibility of an internal critique of Hinduism and the pragmatic and robust alternative of empowerment through colonial education, though finally he found that liberation is unattainable within the Hindu fold, a fact that Ambedkar too was to discover later, though his choice was not Christianity, but Buddhism. *Saraswativijayam* is not a revenge novel, nor a conversion tract; conversion here is a metaphor for the new possibilities opened up by colonialism and modernity. It may be noted that while elite thinkers like Ramakrishna, Vivekananda and Dayanandasaraswati championed an internal critique of Hinduism and found habitation within reformed religion, most of the subaltern thinkers found a solution to caste inequality only in conversion. Sreenarayana was an exception, as, through a philosophical inversion, he could free himself from all religions.

Post-colonial readings, especially informed by Edward Said's theoretical insights have helped unearth the colonial prejudices behind a lot of work on India—not literature alone, but also photographs and paintings. These interrogations, while at times reductive or eclectic, have helped make writers and readers conscious of the dangers of (mis)representation. Romila Thapar has reread Kalidasa's *Abhijnana*

Sakuntalam from a historical point of view to reveal the Orientalist determinations behind its reception. She has shown how Kalidasa's Sakuntala is delicate, shy, meek, faithful and unquestioning in her obedience, returning with tears from Dushyanta's court when he disowns her, as different from the Sakuntala of the *Adiparva* in the *Mahabharata*, where she is strong and independent and boldly interrogates Dushyanta's sense of justice and decorum. She puts certain conditions even before she enters into a *gandharva* relationship with the king. Kalidasa's description fits in very much with the romantic concept of the innocent forest virgin embarrassed by the awakening of desire. In fact there is a whole romantic opposition at work here between the simple, picturesque ashram in the woods that represents rusticity and innocence and the splendid palace of the king that stands for the urban, with its accent on power and cunning. Kalidasa's Sakuntala was the kind of ideal heroine that the romantics were looking for. Goethe describes her as 'a rustic girl', a 'child of nature' with elegant limbs and graceful undulating gait. Popularised in the West through Monier Williams' English translation, from which the German translation was done by Georg Forster in 1791, *Abhijnana Sakuntalam* fitted very well with the Orientalist project of romanticising the East, reflected equally well in colonial photography and the Company paintings. The Germans also exulted in the racial bonds between the ancient Indians and Europeans, whom they considered 'Aryans', whatever that term stands for. For French Indologists like Sylvane Levy and Russian Indologists like Oldenberg, Sakuntala was part of their fantasy about India. She was the ideal Hindoo woman, also for the Indian middle-class Nationalism, who like the Orientalists bemoaned the 'fall' of ideal Indian womanhood. Rabindranath Tagore also upheld Sakuntala, combining in his approach the British Orientalist attitudes of the 19th century, the nascent nationalist sentiment and Victorian moralism. Romila Thapar upholds Shantaram's portrayal of Sakuntala in his film *Stree* as being faithful to her portrayal in the *Mahabharata*, as also the contemporary interpretation one comes across in Nachiket Patwardhan's *Anant yatra* that brings Sakuntala to modern Bombay, where Dushyanta is a business executive. The film hints that any appreciation of the naïve and frail Sakuntala today can only be an escape from today's oppressive patriarchal urban reality. The post-colonial perspective has also helped a better understanding of the politics of the pre-Independent Indian fiction, poetry and travelogues revealing the political in what used earlier to be read apolitically. While the works of poets like Tagore, Nazrul Islam, Vallathol, Subrahmanya Bharati, Sumitranandan Pant and other canonical writers of the period have always been considered anti-colonial in their ethos and aesthetic mode, a poet like P. Kunjiraman Nair, who had earlier been read only as a poet of nature or of devotion, now began to be seen as celebrating pre-colonial spaces and modes of existence in response to the arrival of colonial modernity. The critical works of comparatists like Sisir Kumar Das, Ipshita Chanda, Harish Trivedi and E.V. Ramakrishnan have also been informed to a great extent by a critical understanding of colonial modernity. Ipshita Chanda's *Reception of the Received* rereads Tagore and Nirala who had earlier been seen as influenced by European Romanticism and stands European Romanticism itself on its head to reveal its Indian sources. Sisir Kumar Das's essays in *Indian Ode to the Westwind* and E.V. Ramakrishnan's *Locating Indian Literature* also have many moments of the Empire writing back, not to speak of the many studies of the politically conscious post-colonial Indian English writers like Salman Rushdie and Amitav Ghosh who deal with different phases of Indian history, of slavery and independence. Rita Kothari's reading of Girish Karnad's Kannada *Tuglaq*, T.N. Dhar's reading of Raja Rao's novel *Kanthapura*, Jaidev's reading of post-Independence Hindi fiction, K.C. Belliappa's reading of the novels of Rukun Advani and Shashi Tharoor along with those of Chinua Achebe (all the essays in *Interrogating Post-Colonialism: Theory, Text and Context* edited by Harish Trivedi and Meenakshi Mukherjee), Svati Joshi's reading of Govardhanram Tripathi's Gujarati novel *Saraswatichandra,* Manager Pandey's reading of Premchand, Sumanta Banerjee's reading of Satinath Bhaduri's Bengali novel *Dhonrai Charit Manas,* M. Asaduddin's reading of Qurratulain Hyder's Urdu novel *Aag ka Dariya,* Alok Bhalla's reading of Krishna Sobti's Hindi novel *Zindaginama* and V. Rajakrishnan's reading of Anand's Malayalam novel *Aalkkottam* (all essays in *Narrating India: The Novel in Search of the Nation* edited by E.V. Ramakrishnan) are all informed by insights from post-colonial theory. The assumptions behind the theory have not gone unquestioned: its claim that the major theme of literatures from post-Colonial societies is discursive resistance to the now absent coloniser, its unproblematic assertion that writers who write back to the centre authentically represent their people, its downplaying of the difference between the settler colonial and those colonised in their own territories and the consequent trivialisation of the experiences of those who suffered genocide, pauperisation and cultural deprivation under colonial rule, and its suppression of the internal hierarchies and divisions like class and caste and gender in the societies it describes homogenously as 'the colonised', 'the oppressed', 'the indigenous', etc., have all been under attack from critics. (eg, 'Some Uneasy Conjunctions', Arun. P. Mukherjee).

M.T. Ansari's rereading of the early Malayalam novel *Indulekha* (1889) by O. Chandu Menon assumes a minority point of view and looks at what happens to the Muslim in the process of the formation/translation of the idea of the nation. The novel has a scene where the protagonist Madhavan, on his way from Calcutta to Bombay by train, encounters a handsome Muslim, Sheer Alikhan who introduces himself as a subordinate judge of Allahabad. He is taken in by the man's witty conversation and his handsome looks, but soon finds himself cheated by him at the next station when Alikhan offers him tea and robs him of his luggage with the help of a Pathan who acts like a porter. The police inspector too seems like an accomplice as he, a Turkish Muslim, only beats up the innocent butler who had been after Madhavan for the payment of the food he had been offered by Sheer Alikhan. At the same time Indulekha (Madhavi is her real name) has a feverish dream that Madhavan, her betrothed, has been stabbed by a Muslim. Later in the novel, the man with two accomplices is arrested and confesses to 17 murders. The Muslim becomes a generic term for the 'other' in this narration, as can be seen from the strange description of the man who has the 'colour of a rotten orange' while Madhavan is golden in complexion. Turks,

Pathans, Mappilas, Muslims, all dissolve into one in this figuration of the other. In Indulekha's dream the Muslim becomes the threat to her marital consummation as well as 'our' national consummation. Sheer Alikhan has no nation and not even a proper name, even though he can mute an enlightened woman like Indulekha. Even English language, which to Madahavan is a tool of liberation, becomes a tool of deception in the hands of Sheer Alikhan.

Critics like Krishna Rayan have re-read Sanskrit poetics in the light of the new theories from the West and have come up with extended and flexible interpretations of the central concepts of Sanskrit poetics like *dhvani, rasa, rasadhvani, vakrokti* and *anumana* along with peripheral concepts like *abhidha, loakshana, vibhava, anubhava* etc. In his book, *Text and Sub-text* (1987) Rayan looks at the theory of suggestion and tries to establish that suggestion—the production of unstated, subsurface, indirect, multiple, emotive meaning—is what distinguishes modern literature from the literature of eatrlier periods. Rayan examines texts like Tennyson's *Becket* alongside T.S. Eliot's *Murder in the Cathedral*, Christopher Fry's *Curtmantle* and Jean Anouilh's *Becket ou L'Honneur de Dieu*. Four of Thomas Hardy's novels exploring the notion of a return to the roots are analysed in relation to novels by Margaret Drabble that pursue a similar theme. The book also looks at the practice of suggestion and evocation in Milton's *Paradise Lost* and the poetry of Yeats and the minimalist, micro-suggestive, poetic practice of the *Review* poets like Ian Hamilton, David Harsent, Colin Falck, Hugo Williams and Michael Fried. The critic quotes critical passages from Mallarme, T.S. Eliot, Arthur Symmons, Yeats, A.C. Bradley, Edmund Wilson and W.K. Wimsatt to relate the theory of suggestion to the symbolist practice as well as the Sanskrit concept of *rasadhwani*. He also considers the binary oppositions like emotive/referential meaning (I.A. Richards) Oblique/direct (E.M.W. Tillyard), local texture/ logical structure (J.C. Ransom) and Intensive/extensive meaning (Allen Tate) to be renamings of the suggestion/statement distinction found in Eastern as well as Western poetics. He also associates concepts like 'depth language' (Philip Wheelwright) and 'interiority' (W.J. Ong) with *dhwani*/suggestion. In *Burning Bush: Suggestion in*

Indian Literature (1988) Krishna Rayan extends the *rasadhwani* concept to modern subcontinental texts in various languages, by authors like Nirmal Verma, Kiran Nagarkar, M.S. Sarna, Pranabjoti Deka, Lokenath Bhattacharya, Rajinder Singh Bedi (fiction); P. Lankesh, Kumaran Asan, Jayanta Mahapatra, Nissim Ezekiel, Dina Nath Nadim, Soubhagya Kumar Mishra (poetry); Shrikant Shah, Ediriwira Sarachchandra (play) and others besides some older texts from classical Tamil and Sindhi in order to demonstrate the applicability of the theory to different languages, genres and periods. In *Sahitya: A Theory*, Rayan produces an eclectic theory for Indian critical practice by bringing together Sanskrit, Tamil and Western concepts with plenty of examples and quotations. *Natyasastra* and *Tolkappiyam* are referred to as two basic texts. Here, he also establishes parallels between the *rasa*s of *Natyasastr*a and the *meypadus* of *Tolkappiyam*. For example, *sringara* is identified with *uvakai*, *hasya* with *nakai*, *karuna* with *azhukai*, *raudra* with *vekuli*, *vira* with *perumitam*, *bhayanaka* with *accam*, *bibhatsa* with *ilivaral* and *atbhuta* with *marutkai*. The critic looks at the diverse aspects of literature like literariness, image, narrative, character, style, rhythm, landscape and evaluation. In the chapter on landscape, he introduces the *tinai* concept of *Tolkapiam* with the accompanying *uri* and *mutal* viz., *kurinci* (*mutal*-mountain, *uri-punartal* or premarital union), *marutam* (*mutal*-lowland or riverside, *uri-oodal* or marital union sulking over infidelity) *neytal* (*mutal*-seashore, *uri-iranagal* or anxious pining in the state of separation), *mullai* (*mutal*-forest or pasture, *uri-iruttal* or patient waiting) and *palai* (*mutal*-desert, *uri-pirital* or separation). The landscape here is the signifier and the bond that holds it to the signified is arbitrary and fixed by conventions, which were sustained for several generations during the *Sangam* period. Ayyappa Paniker has also tried to apply the *tinai* theory to Thakazhi Sivasankara Pillai's *Kayar* while V.J. Sebastian has done it to a series of contemporary poems. S. Carlos (Tamilavan) has also tried to extend and apply the theory to modern texts in Tamil. While these are interesting experiments, the method can work fully only in a stable static culture, with a lot of received assumptions and capable of a large number of shared responses. The theory of *rasa*s is also too limited and rigid to make it critically effective, while applied to modern texts where the boundaries of emotions are blurred, moods are in a flux and responses more complex. Behind these theories is a whole static world view and a fixed view of literature and literariness. They have also a tendency to look at literature, especially poetry, as a craft, detached from its time and society. Both classical Sanskrit and Tamil poetics, therefore, fail to historicise its texts and themselves need to be historicised to be understood. Concepts like *dhwani* and *ouchitya* and the linguistic injunctions against *asleela, gramya* and *chyutasamskara* can hardly be isolated from the class that has generated them and hence do not apply to several subaltern forms and movements, both ancient and modern. The traditional concepts of *pratibha* or genius, *sahridaya* or the competent reader, the *sahitatva* or the fixed togetherness of the word and the meaning—compared to the bond of Parvati and Parameswara, meaning as something deposited in the work by the author, and the authorial institution itself emerge from an idealist philosophical premise. The concept of reader as the producer of meaning, of the text as a flux, and the absence or the eternal *differance* of a 'final meaning', literariness itself as the effect of reading, and the historical and ideological determinations of the text are alien to this aesthetic ideology. While the concepts of *dhwani* and *anumana* do take the reader into account, it is an abstract reader outside real history. It is seldom bothered with the question of the historical construction of subjectivity and hence fails to answer several questions about writing, reading and authorship. This also applies to Persian poetics that deals exclusively with forms available in classical Persian or Arabic from which Urdu has adopted them, like *masnavi, nazm, ghazal, rubai, qavvali, manaqib, nama, qasida, qit'a* (or *muqatta'at),* etc., their prosody, rhyme patterns, rules of composition, style and evocation of moods and feelings. The tradition is still alive in the criticism of traditional poetry, but while discussing the new poetry and fiction, critics often depend on modern Western theories, as can be seen in the practices of Shamsur Rahman Faruqi, Shamim Hanfi or Gopichand Narang.

The patriarchal canons are being interrogated, myths revisioned, texts decoded and literary history revised by many feminist critics and theoreticians. Susie Taru and K. Lalita have traced in their introduction to the anthology *Women Writing in India, Sixth Century B.C. to the Present* the evolution of women's writng in India across centuries. Uma Chakravarty, Vijaya Dabbe, Madhu Kishwar, Sonal Shukla, Leela Mullati, Parita Mukta, Vijaya Ramaswamy and others have reread the poetry of women saints like Lal Ded, Akka Mahadevi, Satyakka, Kadire Rammavve, Ayadakki Lakkamma, Muktayakka, Andal, Karaykkal Ammayar, Meerabai, Gangasati, Janabai and Bahinabai to show how Bhakti was to them a tool to escape gender distinction, patriarchal oppression and domestic confinement, just as it was to the Buddhist nuns like Mutta, Ubbiri or Sumangalamata of the sixth century BCE. God becomes a way of dissolving an otherwise impossible situation in these saints. Their worldly marriages, actual as well as potential, represent both the lure and the bondage of the world, while their relationship to God represents a renunciation of the world and the woman's traditional roles in it. Like Susie finds the lyrics of *Terigatha* to be, their poems are epiphanic experiences in which the painful constructions of secular life fall away and the torment of feelings subsides as the peace and freedom of nirvana are attained. While they exult in their new life transformed by Bhakti, they also contrast it to the painful worlds they have left behind. These poets created an alternative family, resisted the oppressive social role imposed upon them by the male-dominated society and simultaneously created a parallel language of experience and emotion.

A lot of scholars and academics like Nabaneeta Dev Sen, Malashree Lal, Vrinda Nabbar, Brinda Bose, Ruth Vanita, Gayatri Chakravarty Spivak, J. Devika, Anita Devasia, G.S. Jayasree and S. Saradakkutty have also done considerable research in women's discourses and the representation of women in literary texts by men. *Same-sex Love in India: Readings from Literature and History* edited by Ruth Vanita and Saleem Kidwai, while being an anthology of gay and lesbian texts, also re-reads a lot of ancient and medieval Indian texts like the *Mahabharata, Krittivasa Ramayana, Manikanthajataka, Panchatantra, Kathasaritsagara, Padmapurana, Bhagavatapurana, Skandapurana* and *Shivapurana* from the homo-erotic point of view.

Eco-criticism is another mode of rereading that focuses entirely on the text without looking at its organic relationship with nature and the larger universe. Even though it was William Rueckert (*Literature and Ecology: An Experiment in Eco-Criticism,* 1978) who introduced the term, it was Joseph Meeker's *The Comedy of Survival: Studies in Literary Ecology* (1974) that first defined the subject. According to Meeker, literary ecology was concerned with the biological themes appearing in literature. Its aim was also to discover the role of literature in human ecology. Literary works, he said, often reveal man's beliefs about the truth of natural processes and the cultural ideologies that have brought the human race to the modern environmental crisis. Cheryll Glotfelty who edited the first eco-criticism reader (1996) describes eco-criticism as an attempt to unravel the exchanges between nature and culture. It has one leg in literature and the other on earth: as a theoretical discourse it connects equally with human beings and non-human ones. The writers' world is not only the social world, but the ecosphere itself. Earth, she says, is at the centre of eco-criticism, just as gender is at the centre of feminist criticism and class at that of Marxist criticism. Eco-criticism according to Lawrence Buel, brings space into the critical agenda that has so far been confined to the theme, plot and characters. He sees it as an umbrella term that embraces various modes and approaches. It has also been called 'ego-criticism' (Sven Birkerts, *Only God can Make a Tree: The Joys and Sorrows of Eco-Criticism*) as it rereads literature to discover what it has to say about man's ego-centrism, greed and craze for wealth and power. Some eco-critics also draw strength from Engels' *Dialectics of Nature*, Raymond Williams's insights into the city-country contradictions and the works of Adorno, Walter Benjamin and other new Marxist thinkers. The anthology *Haritaniroopanam Malayalathil* (Green Criticism In Malayalam) edited by G. Madhusoodanan carries 76 different samples of what can be broadly called eco-criticism in Malayalam—along with 16 theoretical pieces—that began to grow with the environmental awareness generated by the struggle against the proposed dam in the rainforests of the Silent Valley. The book carries re-readings of many Malayalam literary texts based on the concepts of eco-Marxism, eco-Feminism, eco-Ethics and eco-Spirituality in literary criticism.

It was perhaps Sharad Patil's book in Marathi *Abrahmani Sahityanche Saundaryasastra* that first launched an attack on 'Brahmin aesthetics' and spoke of the need for a counter-poetics. Sharan Kumar Limbale in his book *Towards an Aesthetics of Dalit Literature* has attempted a critique of status-quoist Marathi aesthetics, as also of the adulatory as well as negative criticism of Dalit literature by the *savarna* critics. He points out that Dalit literature is not meant to entertain the readers, but to provoke them into rethinking their society and its ethics and aesthetics. It is impossible to investigate Dalit writing with its rebellion, rejection and commitment with the established critical tools meant for the literature of acquiescence and consent. He does not agree with critics like Yadunath Thatte who want to enlarge the *rasa* theory to include revolt and cry as the 10th and 11th *rasa*s. What is needed is a new aesthetics that takes into account the 'differentness' of Dalit writing in content as well as form. Aestheticist criticism cannot digest the non-traditional stance of Dalit literature. For that freedom will have to be recognised as an aesthetic value. The intensity of experience, the way the experience is socialised, its power to cross the boundaries of time and space—these are the standards Limbale proposes for the evaluation of Dalit literature. D.R.Nagaraj in his book *The Flaming Feet: A Study of the Dalit Movement in India* has gone deeper into the specifics of the Dalit sensibility and Dalit imagination and the problem of cultural memory in the context of the cosmologies of caste and the realism in Kannada fiction. He traces the cultural memory of the Dalits to the subaltern, radical, traditions, folk cosmologies, rural myths and oral narratives, which are getting lost in the oppressive process of Sanskritisation pursued by the Hindu revivalists. He looks at the cults of Madeswara and Manteswamy in Southern Karnataka as examples. He points out how the cultural paradigm of the nationalists had no place for the Dalit cultural traditions and practices. The monolithic cultural model erected on the basis of Vedanta by the Hindu Right also precludes all the philosophic and cultural expressions of the Dalits. Nagaraj makes a very insightful comparative rereading of U.R.

Anantha Murthy's *Samskara* and Devanoor Mahadeva's *Kusumabale* to show how caste has been an important factor in determining their modes of representation and imagination. *Samskara* gives the readers an insight into the self-image of the Brahmin by allowing them to see the world through the eyes of Pranesacharya whose attempts to break the system miserably fail, as against that of Naranappa, his alter ego, who completely breaks free of tradition and its taboos. This, according to him, is also the failure of the novel as it cannot establish the sexual contact between the Brahmin and the non-Brahmin as a possible way to break free of the oppressive caste society. Realism frustrates the novel's radical ambitions. But *Kusumabale* rejects the notion of verifiable reality at the very outset and follows a folk narrative form. While *Samskara* ignores the socio-economic power structures, thus turning its concern more metaphysical, *Kusumabale* counter-poses the personal and the political realms of the caste structure, and finds that sexual contact like the one in *Samskara* can only lead to violence within the existing power structure. Devanoor Mahadeva revives the Dalit mode of imagination as when a cot tells a story and a lamp turns into a woman who comments on the events of the day. The narrative is open and works at multiple levels while *Samskara* is highly centered and has an ending that closes the narrative.

Even the random examples we came across in this brief examination of certain trends, I hope, are adequate enough to illustrate the exciting possibilities offered by diverse ways of rereading creative as well as discursive texts and to help us imagine the dynamic scenario of criticism in India today, informed as it is by the visions of an egalitarian future.

TRANSLATION AS WRITING
Text, Translation, Authenticity—
Towards an Indian Perspective

The Lord Buddha addressed Subhuti saying, 'What think you? Did the Lord Buddha formulate a precise system of Law or doctrine?' Subhuti replied saying: 'Honoured of the Worlds! The Lord Buddha did not formulate a precise system of Law or doctrine.'

—*The Vagrakkhedika (The Diamond Sutra)*

Subhuti in The Buddha's *Diamond Sutra* talks throughout in the language of negations. Complete perfection is spoken of as an empty name; Tathagata preaches not about numbers of worlds but about no numbers of worlds, not about selfhood but no selfhood, and finally it is said that there is nothing that was preached by Tathagata. The Buddhist theory of subjectivity also looks at the body as continually changing and realises that man is never the same for two consecutive moments. Sentient beings are but assemblages of different properties or qualities, like the Material Qualities that are like a mass of foam that gradually forms and then vanishes, the Sensations that are like 'a bubble dancing on the surface of water', the Ideas that are 'the uncertain mirage appearing in the sunshine', the mental and moral Propositions that are without firmness or solidity 'like the plantain stalk' and Thoughts that are 'like a spectre or magical illusions'. This idea of self as flux, of the decentred, ever discontinuous subject as also the absence of an Originary central to Buddhist thought I presume is sufficiently post-Structuralist to merit the attention of contemporary scholars and critics. If subjectivity itself is ever in a flux and there is no 'Author'—in a theological sense too there cannot be sacred texts or untranslatable originals. Translation suddenly becomes an act of freedom no more bound to a pre-determined original.

It is not accidental that the Indian equivalents for translation almost always connote other meanings. Look at the Sanskrit words for translation: *Vivarta,* which in the Vedantic sense means alteration or altered condition—as the world is a *Vivarta* of Brahman; *paribhasha* that can mean anything from speech and discourse to reproof and common rule, *bhashantaram,* which means rendering in another dialect or migration into or rebirth in another language and *anuvad,* which denotes a repetitive interpretation. Words like *anukriti* (imitation), *arthakriya* (enacted or performed meaning) *vyaktivivekam* (repetition with individual difference) and the Tamil word *ullurai* (inner speech or sub-textual meanings) were used in the context of translation in the medieval times, none of which, as Ayyappa Paniker points out in a discussion of these terms, is an exact equivalent of the English word 'translation' and all of which recognise the non-identical nature of the source and the target. *Bhashya* or interpretation, and localisation were common to Indian translations of the epics. In pre-colonial India, translations of texts within the same culture maintained not a paraphrasal relationship, but one of intertextuality, allowing plenty of diversity.

While theorising the act of translation, we ought to distinguish between Western and Indian approaches. J. Hills Miller considers translation 'the wandering existence in a perpetual exile', alluding obviously to the Biblical myth of the Fall of Man and his exile from paradise. Translation here is an exile. The myth of the Tower of Babel further underlines the idea that man has been cursed to be multilingual, after the loss of the original common tongue. However, India has accepted and lived with multilingualism for centuries, and the transition from one language to another is as natural to us as a change of body during rebirth. Our poets like Kabir or Meera, Nanak or Vidyapati have themselves been multilingual, without even being aware of it. We have seldom been haunted by the fear of being unparadised; translation does not embarrass us as it is a daily act with us, as physical and as intimate as lovemaking. Ours is traditionally a 'translating consciousness' unlike the monolingual literary cultures of Europe that are too self-conscious of the act. Again, we have never considered deviations from the original as sin; on the other hand, we have admired the imaginative freedom of different translators of the *Ramayana,* whose differences are even more important than their commonalities, since that was what established them as original poets in their languages and often the very founders of the languages themselves. The West was always worried about the authenticity of the translation by which it often meant literality, a concept close to Platonic Mimesis, an attempt to re-situate the original through close imitation. India has no martyrs to the cause of translation like Etienne Dolet, the 16th century French translator of Plato, executed for the freedom he took with the original text. If we had followed this example we would have executed the best of our poets, both the poets of the epics and the Bhakti poets who took every kind of linguistic and intellectual freedom with their 'original' texts. Perhaps the very idea of an 'original' text is foreign to us because of our strong oral traditional that had only perpetually changing texts. While colonial Europe found in the translation of exotic oriental texts a way to contain and dominate them, India sought through translation a living dialogue between its own cultural past and present, as also between its culture and cultures of other lands. For us translation has been a revitalisation of the original through the imagination of a writer of another space and another time. Translation to us has been a version of intertextuality. The original has never been specially privileged; it can never be absolutely repeated. Like any act of reading, translation too is besieged and delivered by the precariousness of intertextuality. The translator's position has never been secondary in India; our greatest poets have been translators and our greatest translators have been poets. From Bharathari onwards—centuries before Derrida—we have believed that meaning exists in language not as a positive presence but as an absence, which reflects its independent presence. Indian linguistics since the days of the Sphota theory has seldom suffered from an anxiety about the loss of the origin. Deviations have not only been tolerated in India, but have been welcomed and encouraged. For example, when Kamban the great Tamil poet wrote *Ramayanam* in his language, he took a lot of freedom with Valmiki's *Ramayana* by editing, condensing, elaborating, adding to, interpreting and modifying the original text in order to turn it into a Dravidian language classic and also to express his own personal tastes and preferences. In his *Ramayanam,* Ravana is an adorable devotee of

Siva, who consciously walks towards death in his search for salvation. *Sitadukham* in Malayalam looks at Rama's tale from Sita's point of view, thus privileging the feminine against the patriarchal versions. In the Malayalam *Adhyatma Ramayana* of Ezhuthachan, when Rama refuses Sita's request to accompany him to the forest, Sita says that in every other *Ramayana,* Sita accompanies Rama, then why not in this *Ramayana:* an example not only of the freedom of the translator, but of a post-modern self-reflexivity and classic intertextuality.

In India we keep translating every moment of our active life: we are always bilingual if not multi-lingual, and often mix languages almost unconsciously in our everyday speech. Our literature too is founded on translations, since the various *Ramayanas, Mahabharatas* and *Bhagavatas* in different languages, including the tribal versions and the performative improvisations, have been the very foundations of our rich literatures. Even the distinction between the original work and the translation was rather blurred and uncertain in India's precolonial discourse. The *Ramayanas* of Pampa, Kamban, Ezhuthachan, Molla, Premananda, Ekanatha, Balarama Das, Tulsi, Kritibas or Madhav Kandali, for example, were taken to be neither translations nor adaptations, but original works, as they were the most brilliant manifestations of the genius of their respective languages. The story of Indian literatures until, say, the 19th century was mostly a story of creative translations, adaptations, re-tellings, interpretations, epitomes and elaborations of classical texts and translations from and into Sanskrit, Persian, Arabic and modern Indian languages knit together communities, languages, religions and cultures. The translations during the days of British occupation, dictated though they were by the colonial ideology of selective appropriation and cautious canonisation, also kept the process alive. Our attempts should be to restore the precolonial openness of the activity, even while relating it and rendering it relevant to our post-colonial context that has made the problematic of translation a site for raising questions of representation, power and historicity. We ought to be aware of the pitfalls of the colonial enterprise that attempted to produce a colonial form of subjectivity through technologies and practices of power/knowledge. Our attempt must be to overcome the asymmetrical relations of power that operated in the colonial era and turned translation into a strategy of containment and reinforcement of the hegemonic versions of the colonised as objects without history. Translation to us today is a way of retrieving our people's histories and recording their past and present.

Translation, especially in a multi-lingual country like India, has deep cultural implications. It is even a measure of the growth achieved by a language and also of the dominance of certain languages over others. Even the use of certain languages as filter languages for translation into other languages involves the question of power. When a work in an Indian language is translated into English, it entails the representation of a regional culture for a more powerful national/Indian regional culture; when made available outside India, it involves representing a national culture for a still more powerful international culture, which today unfortunately means Western culture. There is here an interplay of cross-cultural pride and prejudice, when one world is represented for the other in translation. The practice of translation in post-colonial contexts has given form not only to discourses of domination, but also of resistance. Translation theories so far have mostly been dominated by translations involving Western culture. It is necessary to relocate the theory and practice of translation within hitherto unexplored, Eastern, cultural contexts. Translation activity needs to be examined as policy, prioritisation, empowerment, enrichment and culture learning within post-colonial contexts, since cross-cultural relations are constituted not on an abstract transcultural universal of beauty, but on immediate encounters with other cultural systems. Translation is also a celebration of difference and a re-inventing of cultural identities. The choice of language signifies one's position in the social reality, and the conflict of codes functions as a representation of linguistic diversity. Translation activity constructs cultural identity by reframing the boundaries of the sayable and changing the terms of affiliation.

The question of authenticity became important to translations in India much later. Even the early translators of religious works like the *Bhagavat Gita,* while being true to its spirit were not always true to its words. Jnaneshwar, the Marathi Bhakti poet expounds the Gita, keeping in mind the average Marathi reader of his time. He admits humbly that it is beyond his capacity to expound this text; he compares himself to the *titibha* bird trying to sound the depth of the ocean with its tiny beak. At the same time, he is conscious of the gravity of his mission: 'I have clothed the *Gita* in the garment of Marathi but if there is no one who can recite it, there will be nothing missing. If *Gita is* to be recited, it won't be of less value if this Marathi version is used.'

Later he adds: 'The *Gita* is like a trusting mother from whom, I, her child, have wandered away.'

Thus there is fear of misrecognition, yet confidence that the translator has accomplished his task for public good. A later commentator, Dr S. Radhakrishnan, however, has reservations about translating a text like *Gita.* He says in his preface to his translation.

A translation to serve its purpose must be as clear as its substance will permit. It must be readable without being shallow, modern without being unsympathetic. But no translation of the *Gita* can bring out the dignity and grace of the original. Its melody and magic of phrases are difficult to recapture in another medium. The translator's anxiety is to render the thought, but he cannot convey fully the spirit. He cannot evoke in the reader the mood in which the thought was born and induce in him the ecstasy of the seer and the vision it holds.

Quoting this, R.C. Prasad, a translator of Tulsidas's *Ramcharit Manas,* says the words apply equally well to the translation of this great epic each of whose words evokes very specific native associations. The intertextuality of *Manas* renders the task more complicated as Tulsidas takes passages from Jayadeva's *Prasannaraghava,* Valmiki's *Ramayana,* the *Adhyatma Ramayana,* the *Hanuman-nataka* and Kalidasa's *Meghadoota, Raghuvamsa, Kumarasambhava,* etc., and polishes, sweetens and elevates them to produce a new *rasatmakata.* Agha Shahid Ali finds a similar difficulty in translating the eminent Urdu poet Faiz Ahmed

Faiz, for he used classical forms like *quasida, ghazal, masnavi, qita* and transformed them before his readers. Languages however do not share products but they have corresponding processes. A translation as Dilip Chitre observes, seeks to transcreate the process by which the source text was arrived at by reversing from a surface structure the journey to the inner course of events. The surface structure is not where we stop looking; it is where we intuitively enter the whole underlying process; it is where we begin to see. Translations describe and point to the source by making a model of it. Translation uses the imagination to treat one language as though it were an analogy for another. Referring to his own translation of the Marathi devotional poet, Tukaram, Dilip Chitre observes how in translating Tukaram we are not only translating poetry, but recreating a dramatic ritual of 'possessed' language. The text here is a total cultural performance that embodies a specific tradition and an individual notion of poetry, the poet and his audience. The English translator of Tukaram has to make his work appear here and now and yet suggest also that it is really out there. Tukaram has to remain a 17th-century, Marathi Bhakti poet and not a contemporary Englishman talking of mystical illumination in India.

All these examples show that the concern of the Indian translator has never been literal accuracy: that was an anxiety that came with the translation of the *Bible* and the *Quran*, and grew as a result of the impact of Western understanding. However, after several centuries the West has also begun to realise that 'translation is forever impossible and forever necessary.' The breakdown of traditional theories of linguistics based on the axiomatic relationship between the signifier and the signified, the consequent discovery of discourse as an endless deferral of reality, the loss of the unity of the subject and the redefinition of translation as an intense and intimate mode of reading have together challenged the old concept of the impossibility of translation. Texts are no more believed to be self-identical, having a theological meaning, but as multi-dimensional spaces where a variety of writings blend and clash. There is nothing like an 'authentic' original text and a unique authorial voice. If all works are polyphonic and polysemic, translation, like reading, is a fresh composition, a construction. There is no single authentic translation either; each translation can only be *one* translation, and not *the* translation since there is no pre-existent meaning but meaning depends upon an interventionist reader creating his/her own text. The translator has first to become the intimate reader in order to surrender to the text and respond to its special call. 'The Translator' to quote Gayatri Chakravorty Spivak, 'earns permission to transgress from the trace of the other—before memory—in the closest spaces of the self.' Translating is thus a simple miming of the responsibility to the trace of the other in the self.

All acts of translation are an attempt to mediate between cultures, texts and nationalities. We are however no longer certain about the meanings of these terms; a consensual approach to the definition of notions like Indian culture and sensibility are no longer available to us today. Most of us now understand the interface between translations and colonisation and the complicity of colonial administration, historiography, ethnology and missionary activities in the politics of containment. Literature uses words with which the people of a language community can associate the experience of their composite cultural past. The word is essentially a cultural memory in which the historical experience of the society is embedded. The society remembers and participates in this experience when this is put into a context. The translator has to recreate this participatory experience of the source language culture by recontextualising it in the target language culture so that the target language reader can in some sense participate in an alien cultural experience. Translation as cultural representation is a complex political act, which must foreground a series of significant questions: Who does the translation? Whose experience is being translated? Who is the author of the text? Who forms the target audience? What is the historical position of the respective figures involved in this act? And their affiliation in terms of class, gender and caste? The context, what Neitzsche calls 'effective history', becomes integral and indispensable to the act of translation. But this leads us to the questions related to the politics of translations, the kind of questions discussed by Tejaswini Niranjana and Gouri Viswanathan in the context of colonialism and English education in India. Today, however, India is independent enough to have her own agenda for translation, free from the Orientalist assumptions that underlay the colonial project. There is greater need today than ever before to bring our languages and literatures closer through translations within the country, while also translating from and into foreign languages: these are only two steps in the same direction: uniting the nation without standardising its cultures and bulldozing its diversity, and building bridges between our cultures and other cultures in the context of the growing human concerns that cut across national and linguistic borders, which is the positive aspect of intellectual globalisation.

Part Two
Authors and Texts

ANOTHER LIFE, ANOTHER POETICS
Bhakti, the First Movements

The Bhakti Movement saw a great revival and reenforcement of the alternative tradition of spiritual enquiry, subaltern religiosity and social protest in Indian poetry. Bhakti was by no means a monolithic movement: it was a polyphonic movement spread over 14 centuries—from the sixth to 19th, which accommodated conservatives as well as radicals. But even the conservatives like Tulsidas, the author of *Ramcharitmanas* who supported the status-quoist hierarchy based on *varna,* succeeded in creating a new poetic idiom with fresh dimensions of imagination. Some radical groups like the *Varkaris* of Marathi that included Namdev, Tukaram, Chokhamela and others, the *Veerashaivas* or *lingayats* of Karnataka that included Basavannna, Akka Mahadevi, Allama Prabhu and others and the Radhasoami Movement that included Swami Dayal Singh and Anand Swarup actually created alternative communities based on the principle of perfect equality of caste, creed and gender. The movement included Brahmins like Ekanath and Jnandev of Maharashtra, Chaitanya of Bengal/Orissa or Sankardev of Assam who de-brahminised themselves following *Sramana* ideology, *shudras* and *avarnas* or *atishudras* who approved of Brahmin superiority, like Ezhuthacchan of Kerala, and also marginalised sections like non-brahmin craftsmen, muslims and women who developed a subaltern, egalitarian vision of the new society like Dadu the cotton-carder, Namdev the tailor, Chowdayya the ferryman, Chokhamela the Mahar, Gora the potter, Ravi (Rai) Das the tanner, Kabir the weaver, the Sufis like Sheikh Farid, Bulle Shah and Sultan Bahu and women saints like Karaykkal Ammayar, Andal, Janabai, Bahinabhai, Gangasati, Lal Ded, Muktayakka, Mirabai and others. There were *Vaishnavites, Shaivites* and *Sakteyas* among them; there were also the followers of the *nirguna* cult and practitioners of *tantra.* However, they have enough common features to lend them the appearance of a movement. Some of these, applicable to most of the Bhakti writers and movements are (1) they have a predilection for pre-Aryan patterns of life and thought as implied in its rejection of Brahmin privilege, its egalitarian content and the tribal character of its collective worship, (2) they emphasised the similarities among different religions, found them to be only different paths leading to the same goal and even attempted syntheses of religions as in Sikhism founded by Guru Nanak and the Sufi cults, (3) Most of them rejected the *varna-jati* system and the Brahmin superiority, (4) they problematised the institution of priesthood by directly addressing God, (5) they privileged the oral tradition against the written, (6) they gave up Sanskrit and chose to compose in regional languages and dialects, (7) many of them travelled widely and were multi-lingual (e.g. Meera, Kabir, Nanak, Namdev, Vidyapati), (8) they created or introduced several new forms like *doha, pada, vachana, bijak, vakh, abhang, bharud, barahmasa, qasida, rasa* and *prabandha* and also several group performances like *kirtan, bhajan, dhun, jatra, harikatha, burrakatha, angkiyanat, nagarsankirtana, lila, thungi, Ramleela* and *Krishnaleela*, which gave rise to several classical and semi-classical forms later like *kathakali, thullal, yakshagana, Bharatanatyam, Kuchipudi, Manipuri* and *Odissi*, (9) Poetry and philosophy coexisted and supported each other and the barriers between the physical and the metaphysical became thin in their aesthetic-religious practice, (10) they developed a symbolism of their own, mixing traditional symbols like sky, river, tree, fire, bird etc., with symbols chosen from the kitchen and the workplace like the loom, wheel, knife, ladle, bellows, veil, sindoor etc, (11) they replaced the Vedic gods, mostly by pre-Aryan gods and goddesses. In short it was a comprehensive cultural revolution with profound ideological, aesthetic and practical implications that attempted to create an alternative religion of the people articulating subaltern aspirations.

The Movement exhibited most of these features in its very initial phase in the Tamil Bhakti poetry of the sixth to 13th century, especially of the Siddhas or Cittars qualified by Rev. Robert Caldwell, the linguist, as the anti-Brahmanical cycle of compositions. Thirumular, the sixth-century mystic proclaimed in a famous verse, 'Caste is one and God is one' (Verse 2104). His *Thirumantiram* deals primarily with Yoga and Tantra. He decried bigotry and preached equanimity and love in an age when Vedic and non-Vedic religions, Shaivism and Vaishnavism, Shaivasiddhanta and Sankara's Vedanta quarrelled with each other:

> Those who follow the six religions know him not
> Nor is he confined to those six faiths.
> Seek, and having sought cogitate in your mind
> And then without doubt you will gain salvation.
> (Verse 1533)

K. Kailasapathy points out there are more than 50 names associated with the Siddha School of Poetry. Strangely, Gorakh appears in the list of Siddhas and there is a traditional belief that Tirumular came from Kashmir and some other Siddhas came from Arabia, China and other distant lands; two Sufis, Pir Muhamed and Mastan Sahib, are also listed among them. What interests us here is that orthodox Shaiva Siddhantists held the Siddhas to be religious *panchamas* or outcastes. The Siddhas challenged the very foundations of medieval Hinduism; the authority of the Shastras, the validity of rituals and the basis of the caste system were often questioned by them. To quote Kamil Zvelebil, 'Almost all of them manifest a protest, expressed often in very strong terms, against the formalities of life and religion; denial of religious practices—and beliefs of the ruling classes.' These sentiments are forcefully expressed by the poem of Chivavakkiyar:

> The chanting of the four Vedas,
> The meticulous study of the sacred scripts
> The smearing of the holy ashes
> And the muttering of prayers
> Will not lead you to the Lord!...
> ...You dumb fools performing the rituals
> With care and in leisureliness.
> Do gods ever become stone?
> What can I do but laugh?
> (*Chittar Jnanakkovai*, Verse 121)

> Of what use are temples,
> And of what use are sacred tanks?
> (Ibid, Verse 29)

Pambatti Chittar also ridicules those fools who think that the flaw in a pan will go away if you rub it with tamarind. He goes on:

> We'll set fire to divisions of caste
> We'll debate philosophy in the market places
> We'll have dealings with despised households
> We'll go around in different paths.
> (Ibid., Verse, 123)

The Siddhas often refuted the theory of transmigration and rebirth too. Chivavakkiyar says:

> Milk does not return to the udder
> Likewise butter can never become butter-milk;
> The sound of the conch does not exist once it is broken;
> The blown flower, the fallen fruit, do not go back to the tree;
> The dead are never born again, never!
> (Ibid., Verse 43)

A grand remonstrance against almost everything that was held sacred characterises these poems. One reason for this dissent may lie in the caste/class origins of most of the Siddhas. Tradition tells us they included shepherds, temple-drummers, artificers, robbers, potters, fishermen, hunters, weavers, washermen, oil-pressers, pariahs and others. *Periya Puranam*, the hagiographical work of the 12th century that narrates the lives of 63 Shaiva saints supports this. Sikkilar, the author, a minister in the Chola court, portrays the saints, overcoming their caste origins and attaining spiritual glory through a life of dedication and love. They were well below the Brahmanas, Vellalas (agriculturists) and Vanigas (merchants) who constituted the ruling class in those times. They believed in brotherhood, disbelieved idol-worship and believed in a supreme Abstraction rather than a supreme Person. By imagining an impersonal Godhead, they freed themselves of rituals and other average Hindu observances. They attempted a synthesis of apparently diverse elements of Jnana, Bhakti and Yoga. Like the Indian Sufis, they rejected the mechanical and dreary aspects of Bhakti and cherished love, tenderness and compassion.

The poetry of the Siddhas is sustained by the simple colloquial expressions and speech patterns of the common people. It lacks the 'grammatical finesse' exalted in traditional poetry. These poets did not mind using even 'vulgar' and 'obscene' words; it was a language in which words were on purpose semantically polyvalent. In spite of their obscurities and profundities, the poems were accessible to any native speaker of the language. Over the centuries the Siddhas developed a cryptic, coded, secret, symbolic language of their own best-suited for oral transmission. Images, myths, symbols and histories were deployed by them for communicating their ineffable experience. Their tantric orientation also led them to the use of sexual symbols. Man-Woman intimacy is often used here to express the God-Soul relationship. Manikkavachakar's *Thirukkovaiyar* reads almost like a poem of love, separation and union. It is erotic and allegoric at the same time. The Siddhas were indifferent to accepted language or respectability in modes of expression as they found the established 'literary' culture oppressive. They framed an idiom that was private and colloquial at the same time, full of paradoxes, witticisms, wisecracks, epigrams and earthy adages. Their use of terse and telling phrases soon passed into the common language. They revolutionised Tamil religious-philosophic poetry by bringing into its world the language of folklore, a bold device that became irrevocable. It survived the neglect of the mainstream scholars to be revitalised by Subramania Bharati, Bharatidasan, Turaiyappa Pillai and others. In the best tradition of mystics, they transcended the polarisations of life and literature by mixing the sacred with the profane, the spiritual experience with the external event. Look at this puzzle-like poem by Tirumular:

> I sowed eggplant seed: jack sprouted
> I dug the dust; the pumpkin blossomed
> The garden folk took it away merrily;
> What was fully ripe was the banana fruit.

In this apparently absurd poem, the eggplant seed is yogic practice, the jacktree connotes freedom from worldly desires; digging the dust means philosophical speculations; the pumpkin flower signifies shivam manifesting itself, the garden folk are the sense organs, ripening is obtaining and the banana fruit is spiritual gain.

The Siddhas created and adopted several forms that suited the unorthodox, rebellious, non-conformist and incisive content of their poetry. They used traditional meters outlined in the *Tholkappiyam*, the pre-Christian treatise on grammar and poetics, like *akaval* (used in narratives), *venpa* (for didactical works) and some variations of *Kalippa* (for love poetry and choral music), the fourth meter they did not use being *vanchappa* (for descriptive situations). But they also exploited metrical forms that had no literary or grammatical sanction. They adapted melodies, tunes and meters of folksongs and workers' songs. Idaikkattu Chittar, for example, composed many songs in the form of shepherds' dialogues suggesting a pastoral milieu, Pambatti Chittar followed the model of snake-charmers' songs. Many Siddha songs are in the pliable and popular *chintu* form, with two-line stanzas often broken into four half-lines with initial or end-rhyme. Poets came to be known by the refrains they used, like Akappey Chittar or animals, birds and things that are directly addressed by the poet. Some (*akoppey*, 'the devil of the mind) or Kutampai Chittar (*kutampai*, literally an ear-ring, metonymically a girl wearing it). *Kummi*, a dance-song form and *kanni*, a two-line stanza form were popularised respectively by Kaduveli Chittar and Pattinattar. Form and content were inseparable in their poetry. Sufi mysticism easily co-existed with Siddha philosophy; medieval Tamilnadu and Sri Lanka have several cult sites that are the graves of Muslim sufi saints and pirs. Many celebrated Hindu shrines of Skanda are believed to have been constructed on or near the tombs of Muslim sufi saints as these sites were considered sacred, and the dead saints propitious. Their nonsectarian, anti-establishment philosophy unflinchingly critical of smug religiosity and the oral lore they used together made them extremely popular; they became the voice of the voiceless.

The Siddhas also considered the body sacred. The body according to Thirumular is not only a fit instrument for the progress of the soul in its spiritual journey but it is the actual abode of God: 'The mind is the sacred chamber/the physical body is the temple/for my gracious Lord the mouth is the tower gate.' He also says, 'Those who let the body decay destroy the spirit... I fostered the body, and I fostered the soul.' This is in contrast to much of the mainstream religious teachings that decry the body as evil and unholy. This robust acceptance of life and of physicality must also have endeared them to the common people who led a life of tedium. There was a stoic acceptance even of the saddest experience of life in the Siddhas, barring a few pessimists among them. Thirumular has this famous line, 'May the world be as happy as I am'. The Siddhas, in short, were the harbingers of a vigorous and germane counter-tradition that is part of the dialectics of our cultural history. By 'counter-tradition' I mean what Louis Kampf means by it: not one 'that opposes tradition', but the 'tradition that opposes'.

For the Veersaiva (or Lingayata) poets' religion was not a given, it was something to be attained through faith and constructed through a life-style. Thus it was not a question of chance, but of choice. Hence change and conversion are possible here. Several scholars (Sisir Kumar Das, Birinchikumar Barua, A.K. Ramanujan) have compared this movement to Lutherian reformation that critiqued the Roman Church and provoked the clergy. Lingayatism emerged as a militant religious movement during the reign of the Kalachurya King, Bijjala II (1100–1167). The rule of Kalachuryas was characterised by the dominance of traditional Brahmanical Hindu values, a social system based on caste and a polity and economy governed by feudal principles. Three mutually reinforcing institutions—the court, the temple and the Mahajana Agrahara settlement— supported the Kingdom. The traditional Shaivism of the Kalamukha priests had become indistinguishable from the mainstream Brahmanical Hinduism that perpetuated hierarchy, exploitation and superstition. Lingayatism, while being Shaivite, questioned the status-quoist brand of Shaivism. Basavanna, its master-organiser, wanted to overthrow this exploitative order and replace it with a new society based on freedom, equality, rationality and brotherhood. Basava's *vachana*s (prose-lyrics) are replete with caustic comments on the institution of caste. e.g. 'To him who has self-understanding there is but one caste' (*Vachana,* 878: Tr. R.C. Hiremath) or 'The birthless has no caste distinctions, no ritual pollution' (No. 417) or 'The murderer is an untouchable, the eater of filth is untouchable!' (No. 590). K. Ishwaran points out that the equality of man is associated with his equal right to have access to God. Thus man's belief in God becomes the basis of Basava's egalitarianism. Further, the assumption of equality is related to individuality, since a man should be judged not by the ascriptive criterion of who he is but rather by the achievement criterion of what he has done. He asks in a popular *vachana:* 'Of what avail the reading of the *Veda?* Listening to *sastra*s? Performing ritual meditation?' (No. 598). Again, 'Shall I call *sastra* great? It glorifies Karma. Shall I call *veda* great? It enjoins animal sacrifices.' He points to the futility of orthodox Hindu modes of knowledge and comes close to a form of naturalistic humanism. He rejects the notions of Karma and rebirth and questions bookish religion:

> Sir, isn't the mind witness enough
> for the taste on the tongue?
> Do buds wait for the garlandmakers' word
> to break into flower?
> Is it right, Sir, to bring out the texts
> for everything?
> And, Sir, is it really right to bring into open
> the mark on our vitals
> left by our lord's love-play?
> (No. 848, Tr. A.K. Ramanujan)

He decries also the concepts of heaven and hell: 'There is no other heaven and hell/Truth-speaking is heaven, lying hell./Performance of right conduct, heaven; its non-performance, hell' (No. 239, Tr. R.C. Hiremath). He recommends a rigorous commitment to empirical reality and rejects escapism: 'Let what is supposed to come tomorrow come to us today itself/What is supposed to come today, come to us this moment' (No. 696).

Basava asked the people not to take threats of punishment from Brahmins based on supernatural mechanisms and said that sin and merit—*papa* and *punya*—are creatures of our fashioning. He also pointed to the gulf between precept and practice of the upper castes: 'They tread one path while their *Sastra* treads another' (No. 574). *Sansara* was salvation for him and the only community was the universal community of man:

Our untouchable Channayya is my father,
Drummer Kakayya is grandpa,
Look, Chikkayya is our father,
Flutist Bommayya is brother.
How can they not know me?

The body was important to him also as to the Siddhas:

Make my body the beam of a lute,
Of my head the sounding gourd
Of my nerves the strings
Of my fingers the plucking rods.
Clutch me close
And play your thirty-two songs
O lord of the meeting rivers!

Again,

The rich will make temples for Siva.
What shall I, a poor man, do?

> My legs are pillars, the body the shrine
> The head a cupola of gold.
> Listen, O lord of the meeting rivers,
> Things standing shall fall
> But the moving ever shall stay. (No. 820)

The last two lines reassert the poet's faith in life, movement and change. The stoic acceptance of suffering we found in the Siddhas recurs here: 'He'll grind till you're fine and small./He'll file till your colour shows./If your grain grows fine in the grinding, If you show colour in the filing,/then our lord of the meeting rivers/will love you and look after you' (No. 686). Basava laughed at the multiplicity of gods in India:

> The pot is a god.
> The winnowing fan is a god.
> The stone in the street is a god.
> The comb is a god.
> The bowstring is also a god.
> The bushel is a god
> and the spouted cup is a god.
> Gods, gods, there are so many,
> there's no place left for a foot. (No. 563)

He laughed at religious rituals and customs like holy baths and sacrifices: 'They plunge wherever they see water./They circumambulate every tree they see./How can they know you, 0 Lord,/who adore waters that run dry, trees that wither?' (No. 581) Or:

> In a brahmin house
> where they feed the fire as a god,
> when the fire goes wild and burns the house,
> they splash on it the water of the gutter
> and the dust of the street
> beat their breasts

and call the crowd.
These men then forget their worship
and scold their fire. (No. 586)

He said he cannot believe in a god who ate up lacquer and melted and wilted before fire, or a god that people sold in their need or buried for fear of thieves.

The celebration of the nobility of human labour was another feature of Basava's poetry as well as Veerasaiva philosophy. One *vachana* says, 'Kayaka is Kailasa'. Kayaka is not only the labour for livelihood; it is work for the society. The fruit of labour is to be shared by others. Community co-operation is built into Basava's idea of the work ethic. Basava's efforts to build an alternative community along with the *saranas,* his devoted colleagues, based on modern values was as important as his attempts to revive the oral tradition and employ spoken language instead of Sanskrit to communicate his message. The institution *Dasoha* also tended to generate a sense of sharing between free and rational individuals. The love the *vachanakara*s preached went beyond the human race and had an ecological and cosmic dimension. Dasareswara says in one of his *vachana*s:

Knowing one's lowliness
at every word;
the spray of insects in the air
in every gesture of the hand,
things living, things moving
come sprung from the earth
under every footfall;
and when holding a plant
or joining it to another
or in the letting it go
to be all mercy
to be light
as the dusting brush

of peacock feathers:
such moving, such awareness
is love that makes us one,
with the Lord Dasreswara.

Dasreswara did not even pick flowers to offer them to a god; he gathered only blossoms that fell of themselves. A Kannada saying asks, 'Where is religion without loving-kindness?' The *Vachanas* express kinship with all things, love of man and bird and beast and tree. Basava laughs at those who say 'Pour, pour the milk!' when they see a snake image in stone and cry 'Kill, Kill!' when they meet a real snake. The Veerasaivas shared the principle of *ahimsa* with Buddhism and Jainism, though they rejected the determinist idea of *karma* with its inexorable chain of action and consequence that bound individuals with no hope of grace and also opposed the special privileges Jains enjoyed in contemporary society. Basavanna and Dasimayya desperately struggled against Brahminism and Jainism and had to suffer its consequences. The *vachanakara*s privileged experience over the received (*sruti*) and the remembered (*smriti*). Chowdayya the Ferryman says: 'When the winds of the Lord's grace lash, quickly quickly winnow, winnow' ('winnow when the wind blows' is a common proverb in many languages). This grace cannot be purchased by offerings to god and priest, temple-going, pilgrimage, ritual, following sacred space and sacred time: Veerasaivas were horrified of the bargaining and the manipulation involved in the regular religious practices and believed purely in the Divine Experience that one can only wait for. They believed in an unmediated vision. Like the European Protestants, they returned to what they felt was the original inspiration of the ancient traditions. A.K. Ramanujan, following Victor Turner (*The Ritual Process*) calls the Veerasaiva movement—like some other Bhakti movements—an 'anti-structure' developed out of the elements of the structure they reject. Here the hierarchy of the Guru, the Elders and the Novices is based on mystical achievement and not on birth or occupation. Like the Siddhas, Veerasaivas came from all classes and castes—laundrymen, boatmen, leather workers, etc.

Again, like the Siddhas, the *Vachanakaras* also produced their own form of poetry with its implied oral poetics. As against *sruti* (what is heard) and *smriti* (what is memorised), the *vachana* is something uttered here and now. A.K. Ramanujan observes that both the classical (in Sanskrit and in the regional languages) and folk literature of India work with well-established languages of convention, given personae, and elaborate metrical patterns that mediate and depersonalise literary expression. The literary ideal is impersonality. But vachanas are personal literature, personal in several senses such as:

Many of them express the real conflicts of real persons, represent a life more fully than anything in the older literature. For instance, Basavanna speaks of himself as the minister of a non-Virasaiva king, accused by his own men of betraying his god for a king.

They are uttered, not through a persona or mask, but directly in the person of the poet himself, in his native local dialect and idiom, using the tones and language of personal conversation or outcry.

Even the few given conventional stances of bhakti are expressed in terms of deeply-felt personal relations; the loves and frustrations of bhakti are those of lover and beloved (e.g., Mahadevi), mother and child, father and son, master and servant, even whore and customer.

Compared to other Indian religious literatures like the Vedic hymns, the *vachana*s describe the devotee's state directly and the god only by implication; the concern is with the subject rather than the object (of worship).

Though medieval Kannada was rich in native Dravidian metres, and in borrowed Sanskritic forms, no metrical line or stanza is used in *vachana*s. The saints did not follow any of these models. Basavanna said:

> I don't know anything like timebeats and metre
> nor the arithmetic of strings and drums;
> I don't know the count of iamb and dactyl.
> My lord of the meeting rivers,
> As nothing will hurt you
> I'll sing as I love. (No. 949)
> It is not even he that sings; the Lord sings through him.

The *vachana* is thus a rejection of premeditated art, the *sthavaras* of form. It is not only a spontaneous cry but a cry for spontaneity—for the music of a body given over to the lord.

The traditional time-beat, like the ritual gesture, was felt to be learned, passive, inorganic; too well organised to be organic. Here too, the *sthavara,* the standing thing, shall fall, but the *jangama* shall prevail.

However, in the free-seeming verse, there are always patterns that loom and withdraw, figures of sound that rhyme and ring bells with the figures of meaning. It is not surprising that M. Chidananda Murti has shown how the *vachana* metre actually has a *tripadi-base. Tripadi* is a popular 3-line form of the oral tradition used widely both in folk song and in folk epigram.

Scholars like Parry and Lord have studied the techniques of oral verse-making in folk-epics. They have paid little attention to shorter forms. Several features noted for heroic oral poetry do appear in the *vachana*s: in particular, a common stock of themes that occur in changing forms, repetitions of phrases and ideas and the tendency to use cycles or sequences of poems. But the extensive use of formulae and metonomy in the strict sense and a distinct given prosody, both characteristic of the oral bardic traditions, are generally absent in the *vachana,* a genre of epigram and lyric.

The *vachanakara*s, however, did use stock phrases, proverbs and religious commonplaces of the time. This stock, shared by Southern and Northern saints, the Upanishads and the folk alike, included figures, symbols and paradoxes often drawn from an ancient and pan-Indian pool of symbiology.

Yet it should not be imagined that the common stock was used in exactly similar ways. Only the components were the same; the functions, the emerging meanings, were often startlingly different. For instance, the image of the insect weaving a web out of its body is an ancient one. The *Brhadaranyaka Upanishad* has this description of Brahman, the creator:

As a spider emerges (from itself) by
(spinning) threads [out of its own body]...

So too from this self do all the life-breaths,
all the worlds, all the gods, and all contingent beings
rise up in all directions.

Mahadeviyakka says the following:

Like a silkworm weaving
her house with love
from her marrow,
and dying
in her body's threads winding tight, round and round,
I burn
Desiring what the heart desires.
Cut through, O lord, my heart's greed, And show me
Your way out
O lord white as Jasmine. (Akka: 17)

Note the startling difference in the feeling-tone of these passages, the coolness of the *upanishad* and the woman-saint's heart-rending cry for release. The classical text describes the subject, the Cosmic creator; the *vachana* describes the subject, the speaker's feelings towards herself. The one describes creation by and out of the creator; the other describes the self trammelled in its self-created illusions. One speaks of the birth of worlds, awesome, wondrous, non-human; the other speaks of a death, small, calling for compassion, all too human.

Though Basavanna says in the poem quoted earlier, 'I'll sing as I love,' rejecting conventional patterns of verse-making, the *vachana*s evolve a distinctive structure (as, in the religious dimension, anti-structure develops into a counterstructure). Their metre is not syllabic but syntactic; the regularities and returning units are not usually units of sound, but units of syntax and semantics. The oral origins of the poetry are clear in its favourite structure. The poetics of the *vachana* is an oral poetics.

The range of *vachana* expression spans a pan-Indian stock of figures, homely images of everyday experience, the sense and idiom of the earth, as well as an abstruse esoteric symbolism. The esoteric *vachana*s are called *bedagina vachana* (fancy poems), more riddle than poem and, oftentimes, with a whole occult glossary for key. This glossary is made up of a common pool of symbols and concepts drawn from yogic psychology and tantric philosophy. Allamaprabhu, the most metaphysical of the *vachanakara*s, has many *bedagina vachana*s, e.g.,

> They don't know the day
> is the dark's face,
> and dark the day's.
> A necklace of nine jewels
> lies buried, intact, in the face of the night;
> in the face of day a tree
> with leaves of nine designs.
> When you feed the necklace
> to the tree,
> the Breath enjoys it
> In the Lord of the Caves. (No. 218)

The paradoxical images of this poem have a surrealist brilliance in themselves. To a learned Virasaiva, the poem would mean the following: The night and day are obviously ignorance and awareness. It is in the experience of the ignorant that we find the jewel of wisdom, a necklace of nine lingas. In awareness is knowledge and discrimination (the tree), carefully nurtured. But only when the wisdom of the ignorant experience is fed to the discrimination of the aware, the Linga of the Breath finds true joy.

Such a dark, ambiguous language of ciphers (*sandhyabhasa* or 'intentional language') has been much discussed by scholars of Yoga and Tantra. Riddles and enigmas were used even in Vedic times. In the heterodox and esoteric cults, such systems of cryptography were intended to conceal the secret doctrine from the uninitiated and the outsider. But riddle and paradox are also meant to shatter the ordinary language of ordinary experiences, baffling the rational intelligence to look through the glass darkly till it begins to see. It is 'a process of destroying and reinventing language' till we find ourselves in 'a universe of analogies, homologies, and double meanings'. A related device is a favourite with *vachana*s: extended metaphor, a simile which projects a whole symbolic situation suppressing one part of the comparison. One of the most moving uses of the extended analogue is Mahadeviyakka's love of God, where all the phases of love become metaphors for the phases of mystical union and alienation. For instance:

> I have Maya for mother-in-law;
> the world for father-in-law;
> three brothers-in-law like tigers;
> and the husband's thoughts
> are full of laughing women:
> no god, this man.
> And I cannot cross the sister-in-law.
> But I will
> Give this wench the slip
> and go cuckold my husband with Hara, my lord.
> My mind is my maid:
> by her kindness, I join
> my Lord,
> my utterly beautiful Lord from the mountain-peaks
> my lord as white as jasmine
> and I will make Him
> my good husband. (Akka, 328)

Mahadeviyakka's poem explicitly takes over conventions of Indian love-poetry (available in Sanskrit as in the regional languages). An *abhisarika,* a woman stealing out of a houseful of relatives to meet her lover, is the central image. The method is the method of allegory, explicitly equating, one-for-one, various members of a household with various abstractions: Maya or Primal Illusion is the mother-in-law. Some of the equations are implicit, and they draw on a common background of philosophical concepts. For instance, the three brothers-in-law are the three *gunas,* the three ultimate components which make all the particulars of nature what they are; these three are inescapable as long as one is part of nature, they keep a tiger-vigil. The husband is Karma, the past of the ego's many lives. The sister-in-law, who also keeps the speaker imprisoned, is apparently the *vasana,* the binding memory or 'smell' that the Karma-Past carries with it. The kind confidante or maid is the Mind, who alone helps her meet her Lord and keep the tryst.

A third important movement that created an alternative community is the *Warkari* movement of Maharashtra whose creative influence has been felt in a variety of forms by several social and political revolts in India from Shivaji's rebellion in the 17th Century to Gandhi's in the 20th. The movement was mostly led and sustained by underprivileged classes and survived trying times by its autonomous, unique and broad-based style of life, thought and expression. The 13th century Mahanubhav movement established by Chakradhar (1194–1276), though led by learned Brahmins, had also disregarded the Vedas, attacked Brahmanism, offered equal status to women and *shudra*s and was supported by the marginalised sections of the society. But after Chakradhar was killed by the supporters of the Brahmin orthodoxy, they could not innovate their technique of organisation and expression. Their esoteric scripts, strange costume and monastic establishments alienated them from the people. *Warkaris* adpted a more inclusive approach, welcomed people from all sections, had a simple dress code, discouraged *sanyasa* and *jnanamarga,* had no fixed establishments that could be destroyed by the Muslim rulers, had only small village temples and idols of the tolerant God *Vitthal* used as a symbol and a connecting emblem, left no documents but only preached and sang and gave opportunities to its members to meet one another during the holy pilgrimage to Pandharpur, sacred to *vitthal.* Their saints included Brahmin outcastes humiliated by the orthodoxy like Jnandev and his brothers, liberal Brahmins persecuted for their radical views like Ekanath and Bahinabai as well as *shudras* like Namdev the tailor and Tukaram the pedlar, who was persecuted and tried and had his verses (*abhangs*) thrown into the river by the Brahmin priests.

Namdev (1270–1350) seems to be the first revolutionary saint-poet about whose life some information is available. A closer look at his life is necessary, as he was certainly the first to strengthen the expressive techniques of the movement. Son of a *shudra* tailor, he was the most respected leader of his time because he organised a whole group of active men from all communities under the banner of the *Warkari* cult. A widely travelled man, he is believed to have received the new ideas of *Bhakti* from the South, and there is evidence that he spread them in the North in the early 14th century. As the *Bhakti* cult expounded by him was broad in structure, it spread rapidly in the North in the late 14th century, absorbing spontaneously various regional varieties of worship without any conflict. He was a close associate of the pioneers of the *Bhakti* movement in the North. His ideas even obliterated the borders between Hinduism and Islam by pointing out the bigoted character of both these religions, in effect developing a strategy to criticise the two major enemies—Muslims and Brahmans. He became, therefore, the most popular literary-religious leader of the downtrodden of his times, cutting across both the rigid faiths. He says in one of his Hindi songs:

> The Hindu is blind and the Muslim is cross-eyed,
> A saint is certainly better than both of them.
> The Hindu worships his temple; the Muslim worships his mosque,
> Namadev will worship neither the temple nor the mosque.

In one of the Hindi *pada*s, he says:

> Give up all worship,
> all debates,
> all activity.
> Give up all distinctions,
> Keep your mind on Govind. (*Pada* 63)
> Another *pada* says:
> These clowns

> with their sacred beads
> and rosaries
> know nothing about truth.
> They see nothing
> but claim to give insight
> to others.
> Can deception lead to liberation! (*Pada* 64)

He ridiculed those who performed horse-sacrifices, gave gold in charity, offered rice-balls in Gaya, lived in sacred Banaras, chanted Vedas and carried out the six Brahmin duties (*yajna, yajana, adhyayana, adhyapana, dana and pratigraha*). In a curt statement he says:

> I gather no leaves
> for rituals offerings.
> There is no god
> in the shrine. (*Pada* 65)

His attitude to the body was similar to that of the Veerashaivas and yet different. 'The body is false,/says Namdev./And yet it is real/if Ram is your lover' (*Pada* 78). He gave up idols when he understood the Truth: 'I had my faith in iron and copper./I had chains around my feet./But now I have no fear of this ocean of *samsar*' (*Pada* 68).

With this broad foundation, Namdev spread his cult, which did not even have any particular name. His verses were incorporated in the Holy *Granth Sahib* by the later Sikh *gurus*. His method of challenging Muslim fanaticism and Brahman domineering was subtle and full of humility, disarming and apologetic; but at all stages of his activity he was very sure of his means and ends. Most effective in his quiet revolt, he was the first to accept the untouchable communities in his liberal sect. A contemporary poetess Janabai, a slave-girl, describes him as 'the Head of a Joint family of saint-poets'. She describes him in another lyric as 'a half-naked figure, dancing wildly on the sands of the Chandrabhaga at Pandharpur, singing his lyrics, preaching his radical principles to the crowd.' This is the first reference in *Warkari* lore to the popularity of the revolutionary style of 'preaching while singing' or *Kirtan*. Namdev himself says:

> We will dance in the Kirtan,
> And light the lamps of knowledge in this world.

Namdev advised the common folk, 'We should express openly in order to forget our sorrow, temptation and suffering.' This advice was taken by his family and his followers.

Those were the days when men suffered not only from foreign aggression, war, famine and ruin, but from inner problems which were probably more terrible. In such a society, the poor *Warkaris* gained confidence on the strength of their expression. Without political support or social status, the poor oppressed communities of *shudras* suddenly learned that they had a voice. Now they could protest and question. For example, Janabai could say, 'Nothing wrong to be a woman, the Saints taught me this.' Again, one of Namdev's fellow *Warkaris* and followers, Chokha Mela (d. 1338), an Untouchable, would bitterly address Vitthal in his lyric:

> I am an Untouchable, how can I worship you?
> They drive me out, how can I meet you?
> At my slightest touch, they have to purify themselves,
> My God Vitthal! I pray for your mercy.

His wife, son and brother also speak of the inhuman conditions forced on the Untouchables. Despite starvation, humiliation and helplessness, their struggle to breathe in the free air of equality is characteristic of the liberating influence of *bhakti* on the outcastes. Chokha's son Karma Mela, a young man, describes the wretched condition of his community:

> We never have good food to eat,
> We live disgracefully in this world,
> God! You have a good time,

> Only misery has come to our lot.
> Elsewhere he says, with more confidence:
> God! You have your limitations,
> I'll have to find the way myself.

And about three centuries later, Tukaram (1608–1650), whose daily *kirtan*s at his small village Dehu gathered crowds from distant places, became the most vocal enemy of the Brahman orthodoxy. 'To censure this world has come to my lot,' was his full conviction, so he could fearlessly say:

> A Brahman who believes in contamination is not a Brahman,
> Suicide is the only expiation for such a Brahman.

Thus the *Warkari* tradition developed in the natural course certain effective means of self-expression and mass education which were initiated by Namdev. By any measure, Namdev's revolt was stupendous. He could dissolve the infernal divisions of humanity within Hindu society by the winning strategies of expression.

Apart from the natural functions of literature, such as entertainment and the preservation and dissemination of knowledge within society, the *Warkari* literature is also found to be acting as an agent of social change. Thus, the creative use of language as action became a stylistic device with which the saint-poets influenced the larger plane of society. The predominance of oral expression in the *Warkari* movement has other socio-linguistic dimensions as well, namely, that this verbal expression saved the *Warkari* leaders from depersonalisation, as it was the only available means for the oppressed people to employ safely. The oral techniques of expression needed to be strengthened. For example, Tukaram glorifies the use of words; thus:

> We possess the wealth of words,
> With weapons of words we will fight,
> Words are the breath of our life,
> We will distribute this wealth of words among the people,

Tuka says, look! The meaning of Word is God,
With Word we will extol and worship.

Creative experience made Tukaram feel even superior to the learned Brahmans:

We alone know the real meaning of the Vedas,
Others only bear the burden of it.
Food eaten is not to be compared with food seen...
Tuka says, we have found the root,
Of its own the fruit will be in our hands.

Tukaram believed in the spontaneity of his poetry:
I am no guru.
I rain like a cloud. Listen O Saints,
The sound you hear
Is the falling of rain.
It's baby-talk.
It comes from God,
The beginning of speech.

Tukaram also had a sense of black humour when it came to describing his painful experiences, like his wife's quarrels with him, his growing debts, the death of his children and even his early failures to realise the Lord. He often quarrelled with his God, wept, complained and even abused him, thus proving his God to be all too human:

Whenever I address you,
I find your back turned to me.
That is how I have learned
To understand your feeling for me.

Or, 'A king may not grant land to the landless./But wouldn't he at least ensure/That his subjects get a meal?/After all, a king must protect/The myth of his benevolence' or:

> My wife died:
> May she rest in peace.
> The Lord has removed
> My attachment.
> My children died.
> So much the better.
> The Lord has removed
> The last illusion.
> My mother died
> In front of my eyes.
> My worries are all over.

But when it came to attacking hypocrisy, Tukaram was always sharp:

> In this Age of Evil poetry is an infidel's art:
> The world teems with theatrical performers.
> ...They cite Vedic injunctions but
> Can't do themselves any good.
> The brahmin who flies into a rage at the touch of a mahar
> —That's no brahmin.
> The only absolution for such a brahmin
> Is to die for his own sin.
> He who refuses to touch a chandal
> Has a polluted mind.
> Says Tuka, a man is only as chaste
> As his own belief.

Or see the way he laughs at the tantrics:

> His teaching begins when the sun goes down.
> Drawing mystic squares on the ground,
> decorating them too, he worships occult designs.
> Placing lamps in all four corners and behind curtains
> He assumes a posture and demonstrates tantric gestures...
> His preaching over, time to start the feast

> ...Committing sacrilege is his means of livelihood:
> He sends his followers into the bottomless pit.
>
> Elsewhere he says:
> Nobody becomes a saint by making poems...
> Being a saint's kin
> A saint is not known by the manner of his dress...
> by his family's name
> A saint does not wait for the chance to become a saint
> Nobody becomes a saint by carrying a begging bowl...
> only by wearing rags...
> by delivering songs and sermons...
> by telling sacred myths...
> by reciting the Vedas...
> by performing rites...
> through penance or pilgrimage...
> by living alone in forests...
> merely wearing beads...
> merely wearing ashes.

Later he says a saint is one 'who experiences Cosmic Being' and 'see all through as equal, covet nothing, violate nothing.' The sense of the sacredness of beings we found in Basava reappears in Tukaram:

> Don't kill a snake
> Before the eyes of a saint
> For the saint's being
> Includes all living things
> And he's easily hurt.
> A single hair plucked from one's body
> Causes instant pain
> And the soul that perceives
> Life as a community, always suffers.

In the *Warkari* literary tradition, both the written and the oral cultures, along with several intermediate forms like *purana, harikatha, parayana, pravachana* and *pothi* were popular at one and the same time. These forms of expression needed group co-operation of various communities from Brahmans to the Untouchables, and they reflect several aspects of literature as a social institution. On the whole, they are pointers to the social synthesis of the upper and the lower classes in the making, however slow it may have been. The *Warkari* cult has evolved several oral styles of expression over all these centuries, utilising the traditional as well as folk forms. There are the traditional forms like *purana, pravachana, parayana* and *patha*. The creative literary forms like *ovi, abhang, pada, bhupali, gana, gavalan, virani, shloka, Krishnaleela* and verse biography have been immensely popular. Numerous musical-dramatic forms like *gondhal, rupak, bhedik, lalit, kakad arati and shej arati, goph, garud* and *bharud* are performed on certain occasions. *Mantra, namasmaran* and *haripath* are for individual worship, while *katha, pothi, saptah, kala, palakhi, dindi, vari, bhajan* and *kirtan* demand large social gatherings. In all these forms, the villagers have a full role to play and their creative talents are expressed fully. However, the most characteristically institutional of the *Warkari* forms is *kirtan*.

The *Warkari* cult has evolved styles which are best suited to the resources of the underprivileged classes and, therefore, it never attempted to go beyond the moderate range of social change and preferred to work within the broad Hindu tradition. With these limitations, how far the cult could go towards satisfying the spiritual needs of society as a whole, is itself an independent subject of study.

STRATEGIES OF SUBVERSION
Sramana Elements in Sarala Dasa's Mahabharata

The history of Indian literature has been a history of continuities and discontinuities, consolidation of authority and conflict with it, the hegemony of tradition and innovative heresy, in short, of power and subversion. It is possible to look at these trends as two dialectical if not antithetical streams or first and second traditions of our literature. With some risk of generalisation, I would like to call this second stream the *Sramana* tradition, as opposed to the first that is primarily a Vedic/*Brahmana* tradition. The conflict here, let me clarify at the very outset, is between two world views or ideological systems, not between religions or castes and one's traditions are more a matter of conscious choice and intellectual construction than of mere birth. Proofs of the profound struggle between the two *weltanschauungs* can be found in the writings of Patanjali, the Buddhist and the Jaina thinkers, Asoka's edicts, Megasthenes, ancient Chinese pilgrims like Huen-tsang and in the Arab documents of the second century A.D., that speak of two religious traditions of India called *Breihima* and *Samanya*. These two streams, however, have not always remained in conflict but have also had dialogues and interactions so that they are often found interwoven in the history of our thought and of literature. In later times the two kinds of attitudes were called *Pravrtti-dharma* and *Nivrtti-dharma*. Classical Brahmanical tradition as well as some modern historians attribute both the outlooks to the Vedic tradition—*Pravrtti* to the ritualistic side of the Vedic religion and *Nivrtti* to its agnostic side, or to *Karma-Kancja* and *Alanokancla* respectively. Modern scholars like Jacobi and Oldenberg attribute the gnostic and ascetic traditions of Indian spirituality to a reformist school within the Vedic tradition evidenced by the Upanishadic literature, as also by the *dharmasatras*. Buddhist and Jaina ascetics are then believed to continue this reformist and anti-ritualistic trend. Against this, some scholars (e.g., R.P. Chanda, S.K. Chatterji, and G.C. Pande) attribute them to different ethnic traditions, Aryan and non-Aryan, the ascetic tradition being attributed to the latter.

Some other scholars attribute the rise of the ascetic movements to the social changes implicit in the break-up of tribal society, rise of classes and castes and the various changes ushered in by the Second Urban Revolution. Whatever be the origin of the distinction between *Pravrtti* and *Nivrtti,* the distinction itself is of vital importance in the understanding of composite Indian culture that has its own inner dialectic. G.C. Pande points to a Vedic phase emphasising *Pravrtti,* a post-Vedic phase of ascetic movements emphasising *Nivrtti* and beyond it, a phase of synthesis that led to the creation of an almost uniform religion of asceticism and devotionalism in the medieval period. Sarala Dasa belongs to this Bhakti movement that began in the sixth and seventh centuries A.D. in Tamil with the *alweirs* and *nayanmars,* produced the great *vacanakaras* of Kannada in the 11th and 12th centuries and had its impact in the later centuries in the North, giving rise to great saint poets and philosophers like Lal Ded, Caitanya, Tukaram, Namdeva, Jnanadeva, Gora, Chokkamela, Raidas, Kabir, Meerabai and the great epic poets like Sarala Dasa himself and others like Krittibasa, Balarama Dasa and Ekanatha, joined by their contemporaries from the South like Pampa, Kambar and Ezhutacchan. The Bhakti movement that was undoubtedly the greatest spiritual revolution in the history of our civilisation was essentially a new flowering of the *Sramana* tradition, mostly subaltern in its social origins, as the majority of these poets came from the marginalised sections of the society like workers, peasants and rural craftsmen or were underprivileged by their caste origins, or by being women oppressed by a patriarchal society or Muslims, thus belonging to the minorities. This also defined its—at least in the majority of cases—denial of the Vedas, its rejection of *Pravrtti* or rituals, its opposition to differences of caste and even religion, its suspicion of the priestly class and even its substitution of Sanskrit by the languages spoken by the common people. The whole movement, taken collectively, can be seen as an attempt to form an alternative people's religion that rejects the hierarchies based on birth and the body and on physical, political and economic power, foregrounds the equality of all created beings, and posits a God who is directly accessible to all beings without priestly intervention, visits to places of worship, offerings and rituals. The Sufi literature of India, like the poetry of Bulle Shah, Shah Abdul Latif or Baba Farid is an extension of Bhakti literature in its basic concerns and concepts where the Islamic idea of equality and fraternity is interwoven with the ideas of Indian mysticism, both *Yogic* and *Tantric*.

2

Before examining Sarala Dasa for his subversive and deconstructive reading of *Mahabharata* that takes off from the *Sramana* tradition and employs several of its concepts and its technologies of subversion, I shall briefly examine some of the key *sramanic* ideas that give the tradition a distinct identity. *Sramana* sects did not believe in the authority of the Vedas nor in the existence of God in the sense of a personal creator or determiner of destiny. Hence the *Sramana* philosophies were later described as *nastika* or nihilist, even though originally *nastika* could apply only to materialists like Carvaka. Patanjali speaks of three categories, *astika* who believes that it exists, *nastika* who believes that it does not exist and *daistika* who believes that it is fated. The *Padamanjari* identifies *nastika* with *laukayatika* while *daistika* is a fatalist like Maskari Gosala, the founder of the *ajivikas* the wandering ascetics who deny the freedom of action or will and declare that one should not engage in actions since quiescence constitutes the greater good—an attitude similar to the Taoist one. This denial of free will did not mean the denial of the power of *karman* as the determinant of destiny. Since the belief in the other world also rested on the belief in *karman,* the real issue which divided the three groups was the issue of *karman* that also constituted the essential doctrine of the *gramands* that created a phenomenal thought ferment in the sixth century B.C., which according to R.G. Bhandarkar, was anti-Vedic in the north-east of India and conciliatory and integrative in the north-west. Buddhist and Jaina literatures represent the former tendency, while *Gita* represents the latter. This intellectual ferment can also be traced to the Upanishads that give evidence of heterodox thinkers who did not accept the Vedic tradition (Ranade, Belvalkar); perhaps it can be traced further back, since there are references to *munis* and *yatis* in Vedic literature itself. The essence of this heterodoxy consisted of ascetic practices and the doctrine of *karma* and rebirth—and it may date back to the Indus civilisation. The *sramanic* idea of a beginningless cycle of lives, governed by an overarching law of *karman* from which freedom could come only by total renunciation of all the claims and impulses of instinctive life, falls outside the purview of early Vedic thought. The Upanishadic point of view is a space of possible interaction between *Brahmanism* and *Sramanism* that became real later and had its impact on the origin and development of Buddhism, *Sankhya,* and *Vedanta* for the Upanisads transmute the idea of gods in the Vedas without adopting an atheistic point of view, and seek emancipation from the cycle of existence. One can trace a movement away from the Vedic philosophy to the very early Upanisads like *Brhadaranyaka* and *Chandogya* that culminated in spiritual monism and a devaluation of the non-spiritual world of names and forms. The seventh chapter of *Chandogya* also connects *brahmajijnasa* with the realisation of the sorrowfulness of life, an idea later developed by Buddhist and Jaina thought. The disappearance of the distinction between the subject and the object, the knower and the knowledge, discussed in the *Brhadaranyaka* also foreshadows the Buddhist idea of *nirvana*. *Vijnana* according to the *Vijnanavadins* yields place to *Vijilaptimatrata,* once one transcends the *grahyagrahaka bhava*. That desire is the source of *sansara* and in its absence *karman* does not bind is a principle propounded by Yajnavalkya in *Brihaddranyaka* and also by early Buddhist texts like *Suttanipata*. The distinction drawn by *Kathopanisad* between sensuous pleasures and the true good of man—*anitya* and *nitya, adhruva* and *dhruva, preyas* and *sreyas, bola* and *dhira*—also became important to *sramana* poetry later on. The *Sankhya* thought also is close to the *Sramanic* tradition in that unlike in the Vedas that trace the universe to a sentient, divine being (*Purusavada*), the *Sankhya* stands for a doctrine of material or natural transformations (*Pradhanavada*). While even some Upanishads uphold an optimistic worldview that is almost Vedic (e.g. *Mundaka* says: *visvam idam varis'tham,* this is the best of all worlds, *Katha* advises satisfaction of all desires and recognition of the world). *Sankhya* counts even the supreme happiness of contentment as part of *duhkha* and seeks absolute liberation from it. However, several part of *Katha* and *Mundaka* echo *Sramanic* ideas like the contempt for sacrifices and rituals described as frail boats by *Mundaka* and the celebration of the *munis, yatis* and *bhaiksacharyas* of the forest. The *Sramanic* idea of the renunciation of action is also found in the *Isopanishad.* The later Sankarite development of *Vedanta* became possible only through a full synthesis of *Sramanic* negativism with Vedic positivism. To follow the Buddhist logic, if change is real, eternity is impossible. If Brahmana produces the world really, He must be changeable. The only logical alternative then is to deny the reality of creation. As soon as that is done, life becomes devalued and stark pessimism stares one in the face. This is the starting point of *Sramanic* philosophy, the misery of human life subject to the bondage of passions and actions, birth and death. It seeks not an upgrading of life to the level of the divine, nor its perfection but its transcendence, the return of the soul to its own realm 'far from the sphere of our sorrow.'

Morality, according to the *Sramanas,* lies in conduct, in the equanimous, luminous and untroubled modification of the soul. As a form of self-consciousness, morality synthesises subjectivity and objectivity seeking to realise the ideal and idealise the real. While the Vedic idea of morality stands for a cycle of ritual giving and receiving and stresses man's social dependence through the notion of obligation, *Sramanism* cuts man loose from the dependence on the gods, replacing them with *karman.* What man receives he owes not to gods but to his own past actions and efforts. The individual himself is responsible for the actions and cannot avoid their moral consequences. It is not the cultivation of natural faculties and satisfaction of instincts, but the transcendence of natural and social personality that raises him above the ordinary. If sterility and niggardliness are the main evils in the Vedic tradition, pleasure-seeking, egoism and violence are the main evils in the *Sramanic* view. By the sixth century B.C. many *Sramana* sects had become fatalistic, upholding *akriyavada,* like the *ajivikas* for whom pleasure and pain occur according to *niyati, sangati* and *bhava* and are predestined. This implies a denial of free will and of *kriyei. Samannaphale suttanta* says: 'There is no reason, no cause for the suffering of beings. They suffer without reason and cause. There is no reason for purification, neither is the self a free agent, nor another. There is no freedom of the will, no force, no power, no human strength, no human effort. All beings, all organisms, all creatures and all souls are helpless, powerless, forceless, determined by destiny, conjecture and situation, experiencing pleasure and pain, life and death. Human effort or knowledge cannot hasten or abbreviate this force of *Karman. Karman* is neither one's nor another's according to the negative dialectic of Buddhism, there is no identical agent. It seeks a middleway, rejecting *iisti* and *rasa. Parivrajakas* like the materialist Ajita-Kegakambati and the agnostic Sanjaya Belatthaputta also show a essimism towards life. Life and its pleasures are perishable; death is unavoidable; success is always elusive as man seeks to win happiness through forces that are beyond his control. *Sramanism* advocates asceticism, for the *Mahavaratas* (to use a Jain term) but for the *Anuvratas,* the laity, it advocates an ideal of spiritually inclined ethical humanism, which is a valuable complement to the point of view of mendicancy, as it prepares the soul for rigorous contemplation. While Brahmanical morality is bound up with religious and ritual observations and the fulfilment of traditional social obligations, *Sramanic* tradition rejects much of the traditional ritual, emphasises inward morality and accepts social obligations, not as something absolute but as something which provides an occasion for the practice of certain voluntarily accepted moral laws. Asoka's *dhamma* represents the quintessence of *Sramanism* as it rejects rituals and emphasises non-violence, self-control, equal respect for all beings, mercy, liberality, truthfulness, purity and moderation. It constitutes a system of universal, rational and ethical religion that is wholly non-sectarian. Dharmakirti finds belief in the validity of the Vedas, pride of caste, violence and expectation of ethical merit from ablutions to be the signs of folly. In *Sonadanda Sutta* we find a dialogue between a Brahmin and the Buddha, where finally the Brahmin admits that what really makes a person a Brahmana are conduct and learning —*sila and panditya*, while *varna, jati* and *mantra* are not indispensable. The Buddha says that all men have the same potentiality for moral and spiritual progress even as the same bright fire is produced by all kinds of wood. The source of Brahmanahood is not birth, family, Vedic learning or profession, but purity of heart and other spiritual qualities. Asvaghosa also argues that all men belong to the same race; *varna* is only a functional division (*'kriyavisesena khalu caturvarna-vyavastha kriyate'*). Vaisampayana also says originally it was one race (*'ekavarnamidam purvam'*). In the dialogue between Yudhishthira and the python in the *Ajagaraparvan* of the *Vanaparvan* of *Mahabharata* too, a Brahmana is defined as one who evinces truth, liberality, forbearance, virtue, mildness, austerity and pity; all men are born *s'Fidras* and attain brahmanahood through conduct. The supreme end of man is described as one that is free from pain and pleasure (*'nirduhkhamasukham ca yat'*).

In the Vedic tradition the universe is the expression of a personal will. In the *Sramanic* tradition, it is determined by an impersonal natural law. It stresses the inexorableness of the moral law. Prayers and worship are of no avail against the force of *karman*. Only purification of feelings leads to inward illumination. While in Vedic view illumination comes from outside, from an eternally revealed word or from the grace of God, in *Sramanism* the consolation of a personal God is replaced by the individual dependent on his own resources and guided by a teacher. The world here is seen as ever-existent, without originaries.

3

The originality of our *Bharata-Ramayana* poets is to be sought primarily in the differences of their texts from the Sanskrit texts. These are the free spaces of their creative imagination. An examination of the major deviations of Sarala Dasa's *Mahabharata* from Vyasa's *Mahabharata* will amply prove how the original insertions by the great Oriya poet are inspired, consciously or unconsciously, by the democratic *Sramanic* worldview with its subversive power. He has scrupulously omitted most of the highly philosophical and metaphysical discussions in the original and the stories that generate them. The *Bhagavad Gita* is simply not there except a reference to it in two verses. Bhishma's discourse to Yudhishthira is replaced by a shorter, original one while 20 narratives of the *Vanaparva,* 44, mostly dialectical narratives in the *Seintiparva* and *Anus'asanaparva* have been completely left out. A whole new *parva,* the *Madhyaparva* has been added, carrying some parts of the original *Adiparva.* The Pandavas' *rajasiiya* has been enlarged several times in Sarala Dasa's *Sabhaparva.*

A second technique of the subversion of the original is the transformation of history into mythology: Sarala Dasa's *Mahabharata* gets its specific Oriya character not only from the language with its folk inspiration that I understand continues to be the standard idiom of poetry even today, but also from its geography that encompasses several places in Orissa that the Pandavas visit before their last journey. It includes many incidents of Oriya life and history, clearly interwoven with *Mahabharata* episodes, like the marriage of Old Yudhishthira with Suhani, the young daughter of Hari Sahu of Amaravati; the story of Hasan Gangu, the founder of the Bahamani Kingdom, handing over the treasure he found on his piece of land to his master, enlarged and transmuted into the story of Tapati and Suresvara and the arrival of the *Kaliyuga;* or again the use of some materials from the historical episode of the goldsmith's daughter that caused the war between Vijayanagara and Bahamani Kingdoms in the story of Hiranyakesi in the *Vanaparva.* Sarala Dasa has also adapted several popular stories of his time like the story of Bhima calling Duryodhana the 'son of Golaka' creating a grievance in the latter against his maternal grand-father Gandharasena; that of Duryodhana's daughter under the banyan tree seeing the tiny seeds producing the gigantic trees floating in his urine; or the story of the jackal marrying off his beautiful daughter to the king Bhagyavara, the jackal being a forefather of Sakrajit. At times he uses folktales to laugh at false religiosity e.g. that of the tiger that pretends to be a non-violent *Vaisnava* in order to eat up the monkey on the tree or that of the crane that acts like a saint to lure the fish in the drying pond. There is obviously a greater concern for social issues in Sarala Dasa than in Vayasa as he weaves the myths of a culture into the patterns of collective life, creating new forms, symbols and metaphors in the process.

The unorthodox and irreverent attitude of Sarala Dasa to the original *Mahabharata* is evident from the poet's own statement that the *Mahabharata* war took place not once but 73 times, and each time the same Kurukshetra became the scene of the battle where the naked Kantani danced in ecstasy. Every war, of every time and every place is thus contained in this one battle; it is the mother of all wars. Through this view put in the mouth of Agasti in the *Sabheiparva,* repeated by a jackal in the *Udyogaparva,* and again by Prithvi in the *Chandipurana,* Sarala Dasa turns the *Mahabharata* war into a complex metaphor valid for every age in history. This universalisation, with its hatred of violence, that is also amply evident in the poet's description of various sins, is typical of *Sramana* poetics and ethics with its democratic accent.

The episode where Krishna meets the banished Arjuna in the forest is another example of Sarala Dasa's metaphor-making imagination. Krishna takes the form of a compound beast with the features of nine animals, man and bird: peacock's head, three legs of the elephant, tiger and horse, a human hand holding a lotus, a lion's body with a bull's hunch, cock's plumes and snake's tail. It is a test of Arjuna's friendship and Arjuna does not fail to recognise him: as soon as his alert ears capture the sounds of the animal's three-legged dance and he raises *the gandiva,* he recognises the universal being in its creative dance. The metaphor has been interpreted in various ways, representing the principle of creation, intellect in concentration, harmony and equipoise, the universal essence or Brahman itself. It is diversity in unity, the plural in the singular. One can see in it an expression of folk surrealism characteristic of the *Sramana* poetic tradition that tries to represent the transcendent in terms of the imminent.

Sarala Dasa does not appear to share Vedic faith though he may, by poetic habit, pay lip-service to it. He is conscious of the horrible reality of 15th century Orissa with the Gajapati Kingdom in decline, collapsing under the attack from the north and the south, emasculated, impoverished, breaking asunder. His men and women belong more to earth and history than to heaven and eternity. Look for example at his Ganga: she does not have the grace and sobriety of Vyasa's Ganga. She is the embodiment of revenge against Santanu whom she had mistaken for Siva as the king was moving about the three worlds in Siva's image under instructions from the god himself. She is the virago and the witch, the laughing Medusa, a termagant who finds joy in hurting Santanu, burning his clothes and tearing and piercing his body with teeth and nails. By killing her children, she de-mothers and de-womanises herself, she is a critic of the family, challenging the myth of marriages made in heaven and happy domesticity. In some sense she anticipates the anti-patriarchal heroine of modern feminist fiction, solitary, angry, tongue-tied, trying to communicate her pain through violence. Here Sarala Dasa appears more as a myth-breaker than as myth-maker. Sarala Dasa's Kunti also looks more like a common woman than the *rajamata,* the Queen Mother with her dignity, patience and wisdom. Sarala de-mythifies all his characters, turning them into slaves of passion, devoid of divinity in a world of irrationality and unscrupulous pursuit of selfish ends. This was the world he saw around him, nothing remained great and pure any longer; it was a civilization that was anxious, insecure and nervous, trying to move from nature to culture and facing impediments everywhere.

Even Sarala Dasa's Krishna is a mortal who finally fails and dies. The victory of the Pandavas is ultimately pointless, the question 'Why the number and why the blood' posed at the beginning by Arjuna survives the war. Sarala's Krishna, from whose lips the *Gita* has been taken away, encompasses the entire gamut of human experience as the poet tries to take in all the tales that had gathered around the figure by his time to appeal to the different sections of the society and in the very process, the focus is often lost and Krishna, at times, appears a lecher, as when he wants a tunnel built from the *kadamba* grove to Radha's bedroom. Krishna appears like a sadist in the episode of the sacrifice of Belalasena, Bhima's son, where he seems to enjoy war and blood: an anti-human force that gloats over death and waste. As Prafulla Mohanty observes in his introduction to *Stories from Sarala's Mahabharata*, *lila* and *tattva* in the *Mahabharata* have uneven dimensions. The triumph of good is morally tragic, like the triumph of truth in Greek tragedy. A large area of waste is created by the values of heroism and honour... reason fails. And all the more so when Sarala Dasa makes Krishna the manipulator of the lila of life, devising stories and acts to keep his stories of lila unfolding.

He goes on to say that Vyasa himself is at variance with the Vedic concept of the Brahman: the *lilarupa*, the 'incarnation', is not the totality of the life-force of Brahman. Krishna is incomplete and fails to establish his order without destroying the very people for whom order is meant. Brahman cannot be the creator and the protector as it is detached and free from qualities. In the case of Sarala Dasa, Krishna's manipulatory powers limit the free flow of life; he is a mind 'sick with desire', jealous of greatness and malevolent in the Belalasena episode. Even when he is good and just—as when he rises above familial ties in blessing the beggar Rudrasramana, whose son bashes up Pradyumma, his own son—Krishna is only asserting this will: he can kill or be kind as he wishes. Krishna exhibits 'traits of humanised reality (trying to or) ordering himself on rational values of civilisation...but he also exhibits all excesses which he himself punishes in others.' Thus Sarala's Krishna with his weaknesses and failures appears more of a contemporary minister or bureaucrat than God: his mission appears political-military in the *rajasiiya* that Sarala Dasa describes in finer details summoning up all his powers of imagination.

The concept of suffering that is central to the *Sramana* worldview is crucial to Sarala Dasa's *Mahabharata* too. This irrational suffering is seen not only in the Padmabati episode where King

Sukra's loyal and happy wife is cursed by her husband to carry her four sons as eggs in her womb and live as a skylark for four *kalpas* but in the very conception of the whole epic and its characters, both the Pandava and the Kauravas, who are caught in a maelstrom of irrational evil and pain. Heroes and villains are alike destroyed, neither side wins the war ultimately, since the success that comes to the Pandavas is hardly a success, it is only a right to the ownership of corpses on a wasteland. What remains after all the show of valour is the vision of the fierce wheel—may be the wheel of time itself—slaughtering the tall and the tiny, the good and the bad alike, mercilessly burning the Kauravas and cutting the heads of the Pandavas: a vision described by the head of Belalasena on the auspicious pillar of Kurukshetra to disapprove of the Pandava's claims to heroism. Destruction here is neutral and impersonal, as in modern war or terrorism; it has no logic, both sides have only victims, there is no triumph of good over evil. Even Krishna is not free from this inexorable logic of destruction as he too falls a victim to the curse of Ashtavakra, ridiculed by Samba that wipes out the whole Yadu clan. This is an amoral universe of endless suffering and unreasonable death. Samba's iron-babe is indestructible as its last piece surviving Bhima's hands finally reaches Jara the hunter to make the arrow head that kills Krishna. The orgiastic ritual annhiliation of Yadus as Mohanty suggests, completes a cycle of civilization unworthy to perpetuate itself. Even knowledge doe not save; man is a victim in a world without salvation.

The powerful central metaphor in *Sarala Bharata,* that of Duryodhana crossing the river of blood on the floating corpse of his own son Lakshman Kumara, is like a revelation. The cornered, hunted and humiliated Duryodhana gets no help from his brothers, friends and relations in crossing the deluge of blood he himself has caused: he has to sacrifice his very future, his dreams of continuity and immortality, to cross that river and even that does not finally save him: the present has no way to save itself, none to perpetuate itself, in this cruel struggle for survival. This is a world of unrelieved tragedy to which only the Buddha perhaps has a solution. Sarala Dasa just suggests this possibility of justice, kindness and dispassionate action for the fellow-beings in certain episodes like the one where he gives us a fleeting vision of the nobility of the *candala* worker and the *brahmin* landlord who transcend the love of gold, possible only before the release of Kali into the human world and history. We owe to Sarala Dasa the creation of a parallel world along with that of a great language: what greater mission did Homer, Virgil, Dante, Vyasa or Shakespeare achieve?

I THINK OF THE ENDS OF THINGS
Some Reflections on Ghalib's Modernity

> *I am neither the loosening of song*
> *nor the close-drawn tent of music;*
> *I'm the sound, simply, of my own breaking.*
> —Mirza Ghalib, Tr. Adrienne Rich

These lines full of 'intense moral loneliness' to borrow a phrase from Aijaz Ahmed who has edited a fascinating volume of Ghalib's ghazals in English versions by different poets, could very well have come from a Baudelaire, a Mallarme, a Rimbaud, a T.S. Eliot, a Nelly Sachs or a Sylvia Plath—or any of the modern poets of India, especially of the solipsistic 1960s. Ghalib's times were traumatic: it was a time of fragmentation and despair when the intellectuals felt 'the centre cannot hold,' when a whole civilisation appeared to be breaking up, leaving a cultural and spiritual vacuum that was not easy to fill. Life that was so far intelligible, though challenging, suddenly grew unintelligible; the tradition that had given the poet a secure framework within which he could encounter, evaluate and contain experience was crumbling. In Ghalib's own words, 'a strange time has come upon us like a shadow'. Ghalib seldom observed the rituals of Islam; yet the religion was there, a looming luminous presence that filled him with a sense of the cosmic and made God available to him in moments of crisis. There was too a sense of sharing, there were common experiences, concerns and concepts, of love, anxiety, friendship, brotherhood, equality, giving the poet the secure feeling of being part of a collectivity and a sense of relationship, of harmony with the society, even in times of acute anguish and suffering. But by the beginning of the 19th century, things began to fall apart; order was giving way to disorder, self-doubt began to assail civilisation. The entry of the British commercial interests expedited the break-down of the system. The subconscious of the subcontinent was haunted by a crisis of confidence that soon gave way to disillusionment. Mirza Ghalib (1797-1869) lived and died during these times of turmoil, when relationships were becoming more and more difficult to sustain and the irrational was beginning to dominate society. The utter sense of waste and the desperate longing for lost relationships gave his poetry a tone different from those of Omar Khayyam, with his sensuous wisdom, and Hafiz with his moral grandeur.

Ghalib's Delhi, much like Baudelaire's Paris, Pushkin's St. Petersburg, Lorca's New York, Brecht's Berlin or Eliot's London, was a city of crises and carnage, full of the intensities of cultural friction, the frontiers of experience. The relationship between the metropolises and the experience of modernity has been explored time and again in contemporary literary criticism. Writers and intellectuals have long abhorred the city and dreamt of escaping from its sprawl and speed, its vices and noises. Cultural stability has often been seen as being outside the urban order. And yet the city has fascinated them with its experience of modern history, its turbulent artistic activity, its verve, drive and vivacity. The city has been a metaphor for all that is modern, and modernism itself has been more or less an urban form of art, both in India and abroad. The city, both as a museum of culture and a novel environment, as the foci of migration from the countryside and as centres of political action, as the dissolver of the feudal order and the harbinger of capitalistic relations, has always attracted and repelled artists and writers at the same time. It is here that artists have experienced that modern phenomenon called alienation; that paradoxical position of independence coupled with social indeterminacy. Cities with their vast agglomerations of people of different origins in different roles and situations have always been places of conflict, transformation and novel consciousness that stimulate cultural innovation, along with a feeling of moral and communicative crisis. Chaos, contingency, diversity, heteroglossia: these storm-centres of civilisation have been characterised by these pluralising and surrealising forces of modernism. Exile, disconnection, loss: these experiences of the 'unhoused' writer in the city appear again and again in Ghalib's poetry. 'Dropped like a used light bulb, I won't be shocked', he says in one of his ghazals,

There's no way to fix what's happened inside me.
Even with a door, I probably shouldn't go back in.

He comes to love not the beloved herself, but the spaces between them.

What can you get watching a life run like clockwork?
It time to go when you don't even want loyalty.

He ends the ghazal with the tragic confession, 'I've nothing to be proud of'. Ghalib was literally 'unhoused' in both Delhi and Calcutta. He always rented a house or accepted the use of a house from his patron. He had no books of his own, nor children except the two he adopted in 1852. Ghalib always wished to have a regular income but it never materialised. His marriage was not happy; his relations with his wife were tentative and indifferent. Deprived of both material and moral certainties, Ghalib remained ever vulnerable, ever on the brink of breaking up. He was horrified by the wholesale violence practised by the British rulers, in spite of his admiration for the rationality and the sophistication of the West that he contrasted with the intellectual poverty and the redundancy of the Moghul court. He expressed his horror at the British atrocities in his private letters, though in the public document, *'Dast-Ambooh'*— his diary of 1857 he was generally appreciative of the British, despite occasional remarks against their excesses. It was the onslaught of 1857 that really brought about a transformation in his attitude to the British; he had witnessed the hanging of at least 27,000 patriotic rebels in Delhi itself. In the same year his brother Yusuf, who had been mad since 1826, passed away. Many of Ghalib's friends were among those hanged by the British. His attitude to the British was indeed ambivalent; he admired their liberal ideals, while he was also disgusted with their cruelty and denial of human rights to the Indian subjects.

Nothing comes very easy to you, human creature—
least of all the skill to live humanely.

> Time after time ahead of time, you fool,
> standing in panic at the meeting place
> (Tr. Adrienne Rich)

These lines reflect Ghalib's general attitude to man's inhumanity that left even his body in the grave 'scarred with its disappointments'.

Ghalib's is essentially a poetry of contemplation. His attempt is to draw the subtlest and the most precise distinctions 'between one experience and another and between one shade of an experience and another shade. The questions Ghalib asks are not different from the traditional questions of Persian-Urdu poetry—'What is love? What is God? What is the place of man in this universe?' However, Ghalib is no mystic; even metaphysics attains an earthy character in his poems. Like Baudelaire, he brings together the metaphysical and the temporal to invent a poetics of sudden 'correspondences', of moments when the rapid passage of forms is suddenly illuminated by an intuition of the temporal or spiritual:

> Our time of awareness is a lighting-flash
> a blinding interval in which to know and suffer
> (Tr. Adrienne Rich)

Roland Barthes once observed that around 1850 classical writing disintegrated and the whole of literature became the problematics of language. This was the result of the pluralisation of world views, deriving from the evolution of new classes and communications. In Ghalib's poetry we begin to feel the 'great divide' between the past and the present, the beginning of that break-up, a devolution or a dissolution that characterises modern art. Like all modern artists, Ghalib too confronts a crisis of culture and is under historical strain. His is a poetic art consequent to the collapsing of the conventional notions of causality and traditional notions of the wholeness of individual character. When realities become subjective fictions, the public notions of language become discredited. The dis-establishing of communal reality must have been a great shock to a writer like

Ghalib, who always longed for a meaningful relationship with the community. He is aware of contingency as a disaster in the world of time. The panorama of futility was an immediate experience to him. 'I am a pinched out candle, no longer good for the banquet-table,' he says. He feels he has lost all the campaigns; he is unable to find the truth since 'the world reflects crooked, or the crystal ball distorts'. The seer turns blind... So it's dead in my breast, the zeal, the principle—its only reward was the gleam while it vanished.' (Tr. William Stafford). Even in nature he found the force of pain, 'Spring cloud thinning after rain/Dying into its own weeping'. (Tr. Thomas Fitzimmons).

Virginia Woolf thought that human nature changed in or about December 1910; D.H. Lawrence thought that the old world ended in 1915; Richard Ellman took it back to 1900; but Mirza Ghalib had seen the end of the old world much earlier, in his own youth in the 19th century. 'Images of death piled up everywhere, that's what the world fastens around us,' he wrote in one of his ghazals. He could no more live on the great promise: 'Well, you can believe it, I'd have died of joy and the Great One proved the Word.' He says he would never have had heavenly bliss, even if he had lived longer.

> Exiled, how can I rejoice, forced here from home, and even my letters torn open?
> (Tr. William Stafford)

> 'Be, or be lost,' that was what he felt about life:
> Either one enters the drift, past and whole as one,
> or life is a mere game.

Ghalib found the words of his grief 'fall like a shower of sparks' so that 'out in the world they call me a disciple of fire'. The market place surrounds even the nuanced art of poetry, 'We and the poems we make get bought and sold together'. Nietzsche declared in November 1888, 'I swear that in two years' time the whole world will be in convulsions. I am sheer destiny'. In December he wrote to August

Strindberg, that he now felt possessed of the strength 'to cleave the history of mankind in two'. Ghalib, Nietzsche's contemporary, seems to share this apocalyptic vision, that man is at the terminus of a long era of civilisation, that history had arrived at a point of destiny, that all human values are going to be subjected to total revision. Ghalib appears at times to use a metalanguage that fuses workaday contraries in a new universe of discourse. One feels that Ghalib's ultimate theme is language, the break-down of language that signifies the breakdown of relationships. His inwardness is different from Romantic subjectivity, it comes from the isolation of the poet in the city's commercial chaos; it is a desperate search for a private sense of belonging and of order created out of the cultural fragments strewn around him. He feels spiritually crippled and sterile, subjected to an entropic anarchy:

They are foolish who wonder why I am still living: I am
doomed to live, wanting death, a little longer.

Ghalib is one of the first masters to bring about that radical transformation in the nature of the lyric that is typical of modernism. He very often abandons the traditional subject position of the lyric poet as the lover, the courtier, the patriot and the sage. The aspiration for an inaccessible order, a feeling of doubt, disbelief in the divine promise, the possibility of error, confession of sin, meanness and misfortune: all these characteristics of the modern lyric are discernible in Ghalib's verses. The poet here is no more the celebrant of the culture to which he belongs: he understands the squalor and baseness of urban living as does Baudelaire, and like Rimbaud he often writes a poetry of unorthodox celebrations and chance epiphanies. This is in keeping with the spirit of the modern age, where the epic poem that expresses an ethical choice and the sustained long poem with fully worked-out conceptual schemes appear out-of-tune with the time and the lyric that expresses a transitory mood, or a momentary illusion seems apt and relevant. Ghalib's poetry is like a spiritual diary that follows the contours of his individual experience, where 'every attempt is a wholly new start'. In this attempt the poet is also confronted with the inadequacy of language, its aridity and plenitude. The surface of language seems to grow opaque as the sensibility becomes disassociated. Poetry becomes an attempt to discover 'what flowers might grow amid the ruins of language,' to listen to 'the rattle of pebbles on the shore under the receding wave'. 'I am too old for an inner wildness, Ghalib/when the violence of the world is all around me,' these lines of Ghalib express the feeling of exhaustion and frustration that comes from the confrontation with a world of destruction and ruin. Ghalib's lines 'Anyone who still can hope is seeing visions,' reminds one of what Bertolt Brecht wrote in our own times, 'Those who laugh have not yet heard the terrible tidings'. He too felt that the forehead without wrinkles is a sign of stupidity.

Even love finally left him in a state of disillusionment, and so too wine: 'The walls and doors of the tavern are blank with silence./I am ashamed of the destroying genius of my love;/this crumbling house contains nothing but my wish to have been a builder.' Even creativity is only the expression of a failure: 'Today, Asad, our poems are just the pastime of empty hours;/clearly our virtuosity has brought us nowhere.' (Tr. Adrienne Rich). Here 'The images of collective failure are... fully assimilated in an image of personal lack of worth and effectiveness, and of the irrelevance of the creative act itself', to quote Aijaz Ahmed's comment on this ghazal. Ghalib identifies the totalisation of knowledge in the Hegelian sense with the totalisation of the community itself:

> We make new
> our life is
> an overthrowing
> the great faith gathers to itself
> deaths
> even of its worshippers. (Tr. W.S. Merwin)

He felt that if the poet went on mourning, the cities men inhabit will drift back into the wild.

Ghalib desperately wanted to share his anxieties with others; but he was living in an age when others were beginning to be perceived as hell, as did the existentialists more than a century later.

I'd like to crumple this love, this shame into the fire;
What is this need to share what can't be shared? (Tr. Adrienne Rich)

He felt he was constantly behind bars and yet did not want others to think that it was his nest that the lightning had shrivelled. The agony of living was insufferable: 'What I'm living through now could smash my house in pieces.' He felt love left no children; it always hid itself under the veil of dust. Love, he found, did not have the colour of madness. The heart fails even while it courts disgrace. A sense of impotence seemed frequently to overpower the poet; the heart was in an autumnal state, incapable of registering the meaning of events. 'Without a meaning to perceive, what is perception?' he asks, 'Tears sting my eyes, I'm leaving/lest the other guests see my weakness.' He knew the bitter aftertaste of all sweetness and was aware that the Paradise was but 'a long hangover.' He felt like a runner in a desert whose frontiers seemed to be farther and farther away:

Where I'm going is farther at every step
the desert runs from me
with my own feet.

MY KABIR, MY CONTEMPORARY

I had my first encounter with Kabir in my high school days; Surdas and Meera too had come along. I cannot separate them from the images of our Hindi teachers, one with the tender voice and other with the shrill voice; Kabir, I found, had both the voices. Later I read a lot of Kabir in the original with notes or in English translations. It will be presumptuous to claim that I know him, but I do understand him, and I need him to be myself.

To me Kabir is not a lone voice. I place him in a parallel tradition of Indian poetry, the subaltern traditions of a people's vision—of the physical and the metaphysical words as well as criticism of social and religious practices made from within. This tradition begins with tribal poetry, gets redefined in the major *Upanishads*, assumes a pantheistic form in the *Rigveda*, get enriched by the variety of popular imagination in the thousands of oral, written and performed versions of *Ramayana* and *Mahabharata* in different languages, receives enlightenment from Buddhism and Jainism in the works inspired by them, signs of family, politics and ethics in classical Tamil literature and reaches its visionary height in the Bhakti and Sufi poets, right from the Tamil Siddhas, like the Saivites Thirumular, Chivavakiyar and Manickavachakar, and Vaishnavites like Andal and Auvayar of the sixth and seventh centuries, the Kannada Vachanakaras like Basava and Akka Mahadevi of the 11th and 12th centuries, to the saints and sufi's of North India like Namdev, Tukaram, Jnandev, Eknath, Chokhamela, Kabir, Meera, Surdas, Lal Ded, Shah Abdul Latif, Mir Dard, Baba Farid, Bulle Shah, Sultan Bahu and others. Elsewhere, I have called this the Sramana tradition in Indian poetry that underlines the spiritual equality of all beings, and opposes all form of religious and caste hierarchies as against the brahmana tradition that perpetuates inequality and hierarchy.

While Bhakti poetry is neither simultaneous nor monolithic, the majority of Bhakti poets share certain characteristics—most of them come from the marginalised sections of society. For instance, the Tamil Siddhas, included cowherds, woodcutters, fisherman, hunters, washermen, potters, weavers and pariahs; and in the North we have Namdev the tailor, Dadu the cotton-carder, Chokhamela the mahar, Gora the potter, Raidas the tanner, Akho the goldsmith, Kabir the weaver and Tukaram the pedlar; others were marginalised as Muslims or as women. It is this status that made them advocates of egalitarianism, social justice and spiritual oneness. They seem to share a predilection for pre-Aryan patterns of life and thought, as implied in their rejection of Brahmin privilege the egalitarian content of their credo and the tribal character of their collective worship. They emphasised similarities among different religions, found them to be only different paths leading to the same goal and even attempted syntheses of religions as in Nanak's Sikhism and the Sufi cults. Most of them rejected the *Varna–jati* system and Brahmin superiority. They problematised the institution of priesthood by directly addressing God, privileged the oral tradition against the written and gave up Sanskrit to compose verse in regional languages and dialects. Many of them like Kabir, Meera, Nanak, Namdev, and Vidyapati were multilingual. They created or introduced several new forms of poetry and Allied arts. Poetry and Philosophy co-existed and supported each other and the barriers between the physical and the metaphysical became thin in their aesthetic-religious practice. They developed the symbolism of their own, mixing traditional symbols like sky, river, tree, fire, bird, etc., with symbols chosen from the work place and the kitchen, like the loom, the wheel, knife, ladle, bellows, veil, sindoor, etc. I cannot separate Kabir from this total cultural revolution of profound ideological, aesthetic and practical implications that attempted to shape an alternative religion of the people articulating subaltern aspirations. I see the same Sramana tradition flowering later in the anti-colonial and reformist poetry of Tagore, Nazrul Islam, Sumitranandan Pant, Subramania Bharati, Kumaran Asan, Sri Sri, Kevempu, Ali Sardar Jafri or Faiz Ahmed Faiz and in contemporary poetry by Dalits, women, tribals, as well as various forms of protest poetry and secular-spiritual poetry being written today.

2

Another quality that I like in Kabir is his spiritual unease reflected in verse like this:

> King Ram, here's my condition:
> I can't drop worldly ties.
> A bird that flies to the sky
> But holds to its ropes—so I
> Can't drop hope, won't break
> the rope. How can I fly?
> I try for joy, but find
> Sorrow. I can't
> express it.

The image of the bird striving to fly yet being tied by the rope of hope in this lonely and confessional Sorathi poem of Kabir in the western tradition—with its mood reminiscent of Tukaram's early *abhang*s full of doubt, despair, anger and self-contempt—expresses not only Kabir's spiritual state of incomplete realisation but perhaps too his social condition, the state of the Julaha, the Moslem weaver, caught in the evils snares of poverty, caste and class that defeat his ambitions and tie him down to his loom and shuttle. In the *sabda*s this tone returns when the poet addresses Hari, the silent trickster: 'O childhood friend, when you left me, where did you go to that morning? You're the only man. I'm your woman. Your footstep is heavier that stone' (*sabda* 37); so too is the *bhairun*: 'How can I see you today? Without seeing you how can I believe? Was I a bad servant? Were you unaware? Between the two of us, Ram who is to blame?' (*bhairun* 33) or in the *sakhi*, 'Kabir says, how to work it out: I-he-you?' (*sakhi* 312) or again the first *ramaini*: 'No one knows his ineffable movement. How could tongue describe it?'

Kabir would not have been loved and adored so much as he is but for his intense humaneness that brightens up every line of his verse: pain, doubt, anger, love, tenderness, submission: no human emotion is out of his range. He shows us actual feeling without ceremony, surrounds us with the experience of delusion, and embodies the fragmented nature of everyday life. He does not need to use pathetic fallacy to anthropomorphise flora and fauna like Bhavabhuti, Kalidasa or Tulsidas to reflect ideal human feeling.

3

Kabir's all-inclusive spiritually has always held great fascination for me. He is close to the Upanishads as well as the Sufi poet Jalaludin Rumi in his understanding of Divinity, which is neither inside nor outside and does not recognise religious differences. Kabir's Brahma is the elemental principle of all creation. It is independent, final, unchanging, even while changing everything. It is not on our left or right, above or below, it is free of forms and quality; it cannot be confined to the temple and the mosque. It is truth, pure awareness; it is the minutest and the biggest. It is infinity itself, it is like the Sufi's 'Noor'. Like the Tamil Siddhas, Kabir also does not reject the body. The body is the seat of the Divine, it's the pool where the Lotus blooms. The Divine has no right and left, no front and back. He is formless with no father or mother, only he knows how he is. (*'bayen na dahinem... ahi nahimanem'*) Kabir also identifies *sabd* (word) with the Divine and asks people to worship the word... (*'Sadho, Sabd-Sadhana keeje... Jehi antargati soojhai'*)

The Divine is the Name (*Nam*).

Kabir's concept of the soul (*Atman*) is equally all-comprehensive. It contains all opposites: it is the cosmos embodied, it is the mind and the senses, it transcends gender. It is tree, sun and light, bird and cage, lamp and oil, it is unattached, it is fire and wind and water. (*'Pandit's dekhahu... bako charit anoopa'*).

Maya to Kabir is Nature itself; it is a creeper that grows thicker when it is cut; if you water it, it withers and falls, it is a serpent that generates children like itself. (*'je katon to dahdah... kuch gun khaya na jaee'*)

Salvation (*Mukti*) to Kabir is an ultimate state of fearlessness; it is the end of the duality between oneself and the supreme self. Kabir, like Socrates, focuses on self-knowledge as the path to liberation. To one who has known himself, difference of caste and creed, and rituals and the externals of religion have absolutely no value: (*'jo khodya masjid basat hai... kya bahiro bhya khuday'*). All sacred rivers are but water, all the images are dead, I have never heard them speak (*'theerth mein to sab pani hain... yah sab hai jhitee pol dekha'*).

4

Another aspect that attracts me to Kabir as a poet is his unique voice that sets him apart from all other Bhakti poets. Many of his ideas can be found in other Bhakti poets; the Tamil Siddhas in works like *Thirumantiram* and *Periyapuranam* have decried caste and religion, chanting the Vedas, smearing the body with holy ashes, and rituals and formalities of every kind. The same radical reformist spirit can be found in the Veerasaiva saints of Karnataka like Basavanna, Allamaprabhu and Akka Mahadevi and in the Warkari saints of Maharashtra: in the *bharud*s of Eknath, in the *abhang*s of Tukaram, in the bhajans of Namdev and in the verses of Jnandev, for example; but no one has ever spoken in that special, inimitable voice with its unique flavour and potency full of iconoclastic conceit, startling paradox and pugnacity. Guru Nanak was perhaps more ordered than Kabir as a thinker, doctrinally more consistent; but Kabir alone has that peculiar rhetoric: rough, direct, hard-hitting. The Kabir of the *bijak* is one who shouts and attacks, challenges and teases, who spins out mysterious allegories and tosses bizarre images; who is strong and self-reliant and never takes a stance that emphasises the individual's weakness and impotence. Yet he feels lonely as only rare individuals understood him: 'Nobody listens, nobody believes me, they are happy only if I lie', he says repeatedly. The crazy exuberance of his *ulatbamsi* poems contrasts with the oblique, harsh, grave, austere expression of most parts of *bijak* and the ecstatic realisation of the Kabir poems of the Adi Granth or the Panchvani. Kabir is a poet of many voices and his philosophical eclecticism is perfectly at home with the Indian tradition of the absorption of opposite elements. His 'spontaneous rhetoric'—to use a term A.K. Ramanujan used to qualify the Kannada *vachana*s—that combines the crude and the exciting, the vulgar and the profound and gives muscle to mysticism, refuses to fit into traditional Indian poetics.

Kabir is modern as much for his style as for his universal message that transcends all forms of sectarianism and dogma. He is one of the most personal of bhakti poets, not because he dwells on his private experience, as do Meera or Akka Mahadevi or Tukaram, but because he gets personal with his listeners. While Sur or Tulsi address God, Kabir primarily addresses us. The reader is central to Kabir—*kahai Kabira suno bhai sadho, suno ho santo*: yes, he speaks to us, makes us listen, wants to engage, awaken and affect us. He sabotages passivity through his powerful vocatives: saint, brother, pandit, qazi, yogi, mother, creature, friend, fool. We are drawn into highly charged dialogues that we can never be deaf to. 'Son of a slut! There, I've insulted you. Think about getting on the good road' or 'Your ten doors are full of hell; you smell like a fleet of scents. Your cracked eyes don't see the heart, You haven't an ounce of sense' or 'Monk, stop scattering your mind' or 'seekers, the Brahman is a slicked-down butcher' or 'Pandit, you've got it wrong' or 'Brother, where did your two Gods come from' or 'Qazi, what books are you lecturing on? Yak, Yak, day and night. You never had an original thought'. Here is the style that creates intimacy. We almost identify with the poet as he scorns the greedy Brahmin, the eloquent qazi, the comic pandit and the hypocritical yogi. Questions, riddles, surprises, paradoxes, enigmas; he often appears as a dialectician who disturbs readers by compelling them to scrutinise everything they believe and live by. Distinctions of gender, caste, race and religion simply melt in this scorching lightning that electrifies the dialect of the rural masses of Eastern Uttar Pradesh, charging it with a new meaning, creating structures that bruise and a world of secret, paradoxes where, 'the rabbit devours the lion' and 'the mouse fights the elephant'.

What little unity there may be in Kabir's poetry comes in flashes or in leaps from the disordered surface of the world to a momentary recognition; it is here, in everybody (*ghata ghata mein*), something simple (*sahaja*) a single word (*sabda*). Like modern poets, Kabir adheres closely to psychological and physical reality, speaks in an identifiably original voice close to common speech, saturates his poetry with conflict and tension, dramatises the situation and leads us to unexpected conclusions and fresh insights. There are certain principles that seem to govern the structure of Kabir's verse. They may consist of an extended metaphor, an unfolding argument, a dialogue between poet and audience or a dramatic monologue. Several typical patterns in Kabir depend on repetition with variation. Some poems comprise a series of negotiations whose syntax can be varied for pleasing effects in sound and rhythm. Some are built on an anaphora – the repetition of a word at the beginning of each line. Or the repeated word may be scattered in different positions. Some poems are catalogues of Vishnu's incarnations, famous sages, stereotyped fools. Kabir often turns literary conventions upside down, as when he uses the *dasavatar* sequence to ridicule Vishnu's descents while other poets use it to glorify them. The rain bird (*chataka*) which is usually a symbol of longing and devotion becomes in Kabir a symbol of delusion. Developing a single figure throughout a poem is as common in him as bringing together a series of parallel examples. His conclusions are as powerful as his opening addresses, as they often turn things around unexpectedly, make a wry comment or jam on the brakes with a suddenness that sends us hurtling forward into the darkness. At times he speaks entirely through negatives in the Upanishadic fashion as when he describes truth:

> There is no creation or creator there
> no gross or fine, no mind and fire,
> no sun, moon, earth or water,
> no radiant form, no time there,
> no word, no flesh, no faith,
> no cause and effect, nor any thought
> of the Veda. No Hari or Brahma,

no Shiva or Sakti, no pilgrimage
and no rituals. No mother, father
or guru there...

Kabir opens this piece with a sharp challenge. 'Pandit, you've got it wrong.' Each of these negatives is meant to silence this pandit just as he is about to open his mouth. Kabir is the master of dialectical presentations, of disturbing questions. And his questions continue to reverberate in our own traumatic times when once again dogma, orthodoxy and exclusivity seem to be choking religious discourses and spreading communal poison in our multi-religious society. Kabir satisfies my urge for spiritual realisation, my desire for social transformation and my longing for great poetry at the same time. There are few like him in our tradition. Kabir is our great contemporary speaking to us directly in his clear voice across time, admonishing us for our narrow interpretations of religion, chiding us for our petty communal squabbles, asking us to seek and examine the word, lifting us up to a sublime spirituality that transcends divisions of religion, caste, class, race and gender and teaching us how to write effectively, charging every word with visionary meaning, how to address our dark times honestly and fearlessly. We need him more than he needs us.

THE PATHOGRAPHY OF NATIONALISM
Tagore's Critique of the Idea of the Nation

> *The last sun of the century sets amidst the blood-red colours of the West*
> *and the whirlwind of hatred.*
> *The naked passion of self-love of Nations, in its drunken delirium of greed*
> *is dancing to the clash of steel and the howling verses of vengeance.*
>
> *The hungry self of the Nation shall burst in a violence of fury*
> *from its own shameless feeding*
> *For it has made the world its food,*
> *And licking it, crunching it and swallowing it in big morsels,*
> *It swells and swells*
> *Till in the midst of its unholy feast descends the sudden heaven*
> *piercing its heart of grossness...*
>
> —Rabindranath Tagore (*The Sunset of the Century*, tr. poet from *Naivedya, The English Writings of Rabindranath Tagore, Vol. II*, Delhi: Sakitya Akademi, 1996, 1996, p. 466)

There is only one history—the history of man. All national histories are merely chapters in larger one. ('Nationalism in India', Ibid. p. 453)

When Rabindranath Tagore was composing this poem on the last day of the 19th century and writing his essays on Nationalism, first put-together in the second decade of the 20th (*Nationalism*, New York, 1917), he might not have imagined that by the end of the 20th century several thinkers across the world were going to echo his critique of the nationalist ideology, mostly without ever having read him. Though one may find the rudiments of such a critique in thinkers and conscientious objectors like Bertrand Russell, Aldous Huxley or Jean-Paul Sartre, Nationalism entered modern theoretical discourse in a major way only with Benedict Anderson's acknowledged classic *Imagined Communities* (1983) that was soon followed by a series of treatises on the subject by Ernest Gellner (*Nations and Nationalism*, 1983), Miroslav Hroch (*Social Preconditions of*

National Revival in Europe, 1985), Anthony Smith (*The Ethnic Origins of Nations,* 1986), Partha Chatterjee (*Nationalist Thought and the Colonial World,* 1986) and Eric Hobsbawm (*Nations and nationalism since 1788,* 1990) not to mention innumerable articles in journals and writings in languages other than English.

Benedict Anderson's book, initially provoked by the Vietnamese invasion and occupation of Cambodia in 1978-79 and the Chinese assault on Vietnam, all the countries involved swearing by Marxism and, thus, proving that Nationalism was an ideology that even Marxism could not write off as an anomaly or an aberration, or just the inescapable pathology of modern developmental history often descending into incurable dementia, as described by Tom Nairn[1], defined the nation as an imagined community that belonged more with 'kinship' and 'religion' than with 'liberalism' or 'fascism'. It is 'imagined' because its members can, even without knowing most of their fellow-members, conjure up the image of their communion. In Ernest Gellner's words, 'Nationalism is not the awakening of nations to self-consciousness; it *invents* nations where they do not exist'.[2] For him nation is more a fabrication as it was to Tagore, than something created or imagined into being. The nation, Anderson would say is *limited* as it has finite boundaries demarcating them from other nations; it is *sovereign* as nations like to imagine themselves to be free, the sovereign state being the guage and emblem of this freedom and it is a *community* as it glosses over its inequalities and is conceived as a deep and horizontal comradeship for which you can kill or die. The roots of the nation are cultural and the idea of the nation is close to the religious community and the dynastic realm as most of them have their own epics/sacred texts and whole 'national' literatures, constitutions, hierarchised bureaucracies, anonymous linkages, national anthems that substitute prayers, national census, national celebrations, parades and charades, martyrs, genealogies and selective chronicles that prescribe what to remember and what

---

1. Tom Nairn, *The Break-up of Britain* (London: NLB, 1977), p.359.
2. Ernest Gellner, *Thought and Change* (London: Weidenfeld and Nicolson, 1964), p.169.

to forget, national newspapers and a whole print-capitalist system that helps propagate ideas across the nation, defined borders though less porous than those of kingdoms, maps considered sacred as any deviation is treated as treason, calendars, memorials and museums and a whole paraphernalia of national emblems like national flags, birds and animals, why even national zoos and gardens. Add to this a law against 'sedition' that can be used at will by those who invoke it, as was recently done in India in the case of Binayak Sen, Arundhati Roy and even a Tamil folksinger—and the picture is complete.

2

Tagore's views on nationalism are summed up mainly in three essays, 'Nationalism in the West', 'Nationalism in Japan' and 'Nationalism in India', originally three lectures delivered in Japan and the USA published for the first time, along with translations of five of Tagore's poems, including the one quoted at the beginning of this paper, in the book *Nationalism* (Macmillan, New York, 1917). Europe was at war and E. Thompson points out that though 'the world war is not a central theme of *Nationalism*, it is ever-present in the background as proof of the self-destructive tendency of the organized modern nation'.[3] The publication of *Ghare Baire* in 1917, followed by its English translation by Surendranath Tagore three years later, in some ways complemented these lectures, as the novel was highly critical of the Swadeshi Movement. One may also remember in this context his disagreements with Mahatma Gandhi on the cult of the *charkha* in his article in *Modern Review*,[4] (and on some questions about *Swaraj*[5] as also his essay, 'East and West'[6] besides some of his essays on art and education.

---

3. E. Thompson, *Rabindranath Tagore: Poet and Dramatist* (Calcutta: Rddhi, 1948, [1979 ed.]) p. 8.
4. September, 1925, see *The Mahatma and the Poet,* Sabyasachi Bhattacharya, ed., Delhi, 1997, pp 99-112.
5. *Ibid*, pp. 113–121.
6. Das, op.cit; pp. 530–37.

In 'Nationalism in the West', the first in the series of lectures, Tagore states his position without much ambiguity: 'Neither the colourless vagueness of cosmopolitanism, nor the fierce self-idolatry of nation-worship is the goal of human history.' (Das, p. 419) And he asserts: 'I am not against this nation or that nation, but against the idea of the nation itself' (Ibid, p. 430) He also defines nation in doubtless terms: 'A nation, in the sense of the political and economic union of the people, is that aspect which a whole population assumes, when organized for a mechanical purpose.' (Ibid, p. 421) Tagore recognises the problem of races as the most menacing of the issues faced by India, making our history a continual social adjustment rather than of organised power for defence or aggression or the rise and fall of dynasties as in the case of most other countries. Social regulation of differences with a spiritual recognition of unity has been the twin-strategy for her to cope with her ethnic multiplicity. Tagore is sharply critical of the rigidity of social stratification in India and the resulting crippling of her people's minds, the insularity of world views and the perpetuation of hierarchies. But he is even more critical of the West, where 'the national *machinery* of commerce and politics turns out neatly compressed bales of humanity which have their use and high market value; but they are bound in iron hoops, labeled and separated off with scientific care and precision.' He warns India not to imitate the Western national ideal whose characteristics he sums up in the paragraphs that follow. He makes an important distinction between *society* and *nation*: while society does not have an ulterior purpose and is a natural regulation of relationships and the spontaneous self-expression of man as a social being, nation is an organisation of people with a mechanical purpose, founded on greed, jealousy, suspicion and desire for power. It replaces the living bonds of society with mere mechanical organisation. This also leads to patriarchal power as man, driven to professionalism, turns the wheels of power for his own sake and for the sake of universal officialdom, leaving woman to fight her battles alone. Cooperation gives way to competition; having replaces being; power becomes abstract as a 'scientific product made in the political *laboratory* of the Nation, through the dissolution of the personal humanity'. The integrated human being gets compartmentalised and crushed under the weight of an ever-growing wealth-producing mechanism; interminable economic war is waged between capital and labour, since the greed of wealth and power is limitless; the jealousy and suspicion they breed end in the catastrophe of war. 'The suspicion of man for man stings all the limbs of this civilization like the hairs of the nettle.' (Das, p. 432)

The nation is an outcome of a long history of progressive privileging and fetishisation of competitive accumulation. Tagore makes a distinction between social accumulation as against competitive accumulation: while power had been subsumed under the overall framework of social relations in the early days and considered purely a functional activity over nature and over the distribution of goods, the growth of accumulation led to greed and fear. He clearly sees the choice as one between competition and cooperation and conceives modernity as a moment of brittleness that could take either of the turns. The nation threatens to destroy the global through the enactment of the principle of competition.

Tagore uses a series of tropes and metaphors taken from nature as well as science and the human world to drive home his point. We have already referred to his use of the tropes of 'organisation', 'machine', 'factory' and 'laboratory'. Elsewhere he observes: Nation is like a *hydraulic press* whose pressure is impersonal and hence completely effective. India had been ruled by other foreign powers earlier, but they were like handlooms in whose products the magic of man's fingers gets expressed while Britain is a *power-loom,* relentlessly lifeless, rigorously accurate and immensely monotonous. Elsewhere he speaks of British administration as a *steamroller* whose formidable power may have its uses, but does not help to fertilise the soil. Nation, he says elsewhere, has the callous perfection of an *automaton* and the conscience of a *ghost.*

While the machine is a recurring metaphor in Tagore's writings on nationalism, the poet employs several other metaphors to express the different crippling aspects of the pernicious ideology. For example he characterises the Nation as *a father turning a gambler* to the detriment of the family. Goodness is the end of man, but Nation's end is success. The personal man becomes a phantom: Here we are reminded of W.H. Auden's famous poem, 'The Unknown Citizen' who is just a name in the Census, a tax-payer, a ration-card holder, about whose real happiness and freedom no one seems concerned. India, Tagore observes, is sadly ruled by a Nation, whose symbol, the governor, needs not know our languages, and need have only an official relation with people and can aid or hinder our aspirations from a disdainful distance. It can afford not to take the scantiest notice of calamities happening in areas of India larger than the British Isles. The governed are pursued by suspicions and punished by an abstract force.

After the metaphors of the soulless machine, the loveless man, and the stinging nettle, he turns to the animal world. In nationalism Man is represented by a many-armed octopus of abstractions, fixing its suckers even onto the far-away future. Again, Western nations are *a pack of predatory creatures* that must have their prey. It does not want its hunting grounds to become cultivated fields. So the Western Nation, like a *dam*, checks the flow of Western civilisation, whose great social virtues Tagore praises as complementary to the Eastern spiritual values, into its colonies; it is exclusive and unwilling to share its sources of power with the peoples it exploits. What it has given India most generously are law and order. Here comes another metaphor: the unkind mother. 'While the small feeding bottle of our education is nearly dry, and sanitation sucks its own thumb in despair, the military organisation, the magisterial offices, the police, the Criminal Investigation Department, the secret spy system, attain to an abnormal girth in their waists, occupying every inch of our country.' (Das, p. 426) Nation promotes pace at the expense of life and liberty and regulates our steps with a closed-up system turning the individuals entirely powerless. Before the arrival of the Nation, India made people feel their destiny is in their hands; the hope of the unexpected was always there and there was scope for a free play of imagination by the governors and the governed; the future was no opaque granite wall. Now at the pressing of a button *the monster* of the organisation becomes all eyes; no one can escape the suffocation of its tightening grip. Here we are reminded of Bentham's idea of *panopticon* elaborated by Michel Foucault in his *Discipline and Punish*: the observing eye from the watch tower (Jose Saramago's novel *Blindness* too has it) ever hidden from the observed and hence supposed to be present even when it is not there. People live in a perpetual distrust of its back where it has no eyes. Each footstep and each rustle of movement send a chill through the spine and this terror fathers all that is base in man's nature and makes man unashamed of inhumanity. It petrifies their moral nature. Nation represents the dead pressure of the un-human upon the living human. Tagore prophetically adds: 'Not merely the subject races, but you who live under the delusion that you are free, are everyday sacrificing your freedom and humanity to this fetish of nationalism, living in the dense poisonous atmosphere of world-wide suspicion and greed and panic.' (Das, p. 427). He points to Japan where people voluntarily submit to the trimming of their minds and clipping of their freedom by their government. Tagore certainly had not heard about Antonio Gramsci's concept of 'consent', the voluntary-seeming agreement to its schemes manufactured by the ideological machinery of the State, like education, the State-run press and the whole Goebbelsian State propaganda machine. Yet he understands this process of the legitimation of the Nation when he says that people are 'hypnotized into believing that they are free' (Das, p.428) and they begin to think that bartering the higher aspirations of life for profit and power has been their free choice; the State perfects their instincts of self-aggrandisement and make them believe it is good. It is 'organized gregariousness (of commercial and political) gluttony' (Das, p. 430) Tagore asks whether there has been a greater disaster in human history than the Nation 'fixing its *fangs* deep into the naked flesh of the world'. (Das, p. 428) Another metaphor is that of the *giraffe:* '...Man (in the Nationalist concept) with his mental and material power far outgrowing his moral strength is like an exaggerated giraffe whose head has suddenly shot up miles away from the rest of him, making normal communication difficult to establish. This greedy head, with its huge dental organisation, has been munching all the topmost foliage of the world, but the nourishment is too late in reaching his digestive organs and his heart is suffering from want of blood.' (Das, p. 431). Man's storehouse is growing every day, but his humanity is getting emptied. Tagore is critical of the utilitarian attitude that nationalism engenders: 'Turn a *tree* into a log and it will burn for you, but it will never bear living flowers and fruit'. 'The *bagpipe* of Nation's indignation' goes on changing its tunes according to the needs of diplomacy and alliance to produce a variety performance in the political music hall' (Das, p. 432). The nation's religion is organised selfishness; it gloats on the feebleness of its neighbours. Its wisdom is 'not in its faith in humanity, but in its complete distrust' (Das, p.433). It serves knowledge and efficiency like in a *hotel*; the service is elaborate, but the host is absent; it is more convenient than hospitable.

Tagore finds the idea of the Nation to be the 'most powerful *anaesthetics* that man has invented' (Das, p. 434); it is evil, it cannot check evil. It is manufactory that turns men into ludicrously perfect war-making and money-making puppets. The war in Europe is one of retribution; the cannon roars are the nation's death-rattle. It is 'the fifth act of the tragedy of the unreal'. (Das, p. 435) In his talk in Japan, he advises the Japanese not to imitate the West by organising themselves on the basis of selfishness as the European civilisation is now 'choking itself from the debris carried by its innumerable channels' ('Nationalism in Japan', Das, p. 438) and asks them to minimise the immense sacrifice of man's life and freedom by following their ideals of simplicity and recognition of social obligation. Here Tagore uses new metaphors like *'the weed'* and 'millionaire acquiring money at the cost of his soul' to critique the new political civilisation. Progress has to be judged according to its original objective and contrasts a train's programmed movement to its terminus with the still and spontaneous progress of the tree towards life and light, the latter being the true measure of progress. Japan has realised nature's secrets not by methods of analytical knowledge, but by sympathy. While Europe has felt the conflict of things in the universe, which can only be controlled by war and conquest, Japan has felt in the world the touch of some benign and adorable presence. 'She does not boast of her mastery of nature, but to her she brings, with infinite care and joy, her offerings of love. Her relationship with the world is the deeper relationship of the heart.'

The poet evokes the Buddhist ideal of *maitri* central to Japanese culture and invites the people to come out of the tutelage of European 'school-masters' to create their own modernism, whose core is the freedom of the mind and not a slavery of taste. He is not against Japan acquiring modern weapons of self-protection, but 'it should not go beyond her instinct of self-preservation'. (Das, p. 446) The real power is not in weapons, but in the man who wields them. Japan should avoid the Western path of suicide that is the inevitable end of tyranny. He does not mind Japan following certain other features of Western civilisation, the danger is 'the acceptance of the motive force of the Western nationalism as her own', their belief in 'the survival of the fittest.' 'We can take anything else from the hands of science, but not this elixir of moral death' (Das, p. 447). At the same time he warns against a total rejection of everything Western; we need also to be self-critical; if they have race, we have caste. He acknowledges the living soul of the West that is trying unobserved to combat the power of huge organisations, resisting the markets and the cannons with the ideal of ethical freedom, the sacredness of law, the liberty of conscience, thought, expression and action, the higher obligations of public good above narrower considerations, values that had helped create its civilisation now facing the crisis of commercialism, careerism and competition. The main problem in India, he says in his talk in the U.S. ('Nationalism in India'), is the hierarchisation of her society on the basis of race/caste and a blind faith in the authority of traditions. But he is also happy that India has learnt to contain and tolerate difference rather than exterminate the different, like Europe exterminating the original populations of the countries it came to occupy by force. But in an attempt to provide an order to the society she denied to many the opportunity of movement and expansion. We are also trained to think this system of discrimination is eternal.

Tagore points out that Indians cannot build a political miracle of freedom upon the quicksand of social slavery: a truth that B.R. Ambedkar, more than any other Indian leader realised so well. Tagore wants Indians to realise that our social restrictions are tyrannical enough to turn men into cowards; men with heterodox ideas fear to speak as they can be ostracised. Tagore is against winning political freedom by sacrificing our moral freedom; we need to be free from the tyranny of evil traditions to begin with. Nations of the world have decreed that Indians should remain an agricultural people and the British have killed the process of industrialisation that had been begun in pre-colonial India. Tagore is not against industries, but against turning our civilisation into a commercial one, permitting the values of the market to govern our society and yielding entirely to the temptation of wealth that he considers the new Menaka, whom the European Indra has sent to test our sagacity.

In a response to the letters carried by *The Modern Review of Calcutta* in May, 1921, Tagore points to the need to liberate man from the organisations of 'National Egoism' which he later in the article qualifies as 'racial egoism'. He adds there is no word for 'Nation' in our languages. India has to win freedom for all Humanity, not to join the West's holy feast nor the mad orgy in the name of the Nation. He considers true India an ideal and not 'a mere geographical map'. 'The idea of India is against the intense consciousness of the separateness of one's own people from others, and which inevitably leads to ceaseless conflicts.'[7]

In his discussions on the concept of 'Indian Art' he opposes the blind pursuit of dead habits and argues for a living and creative exchange among diverse aesthetic cultures.

> I strongly urge our artists, vehemently to deny their obligation carefully to produce something that can be labeled as Indian art according to some old-world mannerism. Let them proudly

---

7. Sabyasachi Bhattacharya, ed., 'Tagore's Reflections on Non-cooperation and Cooperation', *The Mahatma and the Poet* (Delhi: NBT, 1997).

refuse to be herded into a pen like branded beasts that are treated as cattle and not as cows.... Art is not a gorgeous sepulcher immovably brooding over a lonely eternity of vanished years. It belongs to the procession of life, making constant adjustment with surprises, exploring unknown shrines of reality along its path of pilgrimage to a future which is as different from the past as the tree from the seed.

—*The Meaning of Art,* Das, pp. 586–7

Tagore questions conformity; art is no plant to be fixed in the narrow soil of tradition producing a monotonous type of leaves and flowers forever.

3

Tagore's observations on nationalism were criticised in his time. It was seen by some critics as a *volte-face* as Tagore had so far been perceived as a fount of inspiration to Bengali patriotism, as well as Indian nationalism. In his early phase Rabindranath did have an alternate concept of the nation as a voluntarist community produced by shared memory and collective will, as pointed out by Partha Chatterjee. ('What is the Nation?', Ref. Dutta, p. 256) It was also regulated by the logic of limits where the nation's self-interest is in harmony with the interests of the people and he believed that the nation is not a problem if kept within limits, but later he found that in actual practice the nations are going beyond the limits and turning violent towards their own people as well as of other countries. The Boer Wars and the First World War proved his apprehensions, turning him a critic of the very idea of the nation. For example, *Ananda Bazar Patrika* in an editorial (5 June, 1923) expressed astonishment at this change of mind, though it was understood as the response of a hurt soul to the destructiveness of the European World War.

But however much the poet's soft and idealistic soul may be hurt... there is no denying that nationalism is a necessity for the oppressed countries like India... In the present world the effort to bind the strong and the weak by the bond of love may be nice to imagine, but it is hopeless as a practical proposition.

—Quoted in translation in *The Mahatma and the Poet,* p. 29

How Sisir Kumar Das in his editorial notes to the book *The English Writings of Rabindranath Tagore, Vol. II,* (Delhi, 1996) remarks: 'Tagore's forthright denunciation of nationalism provoked violent attacks in the American press and severe criticism by the Japanese intellectuals. This work (the above book) made him unpopular not only in America and Japan, but also in India where nationalism had already entered a new phase of growth.' Krishna Kripalani found it 'ill-timed'[8] though he admits he was 'prophetically right in what he said and must be admired for his courage for courting abuse'. In Japan, Tagore was criticised by Inoue Tetsujiro as the representative of a 'ruined nation' while his lecture was recognised by another scholar, Saito Isamu, as a warning and an acceptable call to free themselves from imitation.[9]

Tagore's observations however have to be seen in their proper context of the inhuman and massive violence unleashed by the First World War, the ultimate sources of which can be sought in the aggressive selfishness, mean competitiveness, un-moderated hubris, greed for money and for power and the idea of 'the other as hell' characteristic of the Nationalist ideology. Though Tagore with his loathing of jargons and fondness for metaphors does not use terms like capitalism and the State, his descriptions make it amply clear that he has the capitalist Nation State in mind—though when it comes to the behaviour of the State, the so-called socialist States have not fared any better. Mussolini's Italy, Hitler's Germany and Stalin's USSR are equally guilty of crimes against humanity, and so have been the so-called democracies like USA (the World Wars, Vietnam, Iraq, Afghanistan...) and UK (eg; Ireland). The Indian State has not been

---

8. *Rabindranath Tagore* (O.U.P, 1962), p. 259.
9. Kyoka Niwa, *Rabindranath Tagore and Japan,* Ph.D. Thesis, Jadavpur University, 1987, quoted by Sisirkumar Das, op. cit.

far behind, though its crimes are often more oblique than blatant, most often in the form of collaboration in or silence over crimes. (Look for example at its ambivalent attitudes to violence/suppression of human rights in Palestine, Myanmar, Iraq, Afghanistan or Sri Lanka.) The mass slaughters and various kinds of bombings in the two World Wars, the holocausts starting with the Armenian and the Jewish ones followed by the Cambodian and the Rwandan. Whatever hopes of world peace the dismantling of the USSR and the rhetoric of globalisation had raised for the unthinking have been erased by the post-1980s genocides in Bosnia, Somalia, Iraq, Sri Lanka and Gujarat. As Ashis Nandy observes, 'the ultimate symbols of the (twentieth) century are not space-probes and computers, but gas chambers and Hiroshima'.[10] If we take into account the man-made famines in British India and Mao's China, besides more than 40 wars, more than 200 million people were killed in the last century in avoidable violence. Nations like India that are trying to mimic and replicate the material 'success'—which has meant, so far, the accumulation of wealth and power in a minority within the country that masquerades as the 'nation' with its high Gross National Products and per-capita incomes that conveniently and brutally conceal the real state of life for a majority—of the more wealthy and powerful societies have also recorded a spectacular increase in pathological violence of all sorts, including the necrophilic euphoria over the obscene show of arms and ammunition during the national day celebrations as well as the brutal ecstasy over nuclear tests. One may recall, as Hannah Arendt says, European fascism was an attempt to build a compensatory pseudo-community in place of the ruined communities, cultures and world views. Modern nations also take up this mission and in fact Anderson's 'imagined community' is often imagined as a substitute for real community based on natural bonding. Tagore's refusal—this applies also to Tolstoy, Thoreau and Gandhi—to use rigid intellectual frames and theoretical jargons may be seen as a form of revolt

---

10. Ashis Nandy, 'Violence and Creativity in the Late twentieth Century,' *Time Warps*, (Delhi: Permanent Black, 2002).

against the violence they often imply. While Tagore upholds, what in Benedict Anderson's style may be called a 'rooted cosmopolitanism' his writings clearly indicate that he would not have accepted the jingoist, insular and violent Hindu nationalism modeled on Nazism based on othering, hatred, racial pride, manipulative employment of archetypes and myths and distortion of history on the one hand and the heartless globalisation that is a monologue of power based on an unequal exchange that promotes cultural amnesia in the third world peoples, exports life styles, advocates the hegemony of the materialist aspect of Western culture, places competition above cooperation, destroys environment, turns culture into a tinsel collage and an ethnic branding and transforms the whole world into a market place instead of a creative space, on the other. Remember none of the great figures of European Enlightenment from Vico to Voltaire, so eloquent about reason, seldom spoke of the need for non-violence as a guiding principle of social and intellectual life. To quote Nandy,

> Rabindranath Tagore's creative self was a magisterial protest against the dominant theories of violence and counter-violence. He was probably the first to identify the banal, sanitized machine-violence of our times and, much before Gandhi had entered the Indian political scene, Sisirkumar Das shows that Tagore had anticipated and welcomed the emergence of figures like Gandhi.
> —*Time Warps*; p. 221

Das points out how from the character of Dhananjay Bairagi in *Prayaschitta* (1855) and *Muktadhara* (1922) to the song '*oi mahamanava ashe*' to the self-discovery of Gora in *Gora* (1908) many of Tagore's creative works can be read as attempts to envision the emergence of someone like Gandhi. Even the debates between the two great men presumed some basic agreements. When Tagore argued that 'the foundation of *swaraj* cannot be based on any external conformity but only on the internal union of hearts,'[11] Gandhi declared in

---

11. 'The Cult of the Charkha', *Modern Review*, September, 1925, *The Mahatma and the Poet*, p.106.

Young India: 'Patriotism for me is the same as humanity' (1921), 'it is the narrowness, selfishness and exclusiveness which is the bane of modern nations, which is evil' (1925) and again, 'through the realization of freedom of India, I hope to realize and carry on the mission of brotherhood of men' (1929). (Quoted in the introduction to *The Mahatma and the Poet*, p.30).

Tagore's project can well be seen today as an ambitious attempt to construct a counter-global by conceptualising a process of identity formation that will be free from the form of the nation, as suggested by Pradip Kumar Datta[12]. Globalisation was yet to take the neo-liberal and US-centric form it has taken in the post-USSR decades, but the process has been on for centuries as illustrated by Amartya Sen who looks at the early commercial and cultural interactions between India and the rest of the world as the beginning of the globalising process.[13] Tagore was well-aware of this process and had deep apprehensions about global survival as a watchful traveler traversing all the continents of the world except Africa and Australia, as an anxious observer of the world before and after the First World War and as a pacifist linked to the European movement for world-peace. The gap between the conceptualisation of the global as shared space and the institutional possibilities of describing it as an actually existing reality in his time also,

> allowed greater freedom to reconceive the global, deploying, as Rabindranath did, other historical modes of globalization that he identified with the 'east'. The gap allowed for radical suspension of necessitarian logic. The closing of the gap by the apocalyptic prospect of world-wide destruction also necessitated, at the same time, a fundamental critique of all the principles that propelled the world towards its commitment to destruction.
>
> —Datta, p. 222

---

12. Pradip Kumar Datta, 'Revisiting Rabindranath, Thinking Global', *Heterogeneities: Identity Formations in Modern India* (New Delhi: Tulika, 2010), pp. 214-258.
13. Amartya Sen, *Identity and Violence* (London, W.W. Norton, 2007).

Tagore tapped into this space of opportunity. He tried to puncture the Eurocentrism that had so far characterised the narratives of globalisation. Such interrogation is generally done either by 'pointing to the processes of alternative modernities, involving the identification of local particulars that come into different relationships of complementarity, rupture, hybridisation and so on, with the forces of capitalist modernity' thus revealing 'the limits of universal principles that that cannot exhaust the presence of local particularities' or by 'a historical recuperation of forms of global interconnectedness that exist outside Europe. Tagore rearticulates the global first by using the old civilisational, spatio-temporal categories of 'East' and 'West' without privileging either or turning them into territorial or cultural stereotypes. He defines civilisation by the way it treats others. For him it is something ever in the making, not a finished enterprise. India did not 'other' or exclude successive waves of migrants; it is 'many countries packed into one geographical receptacle' ('Nationalism in India') and thus equipped to confront the problem of diversity and difference the world confronts today. Tagore circumvents the issue of civilisational hierarchy by contrasting civilisations through their respective capacities for handling difference and sees history proceeding through the effects of one civilisation on another, thus placing civilisations symmetrically rather than in a progressive hierarchy. Tagore provides an alternative to the narrative modes of his time by directly critiquing the basis of the global modern located in its homelands in the West through the counter-universal. He neither privileges the 'difference' of the post-colonial world nor critiques universalism itself as an embodiment of Western culture; 'instead he interrogates the basis of a universal, modern Western project of nation-making by posing a counter-universal derived from his location in the East.' He invokes the East as an ensemble of non-instrumentalist modes of social relationships, which can supply the principles for an alternative to the 'Nation', a Western creation. Tagore does not reduce the East to certain fixed values and images as the Orientalists do; it is no unchanging monolith and this applies to the West too: he is not condemning everything Western; there is no binary opposition here; on the other hand he thinks of a common platform where the East and the West interact critically neither compromising their dignity and critical wisdom. Tagore understands that the East has been following organisational principles different from the West so that it provides a perspective to critique the West and offer an alternative. Indeed there is some ambivalence in Tagore's formulation in the three talks, which also comes from his appreciation of the Eastern principles of social organisation combined with a critique of the caste system and the fear that the East is also being taken over by the Western idea of Nationhood. This is especially clear in his talk in Japan that oscillates between admiration for the Japanese heritage and apprehension about its incorporation into the Western paradigm. He found the East nationalising itself, but it was yet an unfinished process with scope for intervention.

> The East is outside the national-Global and yet not free from it. This axis of suspension makes Rabindranath extremely sensitive to the rapid intrusion of the idea of the nation and the urgent need to produce a revised understanding of the East as a basis for the survival of the world. It justifies his counter-universalistic concern as necessary precisely because the very survival of the global life-world is at stake.
>
> —Datta, p. 224

It is possible that Tagore foresaw the rise of Hindu Nationalism, a violent middle-class phenomenon, declaring Muslims to be its other, though it gained momentum only with the economic liberalisation of the 1980s and reached its crescendo in 1992. The middle and elite classes that spearheaded the movement would support the dismantling of the welfare state as what stirred them was 'not the defensive warmth of the community life but the nationalist pride that came with the word Hindu.' (Datta, p. 226) One may well distinguish the secular mainstream nationalism from the identitarianism of Hindutva; but it is dangerous to ignore their continuities, especially on the question of national identity which also spills over to the Hindu diaspora desperately in search of a lost identity. The fetishisation of the nation as a transcendental source of identity prepares the ground for turning nationalism into an identitarian ethic. Rabindranath's critique refutes this insular logic. In *Ghaire Baire* (Home and the World) Tagore critiques this politics by positioning Nikhilesh against Sandip who mobilises people, enshrining the country as a goddess. Nikhilesh sees heresy in attributing divinity that is universal, to the loyalty to a country that is particular. Acts of a blind love of the nation thus becomes a form of self-worship as a nation's divinity comes from its own recognition of its collective power. If nation takes away the powers of the people, this worship of sovereignty becomes hollow, as it is derived more from an identity-fetishism than from a liberal idea of social contract. It is nothing but willed surveillance, and self-subordination: hence Tagore's contention that there is little difference between the colonised subjects and those of a nation founded on hegemonies of various kinds. Selfishness regarded as a vice in individuals becomes a virtue when embodied in a nation. Nations create aliens and isolate them or turn them into slaves. He demonstrates this pointing to the fate of the native blacks in the U.S. (i.e. the children of the slaves of African origin born in the U.S.) and of Indians colonised by the British ('Nationalism in the West') or of Muslims and the Dalits objectified and instrumentalised by the national goddess, who revolt against her. (*Ghare Baire*) Today, as shown by William Mazarella[14] this 'Indian' identity has become a trademark and an advertising strategy in the global corporate market, where it denotes a distinctive ensemble of characteristics that hark back to the Western orientalist construct. Competition seems to have now been normalised by neo-liberal ideologies as the very structuring principle of existence, as can be seen by anyone following the media: success, not happiness, is the keyword and money seems to have become the central quest in life for the already rich, as well as the aspiring middle classes in general. This, we all know, is also at

---

14. William Mazarella. *Shovelling Smoke: Advertising and Globalisation in Contemporary India* (Durham NC: Duke University Press, 2003).

the root of the corruption that, more than ever before, is plaguing our democracy today.

Even if, viewed as a political-theoretical critique, one may come across ambiguities, silences and inadequacies of conceptualisation in Tagore's criticism of the Nation, one cannot miss its power and relevance as a moral critique in our context of neo-liberal globalisation, majoritarian nationalism and an exclusive concept of 'Indianness', described more by 'ideal-typical' definitions than by what Indians are and what is it that 'others' several sections of our people. His arguments can also be used as a critique of the idea of an over-centralised nation seeking some sort of cultural standardisation and a plea for a more open, truly federal polity, where people are free to imagine the nation in the way they want and relate to it on their own terms.

Let me conclude recollecting the elements that go into the making of Tagore's counter-globalisation move: 1. Civilisation is defined by the way it treats others. It works more as a capacity than as a finished and fully articulated trajectory. It is a becoming rather than a formed essence, to use the existentialist phraseology. India's teachers taught the lessons of the spiritual unity of mankind and the ethic of cooperation and appreciation of differences. 2. If Europe is 'one country made into many', India is 'many countries packed into one geographical receptacle.' It has found its own way of coping with difference and diversity: a problem encountered by the world today. The inclusive world view of India has assimilated and not 'othered' the migrants who have settled here and become part of her people. 3. Civilisations do not follow a historicist hierarchisation. East is not 'the waiting room' of history, representing some pre-Western state. Civilisations should be placed symmetrically and synchronically, and judged by their ability to handle difference. 4. History proceeds through civilisational exchanges and their effects and not through competitions. Even invasions introduce new elements into a civilisational identity and help refresh and rejuvenate it. For example, Islam introduced 'religious democracy' and made great contributions to literature, art, philosophy, music and architecture ('An Eastern

University', Das, p. 565). Islam's encounter with Hinduism produced Indian Sufism as also integrationist figures like Akbar ('East and West'. Das, p. 534) The problem with he British is that they refused to be part of India, and introduced their 'Nation' as a superior master, unlike the previous invaders who had respect for Indian civilisation; the British also refused to share their deeper values with India. India's responses were either mindless imitation of the coloniser or an assertion of national pride, both helping increase the cultural distance between the two, as both do not reflect critical respect for the other and are against the principle of assimilation or critical appropriation of elements we need to transform ourselves as well as the other. Tagore saw literature as a major vehicle that introduces new ideas and dispositions into another culture and believed in the creativity of bicultural minds, as other civilisations transform the very parameters of civilisational being and not just add to it. He is not speaking of a 'divided self', but a growing and expanding self that can take in diversity so that movement towards a unity with the universal is possible, though this unity itself is infinitely deferred and is more a goal and a purpose than something fully realised. Boundaries of the self are not constant; identities keep reaching out to the other. Commitment to change is the testament of life, changelessness is death. ('The Problem of the Self', Das, p. 311) Tagore's counter-globality is not just the resistance of the local to the global, which, as we see today, seems a failed project, as the local is easily assimilated into the instrumental commercial logic of the global, but *a unique mode of inhabiting the global*: not a denial, but a new kind of relationship with it. In a way it is also a way of re-imagining the imagined community, where identity is in a constant state of flux with a will to transform itself, and identity and difference do not exist as binary opposites, but are in constant dialogue, ever on the move towards a remote horizon of human unity.

SARATCHANDRA CHATTERJEE AND THE DYNAMICS OF RECEPTION

A century and a quarter have rolled by since Saratchandra Chatterjee was born. It might be rewarding to look at the history of the response to Saratchandra's *oeuvre* in Bengali as well as in other Indian languages, especially at the beginning of a new century and a new millennium that also often signifies a change of sensibility and attitude and ushers in a shift in the episteme revealing the inadequacies of the paradigms of an earlier century. This is particularly true of Saratchandra who had exercised a profound influence on readers and writers across languages in India at least upto the 1960s, an influence that began to visibly wane with the rise of the modern urban fiction in most of the languages of India. While most of the modern authors confess having read Saratchandra in their teens, they tend to dismiss him as overtly sentimental and find his rural sensibility inadequate to articulate the tensions of modern life. Many of them tend to think that the issues he dealt with in his works were relevant to the feudal times and to the life of the Bengali middle classes of those times but have been marginalised, if not rendered obsolete, by the social developments that followed. The radicals of today find him not radical enough; they look at him as a spokesman of the *petit bourgeoisie* with all the conflicts, frailties and uncertainties that go with the term. The modernists find in him a kind of nativist with his narrow range of concerns confined to his age and class. The spurt in Sarat translations in Indian languages has almost stopped; this possibly follows the publishers' perception that modern youth may not be enthusiastic about Sarat's novels. At the same time there is also a vague recognition of Saratchandra as a classic that still impels some to translate his works into English.

2

During Saratchandra's own lifetime he had received wide acclaim across regions and languages. In his own Bengal, even Rabindranath

Tagore, who was known for his reservations about Sarat's fiction openly praised the great contemporary on his 61st birthday on 1 September 1936: 'No other writer has given them (Bengalis K.S.) such intensity of happiness... He has evoked through his words the agony of the Bengali heart.' Nazrul Islam wrote a poem, 'Homage to Saratchandra' where he addressed Saratchandra as the 'autumnal moon' that made the azure brow of the sky aglow: disgraced men could view life's highway by his clear moonlight; the timid feminine heart received a glowing spurt from the moon's vital rays: 'The earthly moon has set holding in silvery net, palaces and hovels and huts.' Subhas Chandra Bose called Sarat a rebel and extolled him for his sympathy for the outcaste and the oppressed.

Later, Suniti Kumar Chatterjee viewed Saratchandra as a product of his milieu. Bankim's robust idealism, he observed, was impossible in Sarat's time of doubtsand difficulties. Sarat's works reflected the spiritual condition of the intelligentsia and the middle class of his age. The linguist-critic praised the novelist for his loyalty to 'the native spirit of Bengali language'. His Bengali was 'pure and undefiled'; he was a master stylist, his expressive idiom and vocabulary revealed his mastery over the secret springs of the language. He was also praised for the diversity of his characters and his humanist spirit. He taught his people to keep their eyes open. Manik Bandopadhyay, the great novelist of the following generation, found in *Ses Prasna* a new Saratchandra, different from the one that wrote *Charitrahin* and *Grhadaha*. He praised Sarat for his courage in having come out of his own fame and unsettled all the preconceptions about himself among his readers. Here was a fresh work, executed with rare artistic restraint. The exuberance of frothy emotion that marred some of his other works was happily absent here. Kamal of the novel was not the female counterpart of Gora, as she was vocal in her support of the West, in its conflict with the ideals of the East. 'Had I written *Ses Prasna* myself, people would have marvelled at my genius,' he concluded. Sukumar Banerjee upheld Sarat's works for their bold heterodoxy, scathing criticism of values and standards and their championship of forbidden love.

Tagore's *Choker Bali,* he felt, anticipated Saratchandra's works in the portrayal of love in all its depth and felicity, its contradictions and struggles. Sarat also completed Tagore's mission of breaking the conventional portrayal of women as passive subjects, as for example in Bankim, who never cared to represent the feminine point of view, and was happy portraying traditional women who never dared question the status quo. Sarat's women, on the other hand, are dynamic and demanding, interrogating even the time-honoured sanctities of wedded loyalty. Again, Sarat wandered along the outer fringes of life in search of the diversity of experience; it was from here that he picked up his Indranath, Bajrananda, Sabitri and Rajlakshmi. These wanderings along the margins gave him that special strength that the aristocratic novelists lacked. It also enabled Sarat to develop a probing critique of Bengali life exposing its weak spots. Subodh Chandra Sen Gupta was fascinated more by the conflict of social ideals and intellectual convictions on the one hand and half-awakened instincts on the other that he found to have been the key-note of Saratchandra's work. He closely analysed the conflict between instinct and institutions in *Ses Prasna* to point to the tragic duality of human life. Dinesh Chandra Sen was struck by the real-life characters in Sarat's novels and the highly focussed nature of his fiction that made no allowances for prolixity or digressions.

Hemachandra Ghosh, a revolutionary of the pre-independence Bengal Volunteers, recalls Sarat's infinite compassion for the tortured and humiliated, his affiliation with the anti-imperial journal *Benu,* and his sympathy for the revolutionaries. He supplied the Bengal Volunteers regularly with bullets with which they shot down many English officials. Sarat collected the material for *Pather Dabi* through his discussions with Hemachandra Ghosh. Shibdas Ghosh, the Marxist thinker, historicises Saratchandra's *oeuvre* and condemns the critics who dub Saratchandra as a *pakshalar Sahityik*—a low-brow writer. He chooses for special praise Sarat's ability to portray independent women characters like Hemangini of *Mejdidi,* Bindubasini of *Bindur Chhele* or Narayani of *Ramer Sumati,* instilling in every woman reader the desire to emulate them. Shibdas Ghosh compares Sarat to the early European Renaissance thinkers. Saratchandra once declared that he would not waste his time in the pursuit of the unknowable. He laughed at the writers who would declare something inexplicable and inconceivable and in the same breath try to vividly explain the very same thing. They wrote book after book on what was beyond forms, properties, words and thoughts: an obvious dig at his 'mystic' contemporaries. Sarat was frequently asked why he had little fiction in his library, while he had plenty of books on physics, chemistry, mathematics, economics, history and psychology. He answered that he had little interest in fiction; these books helped him grasp society and the state of knowledge better. Shibdas Ghosh even agrees with Sarat's view that superstitions and evil customs cannot be fought by legislation; only social movements and the awareness they bring can bring about the change. He takes Sarat's side in the novelist's argument with Tagore on the issue. Tagore had taken the example of cats eating from men's dish or sitting on a Brahmin lady's lap with 'unclean mouth' to ridicule the practice of untouchability; Sarat thought that habits ingrained by centuries of human cultural practice cannot be dismissed by such ridiculous and illogical comparisons. Shibdas Ghosh also defends Saratchandra's refusal to get the widows in his novels like Rama re-married, since the challenges faced by Rama and Ramesh in the fulfilment of their love alone make the society sympathise with their plight and support the idea of widow remarriage. Had the love been fulfilled, it would not only have been unrealistic in the rural context but would not have made the society realise the cruelty of its customs and conventions. Sarat believed in the power of persuasion, rather than an apparently radical stand that would look so unconvincing in the background of the social reality of his times. Ghosh often takes up for discussion *Grhadaha, Charitrahin, Srikanta, Bipradas, Ses Prasna, Niskruti, Baikunther Will* and *Pather Dabi* to expound the subtle relationship between politics and literature, and ethics and aesthetics. He evaluates Saratchandra as a believer in '*petit bourgeois* revolutionism' and '*bourgeois* humanism' and emphasises the need for the working class movement to understand writers like him, since 'the working class movement can destroy the *bourgeois* social system only by means superior in all respects to what the *bourgeoisie* have been able to produce in the fields of ideology, politics and literature'. Subodh Ghose finds Saratchandra to have been to the Bengali soul, what Destoevsky and Turganev were to the Russian soul, Victor Hugo to the French and Charles Dickens to the English. He was, according to Ghose, the creator of a 'national literature,' especially as he appears in *Palli-Samaj* rather than in *Pather Dabi:* a literature whose primary preoccupation is the good of the society, and is concerned with the problems of the age, as manifest within the nation.

Buddhadev Bose perhaps best represents the later critical reaction of the Bengali intellectuals to Saratchandra. Let me quote from his *An Acre of Grass:*

> Saratchandra is a master of sentiment, of the story of sentiments and even of the sentimental story. He has never depicted passion nor life's enchantments or disenchantments, and his sensibility is limited. He has humour, but never achieved comedy, he has pathos, but tragedy was outside his range... His world is bound up in everyday reality, an altogether worldly world full of supremely sociable human beings whose actions and conversations are never intruded upon by animals, children and nature. Life as lived in imagination has no place, not one of his characters is born 'under one law to another bound.' Commonplace reality or domesticity is all.

According to Buddhadev Bose, the finest portraitures in Saratchandra are those of adolescents: the colt-like boy, overflowing with animal spirits, 'moderately blasphemous, immoderately boisterous,' with the appearance of fierce untameability but longing to eat the rice from the woman who mothers him or whom he loves above all else. Hardly one of his characters, according to Buddhadev is really adult, all of them being 'protagonists of chronological adolescence, instead of chronic ones, for, in growing up they threaten to outgrow their author'.

3

Saratchandra, more than any other writer from any other Indian language including Tagore and Premchand, seems to have found the warmest and most spontaneous reception in the other languages of India. While translations of Tagore were most often sponsored by institutions and Premchand's translations were often a product of the Progressive Literary Movement, Saratchandra's translators and publishers were fascinated by the sheer emotional and social appeal of his works. If I can depend on available statistics, the maximum number of translations of Sarat's works is to be found in Hindi: 36 of his works have been translated—quite a few of them having multiple translations: *Biraj Bahu,* and *Palli Samaj* and *Vipradas* have seven each, *Pather Dabi, Ses Prasna* and *Datta* six each, to cite some examples. Kannada has a total of 42 works in translations, Gujarati 33, Telugu and Malayalam 32 each, Sindhi 29, Marathi and Tamil 27 each, Urdu 18, Oriya eight, Assamese six, Nepali five and Punjabi three. This great variation in the number of translations may have many reasons like the difference in the degree of social appeal of the texts depending on the existence or absence of similar concerns, conditions and issues, the general state of translation in the language, the availability of translators with sufficient knowledge of Bengali (or Hindi, since many of these translations have been done from the Hindi versions), the literary needs of specific languages and the dominant sensibility.

Not only was Saratchandra read widely, but exerted a profound influence on the writers of different languages. In Hindi, Yashpal, Phaneeshwarnath Renu, Jainendrakumar, Ilachandra Joshi, Chatursen Sastri, Agyeya, Yogesh, Rajkamal Chaudhuri and Bhagwati Prasad Vajpeyi, among others, have acknowledged their debt to Saratchandra. Sarat's method of delineating the society through the individual and the family was of special appeal to the realists, who aspired to combine emotional appeal with social analysis. Jainendra Kumar felt that Sarat's contribution to the cultural India was no less than that of Gandhi to the moral-political reconstruction of the nation. He commented that Saratchandra 'injected the warmth and liquidity of sentiment in social relations'. He found Sarat's range of experience to have been narrow, but was more than compensated by the intensity of his presentation. He also observed that Sarat's fiction was not political, as it was not meant to inspire action. Mohan Rakesh countered the charge of sentimentality in Saratchandra, pointing out that it was natural to the people of warm tropical countries. It has its positive impact: we have attained tolerance, tenderness and sympathy through the same constitution. Its negative impact expressed itself in our nervous weakness, extreme insistence on tradition on the one hand and blind faith in the new on the other, and the penetration of politics into religion and religion into politics. The eminent critic Nagendra found Sarat to have been more influential than Tagore in Hindi literature. Premchand rejected the 'Bengali sentimentality' in Sarat; but critics have discovered many similarities, even thematic ones, between the two contemporaries. R.S. McGregor, the British comparatist, compares Sarat's Kusum in *Pandit Masai* to Premchand's Kusum in his short story bearing that title, as both reproach their husbands for neglecting them, fear separation and attain an inner calm after the irrevocable separation. The barring of the low-caste persons from an unpolluted well, the central theme of Premchand's *Thakur Ka Kuan* (The Thakur's Well) also can be traced to *Pandit Masai*. However, it is quite possible that these are accidental similarities occasioned by comparable social situations.

Pather Dabi, Ses Prasna, Charitrahin, Bari Didi and *Pandit Masai* seem to have fascinated the readers in Urdu more than the other works of Saratchandra that they find too sentimental. Sarat was the most popular author among the Urdu readers after Tagore and Nazrul Islam. While the critics found his range limited and his canvas rather narrow, they recognised the importance of his search for cultural equilibrium based on social justice. Mohammed Hassan, the Urdu critic, finds in Sarat a synthesis of Mir's pathos and Manto's realism, his faith in man and his rebellious youthfulness.

The Punjab, with its strong progressive proclivities received Saratchandra as a progressive who refused to renounce India's cultural heritage. Sarat laid bare the unequal man-woman relationship under the feudal system and brought home to the victims the tragedy inherent in this dichotomy. It was the brahmanical, feudal ethics that compelled Sarat's protagonists to channelise their love into socially acceptable forms, thus leading them to self-sacrifice or abnegation. Tarsem Raj Vinod examining the dialectics of Sarat's novels points to their essential tension provoked by the conflict of two value systems. Madhabi's love for Surendra has to take a sisterly form; Rama's love for Ramesh is veiled and hence acceptable; Sabitri is only a servant of Satish; Kiranmayi's love for Divakar is again veiled as the love for a brother. Chandramukhi's love for Debdas and Rajlakshmi's for Srikanta are both based on the old ideals of total devotion and service. All are impelled by the fear of the system. Sarat sided with the Western ideal of democracy in its battle against feudal hierarchy and was eager to expose the oppressive nature of the existing system. Surinder Singh Dosanj calls Saratchandra the novelist of transition as his works capture 'at the right moment and in the right manner' the theoretical conflict between traditional Hinduism and the emerging Brahmosamaj whose members were considered *mlechchas* by the orthodox Hindus. The fear of pollution that Rambabu of *Grihadaha* and Apurba of *Pather Dabi* experience is symptomatic of the lower middle class in the cities that felt miserably caught in the incompatibility between the structure of the traditional Hindu society and the demands of modern life. Suresh of *Grihadaha* and Apurba of *Pather Dabi* alike embody the middle-class contradiction between the aspirations of the class and the values and beliefs of their religion and caste. Tarak of *Seser Parichay* escapes this contradiction by being entirely faithful to his class instinct. The reason for Saratchandra's pan-Indian popularity according to Dosanj is his honest analysis of the middle class, particularly lower middle class, from whom his readers came and who shared the same fate all over the country in that period of turmoil. Sarat, as a humanist, was always critical of feudal and patriarchal values, as demonstrated by his characters like Mahim and Mrinal of *Grihadaha,* Lalana of *Subhada* or Sarada, Sabita and Rakhal of *Seser Parichay.* Sarat's characters however are multi-dimensional and throbbing with life; they are sites of conflicts rather than incarnations of virtue and vice; the author does not judge them nor project any single solution to the problems they raise. He is content to capture the individual and social reality of the times through the class he most intimately knows.

Saratchandra is said to have told one of his common admirers, 'Rabindranath writes for readers like me, I write for readers like you'. The common readers of his times obviously placed him above Tagore and loved him more than they did Tagore, perhaps to the chagrin of Tagore himself Sachi Rautray, the eminent Oriya writer, quotes his statement and calls Sarat 'the explorer of ugliness and discoverer of beauty.' He shows how the novelist humanised time and looked at the universe with the eyes of an agnostic. He was the voice of an epoch 'that marked the tradition from a religion-oriented humanistic nationalism to a more rational and radical nationalism.' Sachi Rautray even calls Sarat 'international' as he rose above the barriers of caste, gender and nationality when it came to the analysis of oppression. He could create 'impersonal mothers' like Hemangini, Bindubasini or Narayani because of his liberal character.

Surendra Mohanty, another major Oriya writer does not share this enthusiasm. He finds Saratchandra's attitude to reform rather naïve. His ambivalence reminds him of the Fakir Mohan Senapathy of *Prayaschitha.* Even his radical characters like Bharati and Sabyasachi of *Pather Dabi* suffer from attitudinal confusion. Bharati the terrorist assures Apurba that individuals are free to abide by caste, 'we respect individual sentiment'. Bidhubhusan Das also finds 'sentimentality and sloppiness' in Sarat: yet the 'subtle interrelatedness of human beings' found in Sarat is absent in modern Bengali novel. Surendra Mohanty finds two types of women characters in Sarat's fiction: Sabitri, Rama, Bindu and Parbati are resigned to their destiny and accept and endure every suffering in a mood of renunciation while characters like Kamal, Kiranmayi, Sorati, Sumitra and Bharati are of tougher fibre; they are manifestations of life force and initiators of action comparable to Shaw's Candida or Anne, Ibsen's Nora or Hardy's Eustacia Vye or Bathsheba Everdene.

Sarat was introduced to the Marathi reader chiefly by Mama Varerkar whose translations were published in the 1940s. It was the period of the Second World War and of the Holocaust; war had thrown up new challenges and new sensibilities and upset the quietude of life. The partition of India that followed also had a profound impact on the writers particularly of North India. In this unsettling background, Sarat appeared to belong to the past, dealing as he did with the eternal mysteries of love. Cultural differences of course stood in the way: the Bengali Zamindar was entirely different from the Marathi landlord; the structures of landholding were also different, making Sarat look outlandish. His novels found only limited acceptance among the Marathi readers given to intellectualism and reasoning. Novels like *Srikanta, Debdas* and *Parineeta* did acquire a certain amount of popularity especially among women readers; and writers like Sumati Kshetramade praise Sarat for his depiction of socially condemned women.

In 1923, Mahatma Gandhi asked Mahadev Desai to translate three of Sarat's shorter novels into Gujarati: *Ramer Sumati, Bindur Chhele* and *Mejdidi: Biraj Bau* also was translated the following year. Unlike in Marathi, Sarat found wide acceptance in Gujarati. Chandrakant Mehta, a distinguished Gujarati writer, finds the reason in the sentimental nature of the Gujarati people. Sarat translations—there are versions of 33 of Sarat's books in Gujarati—ushered in a new era called 'Sarat era' in Gujarati in 1923. The name became so popular that translators began to publish their own novels in Saratchandra's name. Kanahiyalal Munshi however finds another, perhaps more plausible, reason for his popularity: patriarchy was very strong in Gujarat, and women were never expected to stray beyond their conventional role. In the context of this enforced silence, Sarat's rebellious, indignant and unconventional women characters fascinated Gujarati women-readers who might have found a release in identifying themselves with those independent women at least in imagination. Sarat questioned the status-quoist concepts of the moral and the immoral. Kamal, Kiranmayi, Chandramukhi, Rajalakshmi, Purabi, Alaka... He created a series of daring women and justified women's love out of wedlock in the oppressive circumstances in which most Indian housewives lived. Gujarati writers like Sneharasmi, Dhiruben Patil, Pannalal Patel, Chunilal Modia and Shivkumar Joshi were deeply influenced by Saratchandra's fictional modes. Raja in Pannalal Patil's *Maavini Bhavai,* Alka in Chandrakant Bakshi's *Ekaltana Kinara* and Uma in Shivkumar Joshi's *Kanchukibandh* take after Sarat's Parbati in *Debdas.* Village life began to feature prominently in Gujarati fiction in this age; independent heroines became the order of the day. Several of the Sarat novels were dramatised on the stage and even non-fiction writers like Chandrakant Mehta, Ramnarayan Pathak and Darshak were fascinated by the phenomenon and attempted critical works on Sarat's fiction. Umashankar Joshi chose *Grihadaha* for special praise. According to him Sarat, more than any other of his contemporaries, teaches us the value of suffering.

Birendra Kumar Bhattacharya, the pre-eminent Assamese novelist, found in Saratchandra's works all the contradictions of India's life in the first half of the 20th century. He noticed the absence of workers in Sarat's fiction and found the reason for Sarat's popularity in the way he reconciled the contradictions of life in his times. In Sindhi, Sarat's example seems to have inspired both the romantic and progressive streams of fiction. Ajhal the Sindhi poet called him the helper of the helpless and awkward masses and the torch bearer of revolution. Gobind Malhi, another major Sindhi writer calls him a creative realist but points out that economic life is lacking in his fiction. As many as 22 of Sarat's novels were translated into Sindhi, mostly after the Partition. Of them *Baridadi, Pather Dabi, Datta, Grihadaha, Srikanta, Debdas* and *Charitrahin* seem to have been the most well-received. Nepali readers too were moved by the primordial energy of Sarat's fiction. Tulsi Bahadur Chhetri praises Sarat's women characters for their motherliness and loyalty. He picks out Biraj Bahu, Annadadidi,

Surabala and Subhada as examples of fidelity and Mrinal, Mejdidi, Narayani, Barididi, Sabita and Rajlakshmi as representatives of the ideal of motherhod. From the delineation of oppressed women like Saraju, Rama, Kusum and Jnanada, Sarat moves to the creation of rebels like Kiranmayi, Sumitra, Sunanda and Abhaya. Chhetri reminds us of Sarat's book of essays on women, *Narir Mulya* that he wrote under the pseudonym, Anila Debi. Kamala Sankrityayan classifies Sarat's178 women characters into five types: loving mothers widowed in their middle age, cruel women with harsh tongues, the simple hearted and loving women who are unmarried, married or widowed, 'serious' women who consider love a sin, and talkative, quarrelsome, old women. She also gives examples to each of these categories.

Sarat's novels were widely welcomed in the languages of South India too. While Tagore appealed chiefly to the intellectuals, Sarat's appeal was much wider. Sarat's novels were avidly read in Kerala and even the village libraries were well-stocked with their translations. Sarat's Parbati was as well-known to the Malayalam readers as Thakazhi Sivasankara Pillai's Karuthamma in *Chemmeen,* C.V. Raman Pillai's Subhadra in *Marthanda Varma* or Uroob's Ummachu in the novel of the same name. At the same time the Malayalam readership does not have much sympathy for the Brahmin community that has been identified with landlordism, extreme cruelty to their own women and to the lower castes. If, in spite of this attitude, the readers have liked Sarat's novels, it can only be because of their universal human element. Primarily, however, he has been seen as a women's writer, a role later appropriated by indigenous writers of serial novels. With the advent of modernism, Sarat has fallen into oblivion in Kerala while more serious writers like Tagore, Tarasankar, Manik Banerjee and Bibhutibhusan are still read with admiration. Sarat's popularity was essentially a transient phenomenon of the 1940s and 1950s in Kerala. He has not had any great influence on serious fiction in Malayalam. In Tamil, *Bindur Chhele, Swami, Dena Paona, Pather Dabi* and *Ses Prasna* have found admirers, while works like *Chandranath, Debdas, Parineeta and Araksaniya* have come under criticism for their weak protagonists. The more radical Tamil critics have found Sarat to be conservative, espeically when it comes to the question of caste. The better novels like *Bindur Chhele* serialised in Kalki's journal, *Anandavikatan* however, immediately became popular. T.N. Kumaraswamy, a novelist, admits that he has been deeply influenced by Sarat's reformist aspirations. Many of Sarat's novels were published in Tamil in abridged translations and several became textbooks in schools and colleges. In Kannada, Sarat was looked upon as a humanist and an idealist, one who fought for social justice, equality and universal brotherhood. In Telugu, again a literature with a strong progressive tradition, Sarat was considered a writer at war with himself and the society he lived in. He was criticised for not providing solutions for social ills and not being sufficiently comprehensive. K.V. Ramana Reddy, a radical leftist Telugu writer, analysing some of the major novels and characters of Saratchandra, comments that the novelist was the intellectual offspring of the middle class social milieu in the Bengal of his times and that this explains his rebellious impulses, as well as his ultimate acquiescence to the system. Sarat, according to him, interrogated the *status quo* within the norms set by the *status quo;* his sentimentality and inconsistency are also products of his class position. But he does hold up for appreciation some of Sarat's women characters like Kamal of *Ses Prasna,* 'a vehement critic of social arrangements,' Abhaya of *Srikanta,* a liberated woman who had gone through life's hell even worse than Ibsen's Nora and Kiranmayi of *Charitraheen,* 'buoyant, intelligent and vibrant' and even Sabitri whom Ramana Reddy calls 'a muted rebel'.

This brief survey of the reception of Saratchandra Chatterjee's novels provided a rare insight into the mechanism and the levels of reception of translated fiction in Indian languages. Reception of literary works in a language has something to do with what may be called the 'temperament' of the language. The warm reception of Sarat in Hindi, Punjabi or Gujarati and his near-rejection in Marathi and critical reception in the South Indian languages seem to be based partly on this linguistic temperament and partly on systemic differences in the communities and the consequent obstacles to communication and empathy. Languages with strong progressive literary movements seem to have looked at Sarat's works from a class point of view and been critical of the ambivalences in their attitude. While Saratchandra has been acknowledged almost universally as a liberal humanist, he has been very often viewed as a sentimentalist confined to domestic life not to be ranked with, say, Bankim, Tagore, Tarashankar or Manik Banerjee, whose concerns went beyond the domestic issues to take up larger social, cultural and philosophic issues. Sarat has won greater appreciation for his portrayal of women than of men and has been a favourite with women readers. The emergence of the modern novel with its urban bias has to a great extent marginalised the exponents of rural life like Saratchandra, who is seldom read today, while Bankim's *Anandamath* or Tagore's *Gora* are still subjects of discussion and analysis because of their cultural-political significance. Saratchandra Chatterjee did have a role to play in the social as well as the literary history of Bengal, as he, more than any other Bengali fiction writer of his time, highlighted the suffering and the struggle of women in the crippling structures of the family and society and convincingly portrayed the contradictions of middle-class life. The changes of time and taste have together marginalised him and rendered his sentimentality overwrought and out-of-tune with modern sensibility. While this is understandable, anyone who wants to evaluate him has to place him in the background of his own times and map the limits of his grasp and genius that while allowing him to be a popular writer with a message also prevented him from growing into a great writer dealing with the larger issues of life, spirit and society. One should not blame the writer if he belongs more to the past than the future; they also serve who deepen our understanding of life, even if in passing.

AGAINST THE GRAIN
The Role of Memory in A.K. Ramanujan's Poetry

It will be unfair to compare the poet A.K. Ramanujan with the greatest poets of Indian languages who could travel easily from the purely aesthetic to the ethical and the political, and from the world of the minute to the world of the cosmic, whose poetry addressed its people and its times with a sense of missionary urgency and stood in the forefront of their great struggles and movements for liberty and equality. Ramanujan, by circumstance as well as by choice, would not play the role of the teacher, the prophet and the visionary that some of the poets he translated from Tamil and Kannada, like Nammalvar or Basava had played in their societies. As a Kannada poet he was overshadowed by his great elders like Gopalkrishna Adiga, Bendre and P.T. Narasimhachar and failed to gain even the recognition received by contemporaries like S.R. Ekkundi or Chandrashekhara Kambara. One reason for this lack of recognition may be his challenging attitude to tradition that is so different from that of many typical Kannada poets. This does not however mitigate his significance as an Indian poet in English, one of those pioneers of the transition of his genre from the ornate, flamboyant, rhetorical and overstated poetry of its early practitioners into a quieter modern mode that shuns sentimentality and exaggeration like the plague and instead chooses counter-strategies like suggestiveness, understatement, irony, objectivity and precision, to create a poetry that is almost atonal and reflective—ideals pursued also by Ramanujan's coevals like Nissim Ezekiel and Keki N. Daruwalla. He has however been more profoundly influenced by Indian bhasa traditions than perhaps any other Indian poet writing in English today. The best possible statement on the constitution of Ramanujan's poetry has been made by the poet himself:

> English and my disciplines give me my outer forms—linguistic, metrical, logical and other such ways of the shaping of experience, and my first thirty years in India, my frequent visits and field trips,

my personal and professional preoccupations with Kannada, Tamil, the classics and folklore give me my substance, my 'inner' forms, images and symbols. They are continuous with each other, and I no longer can tell what comes from where.

The fabric of Ramanujan's poetry is formed by the myriad threads of Indian myth, history, culture, heritage, topography and environment. He says: 'I must seek and will find my particular hell only in the Hindu mind.' Chidananda Das Gupta who interviewed Ramanujan a decade ago commented on his home-bound vision:

'As with so many Indian writers living abroad, it is the Indian experience—a whole storehouse of it that they carry inside, review, relive from time to time and bring into contact with present experience that nourishes Ramanujan's poetry.'

However, Ramanujan is not affectedly Indian. Keki Daruwalla is right when he observes:

he never made heavy weather of exile nor did he exploit his immigration as a poetic tactic to wallow in a maudlin nostalgia or churn out indignant or sordid songs of alienation. He was never away from India: He emphasised the double resource to be in two cultures, though he was not free from the tensions of such a state that led him to constant self-questioning.

Keki Daruwalla refers to a private conversation with Ramanujan in July 1992, where the poet spoke of his obsession with South Indian verse; but he also admitted that he would not have picked up for translation the pieces he did, but for his knowledge of Ezra Pound or John Donne or the Shakespearean Sonnet. Pound especially helped him look at the classical Tamil poetry in a different light and Pound's translations from Chinese poetry remained his models. His own poetry too, echoes Eastern as well as Western texts and makes most amazing connections between the two cultures—for example, between an Upanishadic thought and a Freudian concept. However, it always springs from a very personal context that is distanced and impersonalised by irony or the use of precise, unemotional images. His attitude towards the Indian past is not at all celebratory; he looks at tradition with the scepticism of a materialist or a rationalist and often makes fun of it. The past seldom returns to him as a longing for a lost Paradise; it comes as a childhood fear, anxiety, a ridiculous ritual, as poverty, flood, dead cows, snobbish aunts, suffering parents. Family is indeed an obsession with him and in poem after poem he returns to it; but never do we feel that he wants to return to the actual family or the past he left. Look at the poem, 'Obituary':

> Father when he passed on
> left dust
> on a table full of papers,
> left debts and daughters,
> a bewildering grandson
> named by chance after him
> a house that leans
> slowly through our growing
> years on a bent coconut
> tree in the yard.
> Being the burning type
> he burned properly
> at the cremation
> as before, easily
> and at both ends.

After this quite unsentimental and even cynical presentation he goes on to say how he left for his sons only some half-burnt spinal discs to pick gingerly and throw, facing east as the priest said where the three rivers met near the railway station. This unmistakable eye for detail that marks all of Ramanujan's poems takes an ironic turn as he speaks of two obituary lines given to him by a Madras newspaper 'sold by the kilo exactly four weeks later to street-hawkers, who sell it in turn to the small groceries' where he buys 'salt, coriander and jaggery in newspaper cones' that he usually reads for fun and lately is the hope of finding those lines, and concludes the poem: 'And he left us/a changed mother/and more than/one annual ritual.' This distancing of personal experience creates the impression that the poet is watching himself perform or masking his feelings in irony. Only by penetrating this mask can one touch the tensions from which his poems spring. In the poem 'Still Another for Mother' from *Striders*, for example, the poet watches a short man turning and leaving a buxom woman at the door fumbling with her keys 'beside the wreckage van/on Hyde park street'. He speculates that 'Perhaps they had fought/worse still perhaps they had not fought.' It looks like a casual parting and a catwalk, the poet walks on 'as if nothing had happened to her, or to me'. Then he rounds it off with a memory:

> Something opened
> in the past and I heard something shut
> in the future, quietly,
> like the heavy door
> of my mother's black-pillared nineteenth-century
> silent house, given on her marriage day
> to my father, for a dowry.

In 'Of Mother; among other Things', however, the mask becomes almost transparent as the poet smells 'the silk and white petal' of his mother's youth on a twisted blackbone tree that leads him to the image of the mother running back from rain to the crying cradles. The poem ends with the agony the poet suffers each time his mother's 'four sensible fingers slowly flex to pick a grain of rice from the kitchen floor'.

In poems like 'Conventions of Despair', 'Snakes', 'The River', 'Entries for a Catalogue of Fears', 'Anxiety', 'Cousin on a Swing', 'Self-portrait', 'No Amnesiac King' and 'Extended Family' the poet 'carries his past with him as an inner world of memories and laws that erupt into the present, transformed into anxieties, fears and new insights'. The way memories, future, family and guilt are linked can be seen in 'Entries for a Catalogue of Fears':

> I'll love my children
> without end,
> and do them infinite harm
> staying on the roof,
> a peeping-tom ghost
> looking for all sorts of proof
> for the presence of the past.

However, the poet knows that he has no escape from this painful continuity. We are ever-changing and yet a part of history, in the same way as a growing fruit, which has its origins in earlier trees and seeds. 'A Poem on Particulars' tells us:

> You can sometimes count
> every orange
> on a tree
> but never
> all the trees
> in a single
> orange.

Ramanujan at times makes grand themes like History sound silly by filling a poem with the name 'History' with family gossip, while he also debunks attempts to give grandeur to rituals, traditions, and ceremonies; culture and tradition often appear arbitrary and casual in his poetry. In 'Small-scale reflections on a Great House' he reverses Yeats's worshipful attitudes towards his ancestral house. The house grows into a symbol of tradition and history:

> Sometimes I think that nothing
> that ever comes into this house
> goes out.

Even new ideas become conventional as they enter this house. All things that leave it are returned to it; dead bodies of relatives too return from battlefields across the earth. The house absorbs everything but does not seem to change. Ultimately the house seems to become a symbol of India itself.

The same irreverence marks his poems like 'Prayers to Lord Murugan' where he prays to Murugan, the Lord of the sixth sense to return our five senses to us to cure us of our prayers and to deliver us 'from Sanskrit and the mythologies of night and the several round-table mornings of London'. Similar is the vein in the poem 'Second sight' where he is indifferent to the 'second sight' attributed to him by the foreigner and would only like to regain 'his first and only sight'. He rejects the abstract and the spiritual, the whole idealistic image of India created by the Orientalists and prefers the immediate reality to the vain boastings about tradition. In his essay 'Classics Lost and Found', Ramanujan himself speaks about the origins of his 'Prayers to Lord Murugan':

'I had felt that Sanskrit itself and all that it represented had become an absence, at best a crippling and not an enabling presence; that the future needed a new past.'

Perhaps this was what had led him to translate the Tamil and Kannada classics in an attempt to discover an alternative Little Tradition different from the Great Tradition of Sanskrit. No wonder the Bhakti poets who rebelled against the Brahminical tradition and the caste hierarchy using the same philosophical insights that the Brahmins used to legitimise social inequalities attracted him, as also the secular poets of the past who were blessed with the 'first sight' the natural direct vision of reality through the five senses. His preference for a particular experience over a return to an imagined past or some perfect world is evident also in poems of *The Second Sight* like 'No Amnesiac King', where he is content to watch the 'flat-metal beauty of a whole pomfret with its round staring eyes and scales of silver in the fisherman's pulsing basket' without trying to find out whether its belly has 'an uncooked signet ring and a forest of legend of a wandering king' (an obvious reference to Kalidasa's *Shakuntala*). In 'Extended Family' he compares himself with his grandfather: he bathes like his grandfather before the village crow: but his only

Ganga is the dry chlorine water; the naked Chicago bulb is a cousin of the Vedic Sun. He thinks of proverbs as he soaps his back like his father; and like his mother hears the faint morning song, though here it is in Japanese: like himself he wipes his body dry with an unwashed Turkish towel. He also has many characteristics he shares with his daughter and son; and looks up unborn at himself like his grandson. But he knows too that his future is dependent on several more people yet to come and he may never be like them. At times the poet also feels he has been cheated by time as age sets in and love turns into the arguments of marriage.

There is no smug complacency with the past; Ramanujan's sensing of continuity is always beset with tension. He also senses the unity of the human race as he watches hopscotch—a game of his childhood—being played by Germans and Africans: but the thought of war disturbs this sense of unity as he says the game is played by all, unless a bomb (or polo) has maimed them for life. (See R.C. Sharma's translation of the Kannada poem '*Kuntobille*'). In another poem 'Upanishad, Next Door', originally written in Kannada, the poet watches two birds on the branch of a guava tree, one pecking at a fruit in hunger and thirst and the other watching it, its body all eyes. This immediate, perceivable, little scene of a family next door is to him an Upanishad in itself. Again an example of the poet's preference for the present moment of warm existence over the holy books of the past. His allusion to Mahadeviyakka in the Kannada poem 'When Meditation Works' is also not without irony, as the paper and the table made of the head and trunk of the walnut tree are compared to the legs and head of man compared by the saint poet to the pillars and the tower of a temple. The irony becomes intense as the poem in its entirety is also a critique of the violence man has done to nature. Ramachandra Sharma has aptly said that with his first collection in Kannada *Hokulalli Hoovilla* (No Flower on the Navel, 1969) Ramanujan shook Kannada poetry out of its smugness by offering an alternative way of experiencing the world and giving expression to it. A similar thing in the reverse order happens too in his Chicago poems where he falls into a vision of forest fires and a frothing Himalayan river, as the traffic light turns Orange on 57th and Dorchester (Chicago Zen) or thinks of his funeral in Chicago where they might embalm him in pesticide, bury him in a steel trap and lock him out of nature (Death & the Good Citizen).

Ramanujan's attitude to tradition is neither celebratory, as is the case with several of our poets inclined to be revivalist nor is it nostalgic as in most of our expatriate writers. He recognises continuity, but he also questions its validity. His poetry revolts against the tame, indigenist, Orientalising canon of Indian writing that inclines towards the sacred, the quaint, the nostalgic, the harmlessly lyrical and harmonious, for he knows that the actual movements of life and society have blown apart those tranquil harmonies and the present is too disturbing to permit us to fall back smugly into a self-flattering recounting of the glories of the past. This is where Ramanujan uses his knowledge of tradition subversively, in an attempt to challenge the hegemonic orientalist canons of Indian literature upheld by the establishment. Memory was to him a rich source of images, experiences, fears and anxieties; but he refuses to be drowned in it. He uses it to illuminate a resent context or to question the validity of some relation, ritual or belief glorified by the orthodoxy.

TRANSCENDING THE BODY
On the Poetry of Kamala Das

Women's poetry in India has a distinct tradition of its own that seems to begin with the tribal songs of her early inhabitants, the Pali songs of the Buddhist nuns of the sixth century B.C., the Sangam poets of Tamil like Andal and Avvaiyar, the devotional poets of the middle ages like Meerabai, Ratnabai, Janabai, Atukuri Molla and Akkamahadevi, Muddupalani, Bahinabai, Mahlaq Bai Chanda and Sanciya Hosannainma of the 17th and 18th centuries and reaches up to Kamala Das's mother, Balamani Amma. Indian women poets writing in English, to whose ever-growing tribe Kamala Das belongs, form a little tradition of their own, related in various ways to this great tradition. Kamala's much-discussed poem 'An Introduction' is a comprehensive articulation of the different individual and social components that go into the making of this subgenre.

Kamala Das's poetry has her autobiography written into it. She is not any woman or the incarnation of 'essential womanhood' if at all there is one: she is an Indian poet, writing in English when Indian poetry in English is breaking free from the rhetorical and romantic traditions, when her male counterparts like Nissim Ezekiel and A.K. Ramanujan are struggling hard to form a dense, pithy and ironic idiom in their poems and Jayanta Mahapatra is trying to relate his poetry to his immediate environment with pain and anger. She is a woman poet, acutely conscious of her femininity with all the contradictory demands made on it by the family, society and her radical companions. She is 'aggressively individualistic' according to K.R. Srinivasa Iyengar; yet full of social awareness, even political awareness, to her more careful readers. She is the inheritor of many traditions, the regional cultural traditions of Kerala and the pan-Indian tradition: and within the regional tradition she has a specifically matrilineal background provided by her caste, and a specific provincial background offered by Malabar, where she spent her childhood.

She is also heir to two poetic traditions, that of Malayalam whose roots go back into the ancient Tamil Sangam poetry and medieval folklore, and that of Indian English poetry beginning with Henry Derozio or Toru Dutt. She herself had two poets in the family, Balamani Amma, her mother and Nalapatt Narayana Menon, her maternal uncle. As a child she felt tortured by the 'subtle sadism' of her teachers, who were old maids turned sour with dejection and found refuge in her grandmother and company in the female servants at home. She did not have a university education; she is a bilingual writer, writing mostly stories and memoirs in Malayalam and mostly poems in English. All these have directly or indirectly gone into the making of her poems. 'An Introduction' is itself a polyphonic text with several of the poet's voices seeking articulation in a single verbal construct. The opening statement, 'I don't know politics' has an ambiguous tone that comes from a woman's marginalised position in society. Outwardly it is a confession of ignorance, but it also conceals in it a potential irony as the society does not expect a woman to deal in politics. She is never the master in politics, only the victim, hence her knowledge of the names of those in power who have no content for her. Then she situates herself more specifically using nationality, complexion, place of birth and the languages known, an ironic filling up of an ungiven form. The 'language she dreams in' again is ambiguous enough to warrant many interpretations: it could be that of imagination, woman's language, English, or Malayalam, her mother tongue. She also justifies her choice of English as she believes she is using it with her own angularities and eccentricities, her human joys and longings. It is the voice of her instinct as is the lion's roar and the crow's cawing. She recalls the unconscious terrors of her childhood as she tries to differentiate herself from trees, while monsoon clouds and rains bring in the locale. Speaking of adolescence, her female body inscribes itself on the text and she remembers too her first encounter with masculine violence that belongs to the same frightening world of trees in the storm and the mutterings of the funeral pyre. References to swelling limbs, growing hairs, the pitiful weight of breasts and womb and the 'sad woman body' emphasise the corporeal ground of woman's experience, female physicality often identified with female textuality. It has been said that women suffer cultural scripts in their bodies and women writers are like the mythic woman warrior who went into battle scarred by the thin blades which her parents literally used to write fine lines of script on her body. Woman herself becomes the text and this may explain women writer's preference for confessional modes of writing. (However a crude emphasis on the difference of the body can even be dangerous as that is also the foundation of gender discrimination against women, hence the ironic comment, that the identity of woman's literary practice must be sought in 'the body of her writing and not the writing of her body.') The woman cannot change her body; so the poet changes her dress and tries to imitate men. But the voices of tradition would force her back into sarees, the saree becoming here a sign of convention. She is pushed back into her expected gender roles: wife, cook, embroiderer, quarreler with servants: the gender role also becomes a class role. The elders fill her world with taboos asking her to be her parents' Amy, her friends' Kamala or her readers' Madhavikutty (her penname in Malayalam). Every deviation from the norm is looked upon as perversion or mental illness. Her hurt humiliated soul goes on begging for love; the nature similes of the hasty river and the waiting ocean re-emphasise the element of instinct that drives the woman in her. The many ontological dimensions of her being—lover's darling, drinker of the city nights, one who makes love, feels shame, sinner, saint, beloved, betrayed—are tied together at the end of the poem, where the poet's ego dissolves in others as soon as it is asserted. If the poet finds the male ego, 'tightly packed like the sword in its sheath,' violent, arrogant and exclusive, she finds her identity to be a moment of difference before a final dissolution in others as she finds that her joys and aches are the same as those of her readers. This discovery has a social as well as a metaphysical dimension, both of which in different ways have grown along with her poetry to constitute a spiritual politics of the body and beyond.

2

I am uncertain as to whether Indian literary criticism has developed an indigenous way of decoding gender and reading texts foregrounding the feminine. This is, no doubt, part of a general post-colonial situation where the decolonisation of culture, outlook and modes of reflection has been hampered or slowed down by various factors, including a neo-colonial onslaught. One has, however, to be extremely cautious about any discussion of decolonisation today, since the idea has practically been hijacked by the revivalist discourse that in the Indian context boils down to an invocation of the Vedic ideal of Aryan womanhood: a celebration of domesticity, submission to the father, the husband and the sons in the different stages of life and even the legitimation of inhuman practices like Sati. Orientalists like William Jones and Indologists like Clarisse Bader had idealised this 'ascetic-endurance' of the ancient Indian women as against their later 'fall' into 'sensuousness' and 'debauchery'. Indian nationalist historians too had invoked the same passive ideal in their anxiety to answer the accusations of utilitarians like James Mill, critics like Katherine Mayo and the Evangelicals who attacked the Hindu 'paganism' and imperialists who found in India's moral degradation an opportunity to rationalise and perpetuate the colonial rule. Decolonisation obviously does not mean the retrieval of a 'romanticised' golden past, it means an objective realisation of the complexity of gender construction in India overdetermined as it is by other formations like class, caste, religion, regional cultures and languages, specific traditions, taboos, laws of marriage, sexual kinship and inheritance, contradictions between the country and the city, feudal moral codes and the new roles popularised by the indigenous and Western media. In literary theory, it means challenging the patriarchal canons, deconstructing the phallocentric creative and critical discourses, defining the feminine in literary texts in the Indian context, unearthing the ideological configurations that lay behind the reception and rejection of literary texts in different periods, relating their formal constituents to the specific environment and regional traditions, thus developing an indigenous semiotics that connects signs to their specific space and lineage, decoding gender as an organising principle of experience and relating forms of feminine articulation to the changing social, racial and conceptual permutations in Indian history; for example the employment of dialects and images of domesticity in the quest for spiritual deliverance in the Bhakti period, the tactical redeployment of hegemonic discourses to constitute a new, enlightened middle-class female subject in the colonial reformist period, the creation of new enunciative modalities and rhetorical strategies to express the gender-class nexus in the period of 'progressive' literature, or the use of body-imagery, emphasis on female-bonding, appeal to the pre-Oedipal phase of mental development and open defiance of the set norms and structures of writing in more recent, openly feminist, literature. The kinds of feminist criticism that naturalise the experiences and issues of Western feminism—of whatever kind, Marxist, liberal, lesbian, American or French—are easily co-opted by the academy and align themselves with the apparatus of power. In order to intervene meaningfully in the Indian critical scene, one will have to reconstitute the self, gender, knowledge, social relations and culture—without resorting to linear, teleological, hierarchical, holistic or binary ways of thinking and being—in India's own socio-historical and cultural context. The Procrustean set of critical procedures and the straitjacket of prescriptive categories provided by Western theorists might not help one understand the differences between one's Indian authors from her Western counterpart though they might help one grasp certain similarities at the very fundamental biological and pre-linguistic levels. The universalising theories of Western feminism alone cannot explain Janabai's fervent appeals to Vithoba, the relationships between Raidas and

Meera or Basavanna and Akkamahadevi, Sugathakumari's vision of Devaki dreaming of Krishna the liberator in her prison or Kamala Das's concepts of love and transcendence. Kamala Das, this way, is typically Indian in her identification of the lover with Krishna, in her emancipating compassion for all those who suffer, and in her battles with the body to go beyond it to an unfettered world of humane spirituality. Kamala's poetry shows a gradual widening of concerns over the years as she liberates herself from her initial obsession with her gender identity and extends her sympathies to entire sections of suffering humanity—the marginalised, the poor, the minorities, the fighters for justice, women, children, abandoned youth, victims of war and oppression—until she 'gate-crashes into the precincts of others' dreams' and feels she is 'million, million people/talking all at once, with voices raised in clamour.' This commitment however does not turn her deaf to the call of her inner self; she realises that 'other/journeys are all so easy but/not the inward one, the longest/route home and the steepest/descent....' This tortuous inward journey 'carries you step/by weary step beyond the blood's/illogical arrogance, yes,/beyond the bone and the marrow/into that invisible abode of pain.' She comes to realise that our obsession with physicality is a mistake.

> If only the
> Human eye could look beyond the
> chilling flesh, the funeral pyre's
> rapid repast and then beyond
> the mourner's vanquished stance, where would
> death be then, that meaningless word
> when life is all that there is, that
> raging continuity that
> often the wise ones recognize as God?
> (Anamalai Poems, IV)

This double commitment—to the self and to others—is what defines Kamala's poetics of complementarity and lends to her creative universe a comprehensiveness seldom encountered in the stereotypical feminist poetry of the 1970s and 1980s, with its oppressively repetitive concern with the body, its deliberate and aggressive anti-male stance and its jargonised confessional or indignant idiom.

3

This is not to say that Kamala's poetry transcends gendered subjectivity altogether by resorting to some grand, Tagorean, universal discourse. She does refuse to be 'the invisible woman in the asylum corridor' or the 'silent woman' robbed of all expression; she too is a female Prometheus, one of the *voleuses de langue* (thieves of language) with a manifesto of desire that seeks to escape the paradox of being a prisoner of the hegemonic patriarchal discourse she despises; only she stubbornly resists the temptation to divide the world on the basis of the simple binary male-female opposition since that excludes not only other equally real divisions—of class, caste, nation or race—but even the possibility of authentic love. In this awareness she is closer to her mother and other women writers of that generation, who by the sheer power of experience and intuition, unsupported by any concrete theory, recognised intensely the pains of being a woman, while refusing to surrender to hatred and violence. They would not share the man-made myth of the female being the male's creation reiterated again and again in 'Devee Bhagavata' where Narayana creates Urvashi and other beauties from his thigh, in the 'Book of Genesis' where God creates woman from Adam's rib to alleviate man's loneliness or in Ovid's *Metamorphoses* where Pygmalion's desire lends life to the ivory idol sculpted by him. Man feels ashamed of having been born of woman and tries to overcome the disgrace by 'creating' women and ruling over them though the ways of governance and exploitation differ from age to age. Women are forced to bear the whipmarks of culture on their bodies. They annihilate the distance between life and art by turning themselves into offerings like Devadasis. The openness, the confessional character and the complete identification of the personal and poetic selves characteristic of Kamala's poetry have to be viewed in this context. She reveals rather than conceals, explains rather than suggests. Metaphors fill these poems as naturally as cells from her own body. She transcends ready-made philosophical systems by being honest to the momentary states of her consciousness.

Women's marginalised position in the male-dominated world, while enfeebling and silencing them, also give the survivors a peculiar advantage; women-writers are most unlikely to produce a fixed, authoritarian subject within their discourse. Women's experiences force her to be a yet unformed subject, ever evolving and experimenting with itself.

Women's function in the patriarchal society is primarily one of negation; she tends, by the very fact of her positioning in the social hierarchy, to negate whatever is considered complete, ultimate, well-made and established in her society. Her very act of writing almost inevitably breaks the set rules and norms of the status quo. Kamala Das even while not being consciously political and declaring, 'I don't know politics,' is no exception: the undeniable political dimension of her poetry is an unconscious expression of her longing for a different order of things, where no one will be deprived. She makes fun of her aristocratic great-grandmother who had told her that they had the oldest blood in the world, 'a blood thin clear and fine,' while the blood of the poor and the new-rich was 'as thick as gruel/And muddy as a ditch' (Blood). The poem 'Nani' too turns out to be an indictment of the amnesiac aristocracy that can ruin a poor woman's honour, force her to end her life and, within days, sentence her to the second death, of oblivion. She realises with a pang that the poor were clowns on the lush, opulent stage of the feudal times, when the ancestors nourished the plant of aristocracy during the day and slept with the nieces of their low-caste tenants at night, who, once with child, would be thrown into pools, their dead bodies with bruised throats rising like lilies and lotuses to the watery surface (Honour). The poet wants to exorcise the ghosts of her past and purify her blood of the malignant cells of sin gathered over generations.

Kamala's stance against state-sponsored or patriotic violence and war is an extension of her oblique battle against feudal and patriarchal violence. In 'Toys' her indictment is unambiguous: 'Doomed is this new race of men who arrive/empty slogans to sow dead seeds./ Doomed are their gestures and doomed their/Proud ancestor who moans in shame through their mouths/At the ritual's end.' The genocide of Tamils in Sri Lanka grows into a metaphor of collective violence in her poems on the theme like 'Smoke in Colombo', 'The Sea at Galle Face Green' and 'After July', where she sees a macabre repetition of an earlier holocaust in Colombo: 'Hitler rose from the dead, he demanded/Yet another round of applause; he hailed/The robust Aryan blood, the sinister/Brew that absolves man of his sins and/Gives him the right to kill his former friends. The dark Dravidian aids his three-year-old child/On his lap...' There is more to the lines than meets the eye, for it also invokes the memories of another war in Sri Lanka: that between the fair Rama and the dark Ravana, which in Kamala's poetry becomes the archetypal conflict between the Whites (Aryans) and the 'natives', as references that comes up again and again in her poems as references to her 'nut-brown skin' (Shopper at the Cornells, Colombo) or a defect in the blood 'that made us the land's inferiors,/A certain muddiness in the usual red,/Revealing our non-Aryan descent' (A Certain Defect in the Blood?). But that sympathies go beyond the colour of the skin is proved by her poems like 'Delhi-1984', where she boldly attacks the state-supported terrorism unleashed on the innocent Sikhs in the wake of Indira Gandhi's assassination that turned 'the scriptural chants' into 'a lunatic's guffaw'. 'Any God worth his nab would hasten/to disown these dry-eyed adherents/of the newest cult'. Her denouncement of terrorism is equally vehement in poems like 'If Death is your Wish'. 'If death is your wish, killing becomes/an easy game'. She ridicules the men whose vigour must repose in the guns they tote rather than in their loins. Again she bemoans the growth of the forces of hatred: 'We mated like gods but begot only our killers./ Each mother suckles her own enemy/And hate is first nurtured at her gentle breast...' (Daughter of the Century).

4

Woman's language, like woman's sexuality, is decentred, and in a sense, amorphous. She longs to shape a being from within very much as she longs to carry and mould a child in her body. She is many; her language speaks with a hundred tongues. She finds consistency where man finds only contradiction. She does not want to master anyone, including herself. Kamala Das expresses this state of consciousness in 'The Sensuous Woman III'. 'An Ocean's vast/Languor seizes her blood, the fences between/ The state of life and death fade, and nailed/To the pleasant cross of Being she straddles/The handless clockface of eternity'. Kamala however does not glorify this difference; she realises that matriarchy also, like patriarchy, reinforces gender inequality. She cannot imagine a world without men; her Radha melts in the first true embrace of Krishna until only he remains (Radha) and she tells Krishna in a panic of surrender that his body is her prism, his darkness blinds her and his words of love 'shut out the wise world's din' (Krishna), that their homeless souls will return some day to the old Kadamba tree by the river 'to hang like bats from this pure physicality' (Radha-Krishna). The same embarrassment makes her confess, 'Now that I love you,/ curled like an old mongrel/my life lies, content/in you...' (Love). Woman's instinctive fascination for men, her sad longing for a sacred and perfect love that goes beyond the joy of sex, the disillusionment that follows the realisation that men only lust after her body: the man-woman relationship in Kamala's poetry operates within this emotional triangle. She would like to get out of the binary logic of phallocentrism and isolate the myth called 'woman' from the class called 'women', the solitary struggles for which she presents in 'An Introduction'.

Women poets subvert patriarchal myths either by revising/ 'revisioning' them or by simply denying them and declaring, 'No more masks, no more mythologies!' Kamala belongs to the latter category. But for causal references to the Radha-Krishna myth, as in the poems mentioned above, there are few references to myths in her poetry. She deconstructs myths by exposing them to the text of experience. In 'The Old Playhouse' she uses the mythical concept of metamorphosis to subvert the conventional myth of marriage: 'You called me wife/I was taught to break saccharine into your tea and/to offer at the right moment the vitamins. Cowering/beneath your monstrous ego, I ate the magic loaf and/became a dwarf. I lost my will and reason...' She refuses to glorify the historical past; her nostalgias are confined to certain moments of love and tenderness in her personal past, hence her natural opposition to all forms of revivalism. She rejects the patriarchal value system that is based on egoism, greed for power, expansionism, hero-cult, violence, war, mindless exploitation of man and nature, the misuse of intelligence and the supremacy of reason and theory over sensitiveness and experience. At the same time, she has to express her rejection in a language that still carries a male-bias. This creates an inevitable ambivalence in her poetry: she begins to distrust language or feels uneasy about it. 'Words are birds,' she says, 'where have they gone to roost/Wings tired,/Hiding from the dusk?' (Words are Birds). Again she finds the word to be sin:

> The word then is sin
> nothing better nothing worse
> vain rivers thinning to silver threads
> manicured talons in roses...
> branded cattle on their last long walk
> past mountain passes
> and children's blood on zebra-crossings.

She associates the word with home where the god of sin, and 'the knife sharpened to kill' await us. Man, God and Word together seem to conspire against woman; the poet is aware of the consequences of her struggle against them: 'Tomorrow they may bind me with chains stronger than/Those of my cowardice, rape me with bayonets and/Hang me for my doubts...' (Tomorrow).

Old age, death and nothingness are a recurring presence in Kamala's more recent poems. She realises that 'at my age there are no longer any home comings'. (Woman's Shuttles). In 'A Cask of Nothing' she says, 'If I close my eyes I see nothing./If I shut my ears I hear nothing. Nothing but nothing/inside or outside/the nothing that resides/as an ache within/the only content/the human cask can contain.' In the summer of 1980 she hears only the cry 'kill, kill'. 'Perhaps the malevolent/Alchemy of the city air/Aided us, turning gold to/Lead, so that the familiar/Caressing hands unshaped the clay/And swiftly formed a death-head...' (Summer 1980). She finds a sudden drought to have settled itself down on the 'Sun-bleached estuaries' of her blood and wonders whether she is living or dying; all her gestures seem to have a little of each. Death, according to her, is the obscure parallel of life (Life's Obscure Parallel). She would go in silence 'leaving not even a fingerprint on this crowded earth,' carrying away her 'bird-in-flight voice' and the 'hundred misunderstandings' that ruined her alliances (Death is so Mediocre). Growth, she discovers, is 'the stoicism of the sewers/beneath great cities, accepting the rush/of putrid waste.'

This continuous encounter with physical decay also forces the poet to look beyond death into a state of spirituality that has little to do with conventional religions. She believes that by confessing, by peeling off her layers, she reaches closer to the soul and 'to the bone's supreme indifference' (Composition). Bodily love cannot satisfy this yearning, she knows, as she says in 'The Old Playhouse' that love too must end. 'Bereft of soul/My body shall be bare./Bereft of body/My soul shall be bare' (The Suicide). She finds the body to be a trap and a prison (Prisoner) and longs to conquer the obstacle of the body so that she can go to the sea beyond the river (Advice to Fellow-Swimmers). 'Anamalai Poems' attain special significance from this point of view, for, it is here that Kamala fully articulates her faith in a love beyond flesh:

> There is a love greater than all you
> know that awaits you where the road finally ends

its patience proverbial; not for it
the random caress or the lust
that ends in languor.
(Anamalai Poems, X)

Its embrace is truth; it takes you across death to another womb that convulses 'to welcome your restructured perfection'. Kamala's whole *oeuvre* thus becomes a declaration of the greatness of love that, even while being expressed through the body, also transcends the body.

ON THE LIMITS OF INTERPRETATION
Mahasweta Devi's 'Stanadayini', a case study

It is not easy to summarise Mahasweta Devi's story 'Stanadayini' (Breast-Giver) with all its nuances. It narrates the tragic tale of Jashoda, a tribal woman, wife of Kangalicharan and mother of 20 children, 'living or dead.' Motherhood was her way of living and sustaining her world of countless beings. She was a 'professional' mother, forced into the job of breast-feeding the children of her master's household—the Haldars—after their new son-in-law's Studebaker knocked down her husband and mutilated him. She had herself to be with child almost always, so that her breasts might have enough food for the children of the six daughters of the Haldar household, who used to breed every year and a half— caught by the epidemic of 'blanket-quilt-feeding spoon-bottle-oil cloth-Johnson's baby powder bathing basin' to use the author's jocular idiom. This was necessitated by the demise of Haldarbabu who had promised to look after the family till he was around, to expiate his upstart son's sin towards a poor Brahmin. At this time Gopal, Nepal and Radharani were whining for food and abusing their mother. And Jashoda, in the narrator's words, was 'fully an Indian woman, whose unreasonable, unreasoning, and unintelligent devotion to her husband and love for her children, whose unnatural renunciation and forgiveness have been kept alive in the popular consciousness by all Indian women from Sati-Savitri-Sita through Nirupa Roy and Chand Osmani.' She never blamed her idle husband for her misfortunes.

> Such is the power of the Indian soil that all women turn into mothers here and all men remain immersed in the spirit of holy childhood. Each man the Holy Child and each woman, the Divine Mother. Even those who wish to deny this and wish to slap *current posters* to the effect of *'eternal she'*, 'Mona Lisa', 'La passionaria', 'Simone de Beauvoir', et cetera, over the old ones and look at women that way, are, after all, Indian cubs.

It all started accidentally, when once Jashoda was asked by the Haldar Mistress to breast-feed a grandchild, whose mother was sick. The Lady observed then that Jashoda had such full breasts and was *Kamadhenu,* the legendary Cow of fulfilment herself, while her daughters-in-law did not have 'quarter of that milk in their nipples'. This became a talking point for the men and women of the household at night. They found in Jashoda's full breasts a way to retain the shapes of the wives of the household, even while following the almanac in creating a progeny every year: the women will carry and deliver while Jashoda will suckle the babes: thus they could 'combine multiple pregnancies and beauty'. Jashoda was the divine engine, the paid mother. For this Kangalicharan had also to become a professional father, so that Jashoda might always be with milk in her breasts. She accepted her husband as her guru and would not mind bearing children every year for, 'Does it hurt a tree to bear fruits?' Kangali now took over the cooking at home and Jashoda was well-fed by the Mistress as she was the Mother Cow: she also became important in all the family functions. The young men of the household stopped whistling at the maidservants as they began to look upon these friends of their Milk-Mother also as mothers, and shifted their attention to the girls' school. Jashoda was confined 20 times in 30 years. By then the Haldar Mistress passed away, her grandchildren were swept off by the evil wind of family planning and the household began to split as men began to move to build their own houses or the daughters-in-laws moved to their husband's place of work. Jashoda was as unwanted as the Haldar Mistress's advice. The eldest daughter-in-law promised Jashoda's board if she cooked, but she could not send food for the whole family. Meanwhile Kangalicharan had started a Shiva temple-business. Now he decided to stay in the temple, two of the children also became his assistants. Jashoda was no more of use to Kangali; he also shifted his love to another woman, Golapi. Jashoda was reduced to the state of a mere servant. She also began to feel a strange pain in her breasts: the top of her left tit had grown red and hard like a stone. The nipple had shrunk; her armpit was swollen. The doctor knew it was cancer. The Haldar children who did not want to have the sin of a Brahmin woman's death on their head asked Jashoda's sons to take her away. Kangali heard of this and came back in remorse. He had been tricked by Golapi who had stolen everything from the temple and opened a shop. He took Jashoda home. She was now in the terminal stages of cancer. The doctor at the hospital said she was sick probably because she had borne 20 children and suckled 50. There was little hope of her survival since she was in the secondary stage, of infection and continuous fever. They put her on sedatives, anodynes and antibiotics. She hung on about a month in the hospital. She had no visitors now since the stench in the room was insufferable. Even Kangali stopped coming; he had rejected her the moment the doctor said there was little hope. Jashoda's left breast burst, her limbs grew cold; neither her real sons nor her milksons came to see her. She lay in the hospital morgue for a night and was carried to the burning *ghat* the next day. She was cremated by an untouchable. Mahasweta Devi concludes her story with a characteristically ironic statement: 'Jashoda was God manifest, others do and did whatever she thought. Jashoda's death was also the death of God. When a mortal masquerades as God here below, she is forsaken by all and she must always die alone.' Mahasweta Devi considers this story a parable of India after decolonisation. India is a hired mother abused and exploited by various hegemonic groups and classes, the landlords, capitalists, bureaucrats, diasporics and ideologues of the new state flourishing on the culture of silence, the passive, unarticulated suffering of the people at large. She has grown weak and tired feeding these ungrateful hoodlums and will be consumed by cancer if not assisted scientifically and sustained by those who have benefited by her. Gayatri Chakravorty Spivak— who is also the translator of 'Stanadayini' into English—extends the parable to interpret the end of the story like this:

> The ideological construct of 'India' is too deeply informed by the goddess-infested reverse sexism of the Hindu majority. As long as there is this hegemonic cultural self-representation of India as a goddess-mother (dissimulating the possibility that this mother

is a slave) she will collapse under the burden of the immense expectations that such a self-representation permits.

—G.C. Spivak, 'A Literary Representation of the Subaltern,' *In Other Worlds: Essays on Cultural Politics*, New York and London: Routledge. 1988, p. 244.

Gayatri Chakravarty Spivak warns us about the limitation of this subject-position. India is here represented by way of the subaltern as metaphor. By the rules of a parable, the connection between the tenor and the vehicle of the metaphor must be made absolutely explicit for which the vehicle's reality-effect must have been underplayed. However, here the vehicle is more than the carrier of a greater meaning. It seems too real to be reduced to a symbol. Again the argument that the citizens of the nation must give something to the nation rather than merely take from it, is one of the many slogans of militant nationalism: Indira Gandhi's slogan, 'Talk less, work more', during the Emergency and John F. Kennedy's exhortation at his inaugural, 'Ask not what your country can do for you, ask what you can do for your country', are not very different from this patriotic demand for duty towards the nation. The interpretation that the story 'narrates the nation' as all the so-called Third-World texts are supposed to do, not only fails to explain the details and nuances of 'Stanadayini' but also takes part in the typical homogenisation practised by most foreign critics, who read Indian, or for that matter all Asian-African-Latin American, texts only in the context of nationalism and ethnicity. It also indirectly participates in the ideology of the ruling elite that excludes all forms of subaltern resistance in the pre-colonial, as well as the colonial, histories of these nations, a resistance often suppressed, subsumed or written off by the champions of Big Nationalism who have—if the present Indian context is any indication—colluded with the imperialists in ushering in a new era of neo-colonialism.

Let us not forget, however, that Mahasweta Devi's oeuvre betrays a clear predilection for historicising her fictional narratives by inserting her individual characters in concrete historical contexts. If *Hajar Churashir Ma* (1974) witnesses a crisis following the unexpected interjection of the political into the personal, the stories of *Agnigarbha* (1978) begin to move towards a patently historical form of fiction that achieves fuller results in *Aranyer Adhikar* (1977). Jashoda of 'Stanadayini,' Draupadi of 'Draupadi' in *Agnigarbha* and Birsha Munda of *Aranyer Adhikar* could have existed in real history in specific periods. Since Michel Foucault, we have come to look at the language of historiography also as language and its accounts as another mode of discursive narrativisation of events. If history is no more a value-neutral narration of 'facts', it is not very different in its construction from fiction, as it is guided by theoretical positions and dictated by ideological attitudes. There is indeed a real world of objects and events, but as an object of discourse, it is constituted within thought under certain discursive conditions of emergence. Karl Marx had foreseen this when he distinguished between real-objects and thought-objects. Knowledge works not on real objects but on thought-objects. Louis Althusser has shown how this distinction differentiates Marxist epistemology from the empiricist one. Every 'statement' involves the positioning of a subject, though this subject is not identical with the 'author' of the formulation. No discursive formation is however about language alone; it is as much about the formation of concepts and strategies, as about that of objects and modalities of enunciation. The difference between history and literature, according to this formulation is only that the former deals with real events and the latter with imagined events: a difference more of degree than of kind. Mahasweta Devi's claim that she writes her fiction only after thorough historical research reflects her commitment to the reality-effect of her writing. Her representations in some sense embody modalities of negotiation between factual and fictive events.

If 'Stanadayini' is historical fiction rather than parable or allegory, what is its thematics of production and reproduction? Jashoda is a gendered subaltern: Kangalicharan, a victim of the aggression of a rich upstart who cripples him. By choosing to be the supporter of the family—through continuous gestation and lactation—Jashoda reverses the roles in Marxist as well as feminist terms:

the husband here is the wife's means of production by the logic of sexual reproduction, while by the logic of the production of value both are means of production. Here Jashoda becomes the 'vocal instrument' and Kangali 'the silent working beast'. The Marxist labour theory of value here takes account of sexual production as the feminists demand but the result is not what they expect: the breast-giver is the producer of the surplus, the promoter of exchange value. Mahasweta uses the word 'Jashoda's surplus'— 'surplus' in English itself in the original, to devote her milk in excess of her use, that is, its use for her own children. Only here the Haldars, the owners of her labour power, consume the surplus entirely without leading to capital accumulation, unless, as Gayatri Spivak points out, children are looked upon as an investment in the future. The reversal of roles in the story, the husband as cook and the wife as bread-earner, and the curious mechanics of production-reproduction can hardly be explained by orthodox Marxist or by Marxist feminism. By denying the Marxist assumption that the free worker is male and at the same time asserting that the nature of woman is physical and nurturing, while also turning that reproductive gender role into a productive role, 'Stanadayini' brings both Marxist and feminist analytical models into crisis. To add to this is the fact that both the husband and the wife belong to the highest caste; they are both Brahmins, while the Haldars are not. Brahminhood here at times works as a privilege, as when the landlord respects and feeds the family or when Kangali makes priesthood a profession; but at other times it becomes a source of irony, since ultimately Kangali is driven out of the temple, and Jashoda, out of the Haldar household. The Brahmin who is supposed to receive, becomes also a giver, as Jashoda is by profession the 'breast-giver.' The irony grows when Jashoda's unclaimed body is burnt by an untouchable.

What about a more liberal, non-Marxist, feminist approach? Mahasweta's text is indeed, and quite openly, critical of patriarchy, though it is not all black and white. Describing Jashoda's loyalty to Kangali she remarks:

Jashoda is fully an Indian woman, whose unreasonable, unreasoning, and unintelligent devotion to her husband and love for her children, whose unnatural renunciation and forgiveness have been kept alive in the popular consciousness by all Indian women from Sati-Savitri-Sita through Nirupa Roy and Chand Osmani. The creeps of the world understand by seeing such women that the old Indian tradition is still flowing free—they understand that it was with such women in mind that the following aphorisms have been composed 'a female's life hangs on like a turtle's', 'her heart breaks but no word is uttered', 'the woman will burn, her ashes will fly/only then will we sing her praise on high'. Frankly, Jashoda never once wants to blame her husband for the present misfortune. Her mother-love wells up for Kangali as much as for the children. She wants to become the earth and feed her crippled husband and helpless children with a fulsome harvest. Sages did not write of this motherly feeling of Jashoda's for her husband. They explained female and male as Nature and the Human Principle. But this they did in the days of yore—when they entered this peninsula from another land. Such is the power of the Indian soil that all women turn into mothers here and all men remain immersed in the spirit of holy childhood. Each man the Holy Child and each woman the Divine Mother. Even those who deny this and wish to slap current posters to the effect of the 'eternal she', 'Mona Lisa', 'La passionaria', 'Simone de Beauvoir', et cetera, over the old ones and look at women that way, are, after all, Indian cubs. It is notable that the educated Babus desire all this from women outside the home. When they cross the threshold they want the Divine Mother in the words and conduct of the revolutionary ladies. The process is most complicated. Because he understood this, the heroines of Saratchandra always fed the hero an extra mouthful of rice. The apparent simplicity of Saratchandra's and other similar writers' writings is actually very complex and to be thought of in the evening, peacefully after a glass of wood-apple juice. There is too much influence of fun and games in the lives of the people who traffic in studies and intellectualism in West Bengal and therefore they should stress the wood-apple correspondingly. We have no idea of the loss we are sustaining because we do not stress the wood-apple-type-herbal remedies correspondingly.

This passage is important in more than one way as it contains: (1) a critique of patriarchy, (2) a critique of Indian womanhood that has so completely identified itself with patriarchal notions, (3) a pointer to the difference between Western and Indian women's attitude to men, (4) an exposition of the hypocrisy of Indian men and their double standards at home and outside, (5) a veiled criticism of Saratchandra Chatterjee's concept of woman and wife, (6) a dig at the complicity of intellectual life and alcohol in Bengal and (7) an ironic attack on the projected image of Indian women in general—from legends and epics to the modem media. Mahasweta's text also points to the linkages between the formation of classes under colonial rule and the social emancipation of women. The elder Haldar is described thus:

He lives in independent India, the India that makes no distinctions among people, kingdoms, languages, varieties of Brahmins, varieties of Kayasthas and so on. But he made his cash in the British era, when Divide and Rule was the policy. Haldarbabu's mentality was constructed then. Therefore, he doesn't trust anyone—not a Panjabi-Oriya-Bihari-Gujarati-Marathi-Muslim.

He is also said to have helped the anti-Fascist struggle of the Allies during the Second World War 'by buying and selling scrap iron', a clear reference to the formation of a comprador capitalist class in the India of the late 1940s with a very provincial mindset as the Haldar does not trust anyone outside Bengal and outside the Hindu community. Commenting on the mocking enumeration of people from other regions in the passage that echoes a line in the national anthem that is a regulative metonym for a national identity, Gayatri points out how, while describing the country metonymically, it also measures the distance between regulation and constitution. Haldarkarta finds not even the whole of East Bengal to be the space of his national identity, but only Harisal, his birth place that he thinks is the fountain head of India's cultural heritage. 'One day it will emerge that the Vedas and Upanishads were also written in Harisal'. Brahmin—the source of Vedic knowledge—is presented here and throughout the story, as elite in caste but subaltern in class. The Haldar women move out of patriarchal control into a kind of reproductive emancipation chiefly 'through their access to the circuit of Haldarkarta's political, economic and ideological production'. Jashoda (the proletarian) is useful at the initial stage in giving them freedom from reproductive fear; later the grand daughters-in-law leave the household and take off to the workplaces of their husbands. Thus the liberation of women, at least of the elite classes, is shown to be a result of imperialism that helped the Haldar family to be rich and also of the subalternisation of another set of women represented by Jashoda. The liberal feminist's emotional identification with the 'Third World' women in general, thus becomes a purely benevolent yet unintelligent gesture as it does not take into account the crucial historical factors behind women's liberation in the 'Third World'. Women's empowerment cannot be achieved outside history. Liberal feminism often becomes nothing more than a form of philanthropy prevalent among the elite academic class of women that can neither understand the forces behind the liberation of the Haldar women nor liberate Jashoda from the self-destructive role of the milk-mother. Jashoda's story is not that of the development of a feminine subjectivity, the ideal of liberal feminist criticism. Jashoda does feel a sense of futility at the end as she is left uncared for both by her real children and milk-children; but that is far from an emancipating consciousness that the educated women of the Haldar household develop as they master the reproductive process through family planning and also choose to live outside their ancestral home. Productive rights/are denied to Jashoda by upper-class women as well. Jashoda is a signifier for subalternity as such, while also being a metaphor for the predicament of the de-colonised nation-state, to follow Mahasweta's interpretation. If so, it partly destroys the materiality of Jashoda's copulative/reproductive body, a concept central to most feminisms. If Jashoda is de-colonised

India, her continuous child-bearing becomes an allusion to India's explosive population, and her disease, almost a consequence of it. At another level 'Stanadayini' blurs the distinction between consenting and coercive intercourse since Jashoda, in order to practise her 'right to work' is compelled also to reproduce frequently, to feed the Haldar children. It is partly choice and partly a product of the conspiracy of circumstances. The story also upsets the Lacanian mystification of *Jouissance* and all the care that certain forms of feminism bestow on the female body. It will never be known whether Jashoda really ever knew her body's orgasmic potential, though incidentally she was proud of her ever-full breasts. In this she is like the majority of Indian women who seldom discuss or express orgasm. The same inscrutability of women's pleasure is reflected in another minor narrative in the text where the Haldar boy, driven by lust, attacks the cook 'and the cook, since her body was heavy with rice, stolen fishheads and turnip greens and her body languid with sloth, lay back saying, "yah, do what you like."' She is also happy that her body was found tempting by a young man. When after the event the boy tells her, 'Auntie, don't tell,' the cook only says 'What's there to tell?' and quickly goes to sleep. Throughout the story there are references to men's pleasure and their dreams of women but women's pleasure is never discussed. The mechanical nature of regular sex is suggested at the very opening of the story: 'Jashoda doesn't remember at all when there was no child in her womb, when she didn't feel faint in the morning, when Kangali's body didn't drill her body like a geologist in a darkness lit only by an oil-lamp.' The later discussions of reproductive activity, after she decides to be a professional mother also are devoid of any reference to pleasure. The Haldar women also seem to have more fear of child-bearing than the anticipation of pleasure as their husbands follow the almanac to choose the days for love-making.

If 'Stanadayini' resists monolithic modes of analysis and interpretation and shows up their limits, it is chiefly because it is a polyphonic text that attempts to negotiate the ambivalences inherent in Indian social reality, characterised as it is by class mobility, reversal of gender roles, unevenness of emancipation, the interpenetration of class and caste resulting in odd combinations of material poverty and high caste status, specific forms of patriarchy and bad faith in sexual relationships, the overarching presence of religion and ritual, often in their exploitative forms in the day-to-day, the co-existence of feudal and neo-colonial attitudes and feelings, the dissolution of the joint family and its substitution by unitary system and the solitude the social system thrusts upon the marginalised, especially when they are afflicted by a fatal disease like cancer. My intention is not to mystify literature by stating that it is beyond all systems of interpretation; on the other hand each system problematises the very idea of literature in its own specific way. My purpose is simply to show how even an apparently 'realistic' text—in fact Mahasweta Devi's comments on Saratchandra imply a critique of the realistic mode, as well as the effect of her prose with its awkward syntax and its mixture of streetslang, East Bengal dialect, chaste and elegant Bengali and the everyday language of the household—is far too complex to be studied from a single perspective. Perhaps this also points to the need to decolonise our methodologies and discover tools that are indigenous and at the same time modern enough to grasp the contradictions of the text through a symptomatic reading.

THE TERROR OF THE BLANK PAGE
A Reading of Sitakant Mahapatra's 'The Other View: Yashoda's Soliloquy'

Sitakant Mahapatra's poem, 'The Other View: Yashoda's Soliloquy' based on a famous episode in Bhagavata (Canto X) where Yashoda, Krishna's foster-mother sees the whole universe and herself in the open little mouth of the divine child, transforms the miracle into an oppressive-memory that permanently haunts the perceiver by the sheer terror of its incommunicability. The poem, while being a meditation on an awesome mystery also turns out to be an exploration into the depotentiation of language and its terrified retreat into silence and entropy before the vastness, complexity and inexpressibility of experience. Students of Western poetry are likely to discover in the poem remote echoes of Saint John Perse's 'Anabase' and T.S. Eliot's 'Journey of the Magi', both of which pursue journeys into the interior, into the geography of the spirit rather than of the external world. 'Yashoda's Soliloquy' is more akin to Eliot's poem as the unrelieved weight of an ill-comprehended experience is felt by the speakers in both the monologues, even though the poems have more differences than similarities due to the cultural disparities underlying their perceptions. The Magus had seen a birth whose world-historical significance he knew only vaguely. There is no rejoicing here as in St. Matthew (ii, 1-12); the beginning of the poem is chillingly bleak as it presents the travails of the Magi's journey from the East to Bethlehem. The journey's end too brings no ecstasy; it is, as the Magus says, 'satisfactory' at the most. The flat, anti-climactic conclusion evidently shows that the journey brought no joy, solace or wisdom to the legendary kings, 'Well, they will take Him as they find Him and all this notwithstanding, worship Him for all that', as Lancelot Andrews—from whose sermon Eliot takes off—remarks. The primary significance of the journey, for Eliot, is the retrospective self-examination of the protagonist after the return: his perplexed interrogation of experience, his sense of bewilderment before the mystery of incarnation, his utter sense of alienation born of the loss of his old faith and his longing for release. The poem objectifies what Saint John Perse calls 'the loneliness of action; especially the action of the human spirit upon itself. Saint John Perse's 'Anabase' converts Xenephon's narrative, in Anabasis, of the long trek of the Greek mercenary soldiers from Babylon to the Black Sea after Cyrus's disastrous defeat in the Battle of Cunaxa against Artaxerxes II into an indefinite narrative that achieves, in the words of T.S. Eliot, 'a very allusive and mysterious play... at the extreme verge of what consciousness can grasp'. Eliot too does the same in the 'Journey of the Magi', where the concrete landmarks dissolve into indeterminate symbolic references like the running stream, the watermill, the three trees in the low sky, the green vegetation, the temperate valley, the old white horse in the meadow, the tavern with vine-leaves over the lintel, six hands dicing for pieces of silver and feet kicking the empty wineskins.

'The Other View: Yashoda's Soliloquy' too almost mutes its concrete episodic details in order to turn the whole event into a metaphor for the lonely (wo)man confronting mystery. The Magi are 'no longer at ease' in their palaces, 'in the old dispensation, with an alien people clutching their gods.' They cannot communicate to their pagan subjects the miracle they had witnessed, for three reasons: they themselves were not fully aware of the nature of the spiritual revolution signified by the birth of Christ, their experience was so unique that those who had not personally encountered the mystery would never be able to share its meaning and impact, they lacked the language to express the eerie feeling they had before the Divine Infant. What Yashoda had witnessed too was in one sense an incarnation: a brief rehearsal of the mightier revelation that was to come, of the Cosmic Form before Arjuna in the battle-field of Kurukshetra. On both the occasions, the onlooker was face-to-face with the superhuman and transcendental aspect of a person so close and dear to her/him. Both the encounters produce in their solitary witnesses the same awe the baby in the manger had invoked in the Magi who had followed the star. Yashoda would like to forget it and accept her foster-son as yet another mischievous child consuming earth as stealthily as thieving butter and milk from the milkmaids; but she is accursed to carry forever with her the memory of that spine-chilling vision. While on her daily chores, the scene flashes in her eyes and she feels 'a numbness in my brain, the world reeling about me/overpowering waves of a grim, dark sea rush at me/and in its cloud-black foreboding nets/the sun and moon, planets and stars, forests and hill/squirm and writhe in pain like fishes.'

This is certainly more than what Bhagavata says, for, it is more of a modem poet's vision of the universe than what Yashoda, 'the ignorant milkmaid' as she qualifies herself in the poem, sees in little Krishna's mouth. 'The grim dark sea' and 'the sun and moon, planets and stars, forests and hills' 'squirming and writhing in pain like fishes in her dark nets', reflect the poet's own way of looking at the world, one whose origins may be traced to the Buddha's vision of the tragic life of man on earth tormented by trishna or desire, the advaitic concept of *samsaradukha*, or worldly sorrow that is a product of Maya or illusion, or in the existential 'angst and dread' conceptualised by Kierkegaard or Gabriel Marcel or Sartre. The image of the world's writhing in the net also forebodes Yashoda's own feeling of suffocation as she is unable to understand or translate into words the other-worldly experience she had since she herself is trapped in the illusions of the mundane. That may be why she sees herself in that squirming world. This realisation makes that day for her one of 'darkness'.

The vision confuses the milkmaid: 'I understand nothing'. It throws her into bewilderment about her own identity in relation to herself and to others. No one believes her as she tells them of this demonic play of the child. Her friends, the gopis and Nandagopa, her husband, alike, open the kid's mouth over and over again and burst into laughter finding nothing except the baby's first pair of teeth 'like monsoon-month mushrooms,' his 'lovable red lips' and 'the traces of some stealthily taken earth'—a contrast to Yashoda's bizarre vision. The baby too pretends innocence as he stands with a mischievous half-smile around his lips. Yashoda's attempts at articulating her experience are mistaken for hysteria, since she is a woman; 'Yashoda must be mad', her friends conclude. She is deprived not only of language but even of the trust of others, denied sanity and reason as femininity is ever associated with the irrational and the impulsive. Yashoda does try to forget the event as 'a purposeless passing dream', telling herself that time cannot stand still, 'its billion million years set out as a mere wink on the brink of dark eyes, the endless universes held only in an evening's lamp of worship'. This fear of mystery is expressed by Jara in Sitakant's 'The Song of Jara' too:

> I do not wish to see your universal form
> wherein burns every planet and star,
> moon, nebula, sun and fire.

The baby's mouth obsesses and haunts the milkmaid, however much she might try to sentence it to oblivion. The ruby-red lips 'from which words fly out like the chirruping of tiny birds from an opened cage' fascinate her, while they also terrify her. Like someone awakened by a nightmare, she goes on reminding herself that she is Nanda's wife, her name is Yashoda, Kanha with his peacock-feather crown and flute at his lips is but her own little son and that this is her home. The child still comes to her in the cow-dust hour grimy with dust, playful as ever, asking for food. Yet like Abraham wondering whether it was God's voice he had heard and whether it was he who had been asked to sacrifice his son, Yashoda is unable to determine what is real and what is unreal. Is this Yashoda real, or the one she had seen that day in the whirling worlds? Is this human Krishna real or the divine one who had revealed to her the cosmic longing for salvation? Like Eliot's Magi back in their lands or like Tennyson's Ulysses back in Ithaca, amidst his ignorant subjects who knew nothing about his great adventures, Yashoda feels cut off from her own kith and kin. Husband, son, friends, fairs, festivities, everything appears menacingly alien. They seem to have no substance; things are desubstantiated, de-signified. The *vak* and the *artha*, the word and the meaning, no more stick together like Parvati and Parameswara.

This divine game, this *leela*, has torn her asunder as relationships seem to have lost their content for her. 'Who knows whose husband one is? or whose son?' Doubt seems now to invade all her certainties. She already knows that Devaki, not she, is Krishna's mother and Nandagopa is only playing the role of Vasudeva, the real father. But the present dilemma goes beyond this factual realisation. Can a human mother ever bear such an enfant terrible; can ever a mortal womb carry the immortal God? True she had not suffered any labour-pain to mother this child, but now she feels the profounder pain of being mother to an unnatural child. No physician can cure her of her recurring vertigo or even diagnose the tongueless grief of her unshared mystery that she will soon learn to have been but a prologue to a swelling supernatural theme that would leave many monsters dead during its unfolding—including the child's uncle, King Kamsa himself. It would once again demonstrate to her the meaninglessness of kinships in the battle between good and evil: a lesson Krishna teaches Arjuna too, while the latter is unnerved by the prospect of slaying his own kinsmen in Kurukshetra. Yashoda has not listened to the *Gita*; it is not for the milkmaid, but only for the soldier, Krishna seems to think; the milkmaid is only to be surprised by miracles and shocked into the realisation of her transient, mortal nature. Here she is on the verge of realising the emptiness of mamata, of attachment, but she the poor mother torn between affection and devotion cannot fully grasp the lesson. Perhaps Krishna does not want her to cultivate full detachment too, since her assigned role is primarily that of the loving, tending mother.

Yashoda tries to conceal her wounds behind a cheerful facade. She knows she will grow old sitting among other milkmaids, who have never witnessed the miracle or nursed a god, and waiting for her son's return from the pastures. Time will take its toll: her hairs will turn gray, her senses will become dull, her love and happiness will vanish: yet that awesome vision will stay with her to be buried only along with herself.

Sitakant Mahapatra said in an interview, years ago: '(My Poetry) is a meditation on the mysterious quality of all that exists, a ceaseless negotiation with the world and the self to extract some meaning from the apparent meaninglessness of experience and to find metaphors for what looks inexplicable.'

'The Other View: Yashoda's Soliloquy' may in the light of this statement of authorial intent be taken to be typical of his poetry in its concerns. At the heart of the poem lies silence, a theme central to the creativity of our times. If Schopenhauer found all arts aspiring to the condition of music, John Cage in our century found all music aspiring to silence and George Steiner and Ihab Hassan found silence to be the frontier of language, its inevitable end that leaves for us only uneasy intimations of outrage and apocalypse. Albert Camus thought suicide to be the principal philosophical problem of our times, while to several other writers, from Kafka and Beckett to Coetzee and Perec, it has been silence that confronts mystery or pain. So has it been to poets from Pound to Paul Celan. Pound's cycle 'Hugh Selwyn Mauberly' was an attempt to restore to poetry its missing third dimension. Breton found experience moving round in a cage from which it became more and more difficult to make it emerge. Rilke said he was attempting to discover through Duino Elegies and Sonnets to Orpheus what flowers might grow amid the ruins of language and Tadeusz Rozevicz claimed that he was fashioning his works out of 'a remnant of words, salvaged words, out of uninteresting words, words from the great rubbish dump, the great cemetery'. Yeats found that we have to make do with 'the rattle of pebbles on the shore under the receding waves', since the 'great song' would return no more. Baudelaire had chosen to bury himself in voluptuous surfaces in order to escape the entropic anarchy around and Brecht spoke of 'language-washing', as he wanted to rid poetry of clichés to make it speak afresh. Solitude is the ultimate refuge of the one who finds communication impossible, and feels like imitating Ivan Karamazov who returns his life-ticket to God. The force of absence strikes at the roots and induces, metaphorically, a great silence. This is what happens when Maurice Blanchot finds literature moving towards disappearance and Roland Barthes speaks of 'Writing Degree Zero' and the 'Death of the Author'. Language is held at a discount when Man loses his inner space and his unique world is squashed; he is then reduced to Marcuse's one-dimensional man.

The poet of 'Yashoda's Soliloquy' has explored this theme in poem after poem. In the poem 'This is Why We are Human,' he says that we are human not because we can converse with men from space, but because 'even after sitting hours together/next to someone dear/not even a word rises to the lips.' He accepts the gap between our longing and our expression with calm resignation:

> We are human
> not because we can compel words
> to say whatever, we intend to say
> but we discover that the errant words
> can never be cajoled and persuaded
> to do our bidding.

In the same poem he calls words 'illusory,' those half-truths in half-light and half-shadow' behind which we hide all our life. In the poem 'Shadow' the poet confronts a silent staring shadow that stands, face downward, at his door through all seasons and refuses to come in except in dreams. As he takes tea with his family, 'every piece of conversation seems out of place/and just before a sentence comes to a close/I turn silent, absentmindedly.' Birds forget their songs, plants shrivel and die and words disappear altogether in fear of this shadow. A disbelief for words is reflected also in 'The Ultimate Name of Time'. He feels we are ever drowning under a deluge of words that push, pull, choke and darken:

> ...and before getting lost
> I have only tried to say this much:
> love is what remains
> when all the words have died,
> poetry is what remains
> when all the words have failed.

Lifting the white sheet covering the grandmother's dead body, the poet peers into, 'history's face/as vast as the sky, dumb as the earth/ Once more silence heaved a deep sigh' ('Grandmother'). Here he realises that 'all the tears in life/had to be wept hidden away alone.'

The poet associates silence with solitude in several poems, as he does in 'Yashoda's Soliloquy'. He calls loneliness 'the inexorable author that makes of everything a memory', the transparent vacancy, the crow calling out at noon, a traveller alone on a road stretching away to infinity, 'our final goal, the soul's witness, our only testimony, the ultimate language' ('The Ultimate Name of Time'). Even Krishna awaiting Jara's arrow in the lonesome forest is but subject to the destiny of silent solitude. Poetry, he considers, is more a product of silence than of words. 'With his head bent in prayer/the poet listens/ as in silence words become poems.' And, he asks this poet:

> In the endless pathways of the sun
> in its unfathomed abyss of darkness
> where, dear poet, is the word
> for the ultimate anguish
> the pain without a name?
> ('The Poet in Silence')

In an earlier poem, 'The House', the poet in his childhood, 'the exiled prince', discovers the silence of the rice-field and the palms as well as the silence that reigns on, in spite of the comforting words of the neighbours as his mother lies in the solitary jungle of pain like the exiled queen. It is into silence that one travels as one dies: the poet finds his father, who used to sit silent leaning against the wall while alive, turning into a star and silently taking his place beside his dead mother.

The life of Kubja awaiting Krishna, the liberator, too is made up of silence:

> There is no fragrance, no colour or hue for me
> neither voice nor beauty

everywhere are the same colourless, odourless,
voiceless shadows of silence
(The Song of Kubja)

In the surrealistic world of 'The Brief Encounter', 'the scattered silence at the city's edge/of the fearless flowers of spring/stalk everywhere like a wild tiger.' The poet discovers death in the terrible season of the marigold's drone: 'Death, the orphaned child... ripens in the forlorn darkness inside.' In 'Bhubaneswar, 1972', the poet listens in vain to hear the voices of the town's 'black-robed moss-bearded stones' with their 'Ahalya-pain' a brilliant epithet that suggests the incommunicable sadness of forced silence. The village too is no different. In 'Our Village' the poet presents a hungry boy lying on the river sands: 'Unsung remain his many songs, his anguish and his tears'. Here the poet seems to allude to 'the culture of silence,' a term Paulo Freire uses to denote the silence of the oppressed everywhere. It is to the same silence that the village returns after witnessing a cockfight, they carry 'a lump of startled flesh in silence,' ('Cockfight'). In 'The Arithmetic of Pain', 'Torn words of an empty wind/are brought in on a trembling tray;/moth-eaten-futures/and the dumb music of the timeless dark.' The poet looks for 'the voice of dream in the ash' ('Driftwood') and waits for 'the dead timber to explode in blossoms' ('Woman with Sitar'). Yashoda's silence, thus, has many incarnations in Sitakant's poetry from death to life-in-death, from desperate solitude to the hope of speech and song.

'Terror is the normal state of any oral society for in it everything affects everything all the time,' said McLuhan in *The Gutenberg Galaxy*. It is this terror that stretches from Yashoda's ancient oral society to our own new oral society, where writing is devalued by the growing media that infuse and saturate us as we relive Yashoda's mysterious encounter and share her helplessness with the same intensity.

BETWEEN TWO CULTURES
On Two Poems of Kedarnath Singh

'Country and City are very powerful words,' says Raymond Williams,

> ...and this is not surprising when we remember how much they seem to stand for in the experience of human communities... powerful feelings have been generalised. On the country has gathered the idea of a natural way of life: of peace, innocence and simple virtue. On the city has gathered the idea of an achieved centre: of learning, communication and light. Powerful hostile associations have also developed: on the city as a place of noise, worldliness and ambition; on the country as a place of backwardness, ignorance and limitation.[1]

This rural-urban milieu has been one of the central themes of post-colonial Indian literature, especially since the growth of big modern industrial cities like Bombay and Calcutta. The writers who lived in the metropolises were the first to feel the trauma of the modern experience where 'all that is solid melts into air' to use a phrase from Marx, borrowed by Marshal Berman for the title of his book on modernity and literature. Modernism, and later post-modernism, in Indian languages came chiefly from those writers who had been driven to the urban environment by the pressures of day-to-day life, even while their roots lay in the villages. The alienation, loss of identity, nostalgia, doubt, tension, disenchantment and crisis of confidence, all of which have been identified as the hallmarks of modernist literary sensibility are a product of this encounter between the two worlds. Different writers have negotiated this contradiction using different strategies, for no modernist/post-modernist writer can afford to go back to the binary opposition of earlier writing, where the rural is associated with simplicity, innocence and peace and the urban, with chaos, corruption and evil. Roshan G. Shahani

---

1. Raymond Williams, *The Country and the City* (London, Chatto and Windus, 1973).

has observed how those writings featured the son-of-the-soil syndrome and the earth-mother figure and how socio-political realities were filtered in them through a middle-class consciousness that domesticised, sanitised and blurred the focus of issues like poverty, untouchability, class, caste and gender oppression.[2] At the time when the young nation was consolidating itself, the need for the 'Indianness' of tradition got articulated through a valorisation of the Indian peasant and of the Indian rural scape. Indianness-rusticity-simplicity nexus became a paradigm for Indian literature as well as Indian visual media. There is also the opposite danger, of the city being romanticised. Any authentic expression of India's contemporary experience will have to avoid these extremes; the only way is to pluralise and complexify the representation so that it captures all the nuances of this tension. The fact that our country's halfway industrialisation has not achieved a genuine urbanisation and even for the urban worker, the village is the dream and the nest of kinships, while the city is his reality by compulsion rather than by choice, makes the situation even more subtle and complex.

Kedarnath Singh's poetry articulates this tension between two cultures, two worlds in themselves, through memory and metaphor. He escapes simplification by carefully choosing objects that develop into polysemic symbols with several possible hermeneutic levels. At the level of language, this negotiation is achieved through an interaction between standardised literary Hindi and the dialects of common speech that represent a pre-literary consciousness. Voices from the periphery thus break into the centre of language; interior landscapes of poetry are revivified by evoking multiple perspectives.

In a poem like 'Bile' (The Bullock) in *Zamin Pak Rahi Hai*, the ox from India's agrarian culture represents the brutalising aspect of our rural experience alongwith its meditative and introspective aspect. The poet finds the silent persecution of the trees in his writing paper (*'Ped'*, Tree), seeks his word in the ripening grain (*'Awaz'*, The Voice),

---

2. Roshan G. Shahani, 'Polyphonous Voices in the City' in *Bombay: Mosaic of Modern Culture*, (Bombay, OUP, 1995).

Buddha makes him think of the future of water on earth (*'Buddh ke bare mein Sochna'*, To think of the Buddha), the bridge becomes an improvement on the boat (*'Majhi ka Pul'*, The Bridge of Majhi), the bird shrieks from the wood sawn by the carpenter (*'Badhayi aur Chidiya'*, The Carpenter and the Bird), myth and history penetrate each other in a temple city ('Benaras') or the poet bathes himself in the experience of rural community as in *'Sooryasth ke bad ek Andheri Basti se Guzarte Huve'* (Passing through a Dark Village after Sunset). There are several poems like *'Nadi'* (The River), *'Kuch Sootra Jo ek Kisan Bapne Bete ko Diye'* (A Farmer's Advice to his Son), *'Balu ka Sparsh'* (The Touch of the Sand), *'Chehera'* (The Face), *'Chithi'* (the Letter) and *'Akal mein Saras'* (Cranes in the Drought) that call up the villages of the poet's early life (All in *Akal mein Saras*, Cranes in the Drought). He dreamsof the gold of the December evening raining on the potato plantations (*'Taswir'*, Picture) and thinks of the state of wells that may now be lifted up with cranes and kept in museums. (*'Kuvem'*, Wells). In his house—which is not his, he hears the old, tired, echo of the footsteps of a snowman walking on the snow of his time (*'Goonj'*, Echo). Rivers, he says, know us, as they know the unease of their fish and the temperatures of their shores; the blood of mountains flows in their veins; a little of our blood too. 'Rivers are the beginnings of cities, and cities are the end of rivers.' (*'Nadiyan'*, Rivers) (All in *Uttar Kabir aur Anya Kavitayen*).

I intend to take up two of Kedarnath Singh's poems to illustrate how he transcends the simplifications of some of his predecessors and contemporaries by turning objects into metaphors that operate at different levels. My first example is *'Tuta Hua Truck'* (The Broken-down Truck) about the genesis of which the poet says:

> When I was working in that small town I told you about, I happened to see an abandoned truck beside the road, sprouting all over. A friend of mine commented that it had become a 'natural' phenomenon. Even after coming to Delhi, that theme haunted me. The poem was written in Delhi but it is not a Delhi poem.

The whole life it depicts is that of those people who are like broken trucks. A truck is a modern machine but in a peculiar sense, it is a developed form of bullock-cart. I cannot dissociate the bullock-cart from the truck, just as I can't separate the wooden boat from the huge concrete bridge. The whole story of development is a historical process from bullock-cart to truck and from boat to bridge. So for me, the broken, abandoned sprouting truck was the whole human life in those small towns. Life is there, as sprouting suggests but there is also stagnation. The contrast is striking.
—*Making It New: Modernism in Malayalam, Marathi and Hindi Poetry:* E.V. Ramakrishnan, Shimla, 1995; Interviewed by the Author

The poem, however, is more complex than may seem from this explanation offered by the poet. The little creeper edging along the steering wheel, the leaf that hangs down next to the horn as if it wanted to blow it and the grass that seems eager to change the wheels imply a natural force at work. On the one hand it is life, enveloping death, trying to revive the dead. Hence the poet's fancy that by the next day, everything would be fixed and he would wake up hearing the blare of the horn of the truck roaring off to Tinsukia or Bokajan. The truck also is a bridge between the country and the city as it travels from one to the other and back and also connects the agricultural civilisation to the commercial one. At this level it represents a broken-down relationship that the creepers and the grass are trying to revive.

However, this is only the poet's imagination at work; the truck is still standing there in the evening, 'staring at him.' This 'staring' implies a variety of meanings: It suggests (1) it has now become a menacing presence (2) it is being suffocated by the creepers, with the result its eyes are bulging (3) it is confused as its mechanical order has been challenged by the disorder of the wild vegetation (4) it is an abandoned force created by man, a victim of man's apathy.

The concluding part of the poem is epiphanic. The truck here takes on a new meaning: it becomes a symbol of recognition, the only mark by which the poet can identify his home, his city and his people. Here the poem becomes the intense expression of an alienation. The advancing disintegration of social ties, the growing atomisation of society, the ever-increasing isolation of individuals from one another and the solitude necessarily inherent in such tendencies of fragmentation and privatisation—which are themselves products of alienation—mark the predicament of man today, a state of dehumanisation the poet finds hard to reconcile with. Istvan Meszaros[3] has analysed this phenomenon in the context of the Western society, to point out how all claims for the 'sovereignty of the individual' only make a virtue out of the alienating predicament of solitude, thus affirming what the modern writers orginally intended to negate. Here, however, the poet is sorry for the attenuation of the relationship between individual and society. He does not idealise a situation where an abandoned, broken truck is the only sign by which he may recognise his home and people in the city; he is sorry for the tragic isolation of modern man from his surroundings. Once this little remnant of human touch, a machine made by man slowly turning into a green bush, too is gone, he may have nothing to recognise his city by. If we retrace the lines from here and read backwards, his earlier hope of the truck running again assumes a different dimension: even at the risk of losing his way in the maze of the city, the poet would like the truck to connect the city once again to the village and reestablish a relationship much after his heart. We have seen the city becoming a maze beyond escape in Kafka's *Trial* or in Joyce's *Ulysses* or in several poems of the Urdu tradition from Mir to Faiz and Alchtar-ul-Imam. This is also a major problem in Kedarnath Singh's poetry. Referring to poems like 'The Old Woman Selling Tomatoes', the poet says:

> I was trying to find a locale to Indianise my influences. I went through a crisis of identity. I found my locale in my childhood

---

3. Istvan Meszaros, *Philosophy, Ideology and Social Science: Essays in Negation and Affirmation* (London: Palgrave Macmillan, 1986).

past, in my village. I have been called a poet of *basti*. Bash is neither a village nor city, but has got some collective unity. That was the point where my feelings and experiences got localised for me. (From the interview earlier cited.)

The feeling of estrangement expressed in 'The Broken-down Truck' occurs again and again in Kedarnath Singh's poetry. The latest example perhaps is the long poem 'Uttar Kabir' where he asks:

Suddenly my sleep was disturbed. My sleep, that is whose?... Is it the same one who goes to sleep at night that wakes up on the bed, rubbing his eyes, in the small hours of the morning?... I want to go, but where? From where does this 'where' come screaming every time after each 'here'?

Here the estrangement becomes more abstract. Benares, Maghar and Ammi in the poem are no more associated with Kabir only; they become all places and all rivers. The disjointedness found in 'The Broken-down Truck' affects everything. 'Water has forgotten its relationship with fire; fire no more remembers the touch of the wind, wind flows cut off from every smell; the harmony of earth is delinked from smells; the sky no more talks to earth.' My second example is '*Kudal*' (the Spade) from *Uttar Kabir Aur Anya Kavitayen*. The object raised to the level of a symbol here is an agricultural implement, true to Kedarnath Singh's method of choosing his symbols from ordinary life, a mode inherited from the Bhakti poets who always wove their poems around objects from the kitchen and the workplace. The poet's eyes are disturbed by the sight of a spade left by the gardener at his door. It looks quite out of place there. At the same time he is fascinated by its 'strange, curvaceous, dust-laden beauty'. The word 'dust' is very important here as it is a recurring symbol in Kedarnath's poems. In the poem '*Kasbe ki Dhool*' (The Dust of Kasba [small town]) he says: 'I am aware because/this dust is the most living/and lovely thing of my land/the most restless/the most active/the earth's most nascent/and the most ancient dust.' In a conversation the poet says:

'Dust represents the whole Indian life itself. It is always active and flying in the atmosphere. The darkness and sadness are there in dust. The slowness of its movement represents the rhythm of semi-rural Indian life I am familiar with.' This dust is also related to the past, for the poet sees the spade 'in the pale light of the departing day' (*jate hue din ki dhundhali roshni mein*). The departing day implies also the disappearance of a whole culture represented by the spade:

> There was work
> It is over
> There was soil
> It has been dug to the roots
> And now this spade
> stands at the door
> like a silent challenge.

The spade has already done its work; the rustic culture of the peasant has contributed to an awareness of our roots. Perhaps it also suggests that the village has already played its role in the shaping of the poet's vision and sensibility.

The poet thinks of taking the spade inside the house and leaving it in some corner. First he thinks of keeping it in the drawing room; why not the spade if he can keep the *nagphani* there? But immediately he discovers that the presence of the spade will upset the balance of the whole house. What about the kitchen? But the kitchen had a 'fresh-washed sacredness', before which the dusty spade looked out of place. The products of the peasant can enter the kitchen, but not the peasant himself, nor his earth-laden tool. The spade cannot be kept in the darkness under the cot. It will be an act of cowardice—like concealing one's true origins. The house may, however, become warmer by that odour of mystery that will fill the air. A spade under a cot is a strange image; it makes the poet laugh.

Finally, the poet stops by the spade for a while to meditate over it. He feels he is standing in some invisible court, with the spade on his shoulder, to witness the being of the spade on earth. One cannot but acknowledge the presence of the peasant and his contribution to man's making and civilisation. But for him the cities would not have been; but for him we would go without food and even without culture, for the roots of our literary culture lie in the great oral traditions and our music, dance, painting, sculpture and architecture, even our wisdom, owes much to the folksingers, ritual dancers, carpenters, masons and other artisans, all products of a rural culture with agriculture at its centre. Not only are India's marvelous temples products of rural artistry; our classical dances and music can easily be traced to their folk roots, and our epic *Ramayana*, if we can believe the legends, was authored by a hunter-turned sage, and *Mahabharata* by the son of a fisherwoman. The post-industrial culture of the cities may try to hide these beginnings by hiding them in the darkness under their cots and sleeping over them. But its presence is undeniable, and poetry is perhaps the last witness to that ancestral civilisation. This is why the poet feels the gardener has raised 'the most difficult question of my century.'

The final stanza sounds like a warning. It is like the 'village encircling the city.' As it grows darker, the spade's blade seems to be growing; it is dangerous to leave it at the door. Throwing it to the streets is also impossible. We cannot disinherit or disown our fathers. If Cavafy's people of the city wait for the barbarians to destroy their culture and offer an alternative, the poet here is caught between two cultures, the rural and the urban, the agricultural and the industrial. The poet does not resolve the question; his project is only to present the poser, to highlight the ambivalence of the culture we live. Such an ending is quite natural to a poet who sees the emptiness of the postcard as a message that tells us, 'To write is to see the whole world including the blind' ('Postcard' in *Uttar Kabir*).

To be modern, as Marshall Berman tells us in his preface to *All that is Solid Melts into Air: The Experience of Modernity* is to live a life of paradox and contradiction:

It is to be overpowered by the immense bureaucratic organisations that have the power to control and often to destroy all communities, values, lives; and yet to be undeterred in our determination to face these forces, to fight to change their world and make it our own. It is to be both revolutionary and conservative, alive to new possibilities for experience and adventure, frightened by the nihilistic depths to which so many modern adventures lead, longing to create and to hold on to something real, even as everything melts. We might even say that to be fully modern is to be anti-modern: from Marx's and Dostoevsky's time to our own, it has been impossible to grasp and embrace the modern world's potentialities without loathing and fighting against some of its most palpable realities. No wonder then that, as the great modernist and antimodernist Kierkegaard said, the deepest modern seriousness must express itself through irony.

The irony of poems like 'The Broken-down Truck' and 'The Spade' has to be seen in this paradoxical context of modernism and antimodernism locked in a battle against each other, as in the Indian social context today. The city both constitutes and symbolises the modern predicament. The anonymous massman is cut off from his past and from the nexus of human relations in which he formally existed, and feels anxious and insecure with the dreadful freedom of spiritual choice that the disappearance of God has conferred on him. Only a broken-down truck guides him to his house and the spade from his rural past finds itself awkward in his urban present. The truck and the spade enter a fraternity of the abandoned in an atmosphere of tense estrangement and precarious ambivalence.

SONGS FROM THE UNDERWORLD
The Poetry of Namdeo Dhasal

We are living at a time when Dalit literature is fast being assimilated into the mainstream of Indian literature, which implies a potential loss of its power to provoke and disturb the status quo. The spurt of translations of Dalit poetry, fiction and autobiography in English, in the form of individual works as well as anthologies, while helping to earn the genre a wider audience across the country, can also be seen as a sign of this process of mainstreaming. This is also a reflection of a change in the self-perception of Dalit writers: many of the new generation Dalit writers do not want to be seen as belonging to a special category of writing and to be judged by standards peculiar to them; instead they would like to be seen just as writers and be judged by their innovative use of language and the formal revolution they have pioneered in their respective regional literatures. The avant-garde has always had to face this challenge in the course of their maturing: their works get included in text books, they became an inevitable part of any literary festival or anthology, they win awards from the literary establishment; their works became subjects of formal research, and their structural, syntactic and stylistic values gain greater attention than their thematic radicalism and the social context that in the first place gave rise to the whole Movement. I recall Susie Tharu once pointing to the danger of this appropriation faced by radical woman writers; the Dalit writers like the 'progressive' before them or the 'nativists' after them, are no exception.

But this appropriation, while affecting the transformative social value of Dalit literature in no way reduces the aesthetic value of the textual qualities innate to it. In fact, we begin to perceive those values more clearly in this second phase, when the writing itself has lost something of its initial shock value. That is why a sound thinker like D.R. Nagraj can speak about a specific Dalit memory and imagination, a whole Dalit aesthetics. Dalit writers, we now know, have been redrawing the very map of Indian literature, cleansing and renewing language in order to overcome the stagnation it faced in the practices of the upper castes, challenging the set mores and modes of looking at reality and forcing the entire community to refashion its intellectual tools and observe itself critically. Dalit poetry clearly negates the rules of status quoist poetics by employing words and expressions that the Sanskrit poeticians would have considered inappropriate for literature: *asleela, gramya, chyuthasamskara* (obscene, rustic, uncouth) and challenging the middle class notions of propriety, decency, restraint, and balance. Dalit writing today consists no more of just indignation or pathos as it once did, but it is also now a positive celebration of Dalit identity and Dalit values.

'I did not have to consciously turn to poetry. Ever since I learnt to speak my mother tongue as a child, I started playing with words,' this is how Namdeo opens his statement on himself appended to the poems. He recollects in some detail his early life in his native village of Pur near Pune: watching closely the seasonal performances of the tamasha troupe led by his uncle and grandfather, the robust ribaldry of the Lavani songs, the melodious tamasha songs, ovis, bhajans and lyrics sung by his mother, the nightly community gatherings rich with dance and song, the shehnai played by his grandfather Raoji Buva Dhasal, who was a respected musician acknowledged by the Indore court, the harmonium, table and mridang played with the same expertise by Narayanbuva, his father's brother steeped in the Varkari pilgrims musical tradition, the readings at home of *Shivalilamrut*, the Natha text and *Jnaneshwari*, the Varkari text especially in the month of *shravan*, the *kirtan*s of Gadge Baba, the Shimga festivities following Holi when children put on masks and special dresses to play various roles, his own dance as a woman in a sari that was a real hit with all the villagers...these recollections tell us the story of a sweet childhood spent in the village, full of music, dance and festivities, despite the untouchability and the communal drive that existed there. There is no bitterness here; there is instead a robust acceptance of all that was positive within the community life and even a pride about his family with its artistic and spiritual traditions. Namdeo also remembers the great wave of conversion to Buddhism that swept Pune after 1957, in the wake of the mass movement launched by Ambedkar. The mahars stopped doing their caste–assigned chores; they held concerts and meetings to spread the message of liberation from the hierarchy. Namdeo, then a third-grade student, also wrote a song inspired by what happening around him. He pays glowing tribute to Narayan Shankar Kokate, his teacher at the Baney Compound School in Mumbai who prepared him to be a writer, teaching him classical Marathi literature, nurturing his taste and providing him with a sense of quality in writing. He also mastered Marathi prosody under his training and developed a taste for traditional poetry. The reference library at Janata Kendra opened before him a vast treasure house of literature, complementing what he had learnt from his masters.

Namdeo first wrote romantic lyrics on nature and love; the literary magazine *Satyakatha* and the avant garde little magazines where he came across translations of modern European poets changed his attitude towards writing. The casteim he encountered—in the context of a love-affair—in the apparently 'progressive' sections of the establishment politics led to his disenchantment with the Praja Samajwadi Party, whose activities he had so far been involved with. He revolted against the whole system that sustained communalism and casteism. The frustration made him a rebel: he boozed and visited brothels and plunged headlong into life in the backyards of the city. He threw out all rulebooks and was free as a poet. He sharpened his weapons; nothing could stop him now. He was a taxi driver; he had no fixed time for reading and writing; he wrote at eateries during his brief intermissions. He never consulted others about his poetry nor compared himself with others; he followed his instincts and just decided to be faithful to the nuances and subtleties of the life that opened up before him in all its beauty and brutality.

The poems/excerpts translated by Dilip Chitre from the poet's eight collections so far published, originally written between 1972 and 2006, reflect the range and variety of Namdeo Dhasal's poetic oeuvre. The opening excerpt from *Golpitha*, the poet's first collection, is a powerfully ironic piece that at first appears nihilistic and destructive.

> Man, you should drink human blood, eat spit, roast human flesh, melt human fat and drink it
> Smash the bones of your critics' shanks on hard stone blocks to get their marrow,
> Wage class wars, caste wars, communal wars, party wars, crusades, world wars
> One should become totally savage, ferocious and primitive...

But it turns round towards the end, leading to a wonderfully tender conclusion:

> One should regard the sky as one's grandpa, the earth as one's grandma,
> and coddled by them everybody should bask in mutual love
> Man, one should act so bright as to make the Sun and the Moon seem pale
> One should share each morsel of food with everyone else, one should compose a hymn
> To humanity itself, man, man should sing only the song of man.
> (Man, you should Explode).

'Ode to Ambedkar' is rich with evocative imagery:

> 'The skin of the untouchable life is moistened by your Heavenly stream;
> you have smashed the head of the god–given wind
> That created room for a wobbly nation and its restless people.
> The parrot of existence perennially pecks at the unending agony of thought...
> An earthen owl of compassion and a black rose of blood grow out of my arise,

> If I don't uproot this society of mere onlookers,
> A hard rock will separate you and me; and I will not be able to see
> Your radiant disc surrounded by lotuses growing among crystals,
> rejecting all material things...
> For, at the very point of the needle, one is introduced to love and
> to the green blade of wheat,
> That sun flows perennially through shouts of victory,
> That sun flies like the New Year's butterfly and spreads light,
> That Sun grows parallel to railway tracks,
> That sun loosens the stone walls of universities;
> It moves only from one freedom to the next.

These and lines like these remind the readers of a Neruda or a Vallejo by their raw force and sheer creative energy and one wonders whether to admire the poet or the translator or both for their poetic dynamism. A similar energy characterises 'Water': 'Water is like Siddhartha/Water is like the Ashoka tree/Water is also nitric acid'. At times the lines become soft and fluent like the lines of a folksong: 'Speak water, what colour are you/Son, it's like your eyes.../Tell me water, what your colour is -/Daughter, it is the colour of your thirst.' At times the lines turn red with wrath: 'The rising day of justice, like a bribed person, favours only them/ While we are being slaughtered, not even a sigh for us escapes their generous hands.' ('The orthodox Pity')

The idiom grows darker and more complex as we move forward to poems like 'Approaching the Organized Harem of the Octopus'. Black becomes a positive colour as in the poetry of Senghor and the poets of negritude.

> We are all over the streets spread out long and wide as tar on the body like a prostitute, grotesque people eating starvation underlined in decimals in the womb of 1970, the eunuch cropping up in the harvest to castrate the shit, the sewage that gushes out in a torrent from the face.

Clear and blurred images like these try to capture the horrid reality of our time. 'Mandakini Patel: A young prostitute, My Intended collage' is another poem that foregrounds the gory violence perpetrated upon a sixteen-year old girl by a brutal society. The poet's tone grows tender as he thinks of the girl:

> Manda,/your mind is neither ash nor marble
> I feel your hair, your clothes, your nails, your breasts
> as though they were my own
> They reveal to me, within myself colonies of the dead...
> Never before had I seen a face so devoid of lights/as was yours...

But the poet does not lose hope: 'Manda,/my peahen,/Look out of the window, and a new world, and a new world is born.'

The poet's troubled yet untiring voice goes in recounting atrocity after atrocity, sin after sin in the other poems. The style is basically the same, but sometimes it grows more ironic as in 'The tree of violence', where trees becomes the central metaphor for the state of the nation constantly troubled by waves of violence, whose roots lies in the basic inequalities of society. It is a tree that grows thousand-fold when cut down.

> Those who brought up the tree
> Walked out on their homes
> They laughed their way to the gallows
> Because they knew it for sure
> That as long as the circumstances that gave birth to the tree were not rooted out
> The tree was not destined to die.

The tree finally becomes the cornucopia for the newborn nation. The poems grow even more strident in *Tuhi Yatta Kanchi* (What is your grade?). Poems like 'Kamatipura', 'Hunger', 'Ode to Ambedkar' and 'Sweet Baby Poverty' are all poems of deep anguish and concern for the underprivileged, whose anger and frustration become the poet's own. The poems from *Khel* (Play), however, are more introspective and deal with the questions of the self. 'Untitled Poem' for example, begins like this: 'I have seen him/I have rejected him often/My corpse that wanders/From town to town.' While the next poem begins with: 'The shelf its dead skin in water/Again a growing creeper climbs the new skin.... Each thing unfolds its inner space.' The style also becomes softer and more sober in the later poems: 'There are neither flowers/Nor leaves;/Neither trees/Nor birds./All this is mimicry by mercy of His grace/sealed fragrance of musk/Thus the chains on one's legs are transformed/into music...' (Arsefuckers' park 1). The irony is still there as the poet speaks about the politicised crows listening to the proceedings of pimps confessing to a study of street walkers and homeguards performing their drills on a sterile field of silence. And there is a choking pain: 'Behind every word/There is a naked face hidden', 'A wound has found its home in my heart—even words cannot open the doors'. And the surrealist images: 'Horses are being tattooed on my arms./The creeping plant of my penis is about to flower./Ibsen's doll is about to get married.../The black truth seeks to ride the tortoise.' (Ibid). The poet revolts against the total cleanliness of the shirt of a non-worker and the uncompromising purity that grows heartless: 'A human being shouldn't become so spotless./One should leave a few stains on one's shirt./One should carry on oneself a little bit of sin' (Speculations on a Shirt). 'I am a venereal sore in the private part of language', the poet declares meaningfully in the poem, 'Cruelty', 'The living spirit looking out of hundreds of thousands of sad, pitiful eyes/Has shaken me'. He seeks release from his 'infernal identity' as he sees a sigh 'standing up on lame legs.' The longing for liberation keeps coming back: 'I do not wish to get chained to this God-created hell' ('Worry'); 'Gradually people start coming out of the body' ('People').

The poem 'December 6' is a powerful reminder of the crisis of our secular ethos:

Now
This is city is no longer mine '

> It was only yesterday that you told us
> That this country belonged to us...
> The walls of my own house charge upon me
> They want to assassinate me.
> Digging up dead bodies from the past the enemies are busy
> Playing the politics of chastisement...
> Yesterday they murdered Gandhi
> Now they want to put whole nation to death...

The poet's idiom gets more direct on occasions like these. He finds his face stirred up on the surface of water like Narcissus; he sheds his skin like a snake and asks the reader not to blow a breath on the water, as with that his memoirs will lose their face—a reminder of the fragility of human life. ('Autobiography') Tragedy and comedy become one for him, the fate's *tamasha* and pain's *dasavatar*. He sums up his life thus: 'The soil created me as an outsider;/This air turned its back on me;/What took pity on me in the end was the sky that has no limits' ('Miracle'). He is anxious about tomorrow when people would present nuclear warheads, instead of roses, to one another as symbols of love. ('With a God Who Isn't') He tells van Gogh, 'You have forgotten to paint/One of the colours of Sun!' Kabir has disappeared from the Bazaar, 'This chatter of freedom does not accept my tradition' ('Poetry Notebook'). Still he knows that 'it's started to rain/on the untouchable earth' ('Comes the day, Passes the say'). The poet's testament is summed up in these lines: 'The wicked have injured the earth/Poets know all about it/Only poets can save the Earth/From extinction.'

Dilip Chitre's postscript on the pleasure and exasperation of translating Namdeo's poetry is a real lesson in translation in its specific contexts, while his introduction looks at Naamdeo's poetry as personal expression as well as an expression of his traumatised community. The best way to conclude this short essay would be to quote from Dilip Chitre's introduction to his translation of Namdeo:

It is the nimble and graceful movement across the Faultlines of alienation that gives his poetry its artistic distinctiveness. At times a cleansing fury rages in his writing. At other times, it is moistened by sensitive compassion and a spiritual clarity. Namdeo's is a rooted and located human voice that demands to be heard on its own terms.[1]

---

1. Foreword to Dilip Chitre, trans., *Namdeo Dhasal: Poet of the Underworld, Poems 1972–2006* (Delhi: Navayana Publishing, 2007).

SOURCES AND ACKNOWLEDGEMENTS

- The first three essays ('**The Plural and the Singular**', '**The Modern and the Democratic**', '**Mother Tongue, the Other Tongue**') were originally delivered as a series of Annual Lectures at Central Institute of Indian Languages, Mysore.

- **Indian Literary Criticism Today**: First presented in summary form as an editorial in the journal *Indian Literature*, published by Sahitya Akademi, New Delhi, 1993.

- **Indian Literature:** Contribution to a seminar on 'Nativism' held at I.I.T. Kanpur; included in Makarand Paranjape (ed.) *Nativism* (New Delhi: Sahitya Akademi, 1997).

- **Sex, Text, Politics**: Originally a talk delivered at IGNCA, Delhi 1993; published in *Word-Plus*, Trivandrum, 1994. Also developed as a keynote address at the National Seminar on 'Women's Writing in India', Delhi, 2014.

- **Imagined Communities:** Abridged version of the Agyey Memorial talk at I.I.T., Kanpur, 1996; a shorter version presented at the SAARC Seminar, Calcutta and published in *The Journal of Comparative Literature*, Jadavpur University, Calcutta, 2000.

- **Of Many Indias**: Paper presented at the seminar on 'Indianness in Indian Literature' at the Department of Oriental Studies, University of Leiden, Netherlands, 1999.

- **That Third Space**: Inaugural Address at the seminar on 'The Literature of the Indian Diaspora' held at Jawaharlal Nehru University, New Delhi, 2000.

- **The Politics of Rereading**: Delivered as the valedictory lecture at the National Seminar on 'Indian Literary Criticism Today' organised by Sahitya Akademi, Delhi, 2014.

- **Translation as Writing**: Paper presented at the International Seminar on 'The Problems of Translation' organised by the National Book Trust, India, New Delhi, 2014.

- **Another Life, Another Poetics**: This is part of an ongoing study on the social dynamics and poetics of the Bhakti Movement in India. Excerpted from the Purohit Swamy Memorial Lectures delivered at the Banaras Hindu University, Varanasi, 1999.

- **Strategies of Subversion**: Chief Guest's Speech delivered on the occasion of the Sarala Samman Ceremony, Cuttack, Orissa, 1999.
- **I Think of the Ends of Things**: Speech delivered at the International Seminar on Mirza Ghalib, Sahitya Akademi, Delhi, 1998.
- **My Kabir, My Contemporary**: Talk delivered at the Kabir Seminar organised by Sahitya Akademi at Jamnagar, Gujarat, 2003.
- **The Pathography of Nationalism**: Paper presented at the International Seminar on Tagore at the University of West Australia, Perth, 2011, further developed and presented at the National Seminar on 'Tagore and Nationalism' at IIAS, Shimla, 2015.
- **Saratchandra Chatterjee and the Dynamics of Reception**: Written for a Sahitya Akademi seminar on Saratchandra Chatterjee, in Calcutta, 2001.
- **Against the Grain**: Talk delivered at a symposium at Lady Shri Ram College, New Delhi, 1993.
- **Transcending the Body**: Introduction to Kamala Das's collection of poems, *Only the Soul Knows How to Sing*, Kottayam: DC Books, 1996.
- **On the Limits of Interpretation**: First published in *Indian Literature: Positions and Propositions*, New Delhi: Pencraft International, 1999.
- **The Terror of the Blank Page**: Paper written for a collection of articles on Sitakant Mahapatra, first published in *Indian Literature, Positions and Propositions*, Pencraft International, Delhi, 1999.
- **Between Two Cultures**: Originally published in Hindi in *Uttar Kedar*, ed. Sudhish Pachauri, Delhi, 1996.
- **Songs from the Underworld**: Article written for *The Book Review*, Delhi, 2008.

SELECT BIBLIOGRAPHY

Ahmad, Aijaz. *In Theory: Classes, Nations, Literature.* New Delhi: Oxford University Press, 1992.

Berman, Marshall. *All that is Solid Melts into Air: The Experience of Modernity,* London: Verso, 1982.

Callewaert, Winand M., and Mukund Lath. *The Hindi Padavali of Namdev.* Delhi: Motilal Banarsidas Publishers Ltd, 1989.

Chitre, Dilip, trans. *Says Tuka,* Delhi: Penguin Books, 1991.

Dalmia, Vasudha and Theo Damsteegt. *Narrative Strategies: Essays on South Asian Literature and Film.* Leiden: Research School CNWS, 1998.

Das, Sisir Kumar. *A History of Indian Literature* (3 vols). New Delhi: Sahitya Akademi, 1993.

Dharwadker, Vinay, trans. *Kabir, The Weaver's Songs.* Delhi: Penguin Books, 2003.

Duggal, K.S., trans. *Sain Bulleh Shah, the Mystic Muse,* Delhi: Abhinav Publications, 1996.

Eagleton, Terry. *Significance of Theory.* Oxford, UK: John Wiley and Sons Ltd. 1992.

George, K.M. *Comparative Indian Literature* (2 vols). New Delhi: Sahitya Akademi, 1984.

Limbale, Sharan Kumar. *Towards an Aesthetics of Dalit Literature.* New Delhi: Orient BlackSwan 2004.

Meeker, Joseph. *The Comedy of Survival: Studies in Literary Ecology.* New York: Scribner, 1974.

Meszaros, Istvan. 'Philosophy, Ideology and Social Science,' *Essays in Negation and Affirmation.* London: Palgrave Macmillan, 1986.

Mills, Sara. *Discourses of Difference: An Analysis of Women's Travel Writing and Colonialism,* London: Routledge, 1991.

Mukherjee, Sujit. *Towards a Literary History of India.* Simla: IIAS, 1975.

Nagaraj, D.R. *The Flaming Feet: A Study of the Dalit Movement in India.* Kolkata: Seagull Books, 2011.

Pollock, Sheldon, ed., *Literary Cultures in History: Reconstructions from South Asia.* Berkeley: University of California Press, 2003.

Punekar, Rohini Mokashi, trans. *Songs of Chokhamela.* New Delhi: The Book Review Literary Trust, 2002.

Ramakrishnan, E.V. *Making It New: Modernism in Malayalam, Marathi and Hindi Poetry.* Shimla: IIAS, 1995.

———. *Narrating India: The Novel in Search of the Nation.* New Delhi: Sahitya Akademi, 2005.

Ramanujan, A.K., trans. *Speaking of Shiva.* New Delhi: Penguin Books, 1973.

Ravindran, P.P., 'Genealogies of Indian Literature', *Economic* and *Political Weekly*, 24 June, 2006.

Rayan, Krishna. *Text and Sub-text: Suggestion in Literature.* London: Hodder Arnold, 1987.

———. *Burning Bush: Suggestion in Indian Literature.* New Delhi: BR Publishing Corporation, 1988.

———. *Sahitya: A Theory for Indian Critical Practice.* New Delhi: Sterling Publishers, 1991.

Satchidanandan, K. *Authors, Texts, Issues.* Delhi: Pencraft International, 2003.

———. *Indian Literature: Positions and Propositions.* Delhi: Pencraft International, 1999.

Shahani, G. 'Polyphonous Voices in the City' in *Bombay: Mosaic of Modern Culture.* Bombay, Oxford University Press, 1995.

Sharma, T.R.S., C.K. Seshadri and June Gaur, Introduction to *Ancient Indian Literature.* New Delhi: Sahitya Akademi, 2001.

Subramaniam, Arundhati, ed. *Eating God: A Book of Bhakti Poetry.* New Delhi: Penguin Ananda, 2014.

Tagore, Rabindranath. *Nationalism*. New York: Macmillan, 1917.

Thapar, Romila. *The Aryan: Recasting constructs*. New Delhi: Three Essays Collective. 2008.

———. *Which of us are Aryans?* New Delhi: Aleph, 2019.

Tharu, Susie and K. Lalita. *Women Writing in India, Sixth Century B.C. to the Present*. New Delhi: Oxford University Press, 1997.

Trivedi, Harish and Meenakshi Mukherjee, eds. *Interrogating Post-Colonialism: Theory, Text and Context*. Shimla: IIAS, 1996.

Vanita, Ruth and Saleem Kidwai, eds. *Same-sex Love in India: Readings from Literature and History*. London: Macmillan, 2000.

Williams, Patrick and Laura Chrisman, eds. *Colonial Discourse and Post-colonial Theory*. New York: Columbia University Press. 1994.

Williams, Raymond. *The Country and the City*. London: Oxford University Press, 1985.

SUGGESTIONS FOR FURTHER READING

Alexander, Meena, ed. *Name Me a Word: Indian Writers Reflect on Writing*. New Haven and London: Yale University Press, 2018.

Bassnett, Susan. *Translation Studies*. London and New York: Routledge, 2002 (First published, London: Methuen, 1980).

Bassnett, Susan and Andre Lefevere. *Constructing Cultures: Essays in Literary Translation*. Clevedon: Multilingual Matters, 1998.

Basu, Tapan, ed. *Translating Caste*. New Delhi: Katha, 2002.

Bose, Brinda, ed. *Translating Desire*. New Delhi: Katha, 2002.

Cama, Shernaz, and Sudhir Chandra Mathur, eds. *The Muse and the Minorities: Social Concerns and Creative Cohesion*. New Delhi: The Steering Committee, The Muse and the Minorities, 1998.

Chanda, Ipshita. *Reception of the Received: European Romanticism: Rabindranath and Suryakant Tripathi 'Nirala'*. Kolkata: Jadavpur University, 2006.

Das, Bijay Kumar. *The Horizon of Translation Studies*. New Delhi: Atlantic publishers and Distributors, 1998.

Das, Sisir Kumar. *A History of Indian Literature. 500-1399*. New Delhi: Sahitya Akademi, 2005.

———. *A History of Indian Literature, 1800-1910*. New Delhi: Sahitya Akademi, 1991.

———. *A History of Indian Literature 1911-1956*. New Delhi: Sahitya Akademi, 1995.

Dasan, M., V. Pratibha, et al., eds. *The Oxford India Anthology of Malayalam Dalit Writing*. New Delhi: Oxford University Press, 2012.

Dasgupta, Subha Chakraborty. *Regionality and Comparative Literature*. Kolkata: Jadavpur University, 1998.

Deshpande, G.T. *Abhinava Gupta*. New Delhi: Sahitya Akademi. 1989.

Eco, Umberto. *Mouse or Rat? Translation as Negotiation*. London: Phoenix, 2003.

Ferro-Luzi, Gabriellla Eichinger. *Glimpses of the Indian Village in Anthropology and Literature.* Napoli: Instituto Universitario Orientale, 1998.

George, K.M., ed. *Masterpieces of Indian Literature*, 3 Volumes. New Delhi: National Book Trust, 1997.

———, ed. *Modern Indian Literature: An Anthology:* Three Volumes, New Delhi: Sahitya Akademi, Vol. 1, 1997; Vol. 2, 1999; Vol. 3, 2000.

Goldman, Jane. *Modernism 1910-1945: Image to Apocalypse.* Hampshire and New York: Palgrave Macmillan, 2017 (First published 2004).

Jain, Jasbir, *The Diaspora Writes Home: Subcontinental Narratives.* Jaipur and Delhi: Rawat Publications, 2015.

———, ed. *Feminizing Political Discourse: Women and the Novel in India.* Jaipur and Delhi: Rawat Publications, 1997.

———. *Growing Up as a Woman Writer.* New Delhi: Sahitya Akademi, 2007.

Joseph, Ammu et al., ed. *Just Between us: Women Speak about Their Writing.* Delhi: Women Unlimited, 2004.

Kar, Angshuman, ed. *Contemporary Indian Diaspora: Literary and Cultural Representations.* Jaipur: Rawat Publications, 2015.

Kar, Prafulla C. et al., ed. *Journal of Contemporary Thought. Special Number on Postcolonialism and the Discourse of Marginality.* Forum on Contemporary Theory, MS University, Baroda and Louisiana State University, USA, Summer, 1999.

Karickam, Dr Abraham, ed. *Comparative Literature and Translation*, Tiruvalla: CLRSC, 2000.

Kaul R.K., and Jaidev. *Social Awareness in Modern Indian Literature.* Shimla: IIAS, 1993.

Kothari, Rita. *Translating India.* Manchester, UK and Northampton MA: St Jerome Publishing, 2003.

Kumar, Akshaya. *Poetry, Politics and Culture, Essays on Indian Texts and Contexts.* New Delhi: Routledge, 2009.

Kumar, Udaya. *Writing the First Person: Literature, History and Autobiography in Modern Kerala.* Ranikhet: Permanent Black, 2016.

Lal, Malashri, *The Law of the Threshold: Women Writers in Indian English.* Shimla: IIAS, 1995.

Landry, Donna and Mac Lean, Gerald, *The Spivak Reader.* New York and London: Routledge, 1996.

Mangalam, Harish, and M.B. Gaijan, eds. *Pristine Land: Gujarati Dalit Literature.* Delhi: Yash Publications, 2009.

Mukherjee, Sujit. *Translation as Recovery.* Delhi, Pencraft International, 2004.

Nagaraj, D.R. *The Flaming Feet: A Study of the Dalit Movement.* Bangalore: South Forum Press, 1993.

Nair, Rukmini Bhaya. *Poetry in a Time of Terror: Essays in the Post-Colonial Preternatural.* New Delhi: Oxford University Press, 2009.

Nanavathy U.M., and Kar, Prafula C. *Rethinking Indian English Literature.* Delhi: Pencraft International, 2000.

Narasimhan, Raji, *Translation as Touchstone.* New Delhi: Sage Publications, 2013.

Narasimhaiah, C.D., ed. *East West Poetics at Work.* New Delhi: Sahitya Akademi, 1994.

Narasimhaiah, C.D., and Srinath C.N., *Bhakti in Indian Literature.* Mysore: Dhvanyaloka, 1989.

Nehru Memorial Museum and Library, *Gender and the Nation.* New Delhi: NMML, 2001.

Omvedt, Gail. *Dalit Visions.* Hyderabad: Orient Longman Ltd, 1995.

Pandey S.M., *Poetic Influence on Bhakti.* New Delhi: Aravali Books International (P) Ltd, 1999.

Paniker, K. Ayyappa. *Indian Narratology.* New Delhi: IGNCA, 2003.

———. *Medieval Indian Literature: An Anthology.* Four Volumes, New Delhi: Sahitya Akademi, Vol. 1, 1997; Vol. 2, 1999; Vol. 3, 1999; Vol. 4, 2000.

———. *Spotlight on Comparative Indian Literature.* Kolkata: Papyrus, 1992.

Patil, Anand B. *The Whirligig of Taste: Essays in Comparative Literature.* New Delhi: Creative Books, 1999.

Pieterse, Jan Nederveen, and Bhikhu Parekh. *The Decolonization of Imagination.* New Delhi: Oxford University Press, 1997.

Poduval, Satish, ed. *Re-figuring Culture: History, Theory and the Aesthetic in Contemporary India.* New Delhi: Sahitya Akademi, 2004.

Rajendran, C., *Studies in Comparative Poetics.* Delhi: New Bharatiya Book Corporation, 2001.

Ramakrishnan, E.V. *Locating Indian Literature: Texts, Traditions, Translations.* Hyderabad: Orient BlackSwan, 2011.

Ramakrishnan E.V., et al, ed. *Interdisciplinary Alter-natives in Comparative Literature.* Sage, Delhi, 2013.

Ravikumar, Azhagarasan R., ed. *The Oxford India Anthology of Tamil Dalit Writing.* New Delhi: Oxford University Press, 2012.

Sangari, Kumkum, and Sudesh Vaid, ed. *Recasting Women: Essays in Colonial History.* New Delhi: Zubaan, 2006.

Sharma, T.R.S, *Ancient Indian Literature*, Three Volumes, New Delhi: Sahitya Akademi, 2000.

Sherrif, K.M. ed., and trans. *Ekalavyas with Thumbs.* Ahmedabad: Pushpam Publications, 1999.

Singh, Avadhesh K. *Translation: Its Theory and Practice*, New Delhi: Creative Books, 1996.

Singh, Sushila. *Feminism: Theory, Criticism, Analysis.* Delhi: Pencraft International, 1997.

Spivak, Gayatri Chakravorty. *A Critique of Postcolonial Reason: Towards a History of the Vanishing Present.* Harvard University Press, Cambridge, 1999.

———. *Death of a Discipline.* Columbia University Press, 2003.

———. *Outside in the Teaching Machine.* New York and London: Routledge, 1993.

Srilata, K., ed., and trans. *The Other Half of the Coconut: Women Writing, Self-respect, History.* New Delhi: Kali for Women, 2003.

Sunder Rajan, Rajeswari, ed. *Signposts: Gender Issues in Post-Independent India.* New Delhi: Kali for Women, 2000.

Thapar, Romila. *Sakuntala: Texts, Readings, Histories.* New Delhi: Kali for Women, 1999.

Trivedi, Harish, *Colonial Transactions: English Literature and India.* Kolkata: Papyrus, 1993.

Trivedi, Harish and Meenakshi Mukherjee. *Interrogating Post-Colonialism: Theory, Text, Context.* Shimla: IIAS, 1996.

Trivedi, Harish, ed. *The Nation across the World.* Delhi: Oxford University Press, 2007.

Trivedi, Harish, Susan Bassnett, and Meenakshi Mukherjee, eds., *Post-Colonial Translation: Theory and Practice.* London: Routledge, 1999.

Usha, V.T., and S Murali, *Figuring the Female: Women's Discourse, Art and Literature.* Delhi: The Women Press, 2006.

Vanita, Ruth and Saleem Kidwai, ed., *Same-Sex Love in India: Readings from Literature and History.* Delhi: Macmillan India Ltd, 2001.

Venuti, Lawrence. *Rethinking Translation: Discourse, Subjectivity, Ideology.* London and New York: Routledge, 1992.

———. *Scandals of Translation: Towards an Ethic of Difference,* London: Routledge, 1998.

———. *The Translator' Invisibility,* London and New York: Routledge, 1995.

———, ed. *The Translation Studies Reader.* London and New York: Routledge, 2000.

Verma S. Dominique and T.V. Kunhikrishnan, eds. *Memories of the Second Sex: Gender and Sexuality in Women's Writing.* Mumbai: Somaiya Publications Pvt Ltd, 2000.

Vijayasree, C., ed., *Writing the West: 1750-1947: Representations from Indian Languages.* New Delhi: Sahitya Akademi, 2004.

Wiemann, Dirk. *Genres of Modernity: Contemporary Indian Novels in English.* Amsterdam-New York: Rodopi, 2008.

INDEX

A

Adiga, Gopalakrishna, 47
African and Caribbean encounters with English, 86–87
Afternoon Raag (Amit Choudhuri), 83
Agnigarbha (Mahasweta Devi), 311
agricultural civilisation of India, 147
  significance of spade, 148–149
Ahmed, Aijaz, 12
  In Theory, 41
Akhtar-ul-Iman, 47
Alamkara-shasthra, 44
Alexander, Meena, 76
alienation, 237
Anand, Mulk Raj, 76–78
Ananthamurthy, U.R., 13, 49–50, 52, 95
  Samskara, 38, 69, 106
ancient Indian women, 119
Aranyer Adhikar (Mahasweta Devi), 311
Arthashastra, 40
Aryan family of languages, 17–18
Aryans, 17–18
Aryan womanhood, 119, 297

B

Bakhtin, Mikhail, 11
Barthes, Roland, 95
Basava's *vachana*s (prose-lyrics), 30–31, 204–207, 209–210
  nobility of human labour, 207
bedagina vachana (fancy poems), 212
Bedi, Rajinder Singh, 46
Beethoven among the Cows (Rukun Advani), 83

Bhagavad Gita, 40, 230
Bhakti Movements, 27–29, 197, 224
  Namdev, 215–218
  oral techniques of expression, 218–222
  in Tamil Bhakti poetry, 198–199
  Tukaram's poems, 218–221
Bhakti poetry, 244–245, 248
Bhakti-Sufi movements, 27–29, 36–37, 56
  features of, 27–29
Bhili *Ramayana*, 24
Bhils, 15
Big Nationalism, 310
Bijjala II, King, 203
bourgeois social system, 276
Brahmanical Hinduism, 203–204
Brahminism, 78–79
Brahmin outcastes, 214
Brahmin superiority, 197–198
Brhadaranyaka Upanishad, 210–211
Buddhacharitam (Asvaghosha), 26
Buddhist and Jain literature, 55–56
Buddhist theory of subjectivity, 185
Bulcke, Camille, 23
Bulle Shah, 34–35
Burger, Peter, 49

C

caste system, 20, 144, 198
Chander, Krishan, 46
Chicago poems, 292–293
Chintavishtayaya Sita (Kumaran Asan), 25
Chitre, Dilip, 343–344
Chivavakkiyar, 29

Chokhamela, 32
colonial historiography, 40, 40
colonialism, 42
Comparative Indian Literature (K.M. George), 10
contemporary Indian poetry
    Dalit woman, 154–156
    expected gender roles of women, 152–154
    female subject, 159
    Hindi poetry, 156–158
    idea of nationhood, 147
    illiterate rural woman, 149–151
    image of violence, 146
    '*Kasbe ki Dhool*', 147–148
    language and region, 156
    'Mother,' 149–151
    political, 145–147
    regional against the national, 158–159
    relationship between English and Hindi, 157
    semi-rural Indian life, 148
    transformation of woman into an embodiment of revenge, 151–152
contemporary literature, 126
contemporary poetry of independent India
    rural peasant *vs* city dweller, 147–149
cultural identity, 166
cultural nationalism, 50, 52, 142
cultural pluralism, 160
cultural politics, 110
cultural stability, 237

D

Dalit literature, 14, 183, 336
Dalit movement, 85
Dalit poetry, 133–135, 159–160, 337
Dalit writing, 88, 105–108, 336
Dandekar, R.N., 22
Darius I, emperor, 18
The Dark Holds No Terrors (Shashi Deshpande), 84
Das, Kamala, 67
Das, Sisir, Kumar, 10
Dasareswara's *vachana*s (prose-lyrics), 207–208
'*Dast-Ambooh*', 238
democratisation, 45
Desani, G.V., 76
Deshpande, Shashi, 67, 84–85
desivadi writers, 65
Dey, Bishnu, 46–47
Dhangars, 15
Dhoorjati, king, 44
diaspora, 163–164
diasporic ideologies, 168–169
    experience of exile, 164
    forms of othering, 166–168
    idea of 'Indianness,' 168
    of neo-colonial and post-colonial world, 166
    in relative, linguistic and regional-cultural terms, within the country, 169
diasporic communities, 164
diasporic writer, 164, 169
    class component in literature, 166
    negotiation of cultural identity, 165
divided self, 271
Doll for a Child Prostitute, A (Kamala Das), 116
Doosari Parampara (Namwar Singh), 107

Dravidians, 17
Duggal, K.S., 46

E
ecocentric writing, 88
eco-criticism, 182
Engels' *Dialectics of Nature* (Raymond Williams), 105
equality of man, 204
Eurocentrism, 267
European Enlightenment, 265
European fascism, 264
European Literature, 12
European stereotypes of India, 143
European World War, 262–263
Ezekiel, 73–74

F
Faiz, Ahmed Faiz, 46
feminist criticism, 298
Flaming Feet: A Study of the Dalit Movement in India, The (D.R. Nagaraj), 106
folk narratives, 20
Foucault, Michel, 116

G
Gandhi, Mahatma, 46, 68
Gangopadhyay, Sunil, 46
Gathasaptasati, 26–27
George, K.M., 10
Ghalib's ghazals, 236–237
    anxieties, 243
    attitude to man's inhumanity, 238–239
    feeling of exhaustion and frustration, 242
    'great divide' between past and present, 239
    language, 241
    relationship between metropolises and experience of modernity, 237
    as spiritual diary, 241–242
    totalisation of knowledge, 242
    'unhoused' writer, 237–238
'Girl child in the Nineties' (Sugathakumari), 116
globalisation, 266–267
Glofelti, Cheryll, 104
Goddess of Revenge, The (Lalitambika Antarjanam), 116
Gora (Tagore), 37–38
Guha, Ramachandra, 57
Gutenberg Galaxy, The (McLuhan), 326

H
Hajar Churashir Ma (Mahasweta Devi), 310
Haritaniroopanam Malayalathil (G. Madhusoodanan), 105
Hindi language, 57
Hindu nationalism, 265
Hindu paganism, 119
History of Indian Literature (Sisir Kumar Das), 10, 107
'The House' (Sitakant Mahapatra), 325
Hyder, Qurratulain, 46

I
Imagined Communities (Benedict Anderson), 252–253
India after Gandhi: The History of the World's largest Democracy (Ramachandra Guha), 57
Indian Art, 261–262
Indian culture, 14, 109, 142–143
    dharma, 143–144, 146

Indian identity, 269
Indian literary criticism, 88, 297
    approach of Progressives, 93–94
    comparison of Eastern and Western concepts of poetics, 90
    of Dalit literature, 105–108
    diverse aspects of, 91
    eco-criticism, 104–105
    feminist critics, 101–104
    gender construction in India, 103
    history of, 89
influence of Western criticism, 93–101
    Marxist criticism, 94–96
    post-Colonial theory, 99–101
    pratibha (genius) *vs sahridaya* (competent reader), 92
    reading of Kalidasa's Sakuntala, 98–99
    reading of Kunhambu's, 97
    readings of Sreenarayana Guru, 96–97
    re-readings of canonical texts, 96–97
    Said's formulations in *Orientalism*, 101
    theories, 91–92
Indian literature, 9
    attitude of European scholarship towards, 41–42
    based on identity, 39
    Bhakti-Sufi movements, 36–37
    criterion of, 11
    Dalit perspective, 11
    division on basis of language, 12
    evolution of, 39–40
    folk narratives, 20
    genres and forms, 12–14, 37
    Hindi-Urdu tradition, 12
    history of, 10
    ideals of Progressive Movement, 38–39
    Indian thinkers on, 41
    intellectual and spiritual traditions, 37
    literary influences, 13
    multilingualism in, 12
    oriental and occidental concepts in, 12–13
    Ramayana and its sub-traditions, 23–25
    roots of, 15
    translations, 40
    trends and movements, 13–15, 37
    Vedic poetry, 18
    view of, 11
Indianness, 51, 109–110, 138, 142, 160, 328
Indian poetry, 127
Indian spirituality, gnostic and ascetic traditions of, 223
Indian Sufism, 271
Indian writing in English, 10, 67
    charge of 'elitism' against, 71–72
    critics of, 84–87
    immigrant experience, 81
    Indianisation of themes, 81–84
    influence of English novels, 70–71
    linguistic problems, 77
    literal translations, 78
    merging of English words with Indian languages, 68–69
    myths, 82

nativisation of English, 71–75
new writers, 79–80
Raja Rao's observation, 69–70
relation between idealism and renunciation, 81–82
sources of, 75–76
Western trends, movements and techniques, influence of, 71
women, 294
Indo-Aryan Gods, 17
Indo-Aryan languages, 18
Indulekha (O. Chandu Menon), 70–71
Indus valley civilisation, 15–17

J
Jameson, Fredric, 48
Joshi, Umashankar, 46

K
Kabir's poetry, 33–34
    bijak, expression of, 248–249
    Brahma, 247
    Maya, concept of, 247
    as reformist, 245
    repetitions in, 250
    salvation *(Mukti),* concept of, 247–248
    soul *(Atman),* concept of, 247
    spiritual state of, 246
    truth in, 250–251
    typical patterns in, 25
Kafka, 94
Kakkad, N.N., 47
Kalachuryas, 203
Kalidasa's poetry, 26
    Abhijnanasakuntalam, 26, 99
    Malavikagnimitram, 26
    Meghadootam, 26
    Raghuvamsam, 26
    Ritusamharam, 26
    Sakuntalam, 40
    Vikramorvasiyam, 26
Kamala Das's poetry, 76
    'A Cask of Nothing,' 305
    'Anamalai Poems,' 305–306
    'An Introduction,' 303
    complementarity in, 299–300
    conventional myth of marriage, 304
    'Delhi-1984,' 302
    experiences of terrors of her childhood, 295–296
    gendered subjectivity, 300
    identification of lover with Krishna, 299
    individualistic nature of, 294
    man-woman relationship in, 303
    metaphors, 301
    ontological dimensions of her being, 296, 299
    patriarchal myths, 303–304
    personal and poetic selves characteristic of, 300–301
    stance against state-sponsored or patriotic violence, 302
    'The Old Playhouse,' 304
    traditions, 294–295
    women's marginalised position in patriarchal society, 301
    'Words are birds,' 304
karman, 225
Kedarnath Singh's poetry
    Akal mein Saras, 329
    Awaz, 328
    Badhayi aur Chidiya, 329
    Balu ka Sparsh, 329
    Buddh ke bare mein Sochna, 329
    Chehera, 329

Chithi, 329
Goonj, 329
Kuch Sootra Jo ek Kisan Bapne Bete ko Diye, 329
Kuvem, 329
   Majhi ka Pul, 329
   method of choosing symbols, 332
   Nadi, 329
   Nadiyan, 329
   Ped, 328
   poet's imagination at work, 329–330
   Sooryasth ke bad ek Andheri Basti se Guzarte Huve, 329
   Taswir, 329
   tension between two worlds, 328
   'The Broken-down Truck,' 332, 335, 329
   'The Old Woman Selling Tomatoes,' 331–332
   'The Spade,' 332–335
   'Uttar Kabir,' 332
   word 'dust' in, 332–333
   Zamin Pak Rahi Hai, 328
Khalistan movement, 112
Kluckhohn, Clyde, 81
Kolatkar, Arun, 76
Kosambi, D.D., 16–17, 19, 21
Kusumabale (Devanoor Mahadeva), 106

L

Lalleswari (Lal Ded, Lalla Arifa), 36
liberation movements, 126
Lingayatism, 203
Linguistic Survey of India (George Grierson), 9
Literary Cultures in History: Reconstructions from South Asia (Sheldon Pollock), 42
literary ecology, 182
literary historiography, 120
literary modernism, 128
literary theory, 120
literature
   criterion of, 11
   known in name of nations, 12
   The Little Soldier (Kiran Nagarkar), 83
Looking through Glass (Mukul Kesavan), 83
'Loss of a Halo' (Baudelaire), 45

M

Mahabharata, 20–23, 144, 149, 160, 171, 334
Mahadevi, Akka, 35–36
Mahadeviyakka's poem, 213–214
Mahajana Agrahara settlement, 203
Mahanubhav movement, 214
Mahapatra, Jayanta, 75
Mahasweta Devi's 'Stanadayini'
   Brahminhood, 312
   critical of patriarchy, 312–314
   G.C. Spivak's translation, 309–310
   gendered subalterns in, 311–312
   Haldar family, 314–315
   historical fiction, 311
   Indian social reality in, 316–317
   linkages between formation of classes and social emancipation of women, 314
Marxist labour theory of value, 312
Making It New: Modernism in Malayalam, Marathi and Hindi

Poetry (E.V. Ramakrishnan), 10, 48
Malayalam literature, 11
Manimekalai (Chathanar), 27
Manto, Saadat Hasan, 46
Manusmriti, 40
Marxism, 253
Meeker, Joseph, 104
Meluhha, 16
Menzes, Armando, 46
Mesopotamians, 16
Midnight's Children (Saleem Sinai), 82–83
Mitro Marjani (Krishna Sobti), 116
modern folk writing, 88
modernisation, 45
modernism, 48, 54–55, 327
   in Indian poetry, 128–129
Mohiuddin, Makhdoom, 46
Mricchakatikam (Soodraka), 26
Mukherjee, Arun P., 99
Muktibodh, Gajanan Madhav, 47
Muslim priesthood, 34

N
Nagaraj, D. R., 50
Nagraj, D. R., 336
Nair, Rukmini Bhaya, 76
Namdeo, 337–338
   'Approaching the Organized Harem of the Octopus,' 340
   'December 6,' 342–343
   Golpitha, 339
   irony in poems, 341–342
   Khel (Play), 342
   'Mandakini Patel: A young prostitute, My Intended collage,' 341
   'Ode to Ambedkar,' 339–340
   romantic lyrics, 338
   'Untitled Poem,' 342
   use of idioms, 340, 343
Namdev, 31–32
Narayan, R. K., 77
Narrative Strategies: Essays on South Asian Literature and Film (Vasudha Dalmia and Theo Damsteegt), 41
nation, 253
nationalism, 42, 253, 310
   Ernest Gellner's views, 253
   Tagore's views, 254–271
Nativism, 109–114
   community implicit in, 111–112
   cultural and political homogeneity, 113
   ethnic and linguistic ties, 112
   ideological formations, 110–112
   margi, desi and *videsi* elements, 113
   positive aspects of, 114
nativism, 88
Natkeeran, 44
Natyasastra, 91
Naxalite movement, 131–132
Nehru, Jawaharlal, 68
Niranjana, Tejaswini, 40
Nivrtti-dharma, 223–224

O
Oorubhangam (Bhasa), 26
oral folk literature, 132
oral literary practices, 89

P
Paniker, Ayyappa, 47–48
Panis, 19
Patalaramayanam, 24

patriarchal power, 115, 255
Paumachariya, 23
Piratapa Mutaliyar Charittiram
  (Samuel Pillai), 71
pluralistic religious tradition of
  India, 113
poetry of independent India,
  45–47
  avant-garde tradition, 49–50
  confessions or sighs of
    frustration, 132
  in context of industrialisation
    and urbanisation, 52
  cultural nationalism, 50, 52
  Dalit poetry, 62–64, 133–135
  democratic tradition (*sramana*
    or *samanya* elements), 55–60
  feature of 'Indianness,' 51
  feminist, 136
  free verse and prose, 48
  identities, 50–51
  idioms and approaches, 48, 57
  Kannada, 138
  'Love' (Murari Mukhopadhyay),
    130–131
  Maoist poetry, 58
  modernism in, 128–129
  multi-layeredness of Indian
    life, 53–54
  of nativist or *desivadi* writers,
    65–66
  Naxalite movement and, 131–
    132
  new/modern, 47–55
postmodernism in, 140
progressive-modernist, 129–131
  regional and linguistic identity,
    137–141
  series of transversal struggles,
    56

social critical functions, 133
socialist vision of Progressives,
  57–58
social reality, 60
style and ideology, 50
Tamil *cankam*, 144
Tamil Sangam, 138
tradition of women's, 60–62
of tribal communities, 64–65
women poets, 136–137
Pravritti-dharma, 223–224
'Primitive Communist' society, 18
print-capitalist system, 254
Pritam, Amrita, 46
private property, concept of, 18
Progressive Literary Movement, 14,
  38–39, 56, 57, 93–94
progressive-modernist, 129–131
public sphere, 37

R
Radhakrishnan, S., 13
Radhasoami Movement, 197
Ramakrishnan, E. V., 10–11, 48–49,
  51
  Making It New, 107
Ramanujan, A.K., 9, 12, 29, 44,
  73–75, 109, 286
  'A Poem on Particulars,' 290
  attitude to tradition, 293
  'Classics Lost and Found,' 291
  collapsing of nature and
    culture, 144
  constitution of poetry, 286–
    287
  'Entries for a Catalogue of
    Fears,' 289–290
  'Extended Family,' 292
  memories in poems, 289, 293
  modernisation in India, 144

'No Amnesiac King,' 291
'Obituary,' 288–289
'Of Mother; among other Things,' 289
'Prayers to Lord Murugan,' 291
'Second sight,' 291
sensing of continuity, 292–293
'Small-scale reflections on a Great House,' 290
'Still Another for Mother,' 289
'Upanishad, Next Door,' 292
on Veerasaiva movement, 208
'When Meditation Works,' 292
Ramayana, 334
Ramayana and its sub-traditions, 23–25
   Bhili Ramayana, 24
   Buddhist Ramayana, 23
   Jain Ramayana, 23–24
   Patalaramayanam, 24
   Valmiki's Ramayana, 24
Ramayanas, 9, 109–110, 143, 149, 160, 171, 187–188
Rao, Raja, 69–70, 78–79
   Kanthapura, 77, 82
Rao, Velcheru Narayana, 23
rasadhwani, 178–179
Ravan and Eddie (Kiran Nagarkar), 83
Ravindran, P.P., 41
Ray, Annada Shankar, 48
Ray, Nihar Ranjan, 9, 11, 13
Rayan, Krishna, 90
Red Earth and Pouring Rain (Vikram Chandra), 84
religious democracy, 270
re-readings and counter-readings
   aestheticist criticism, 183
   anti-colonial, 176–177
   application of rasadhwani concept to modern subcontinental texts, 179
   binary oppositions, 178
   of canonical texts, 172
   caste in modes of representation and imagination, 183–184
   concept of body in Sreenarayana Guru, 173
   Dileep Menon's reading of Saraswativijayam, 173–174
   eco-criticism, 182
   evaluation of Dalit literature, 183
   M.T. Ansari's rereading of novel Indulekha, 176–177
   parallels between the rasas, 179
   radical, 171
   representation of women, 180
   re-read Sanskrit poetics, 178
   Romila Thapar reading of Kalidasa's Abhijnana Sakuntalam, 174–176
   social and literary context, 171–173
   theory of suggestion, 178–179
   women's writng, 181
resident aliens, 165
re-writings, 171
Richman, Paula, 23
Rigveda, 18–19
Romance languages, 18
rooted cosmopolitanism, 265
Roots and Shadows (Shashi Deshpande), 84
Roy, Arundhati, 79
Rueckert, William, 104
Rushdie, Salman, 67–68, 79
   Enchantress of Florence, 83
   Satanic Verses, 83

S

Sahni, Bhisham, 46
Said, Edward, 38, 99, 116
    formulations in *Orientalism*, 101
Sakuntala (Kalidasa), 26
samsaradukha, advaitic concept of, 320
Samskara (U.R. Ananthamurthy), 38
Sangam literature, 27, 56
Sanskritisation, 183
Sanskrit literature, 39, 88
    age of epics, 25–26
    Buddhist and Jain texts, 26
    Tamil texts, 27
Sanskrit poetics, 14, 89
    central concepts of, 90
    rasadhvani concept, 90–91
Sarala Dasa reading of *Mahabharata*
    Brahman, concept of, 233
    Ganga, 232
    Krishna, 232–233
    Kunti, 232
    metaphor-making imagination, 231
    Pandavas' *rajasiiya*, 230
Sramana elements in, 225–235
suffering, concept of, 233–234
Saraswativijayam, 97–98
Saratchandra's works
    Assamese readers, 282
    characters in, 280–282
    Charitrahin, 273
    conflict between instinct and institutions, 274
    conflict of two value systems, 279
    contribution to cultural India, 278
    critics, 278
    dramatised on stage, 282
    Grhadaha, 273
    Gujarati readers, 281
    influence on writers of different languages, 277
    Kusum in *Pandit Masai*, 278
    Marathi readers, 281
    method of delineating the society, 277–278
    Nazrul Islam on, 273
    popularity, 277–283
    portrayal of love, 274
    progressive literary movements and, 285
    Punjab readers, 279
    recognitions, 273–274
    reformist aspirations, 284
Ses Prasna, 273, 284
    Sindhi readers, 282
    in South India, 283
    spirit of Bengali language in, 273
    Subhas Chandra Bose on, 273
    Sukumar Banerjee on, 273
    Suniti Kumar Chatterjee on, 273
    on superstitions and evil customs, 275
    Tagore on, 273
    translations of, 277
    Urdu readers, 278–279
    women characters, 274, 280–283
Schlegel, Wilhelm von, 39
    A Sea of Poppies (Amitav Ghosh), 83
sedition, 254
selfishness in politics, 47
'Shadow' (Sitakant Mahapatra), 324
Shadowlines (Amitav Ghosh), 83
Shahani, Roshan G., 327
Shaiva saints, 29
Shaivism, 203–204

Shankar, Annada, 46
Sharma, T.R.S., 41
   Ancient Indian Literature, 41
Siddhas, 29
Siddha School of Poetry, 199–200
   acceptance of suffering, 206
   Chittar's poem, 200
   Chivavakkiyar's poem, 199–200
   dissent against class and caste, 200
   as expression of common people, 201
   form and content, 202–203
   sacredness of body, 203, 205
   symbolic language, 201
   Tamil religious-philosophic poetry, 201–202
   tantric orientation, 201
   vigorous and germane counter-tradition, 203
   'vulgar' and 'obscene' words, use of, 201
Significance of Theory (Terry Eagleton), 108
Silappadikaram (Ilango Adigal), 27
Singh, Kedarnath, 47
Singh, Khushwant, 46, 78
Singh, Nanak, 46
Sitakant Mahapatra's 'The Other View: Yashoda's Soliloquy'
   concept of silence, 323, 325–326
   echoes of Western poetry, 318–319
   poet's vision of the universe, 320
   sense of incarnation, 319–320, 326
   Yashoda's experience of bizarre vision, 320–321
Slavic languages, 18

Small Remedies (Shashi Deshpande), 84
Sphota theory, 187
Sramana tradition, 55, 197, 223, 244–245
Sarala Dasa reading of *Mahabharata*, 225–235
Strange and Sublime Address, A (Amit Choudhuri), 83
subversion technique, 230
Sufi poets, 34
Suitable Boy, A (Vikram Seth), 69, 84
Swadeshi Movement, 254
Swapna vasavadattam (Bhasa), 26

T

Tagore's views on nationalism, 37–38, 254–271
   Buddhist ideal of *maitri*, 260
   in context of inhuman and massive violence, 263–264
   counter-globalisation, 270–271
   criticism against, 262–263
   criticism of the Nation, 269–270
   distinction between social accumulation and competitive accumulation, 256
   distinction between *society* and *nation*, 255
   foundation of *swaraj*, 265–266
   Ghare Baire, 254, 269
   Gora, 37–38
   Hindu nationalism, 265, 268–269
   idea of nation, 255–259
   issue of civilisational hierarchy, 267
   legitimation of the Nation, 258

moral freedom, 261
organisations of 'National Egoism,' 261
principle of competition, 255–256
on social stratification in India, 255
in terms of material 'success,' 264
usage of tropes and metaphors, 256–259
in the West, 255
Tagore syndrome, 50
Tamil Bhakti poetry, 28–29
Tamil literature, 14
Tamil poetry, 287
Tamil Sangam poetry, 295
Tamil Siddhas, 244–245, 248
Tara Lane (Shama Futehally), 83
Teeka Swayamvar (Bhalchandra Nemade), 107
Terhi Lakeer (Ismat Chughtai), 116
Teutonic languages, 18
Thapar, Romila, 17
   critique of televised *Ramayana*, 23
   on languages, 17
   reading of Kalidasa's Sakuntala, 98–99
   Shakuntala: Texts, Readings, Histories, 40
That Long Silence (Shashi Deshpande), 84
theory of suggestion, 178
third space, 164
Third World status, 126
Thirukkural, 27
Thirumantiram (Thirumular), 198–199
Thirumular, 28–29
'This is Why We are Human' (Sitakant Mahapatra), 324

Tholkappiyam, 27, 91
A Thousand Faces of Night (Gita Hariharan), 84
Towards a Literary History of India (Sujit Mukherjee), 9–10
Towards an Aesthetics of Dalit Literature (Sharan Kumar Limbale), 105
translation
   colonial era, 188–189
   cultural implications, 189, 192
   intertextuality in, 187–188, 190
   poetry, 191
   politics of, 192–193
   post-colonial era, 189
   in pre-colonial India, 186
   question of authenticity, 190–192
   Ramayanas, 187–188
   of religious works, 188, 190–191
   Sanskrit words, 185–186
   translator's position, 187
   Western and Indian approaches, 186–187
tribal writing, 88
Trotternama (Allan Sealy), 83
Tukaram, 32–33
Turner, Victor, 29
Tyrewala, Altaf, 80

U

'The Ultimate Name of Time' (Sitakant Mahapatra), 324
universal community of man *(Sansara),* 205
Urdu literature, 14

V

vachana expression, 207–212
   metaphors in, 213

*vachanakara*s, 207–210
varna-jati system, 198, 245
Vedas, 18–19
    Gods in, 18
Vedic gods, 22
Vedic poetry, 18
Vedic tradition, 119, 198–199, 209, 212, 223–227, 229
Veerasaiva philosophy, 207–208

W
Warkari movement of Maharashtra, 214, 218, 222
Western concepts in poetics, 14
Western feminism, 298
White Tiger (Aravind Adiga), 80
Williams, Raymond, 327
women saints, 35–36, 36
    Akka Mahadevi, 35–36
    Lalleswari, 36
    Meerabai, 36
women's poetry in India, 60–61, 294
    Dalit women, 61–62
    urban Muslim women, 61
women's writing, 88
    Bhakti movement and, 123–124
    borders between imagination and reality, 116–117
    buried or censored, 118
    feminist reading, 118–119
    literary historiography, 120
    lost identity of individual, 129
    magazines and studies on, 117
    poetry, 123–125
    portrayal of women in men's literature, 119
    present times, 115
    ranks of writers, 118
    reading of, 116
    in regional languages, 117
    strategies of reading, 121–123
    study of Mirabai, 123–125
    translations, 117
    Western feminist critical trends on, 120–121
working class movement, 276

Y
Yashpal, 46
Yeats, W.B., 47

PRAISE FOR EARLIER WORKS OF CRITICISM

On *Indian Literature: Positions and Propositions*
An acute critical mind that plots out both the complete historiography of Indian literatures and a forward-looking agenda... Very illuminating, always graceful... a stimulating collection
—*World Literature Today*, USA

A ground-breaking statement on how to approach the composite body of Indian literature with the pedagogical tools of serious critical study
—*The Book Review*, Delhi

A work that provides insights into how one of the most vital creative minds of contemporary India relates itself to the various literary debates alive around it
—*Journal of Aesthetics and Literature*, Kerala

For anyone who is a serious reader, a practitioner f literature, or wants to have the best of Indian writing in his library shelf, this book is a must-buy, must-read and must-re-peruse in 'the bliss of solitude'
—*IIC Quarterly*, Delhi

On *Authors, Texts, Issues*
The book evokes in an intense poetic manner many a pause and rupture central to the cultural discourse of our times
—*The Book Review*, Delhi

Raises many questions and articulates them with clarity and force; supportive evidences are presented in plenty with astonishing range and variety
—*The Hindu*, Madras

K Satchidanandan shows us how complex issues like the notion of Indianness can be dealt with... There is an ease with which he tackles the general as well as the specific
—*Journal of Indian Writing in English*